WITHDRA  OCK

D1327843

100486329

Migration and International Legal Norms

100486329

Published in cooperation with

the Migration Policy Institute, Washington D.C.
the Graduate Institute of International Studies, Geneva
the International Organization for Migration, Geneva

and with the support of

the Swiss Federal Office for Refugees

Migration

and

International Legal Norms

Editors

T. Alexander Aleinikoff
Georgetown University Law Center, Migration Policy Institute (Washington, D.C.)

Vincent Chetail
Graduate Institute of International Studies (Geneva)

T·M·C·Asser Press
The Hague

Published by T.M.C.ASSER PRESS
P.O.Box 16163, 2500 BD The Hague, The Netherlands

ISBN 90-6704-157-2

All rights reserved.
© 2003, T.M.C.ASSER PRESS, The Hague; Migration Policy Institute, Washington D.C.;
Graduate Institute of International Studies, Geneva; and International Organization
for Migration, Geneva

No part of the material protected by this copyright notice may be reproduced or utilized in
any form or by any means, electronic or mechanical, including photocopying, recording, or
by any information storage and retrieval system, without written permission from the copyright
owners.

PRINTED IN THE NETHERLANDS

SUMMARY OF CONTENTS

Labor, Trade and Development

Emerging Topics

International Cooperative Efforts

FOREWORD

Since 1965, the number of international migrants has doubled. As of the year 2000, there were approximately 175 million migrants throughout the world. Thus, approximately 2.59% of the world population, or one in every thirty-five persons, are migrants. There are multiple reasons for this: the collapse of long-standing political barriers to movement, the development of worldwide communication systems, and the relative cheapness of modern means of transport – to name but a few. None of these trends is likely to be reversed in the foreseeable future. Hence, the growing awareness of the phenomenon of international migration among both policy makers and academic experts.

Both countries of origin and countries of destination benefit from migrants. Countries of origin are in great need of foreign financial resources to foster their economic development. It is estimated that worldwide remittances now amount to more than 73 billion US$ per year. Abroad, migrants have access to education and training indispensable for creating enterprises when they return to their countries of origin. They are also among the first investors in their home economy and can in that way compensate for the "brain drain" caused by their departure. Countries of destination, on their part, have a lack of certain types of labor, e.g., nurses, computer specialists, agriculture workers. Moreover, many destination countries have a significant demographic imbalance. Europe's population would rapidly decline to an even greater extent – with dramatic economic and social impact – if not compensated in some measure by migrants.

However, migration is to a large extent perceived negatively in countries of destination. Migrants are often seen as potential competitors by the domestic labor force; they are blamed for the rise in criminality; in case of recession they are the first to lose their jobs and burden the social security system; even the cultural identity of the local population is said to be at stake if faced with too many immigrants. Disruptive and disorderly movements are considered to be a threat to internal order and stability. Worse, since September 11, 2001, migrants are perceived as potential terrorists. The situation is exacerbated by the reluctance of some countries of origin to readmit their own citizens as well as by the perceived tolerance on the part of these same states of smuggling and trafficking of human beings.

Not surprisingly, many countries of destination, alarmed by the public mood, are resorting to unilateral measures to reduce immigration. A number of them are limiting immigration to qualified workers and reduce, if not eliminate, social assistance to foreigners. Several countries of destination are also imposing more severe penalties on those who enter illegally and forcibly return migrants in an irregular situation. Some go as far as to discourage marriages between nationals and foreigners.

The regional and international repercussions of such unilateral restrictive measures are rarely considered. Neighboring countries are suddenly confronted with an unexpected shift of the stream of migrants to their borders and have to take comparable measures thus accelerating the spiral of restrictions. Countries of origin are blamed for being at the root of the problems; at best, a discussion with them is start-ed on how to return undesirable migrants.

This does not mean that there are no international treaties dealing with migration. On the contrary, there are many agreements, as well as bilateral, regional, and multi-lateral conventions aimed at managing aspects of migration, in particular in the hu-manitarian field. Some of these rules work satisfactorily whereas others are not fully implemented. In certain areas, however, no rules or guidelines to regulate interstate cooperation exist.

With the exception of the European Union and of the limited scope of the General Agreement on Trade in Services in the World Trade Organization (WTO), there is no comprehensive regional or multilateral institution that deals with the relations among States, or tries to bring order to the myriad of conventions, agreements, guidelines, and best practices, on migration. There is no global system of orderly movements, managing in a cooperative way and combining efficiency, equity, and respect for the interests of the countries of origin, of transit and destination. There is also no umbrella agreement like the WTO that stipulates minimum standards with which unilateral action or bilateral agreements must comply.

In view of the importance of the issues involved, the question arises – why? The most important reason is no doubt State sovereignty; migration is thought to be too sensitive an issue to be dealt with in a binding multilateral context. Understandably, Governments want to maintain sovereign authority, and international organizations active in the field of migration are reluctant to relinquish any of their responsibilities to an overall framework of migration.

The uncoordinated approach to migration may have functioned well enough until now. However, without better cooperation and partnership between concerned coun-tries, irregular migration will continue to increase and to foster lasting negative per-ceptions towards aliens. The consequences of such developments may affect rela-tions among States, as well as the delicate balance in the international trade and financial regimes and global security.

Although policy makers are becoming gradually more aware that domestic mea-sures alone are not sufficient to cope with the occurrence of migration and that the problem is now increasingly discussed at the international level, there has been, until now, no broad-based initiative to open up for a dialogue between countries of origin, countries of transit, and countries of destination on the full range of migration is-sues. This is astonishing. While it is true that countries of origin, of transit, and of destination have different interests, these countries also have many common con-cerns. All stakeholders involved and, last but not least, the migrants themselves, would benefit from a better management of migration at the international level.

It is with this in mind that the Federal Office for Refugees in Switzerland launched in June 2001 the *Berne Initiative*. Government representatives of migrant origin, transit, and destination countries, international organizations, non-govern-mental agencies and academics gathered at a symposium in order to start up a States'-owned process with the objective of obtaining better management of migra-tion at the regional and possibly at the global level through cooperation between States. The process should ideally lead to a dialogue between countries of origin and destination first regionally, then globally. This dialogue could lead to the establishment of a suitable general intergovernmental framework with guidelines and best practices to assist Governments when confronted with challenges in the field of migration policy development.

Such a framework of guidelines and best practices would have to strike a balance of interests between countries of origin and countries of destination. It should not be governed by a laissez-faire attitude, but by the principle of orderly or regulated movement of people. It should also lead to a reduction of forced and disruptive migration. Orderly migration should be promoted and illegal migration and the criminal aspects related thereto, including trafficking, should be prevented.

However, in order to aim at such ambitious results, a series of intermediary steps are necessary. One of these is a stock-taking of existing international legal standards on migration as presented in this volume. An expert study comprising contributions of some of the most renowned legal scholars in the field of migration – led by the Migration Policy Institute (MPI) of Washington, D.C. and the Graduate Institute of International Studies (HEI) in cooperation with the International Organization of Migration (IOM) – will serve as background for further work. The aim of this expert study is to highlight existing regulations, standards, and norms on migration as well as to point out clear legal gaps in that area.

The present study – financed by the Federal Office for Refugees in Switzerland – lays the ground for further work, which may eventually lead to the establishment of the intended framework. It will certainly facilitate the global dialogue on interstate migration and serves not only as an important reference work for legal experts on migration norms, but moreover offers valuable information for government officials and practitioners.

The publication of this study would, of course, not have been accomplished without the work and support of a number of people. There is, first of all, T. Alexander Aleinikoff, professor of Law and Senior Associate of MPI in Washington who has mastered the challenging task of supervising the work of all authors by collecting, analyzing, improving, and editing the various articles which have been written in the course of this project.

There is, moreover, the entire team of the Migration Policy and Research Programme (MPRP) of the IOM who, under the direction of its Director, Gervais Appave and his Deputy-Director, Michele Klein-Solomon, has organized and managed the publication of the expert study. Moreover, I owe special gratitude to Brunson McKinley, Director General of IOM, and to Ruud Lubbers, High Commissioner for Refugees, for supporting the entire Berne Initiative process.

Additional thanks go to Rolf Jenny and Colleen Thouez of the International Migration Policy Program (IMP), as well as Gerry van Kessel of the Inter-governmental Consultations on Asylum, Refugee and Migration Policies in Europe, North America and Australia (IGC), who have offered valuable support and constructive criticism.

And last, but certainly not least, my deep gratitude to all legal experts who have taken the time to clarify the scope of legal norms in the field of migration for the purpose of this study: Jacqueline Bhabha, Steve Charnovitz, Vincent Chetail, B.S.

Chimni, David Fisher, Joan M. Fitzpatrick, Guy Goodwin-Gill, Vera Gowlland, Kay Hailbronner, Walter Kälin, Kate Jastram, Peter van Krieken, Virginia Leary, Eve Lester, David Martin, Susan Martin, Vitit Muntarbhorn, Gerald Neuman, Kathleen Newland, Gregor Noll and Andrew Schoenholtz. Many thanks also to Peter Tschopp, Director of the Graduate Institute of International Studies in Geneva, as well as Daniel Warner and his assistant Valérie Clerc for hosting a seminar for the experts involved.

Jean-Daniel Gerber
Director of the Federal Office for Refugees
Berne, Switzerland, December 2002

FOREWORD

International migration is an established feature of contemporary social and economic life. As governments the world over come to terms with this reality, they are
faced with the challenge of developing effective modes of cooperation in this field.

With its rapidly increasing membership (expected to reach at least ninety-eight
Members States at the December 2002 Council, up from fifty-nine in 1997) grap-
pling with the complex and varied issues related to migration management, IOM is
in a unique position to share the knowledge and expertise it has acquired over the
past fifty years. As the principle inter-governmental organization focusing on the
broad range of migration issues, it is well placed to assist governments through enhancing understanding and building capacity for more effective migration management. At the request of Member States for IOM to play a more dominant role in the
migration policy debate, IOM launched, as an integral component of its Eighty-sec-
ond Session of the Council held in November 2001, its first International Dialogue
on Migration. This session of the dialogue emphasised the requirement for a comprehensive approach to managing migration, as well as the need to better understand
migratory phenomena. Of most relevance to the current publication, governments
emphasised the need to understand the existing international legal framework relevant to migration management.

The Berne Initiative, launched by the Swiss Federal Office for Refugees in June
2001, has been following a similar orientation. One of its main purposes is to open
up avenues of study, reflection, and consultation among governments and other migration stakeholders with a view to enhancing cooperation.

Migration and International Legal Norms is an important contribution to this process and a response to numerous requests from policy makers for a concise guide to
international legal norms and standards in the field of migration. This study provides
a ready tool for policy makers and migration practitioners by gathering and analyzing in one place relevant international legal norms for the management of migration.

Migration and International Legal Norms was commissioned by the International
Organization for Migration under the sponsorship of the Swiss Federal Office for
Refugees and the Swiss Department of Foreign Affairs as part of the Berne Initiative, and provides sixteen distinct papers on different migration issues prepared by
international law experts in each of the identified fields relevant to migration management. It includes chapters on the authority and responsibility of States, freedom
of movement and transnational migration, return to States of origin and third states,
migration and security, nationality, forced migration, combating smuggling and trafficking, protection of asylum-seekers and refugees rescued at sea, human rights of
migrants, family unification, children and migration, labor migration, trade law
norms, migration and development, migration and health, integration and inter-state
cooperation on migration. An introductory chapter provides an analysis of each of

the individual studies and offers an integrated view of the legal landscape in the field of international migration.

IOM would like to thank the many experts who contributed their time and expertise to this study. In addition, IOM would like to thank Mr. Daniel Warner and Mr. Vincent Chetail of the Institut Universitaire de Hautes Etudes Internationales, Geneva, for their organization of the expert seminar in connection with the study and careful editing of the expert chapters. IOM would like to especially thank the editor, Mr. T. Alexander Aleinikoff, Senior Associate of the Migration Policy Institute, Washington, D.C., and professor of constitutional and immigration law at Georgetown University Law Center, for his excellent work and tremendous patience and flexibility in the preparation of this work.

Brunson McKinley
International Organization for Migration
Geneva, Switzerland, December 2002

ACKNOWLEDGEMENTS

This project began with a conversation initiated by Michele Klein-Solomon of the International Organization for Migration's Migration Policy and Research Programme (MPRP). She wondered whether she could interest the Migration Policy Institute in conducting a study of international legal norms relating to migration to provide a framework and background for the policy discussions being undertaken by participants in the Berne Initiative. The Swiss Federal Office for Refugees was ready to provide the necessary financial support.

The idea of a study grew into a conference bringing together some of the world's leading experts on migration and international law. Daniel Warner, Deputy Director of the Graduate Institute of International Studies, graciously lent his substantive expertise and organizing skill in planning and hosting the meeting of experts in Geneva in May 2002.

This volume, then, is the product of an extraordinary confluence of talent and cooperation. Front and center are the scholars who took the time to write papers and then rewrite them based on the lively and challenging discussions held in Geneva.

IOM staff have also played a major role. From MPRP, Gervais Appave, Kerstin Barsch, Michele Buteau, Michele Klein-Solomon, and Erica Usher have provided invaluable support. Other people at IOM have aided the project: Brunson McKinley, Director General; Drs. Danielle Grondin and Akram Eltom, who assisted in the preparation of the chapter on Health and Migration; and Heikki Mattila and Carol San Miguel, from the Publications Unit. Heikki and Carol, together with MPRP, also managed the production of the publication "International Legal Norms and Migration: An Analysis" (IOM International Dialogue on Migration 2002), based on chapter one of this volume. Colleagues in other international organizations – the International Committee of the Red Cross, the International Labor Organization, the Office of the UN High Commissioner for Human Rights, and the Office of the UN High Commissioner for Refugees – generously gave of their time in reviewing parts of the volume.

At the Graduate Institute, Valérie Clerc's efficiency and thoroughness made the Geneva conference an ideal environment for the legal discussions that ensued. Lisa Krähenbühl likewise provided important support. Georgetown University Law Center has materially aided in the preparation of this volume, and special thanks goes to Anna Selden whose tireless efforts in communicating with far-flung authors and copy-editing and correcting the drafts have made this a better book.

The conference and this volume were made possible by the generous financial support of the Swiss Federal Office of Refugees. Particular recognition and thanks is due to Jean-Daniel Gerber, Director of the Swiss Federal Office for Refugees, and Anne-Grethe Nielsen, the head of International Affairs for the Office. This book would not have been possible without their foresight and insight, and their dedication to the advancement of policy discussions informed by law and principle.

T. Alexander Aleinikoff, *Washington, D.C.*
February 2003   Vincent Chetail, *Geneva*

TABLE OF CONTENTS

State Authority and Responsibility

Forced Migration

Chapter 7
FORCED MIGRATION AND INTERNATIONAL LAW
Guy S. Goodwin-Gill and Kathleen Newland

Chapter 8
THE PROTECTION OF ASYLUM-SEEKERS AND REFUGEES RESCUED AT SEA
Office of the United Nations High Commissioner for Refugees

Human Rights of Migrants

Chapter 14
TRADE LAW NORMS ON INTERNATIONAL MIGRATION
Steve Charnovitz   241

Chapter 15
DEVELOPMENT AND MIGRATION
B.S. Chimni   255

Emerging Topics

International Cooperative Efforts

LIST OF ABBREVIATIONS

AALCC	Asian-African Legal Consultative Committee
AALCO	Asian-African Legal Consultative Organization
ACHR	American Convention on Human Rights
AFTA	ASEAN Free Trade Area
AJIL	American Journal of International Law
ALOs	Airline Liaison Officers
ANZCERTA	The Australia-New Zealand Closer Economic Relations
ANZUS	Security Treaty Between Australia, New Zealand, and The United States of America
APC	Inter-Governmental Asia-Pacific Consultations on Refugees, Displaced Persons and Migrants
APEC	Asia-Pacific Economic Co-operation Forum
ARIAT	Asian Initiative against Trafficking
ASEAN	Association of Southeast Asian Nations
ASEM	Asia-Europe Ministerial Conference on Co-operation for the Management of Migratory Flows between Europe and Asia
AWR Bulletin	Association for the Study of the World Refugee Problem
BDIM	Bangkok Declaration on Irregular Migration
BHRC	Butterworth's Human Rights Cases
BLM	Border Liaison Mechanism
CARICOM	Caribbean Community
CAT	Convention Against Torture and Other Cruel, Inhuman or Degrading Treatment or Punishment
CDPD	Cairo Declaration on Population and Development
CEDAW	Convention on the Elimination of All Forms of Discrimination Against Women
CEECs	States of Central and Eastern Europe
CERD	American Convention, Convention on the Elimination of All Forms of Racial Discrimination
CESCR	Committee on Economic, Social and Cultural Rights
CIREFCA	Declaration and Concerted Plan of Action in favor of Central American Refugees, Returnees and Displaced Persons
CIS	Commonwealth of Independent States
CLR	Commonwealth Law Reports
CMLR	Common Market Law Review
COE	Council of Europe
COMESA	Treaty for a Common Market for Eastern and Southern Africa
CPA	Comprehensive Plan of Action

CRC	Convention on the Rights of the Child
CSR	Convention on the Status of Refugees
DDR	Demobilization and reintegration
DISERO	Disembarkation Resettlement Offers Scheme
DLR	Dominon Law Reports
DRD	Declaration on the Right to Development
ECHR	European Convention for the Protection of Human Rights and Fundamental Freedoms
ECHR	European Court of Human Rights
ECLAC	Economic Commission for Latin America and the Caribbean
ECN	European Convention on Nationality
ECOSOC	United Nations Economic and Social Council
ECOWAS	Economic Community of West African States
ECR	European Court Reports
ECRE	European Council on Refugees and Exiles
EEA	Agreement on the European Economic Area
EFTA	European Free Trade Association
EHRR	European Human Rights Reports
ESC	Economic, social, and cultural
ESC	European Social Charter
ESCAP	United Nations Economic and Social Commission for Asia and the Pacific
ETS	European Treaty Series
EXCOM	Executive Committee Conclusions
FCN	Friendship, commerce and navigation
GAATW	Global Alliance Against Traffic in Women
GATS	General Agreement on Trade in Services
GATT	General Agreement on Tariffs and Trade
HEI	Hautes Etudes Internationales
HRC	Human Rights Committee
IACHR	Inter-American Commission on Human Rights
ICARA	Declaration and Program of Action of the First and Second International Conference on Assistance to Refugees in Africa
ICCPR	International Covenant on Civil and Political Rights
ICERD	International Convention on the Elimination of All Forms of Racial Discrimination
ICESCR	International Covenant on Economic, Social and Cultural Rights
ICJ	International Court of Justice
ICJ Reports	International Court of Justice, Reports of Judgments. Advisory Opinions and Orders
ICMW	International Convention on the Protection of the Rights of All Migrant Workers and Members of their Families
ICMPD	International Centre for Migration Policy Development

ICPD	International Conference on Population and Development
ICRC	The International Committee of the Red Cross
IDB	Inter-American Development Bank
IGC	Inter-governmental Consultations on Asylum, Refugee and Migration Policies in Europe, North America and Australia
IHRR	International Human Rights Reports
IJRL	International Journal of Refugee Law
ILA	International Law Association
ILC	International Labor Conference
ILC	International Law Commission
ILM	International Legal Materials
ILO	International Labor Organization
ILR	International Law Reports
IMP	International Migration Policy Program
IMO	International Maritime Organization
IOM	International Organization for Migration
IT	Information Technology
ITO	International Trade Organization
LNTS	League of Nations Treaty Series
MERCOSUR	Southern Common Market Pact
MIDSA	Migration Dialogue for Southern Africa
MIDWA	Migration Dialogue for West Africa
MPRP	Migration Policy and Research Programme
MPI	Migration Policy Institute
MWC	International Convention on the Protection of the Rights of All Migrant Workers and Members of the Families
NAFTA	North American Free Trade Agreement
NATO	North Atlantic Treaty Organization
NGOs	Non-governmental organizations
OAS	Organization of American States
OASTS	Organization of American States, Treaty Series
OAU	Organization of African Unity
OCAM	The Central American Organization on Migration
OCED	Organization for Economic Cooperation and Development
OCHA	United Nations Office for the Coordination of Humanitarian Affairs
ODIHR	Office for Democratic Institutions and Human Rights
OJ	Official Journal
OSCE	Organization for Security and Cooperation in Europe
PCIJ	Permanent Court of Justice
PTSS	Post Traumatic Stress Syndrome
RASRO	Rescue-at-Sea Resettlement Offers Scheme
RCM	Regional Conference on Migration
RCPs	Regional Consultative Processes
RQN	Return of Qualified Nationals

RTA	Regional Trade Agreements
RTD	Right to development
SAARC	The South Asian Association for Regional Cooperation
SADC	South African Development Community
SAI	Andean Integration System
SAP	Structural adjustment programs
SAR	International Convention on Maritime Search and Rescue of 1979
SICA	Information System on Migration in Central America
SIS	Schengen Information System
SPS	Sanitary and Phytosanitary Measures
SOLAS	International Convention for the Safety of Life at Sea of 1974
TBT	Technical Barriers to Trade
TCI	Traditional countries of immigration
TIAS	Treaties and Other International Agreements
TOKTEN	Transfer of Knowledge Through Expatriate Nationals
TPS	Temporary protected status
TRIPS	Trade-Related Aspects of Intellectual Property Rights
TS	Treaty Series
UDHR	Universal Declaration on Human Rights
UEMOA	West African Economic and Monetary Union
UNAIDS	Joint United Nations Programme on HIV/AIDS
UNCLOS	United Nations Convention on the Law of the Sea
UNDP	United Nations Development Programme
UNEP	United Nations Environment Program
UNGA	United Nations General Assembly
UNHCR	United National High Commissioner for Refugees
UNHRC	United Nations Human Rights Commission
UNICEF	United Nations International Children's Emergency Fund
UNITAR	United Nations Institute for Training and Research
UNRISD	United Nations Research Institute for Social Development
UNSC	United Nations Security Council
UNTS	United Nations Treaty Series
UNTAET	United Nations Transitional Administration in East Timor
UST	United States Treaties and Other International Agreements
VDPA	Vienna Declaration and Program of Action
VTC	Vienna Convention on the Law of Treaties
WFP	World Food Programme
WHO	World Health Organization
WIPO	World Intellectual Property Organization
WLR	Weekly Law Reports
WTO	World Trade Organization
ZaöRV	Zeitschrift für ausländisches öffentliches Recht und Völkerrecht

Chapter 1
INTERNATIONAL LEGAL NORMS AND MIGRATION: A REPORT

T. Alexander Aleinikoff*

We are a world of states and a world of people on the move. We are also a world of borders. People cross borders for a wide range of reasons: to work, to visit family, to escape violence and natural disaster, to seek an education or medical care, or to return home. Virtually all states attempt to manage their borders, controlling the flow of persons in and out of the state.

It is sometimes said that states have complete authority to regulate the movement of persons across their borders – that anything less than complete authority would undermine their sovereignty and threaten their ability to define themselves as a nation. Against this claim, it is regularly asserted that migrants have fundamental human rights that state regulations of migration cannot abridge.

This debate misses crucial aspects of the current international legal regime, and it insufficiently values the possibility for cooperative efforts at managing migration in the interest of both states and migrants. There is, in fact, a fairly detailed – even if not comprehensive – set of legal rules, multilateral conventions, and bilateral agreements that constrain and channel state authority over migration. The claim of unbridled state authority cannot be sustained. Importantly, the extant norms are not imposed from above, the product of some worldwide legislature that has established a master plan for the movement of persons with which states must comply. Rather, the norms have been created from the ground up, through state-to-state relations, negotiations, and practices. States, that is, have sought to manage migration in the interests of both their populations and of friendly relations with other states. They have affirmed human rights norms both on principle and because they expect such norms to followed by the states to which their citizens travel and in which they take up residence. In short, because human migration has always occurred, because it is a natural human process – indeed, more natural than the state borders that people cross – it is not surprising that states have sought to work with other states in managing such movement.

Accordingly, this chapter examines international legal norms from a different perspective than the win-lose debate of state control versus migrants' rights. It seeks to identify the legal norms that constitute the framework of and cooperative management in the interests of states, their citizens, and interstate relations. It is therefore

* Professor, Georgetown University Law Center, and Senior Associate, Migration Policy Institute.

T.A. Aleinikoff and V. Chetail (Eds.), Migration and International Legal Norms
© 2003, T.M.C. Asser Press, The Hague, The Netherlands, et al.

consistent with the purpose of the UN expressed in its Charter, under which Member States commit themselves "[t]o achieve international co-operation in solving international problems of an economic, social, cultural, or humanitarian character, and in promoting and encouraging respect for human rights and for fundamental freedoms for all without distinction as to race, sex, language, or religion."

We will see that there is both more and less international law than might be supposed. On a number of issues there are easily identified norms relating to migration. Many are enshrined in interstate conventions (such as the principle of *non-refoulement*, which prohibits the return of persons to states where they face a risk of persecution). Other issues have evolved over time, and form part of customary international law (for instance, the duty of states to readmit nationals who seek to return). Furthermore, there are literally scores of international, regional, and bilateral agreements pertaining to migration that establish reciprocal obligations for ratifying states. These cover such diverse areas as trafficking, trade, the free flow of migrants within regions, and the rights of migrant workers.[1]

International norms are less clear or have not yet fully crystallized on other issues. Examples include: (1) a right to family unity is recognized in widely ratified human rights conventions, yet it is more difficult (outside the refugee context) to speak of an established right to migrate in order to unify a family; (2) while the duty to rescue persons at sea is clear, there is no firm rule on where such persons may disembark; and (3) states are permitted to draw lines based on citizenship status, but the standard for assessing the permissibility of discriminatory treatment is not firmly established. And in other areas, no clear legal norm has been established or is on the horizon. For example, there are no general international norms that manage dual nationality or regulate the integration of immigrants.

Each of these categories of issues implicates cooperative state efforts. Established norms evidence general international agreement; emerging and vague norms are areas where joint interpretive work may be productive; and "gap" areas provide obvious issues for further international consideration.

The migration process is frequently conceptualized as a triangular relationship among a person, a sending state, and a receiving state. A more complete description considers the role, *inter alia*, of countries of transit; social networks of migrants in home and settlement states; employers in receiving states; carriers, smugglers, and traffickers; and non-state agents of persecution whose acts cause persons to flee. This produces a complex web of connections among these various persons, groups, and states. International legal norms, accordingly, operate on several levels and have a range of addressees. They may describe state-to-state obligations (such as the duty to accept the return of one's nationals); state-to-individual obligations (such as the principle of *non-refoulement* of refugees); or individual-to-individual obligations (such as a ship captain's duty to rescue persons in distress at sea).

The chapters that constitute the bulk of this book describe in full these crosscutting legal norms.[2] The purpose of this introductory chapter is to extract from and

---

[1] See IOM, "Multilateral, Regional and Bilateral Cooperative Arrangements in the Management of Migration," this volume.

[2] It does not purport to be a survey of domestic norms, nor is it a comparative study of different kinds of domestic regimes of regulation.

organize that work in a manner that can be useful for policy-makers. It thus groups themes under broader categories, such as the authority and responsibility of states and the legal regime regarding forced migration. Legal citations have been kept to a minimum; for detailed legal references and discussions, the reader is urged to consult the expert papers.

STATE AUTHORITY AND RESPONSIBILITY

Authority

International law affirms the authority of states to regulate the movement of persons across their borders. Such power is understood to flow from the concept of an international system of states, with states possessing primary authority over their territory and population. State power over immigration is generally stated in broad terms; that is, states are deemed to have wide discretion in crafting admission, residence, expulsion, and naturalization policies for non-citizens.

Managing Admissions and Residence

In the modern era, states have exercised authority to manage admissions to their territory by defining classes of admissible and inadmissible non-citizens, by removing non-citizens deemed undesirable, and by making certain benefits and opportunities available only to citizens. Grounds for refusing admission (or mandating expulsion) typically include disease, criminal activity, violations of immigration laws, national security or *ordre public* concerns, and lack of economic means. Virtually all states have also specified documentary requirements – such as possession of a valid passport, visa, or travel document – for the entry of non-citizens into state territory.

Securing Integrity of Borders

State authority has also been exercised against persons and organizations that seek to transport migrants in violation of law.

The UN Convention Against Transnational Organized Crime (adopted by the General Assembly in 2000, not yet in force[3]) includes protocols dealing with smuggling and trafficking.[4] Under the protocols, *smuggling* is defined as the organized

---

[3] United Nations Convention Against Transnational Organized Crime, 9 January 2001, GAOR 55th Session, U.N. Doc. A/Res/55/25, 40 *ILM* 335 (2001) (not yet in force at time of publication). The Convention has been signed by 143 states and ratified by 24 states. It will enter into force after the fortieth ratification. Id. at Art. 38.

[4] See Protocol Against the Smuggling of Migrants by Land, Sea and Air Supplementing the United Nations Convention Against Transnational Crime (Smuggling Protocol), Art. 18, 15 November 2000, ch. II, U.N. Doc. A/55/383 (2000), 40 *ILM* 335 (2001) (not yet in force at time of publication); Protocol to Prevent, Suppress and Punish Trafficking in Persons, Especially Women and Children, Supplementing the United Nations Convention against Transnational Organized Crime (Trafficking Protocol), Art. 8, 15 November 2000, UN Doc. A/55/383 p. 53, 40 *ILM* 335 (2001) (not yet in force at time of

movement of persons into national territory for financial or other material benefit in violation of domestic laws;[5] *trafficking* is defined as recruiting, transporting, or harboring of persons involving the threat or use of force, coercion, fraud, deception, or abuse of power or of a position of vulnerability for the purpose of exploitation.[6] The protocols call for criminalization of certain acts and for interstate cooperation in exchange of law enforcement information and return of smuggled and trafficked persons.[7]

Regional efforts have also been undertaken, such as the Bangkok Declaration of 1999 (under which states pledge to coordinate efforts on irregular migration, smuggling, and trafficking). Bilateral arrangements between receiving states and states of origin have provided training and assistance to law enforcement officers and carrier personnel in states of origin to prevent illegal transit.

International conventions also deal with specific crimes sometimes associated with cross-border movements, such as terrorism, narcotics trafficking, and transnational organized crime.[8] These instruments generally call upon states to criminalize the activity, take steps to prevent its preparation within state borders, and cooperate with other states in prosecuting offenses (through, for example, extradition and legal assistance).

A number of consultative processes have been initiated in various regions of the world that seek to foster cooperation in stemming irregular migration.[9] More than forty European governments and ten international organizations participate in the Budapest Process, begun in 1991, which deals with such issues as smuggling, visa policy harmonization, readmission agreements, and sharing of information on unauthorized migration. The Regional Conference on Migration (commonly known as the Puebla Process) was initiated in 1996 to bring together North and Central American sending and receiving states on issues of common concern. Sixteen governments, the International Organization for Migration (IOM), and the United Nations High Commissioner for Refugees (UNHCR) participate in the Inter-governmental Consultations on Asylum, Refugee and Migration Policies in Europe, North America and Australia (IGC), which provides a forum for the exchange of information and comparative policy analysis.

---

publication). States Parties must also "take or strengthen measures ... to alleviate the factors that make persons, especially women and children, vulnerable to trafficking, such as poverty, underdevelopment and lack of opportunity." Trafficking Protocol, Art. 9(4).

[5] See Smuggling Protocol, Art. 3(a).

[6] See Trafficking Protocol, Art. 3(a).

[7] Importantly, each protocol includes a "saving clause" which notes that nothing in the provisions of the protocol "shall affect other rights, obligations, and responsibilities of State and individuals under international law, including international humanitarian law and international human rights law, and, in particular, where applicable, the 1951 Convention and the 1967 Protocol Relating to the Status of Refugees and the principle of *non-refoulement* as contained therein." Smuggling Protocol, Art. 19(1); Trafficking Protocol, Art. 14(1).

[8] See D. Fisher, S. Martin, and A. Schoenholtz, "Migration and Security in International Law," this volume.

[9] See generally A.K. von Koppenfels, "The Role of Regional Consultative Processes in Managing International Migration," *IOM Migration Research Series*, No. 3 (2001).

Nationality[10]

Every state possesses authority to determine who its nationals are, subject to conventional and customary law norms. So states may choose whether to adopt *jus soli* or *jus sanguinis* rules (or both) for birthright citizenship; and there is no international law requirement that a state extend citizenship to the children of immigrants (international instruments do, however, urge steps to avoid statelessness).[11] The state's power to make membership rules as well as its power to regulate immigration support state authority to make rules for the granting of citizenship to immigrants (naturalization). (Nationality is discussed in greater detail below.)

National Security

The power of a state to protect its security is a core attribute of sovereignty. Although there is no comprehensive instrument relating to migration and security, it is clear that states possess authority, under international law, to limit and control migration on national security grounds; and the exclusion and expulsion of persons thought to pose a threat to the national security of a state is firmly embedded in state practice.

In the wake of the September 11 attacks on the United States, the UN Security Council adopted Resolution 1373, calling on states to "[p]revent the movement of terrorists or terrorist groups by effective border controls and controls on issuance of identity papers and travel documents, and through measures for preventing counterfeiting, forgery or fraudulent use of identity papers and travel documents."[12]

National security grounds sometimes arise in international law as exceptions to rights secured under human rights and other conventions. These exceptions take the form of limitations on rights ("clawbacks") or as grounds for derogating from rights protected in the convention. The International Covenant on Civil and Political Rights (ICCPR) includes both kinds of provisions. Under Article 12(3), for example, freedom of movement within state territory and the right to leave a state "shall not be subject to any restrictions except those which are provided by law, *are necessary to protect national security*, public order (*ordre public*), public health or morals or

---

[10] In this paper, the terms "citizenship" and "nationality" are used interchangeably, although their meanings may have different connotations under the domestic laws of states.

[11] E.g., Convention on the Rights of the Child (CRC), Art. 8, 20 November 1989, U.N. Doc. A/RES/44/25 (1989), 28 *ILM* 1457 (1989).

[12] Efforts at drafting a comprehensive convention of terrorism have foundered on reaching agreement on the definition of terrorism. However, two conventions dealing with specific aspects of terrorism have recently entered into force: (1) the International Convention for the Suppression of Terrorist Bombing, GA Res. 52/164, annex (15 December 1997), 37 *ILM* 249 (1998) (entry into force 23 May 2002)(obligating States Parties, *inter alia*, to criminalize terrorist bombing and to extradite persons wanted by other States Parties); and (2) the International Convention for the Suppression of the Financing of Terrorism, GA Res. 54/109 (9 December 1999), 39 *ILM* 270 (2000) (entry into force 10 April 2002) (requiring States Parties to take appropriate steps for detecting, freezing, and seizing funds used in terrorist activities and to cooperate with other States Parties in preventive and enforcement efforts).

the rights and freedoms of others, and are consistent with the other rights recognized in the present Covenant."[13] Similarly, Article 13, provides:

> "An alien lawfully in the territory of a State Party to the present Covenant may be expelled therefrom only in pursuance of a decision reached in accordance with law and shall, *except where compelling reasons of national security otherwise require*, be allowed to submit the reasons against his expulsion and to have his case reviewed by, and be represented for the purpose before, the competent authority or a person or persons especially designated by the competent authority." (Emphasis supplied.)

States Parties may also derogate from certain of their obligations under the Covenant "[i]n time of public emergency which threatens the life of the nation ... to the extent strictly required by the exigencies of the situation, provided that such measures are not inconsistent with their other obligations under international law and do not involve discrimination solely on the ground of race, color, sex, language, religion or social origin."[14] The appropriateness of a limitation or derogation is judged on a case-by-case basis; but it is certain that a significant threat to national security would rank high among the state interests that could trigger restriction of a right.

Security grounds also provide an exception to the right of *non-refoulement* under international refugee law.[15] However, the Convention Against Torture does not provide such an exception, and the Committee Against Torture (the monitoring body for the treaty) has criticized national legislation that appears to permit the return to torture of persons deportable on national security grounds.[16]

Enforcement on the High Seas and Air Carriers

States increasingly seek to project enforcement of their immigration laws beyond their borders, deterring unlawful entries by sea and air. Under customary and conventional international law, state authorities may stop and board ships bearing their flags, stateless ships, and ships that have entered their territorial waters. States may enforce their immigration laws on ships in international waters flying foreign flags only with the consent of the flag state.[17]

Ships transporting migrants are sometimes overcrowded and present dangers to their passengers. Shipmasters have a duty under international law to rescue persons on ships in distress on the high seas;[18] and states have a duty to adopt legislation that

---

[13] Emphasis supplied. For references to clawback provisions in other treaties, see D. Fisher et al., this volume, at n. 69.

[14] Art. 4(1). See procedural requirements in Art. 4(3).

[15] Convention Relating to the Status of Refugees, Art. 33(2), 28 July 1951, 189 *UNTS* 150.

[16] E.g., CAT/C/SR.13 para. 27 (1989). See ICCPR, Art. 4(2), not permitting derogation from Art. 7 of the Covenant, which prohibits torture and cruel, inhuman, or degrading treatment or punishment.

[17] Convention on the High Seas, 29 April 1958, 450 *UNTS* 82 (entry into force 30 September 1962); United Nations Convention on the Law of the Sea of 1982 (UNCLOS), 10 December 1982, Art. 98(1), 1833 *UNTS* 397; Fisher et al., this volume.

[18] UNCLOS, Art. 98(1); International Convention for the Safety of Life at Sea, 1 November 1974, Chapter V (Reg. 10), 32 *UST* 47 (entry into force 25 May 1980).

establishes penalties for shipmasters who violate the duty to rescue.[19] Two difficult situations arise in regard to persons rescued at sea. First, international law does not provide clear guidance on where they should be taken – possibilities include the next scheduled port of call for the vessel or the nearest port. Second, persons rescued may frequently fear return to their home states and may have valid claims to *non-refoulement* under the Refugee Convention or other human rights instruments.[20]

Persons arriving in state territory by air are generally subject to inspection and admissibility procedures. Under Annex 9 to the (Chicago) Convention on International Civil Aviation, air carriers must "take precautions at the point of embarkation" to ensure that passengers possess valid travel documents as required by the state of disembarkation.[21] Passengers found to be inadmissible are transferred to the custody of the carrier, who is responsible for their "prompt removal" to the place where they began their journeys or to any other place where they are admissible. States Parties to the Convention commit themselves to receiving a passenger denied admission elsewhere if he or she had stayed in state territory before embarkation (other than in direct transit), unless the person had earlier been found inadmissible there. Many states impose fines and other penalties on air carriers landing passengers who do not possess proper documents, although penalties are not permitted where the carrier can demonstrate that it has taken "adequate precautions" to ensure compliance with documentary requirements.

In sum, international law recognizes a significant – if not primary – role for unilateral state action in regulating migration. Nonetheless, in many areas states have entered into cooperative interstate arrangements in pursuit of state interests and of better management of international migration.

Responsibility

Recognizing the existence of authority does not imply that such authority is unconstrained. As the regulation of migration implicates the interests of countries of origin and transit as well as the interests of migrants, states have entered into bilateral and multilateral agreements that limit and channel their authority over immigration. So too international law may establish substantive and procedural norms for the exercise of state power – including, most importantly, human rights norms embraced in customary law.

International Commitments

It is a bedrock norm in international law that treaties freely concluded and in force between states are to be respected and implemented. This principle – *pacta sunt*

---

[19] UNCLOS, Art. 98(1). See also International Convention on Maritime Search and Rescue, 1979 Annex, *TIAS* 11093 ch. 2, para. 2.1.10 (entry into force 22 June 1985).

[20] See UNHCR, "The Protection of Asylum-Seekers and Refugees Rescued at Sea," this volume. The United States Supreme Court has held that, under U.S. law, the Refugee Convention does not apply to actions of U.S. authorities beyond the territorial waters of the United States. *Sale* v. *Haitian Centers Council*, Inc., 509 U.S. 166, 113 S.Ct. 2549 (1993).

[21] 3.52-3.71.

servanda – is recognized in Article 26 of the 1969 Vienna Convention on the Law of Treaties: "every treaty in force is binding upon the parties to it and must be performed in good faith." It is further established that, under international law, treaty obligations between parties take precedence over conflicting provisions of municipal law.[22]

Respect for and Protection of International Human Rights Norms

States are bound by commitments in human rights conventions that they ratify and by customary international law norms. Most human rights are guaranteed irrespective of an individual's immigration status; they are a function of a person's status as a human being, not as a citizen of a particular state.[23]

As will be detailed below, of particular importance to regulation of immigration and immigrants are non-discrimination norms, general protections regarding due process, detention, and access to courts, specific protections pertaining to immigration proceedings, and norms relating to family unity.

Non-refoulement

Several widely ratified conventions prohibit the return of persons to particular kinds of harm. Most important among these are the 1951 Convention Relating to the Status of Refugees, the Convention Against Torture and Other Cruel, Inhuman or Degrading Treatment or Punishment, and the Fourth Geneva Convention relative to the Protection of Civilian Persons in Time of War, discussed below. These obligations also call into question some state practices directed at preventing illegal entry that have the effect of deterring or punishing asylum-seekers and other persons in need of international protection.

Duty to Accept Return of Nationals

Numerous authorities report that states have a duty to accept the return of their nationals from other states.[24] Although this duty is not established by a multilateral convention, it is generally deemed to follow from the recognized authority of a state to expel non-nationals. That is, for the right of a state to remove non-nationals to be effective, another state must accept those removed; and in a world that understands citizenship as state membership, that obligation is said to fall on home state of which the expellee is a citizen. Widespread state practice of accepting the return of

---

[22] *Greco-Bulgarian Communities* case, *PCIJ Reports*, Serie B, No. 17, p. 32. It remains, however, a question of domestic law whether international law will be given priority in domestic courts over inconsistent domestic law.

Although it is difficult to speak of a general duty of states to cooperate with one another on common issues, the U.N. Charter requires states to "settle their international disputes by peaceful means in such a manner that international peace and security, and justice are not endangered." Art. 2(3).

[23] General Comment No. 15, para. 7 (1986) (stating that aliens are entitled to recognition before the law).

[24] See sources cited in G. Noll, "Return of Persons to States of Origin and Third States," this volume.

one's citizens, including the conclusion of readmission agreements, is said to support the existence of such a norm of customary international law.

Despite the notice of such a norm in leading international law treatises, there are some difficulties with the position that one state must make perfect another's state exercise of the power to remove non-nationals. The home state may possibly object that *its* authority is being compromised by the demand of the expelling state; perhaps, then, only a more limited duty of non-interference exists – that is, not to hinder removal efforts of another state. Furthermore, it is arguable that the duty to accept the return of one's nationals applies only to those voluntarily returning. In this way, it would complement the individual's right to return rather than represent a duty imposed on one state because of the exercise of power of another state. Finally, the evidence of readmission agreements can be argued two ways: either they demonstrate the lack of a norm (and hence the necessity for an agreement), or they demonstrate the fleshing out of a recognized extant norm.[25]

In all events, it is clear that difficulties attending the return of non-nationals to their countries of origin have been a significant irritant in interstate relations. Readmission agreements are evidence of one kind of inter-state cooperation that is possible;[26] broader international commitments may also be feasible and advisable.[27]

Consular Access

Under the 1963 Convention on Consular Relations, a state that arrests or detains a non-citizen must inform him of his right to contact consular officials of his home state and must communicate such a request to consular officials "without delay." Consular officials are given the right "to visit a national of the sending State who is in prison, custody or detention, to converse and correspond with him and to arrange for his legal representation."[28]

FREEDOM OF PERSONS TO LEAVE AND RETURN

Numerous international and regional conventions affirm the right of persons to leave any country and to return to his or her country.[29] Importantly, this norm is narrower

---

[25] See id.

[26] See, for example, the European Council Recommendation of 30 November 1994 concerning a model bilateral readmission agreement between a Member State and a third country, *Official Journal* C 274, 19 September 1996, p. 20 (Art. 2(1): "The Contracting Party via whose external frontier a person can be proved, or validly assumed, to have entered who does not meet, or who no longer meets, the conditions in force for entry or residence on the territory of the requesting Contracting Party shall readmit the person at the request of the Contracting Party and without any formality.").

[27] See also Trafficking Protocol, Art. 8 (requiring State Parties to facilitate and accept return of trafficking victim who had right of permanent residence in the state at the time of the victim's entry into the receiving state); Smuggling Protocol, Art. 18.

[28] Art. 36.

[29] E.g., Universal Declaration on Human Rights (1948) (UDHR): "Everyone has the right to leave

than a general right to cross international borders or to be admitted to whatever country one chooses. Rather, it establishes a right to be free from arbitrary departure restrictions and an affirmative duty on states to provide travel documents. The right is not absolute. States may prevent departure, for example, to enforce criminal sanctions, the payment of taxes, military service requirements, and attendance at legal proceedings.

The right to leave is an "incomplete" right.[30] In a world of nation-states and controlled borders, exercise of the right depends upon a person's ability to locate a state willing to take him or her in. Because there is no right to enter a state other than one's own, persons who find that door closed or who seek to depart their home state but can find no other state to admit them will be unable to exercise their right to depart – except, perhaps, through unauthorized means.[31]

The right to leave applies to both nationals and non-nationals of the state of residence. Categories of persons able to assert a right to return, however, are more limited; it pertains to citizens and nationals of a state, and – it is generally agreed – to persons stripped of their nationality in violation of international law and perhaps to settled immigrants as well.[32] At the same time, the right to return is recognized as subject to fewer restrictions than the right to depart. According to the Human Rights Committee, charged with monitoring implementation of the widely ratified International Covenant on Civil and Political Rights, "there are few, if any, circumstances in which deprivation of the right to enter one's own country could be reasonable."[33]

FORCED MIGRATION

Because it is commonplace to note that increasing numbers of persons seek to travel across international borders, it is sometimes forgotten that the vast majority of the world's people seek to remain in their country of origin. Staying is the rule; moving is the exception. Indeed, it has been suggested that people have a "right to remain" in their home countries[34] – a right that is put under pressure by human causes and forces of nature.

International law does not recognize a general category of forced or involuntary migrant, but important and well-engrained norms pertain to certain classes of such persons. Indeed, a fairly elaborate regime has been established for the international protection of refugees and for victims of torture.[35] At the regional level, interstate

---

any country, including his own, and to return to his country." See V. Chetail, "Freedom of Movement and Transnational Migrations: A Human Rights Perspective," this volume.

[30] See id.

[31] The failure to provide lawful routes for departure and entry fall particularly hard on refugees and asylum-seekers who seek safety outside their countries of origin.

[32] Human Rights Committee, General Comment No. 27, CCPR/C/21/Rev.1/Add.9, para. 20 (1999) (noting that Art. 12(4) of the ICCPR uses the phrase "his own country," rather than the phrase "country of his nationality").

[33] Id. at para. 21.

[34] G. Goodwin Gill and K. Newland, "Forced Migration and International Law," this volume.

[35] See also Geneva Convention (IV) Relative to the Protection of Civilian Persons in Time of War,

agreements and arrangements have extended protection to persons who cross state borders in flight from other forms of inhumane treatment, civil war or disorder, and natural disasters. Furthermore, human rights principles condemn many of the practices that force persons to flee.

Refugees

More than 140 states have ratified either the 1951 Convention relating to the Status of Refugees or its 1967 Protocol. Under these instruments, a refugee is defined as a person who "owing to well-founded fear of being persecuted for reasons of race, religion, nationality, membership of a particular social group or political opinion, is outside the country of his nationality and is unable or, owing to such fear, is unwilling to avail himself of the protection of that country." States are obligated to grant recognized refugees a range of benefits and opportunities afforded to immigrants and nationals. Most important, Article 33 prohibits the return of a refugee to a country "where his life or freedom would be threatened" on one of the Convention grounds (the principle of *non-refoulement*).[36]

The Convention establishes a regime of "surrogate protection."[37] That is, the States parties have committed themselves to protecting persons forced to flee their home state who cannot rely upon that state to safeguard their fundamental rights and interests.

Prior to adoption of the 1951 Convention, the General Assembly established the Office of the United Nations High Commissioner for Refugees (UNHCR) to provide international protection to, and seek permanent solutions for, refugees. The Convention also charges UNHCR with the supervision of the application of its provisions.[38]

Although these refugee protection norms and practices constitute the most well-established and widely adopted international regime pertaining to migration, there are nonetheless numerous gaps in the system:

1. Although there is a recognized right to "seek asylum,"[39] states are under no duty to grant asylum or even to admit persons so that asylum claims may be pursued.[40] The crucial state obligation is *non-refoulement*, not admission or a grant of residence.

---

75 *UNTS* 287 (1949), Art. 45 (stating that "[i]n no circumstances shall a protected person be transferred to a country where he or she may have reason to fear persecution for his or her political opinions or religious beliefs").

[36] The principle of *non-refoulement* is also, arguably, a norm of customary international law. See G. Goodwin-Gill, *The Refugee in International Law* (2nd edn. 1996), p. 225; V. Chetail, "Le principe de non-refoulement et le statut de réfugié en droit international," *in* V. Chetail (ed.), *La Convention de Genève du 28 juillet 1951 relative au statut des réfugiés – 50 ans après: bilan et perspective* (2001), p. 65.

[37] James Hathaway, *The Law of Refugee Status* (1991), p. 135.

[38] Art. 35.

[39] UDHR, Art. 14(1).

[40] But see Ex. Comm. [of the UNHCR Programme] Conclusion No. 22 (XXXII), Protection of Asylum-Seekers in Situations of Large-Scale Influx (states should admit asylum-seekers in cases of large-scale influx pending arrangements for a durable solution).

2. States have adopted varying interpretations of the term "refugee" that have led to inconsistent application of the Convention. UNHCR has authority to issue guidance on interpreting the Convention's provisions, but such guidance is not binding on State Parties.

3. The Convention and Protocol do not apply to all persons forced to cross international borders – such as some victims of civil war or disorder, and persons who flee extreme poverty, famine, or other natural disasters. (Regional instruments and declarations include some of these categories.)

4. States, in efforts to deter unlawful migration, have adopted numerous measures – such as visa requirements, carrier sanctions, and detention policies – that hinder the ability of persons seeking asylum to leave their countries of origin or to gain access to refugee status determination procedures.

5. Asylum-seekers frequently travel through other countries before reaching the state in which they assert a claim to refugee status. Norms are not well established, however, regarding the duties of transit countries or return of asylum-seekers to such countries.

6. The Convention does not supply standardized status determination procedures. Accordingly, procedures vary considerably among states.

In each of these areas, frictions among states have developed. For instance, some states seek to return asylum-seekers to states through which they transited with the idea that they request asylum there; and differing treatment of classes of persons who do not meet the formal definition of refugee may deflect flows from one state to another. Nor does there appear to be emerging a norm that a state that creates a refugee flow has breached a duty owed to the state burdened by that flow.[41] Some of these matters have been dealt with on a bilateral or regional basis,[42] and the opportunity for mutually advantageous state cooperation – consistent with the overriding norm of protection for bona fide refugees – is apparent. For example, in 2001, the EU Council issued a directive establishing minimum standards for temporary protection programs in situations of mass influx.[43]

---

[41] See L. Lee, "The Right to Compensation: Refugees and Countries of Asylum," 80 *American Journal of International Law* (1986) p. 532.

[42] See IOM, G. Goodwin-Gill and K. Newland, this volume; See also U.S.-Canada Smart Border Declaration (12 December 2001), available at www.canadianembassy.org/border/declaration2-e.asp.

[43] Council Directive 2001/55/ED (20 July 2001). The EU is also in the process of developing a common policy on asylum, as mandated by Art. 63 of the Treaty of Amsterdam.

See also 1969 Organization for African Unity Convention on the Specific Aspects of Refugee Problems in Africa (extending refugee definition to persons who flee "external aggression, occupation, foreign domination or events seriously disturbing public order" as well as persons protected as refugees under the 1951 Convention, Art. I(2)); 1984 Cartagena Declaration, pertaining to forced migrants in Central and South America.

Beyond the protection of the *non-refoulement* principle, the 1951 Convention establishes fairly robust non-discrimination norms (e.g., to work, social welfare programs, religious freedom) for refugees lawfully in their countries of settlement. Refugees are guaranteed the right of access to courts and freedom of movement and are protected, with certain qualifications, against penalties for unlawful entry. The Convention also establishes limits on the detention of refugees.

International law recognizes the special case of children refugees and asylum-seekers.[44] Children may be entitled to refugee status on grounds similar to those of adult asylum-seekers or as members of a "particular social group," such as victims of abuse or trafficking. Furthermore, it cannot be assumed that a child's asylum claim necessarily merges with a parent's claim – most obviously in cases where the child is asserting abuse within the family. Guidelines have been developed at the international, national, and regional level to address substantive and procedural issues specific to child asylum-seekers.[45]

Torture Victims

International and regional conventions and customary international law protect other victims of human rights abuses from *refoulement*. Most states have ratified the 1984 Convention against Torture and Other Cruel, Inhuman or Degrading Treatment or Punishment (CAT), under which they commit themselves not to return a person "where there are substantial grounds for believing that he would be in danger of being subject to torture."[46] The protection in the European Convention on Human Rights and Fundamental Freedoms against torture and inhuman or degrading treatment and punishment has been interpreted to prohibit the return of a person to a state when there is a "real risk" he or she would suffer such treatment.[47]

Trafficked Persons

The recently adopted Trafficking Protocol goes beyond traditional law enforcement approaches that viewed trafficked aliens as illegal migrants. In addition to promot-

---

[44] Art. 22(1) of the Convention on the Rights of the Child, *supra*, provides:

States Parties shall take appropriate measures to ensure that a child who is seeking refugee status or who is considered a refugee in accordance with applicable international or domestic law and procedures shall, whether unaccompanied or accompanied by his or her parents or by any other person, receive appropriate protection and humanitarian assistance in the enjoyment of applicable rights set forth in the present Convention and in other international human rights or humanitarian instruments to which the said States are Parties.

[45] See J. Bhabha, "Children, Migration and International Norms," this volume.

[46] Art. 3. While the *non-refoulement* provision of the Refugee Convention, Art. 33(2), does not extend to refugees who pose a danger to the security of the country of refuge or who have committed a "particularly serious crime" there, the Torture Convention's prohibition against *refoulement* is absolute.

[47] *Soering* v. *UK*, 7 July 1989, Series A No. 161, pp. 35-36, paras. 90-91; *Chahal* v. *UK*, 15 November 1996, Reports of Judgments and Decisions 1996-V, p. 1853, paras. 73-74. See also ICCPR, Art. 7 (implicit *non-refoulement* obligation for persons facing torture or cruel, inhuman, or degrading treatment or punishment).

ing the suppression of trafficking, the Protocol states a purpose of protecting and assisting victims of trafficking "with full respect for their human rights."[48] It thus mandates that State Parties take steps to protect the physical safety, privacy, and identity of victims; to assist victims in legal proceedings; and to consider implementing measures to provide for the physical, psychological, and social recovery of victims. States are also urged to consider adopting laws or regulations that permit victims to remain in the territory on a temporary or permanent basis.[49]

Children are particularly vulnerable in trafficking situations, and they are frequently the victims of sexual exploitation, abusive adoptions, or coerced labor. International norms prohibiting child exploitation[50] thus complement anti-trafficking norms.

THE HUMAN RIGHTS OF MIGRANTS

The human rights of individuals – including immigrants – are frequently conceptualized as rights that challenge the sovereignty of states. This approach, however, fails to recognize that such rights are often memorialized or protected in exercises of state sovereignty. States may be bound by human rights norms because they have ratified conventions protecting such rights; in such cases, any resulting limit on state sovereignty has been expressly consented to by the state. States may also be bound by norms of customary international law. These norms are established only after they have received widespread support in state practice and are generally recognized by states as binding legal obligations. Under prevailing international law, states are not bound by norms to which they objected during the crystallization of the norm. In short, human rights norms do not appear *deus ex machina*; they reflect state deliberation, practice, and commitment.

Non-discrimination

The principle of non-discrimination – fundamental to international law – protects immigrants and citizens.[51] It does so in two ways. First, non-citizens, like citizens, are protected against discrimination based on race, religion, sex, and other protected grounds. Second, differential treatment based on a person's alienage is subject to scrutiny under prevailing human rights norms. Both these concepts are found in the ICCPR. Article 26 provides:

> "All persons are equal before the law and are entitled without any discrimination to the equal protection of the law. In this respect, the law shall prohibit any discrimination and guarantee to all persons equal and effective protection against discrimination on any

---

[48] Art. 2.

[49] Arts. 6 and 7.

[50] E.g., CRC, Art. 36; ICESCR, Art. 10(3).

[51] See also id. at Art. 26 (guaranteeing to "all persons" equality before the law and equal protection of the law without discrimination).

ground such as race, colour, sex, language, religion, political or other opinion, national or social origin, property, birth or other status."

A law, for example, that denies job opportunities to members of a particular religion would be evaluated in the same manner under the Covenant's protections whether a member of that religion is a citizen or a non-citizen. Furthermore, a law that denied non-citizens, but not citizens, a right to go to school or to own land could also give rise to claim because alienage could constitute a protected "status" under the provision.[52]

It is clear, however, that neither the ICCPR nor other human rights instruments purport to prohibit all distinctions between citizens and non-citizens. While different formulations have been proposed to describe the alienage non-discrimination norm,[53] it is clear that (1) the state must be pursuing a legitimate end, and (2) there must be a demonstrable connection between that end and the means used to advance it. As noted in a General Comment of the Human Rights Committee (established under the ICCPR to monitor States Parties' compliance with the Covenant), "not every differentiation of treatment will constitute discrimination, if the criteria for such differentiation are reasonable and objective and if the aim is to achieve a purpose which is legitimate under the Covenant."[54] In the context of discrimination based on alienage, the status of the alien (settled immigrant, temporary visitor, unauthorized migrant) is likely to influence the evaluation of the differential treatment.

States would have a difficult time justifying policies that deny to non-citizens core civil rights and political freedoms that are granted to citizens – such as access to courts and freedom of speech. It is generally recognized, however, that restricting the franchise and political office holding to citizens does not constitute unjustifiable discrimination against immigrants.[55]

Rights protected under the International Covenant on Economic, Social and Cultural Rights (ICESCR) – such as the right to work, to an adequate standard of living, to health, and to education – are generally guaranteed to "everyone" within a state. Furthermore, the Covenant provides that such rights "will be exercised without dis-

---

[52] Regional conventions are to the same effect. W. Kälin, "Human Rights and the Integration of Migrants," this volume. The International Convention on the Elimination of All Forms of Racial Discrimination specifically provides that its prohibition of racial discrimination does "not apply to distinctions, exclusions, restrictions or preferences made by a State Party to this Convention between citizens and non-citizens." Art. 1(2). But the precise meaning of this – rather odd – exception is unclear, and does not appear to prevent immigrants from asserting a right to be free from racial discrimination. J. Fitzpatrick, "The Human Rights of Migrants," this volume.

[53] Compare J. Fitzpatrick, this volume ("differential treatment is permitted where the distinction is made pursuant to a legitimate aim, the distinction has an objective justification, and reasonable proportionality exists between the means employed and the aims sought to be realized") with D. Martin, this volume (suggesting that a lower standard – that there be "some rational basis for the differentiation relevant to the purpose that is sought to be achieved" – better reflects real-world application).

[54] General Comment No. 18, Non-discrimination (1989), para. 13.

[55] See ICCPR, Art. 25 (limiting to citizens the rights to take part in public affairs, to vote, and to have access to public service).

crimination of any kind."[56] Thus non-citizens are protected against discrimination based on their alienage as regards rights secured by the Covenant.[57] The ICESCR includes a provision authorizing a particular kind of discrimination against non-citizens: developing states are permitted to determine "to what extent they would guarantee the economic rights recognized in the present Covenant to non-nationals."[58] But express recognition of this limited form of discrimination supports the proposition that the Covenant generally prohibits discrimination based on alienage for Covenant rights. Nonetheless, state practice demonstrates widespread limitations on economic and social rights, restricting, for example, the right to work and participation in social welfare programs for various classes of immigrants.

Substantive Rights

Instruments protecting human rights generally apply to all persons within a state's jurisdiction.[59] In other words, a person's status as an alien does not take him or her outside the protections of human rights law.

Non-citizens, like citizens, are entitled to rights that are absolute or not subject to derogation or limitation. They are also entitled, on equal terms with citizens, to those rights whose denial on the basis of alienage would never be justifiable. These include, for example, the right to life; rights guaranteed in the criminal process; freedom of thought, conscience and religion; the right to leave a country; the prohibition on retroactive criminal penalties; and the right to marry.

For other categories of rights, immigration status may be a relevant consideration. Some state practices that pertain only to non-citizens might not be deemed "arbitrary" under various provisions of human rights instruments. For example, the prohibition in Article 9(1) of the ICCPR of "arbitrary arrest and detention" cannot be read as prohibiting all detentions of immigrants in immigration proceedings. Nor would the Covenant's protection against "arbitrary" interferences with family (Article 17) erect a total bar to deportation of an immigrant who has family members in the state of settlement.

---

[56] ICESCR, Art. 2(2). Such discrimination would also be subject to the non-discrimination norm of Art. 26 of the ICCPR.

The ICESCR recognizes that the provision of social, economic, and cultural rights frequently requires affirmative conduct by states (including expenditure of state resources). It thus commits States Parties to "achieving progressively the full realization of the rights recognized in the present Covenant," subject to "the maximum of its available resources." Art. 2(1). This provision, however, does not authorize discrimination against non-citizens as a way for states to progressively realize Covenant rights.

[57] State laws excluding settled immigrant children from primary education would be particularly difficult to justify, given the importance of education to a child's development and his or her ability to enjoy other rights. See CRC, Art. 28(1); ICESCR, Art. 13.

[58] ICESCR, Art. 2(3).

[59] See ICCPR Art. 2(1), requiring states to ensure Covenant rights to "all individuals within its territory and subject to its jurisdiction." This mandate mentions neither nationality nor reciprocity (i.e., there is no requirement that in order for a citizen of State X to be protected in State Y, State X must grant similar rights to citizens of State Y residing in State X).

Some rights established in conventions are subject to limitations based on grounds of national security or *ordre public*.[60] To the extent that such rights may be limited for citizens, they may be limited for non-citizens within the jurisdiction of a state as well. Furthermore, alienage itself may be a factor in considering whether a particular limit serves a legitimate state purpose and is proportional to the end sought by the state.

Certain rights are expressly limited to citizens. For example, although most of the rights in the ICCPR are guaranteed to all persons, Article 25 states that "[e]very citizen" shall have the right to take part in the conduct of public affairs, to vote and be elected, and to have access to public service. Other rights are guaranteed only to citizens and lawfully present migrants, such as the right to freedom of movement within a state secured by Article 12(1) of the ICCPR.

Some rights apply only to non-citizens, or a subset thereof (such as those concerning immigration proceedings).[61]

Some human rights treaties state that their protections do not apply to certain differential treatment based on citizenship status.[62]

Family Unity

The right to family unity is widely recognized in international and regional human rights instruments. As the "fundamental group unit" in society, the family is entitled to protection and support.[63] Furthermore, under the Convention on the Rights of the Child (CRC), a child may be separated from his or her family only when competent authorities subject to judicial review determine that such separation is necessary for the best interests of the child.[64] Family unity rights pertain to non-nationals as well as nationals. Thus immigrants are protected in their rights to marry and form and raise a family.

Immigration regulation interacts with family unity in a number of ways. Most states permit the entry of immediate family members (spouses and minor children) to join a lawful resident immigrant. At the same time, however, it is increasingly apparent that some immigration policies pose significant challenges to family unity. For example, admissions policies frequently engender long delays in the entry of close family members or deny entry altogether. Expulsion measures may also threat-

---

[60] See ICCPR, Arts. 18 (manifestation of religion), 19 (freedom of expression), and 22 (freedom of association).

[61] E.g., ICCPR, Art. 13.

[62] See International Convention on the Elimination of all Forms of Racial Discrimination (CERD), 21 December 1965, Art. 1(2), 660 *UNTS* (entry into force 4 January 1969) (Convention "shall not apply to distinctions, exclusions, restrictions or preferences made by a State Party to this Convention between citizens and non-citizens"); ICESCR, Art. 2(3)("Developing countries, with due regard to human rights and their national economy, may determine to what extent they would guarantee the economic rights recognized in the present Covenant to non-nationals").

[63] K. Jastram, "Family Unity," this volume.

[64] Art. 9(1). Plainly, this rule would not prohibit all separations. For example, imprisonment of a parent after conviction for a criminal offense would not barred. See Art. 9(4).

en to separate families.[65] And the definition of family applied by the receiving state may be different than that used by the immigrant family.

It has been suggested that family unification across borders is a necessary corollary to the right of family unity. But this norm of international law has yet to crystallize, and state practice is frequently to the contrary. Human rights instruments exhort states to take best efforts to foster family unity, as does international refugee and humanitarian law. For example, the Convention on the Rights of the Child provides that "family unification shall be dealt with by States Parties in a positive, humane, and expeditious manner."[66] Furthermore, it is not obvious that such a norm would require a state to admit family members of settled immigrants; it might be possible for the family to unify in another state (most particularly the state origin). An emerging right to family unification across borders is strongest for refugees and settled lawful immigrants; it would be more difficult to sustain such a right for unauthorized entrants or asylum-seekers. It is clear, in any event, that the problem of separated families is significant both for the families and the states of residence, and that this remains an area for which interstate cooperative efforts would be important.

The right of a family to stay together has been more fully developed in expulsion cases. Thus, the Human Rights Committee, in a case raising a claim that the deportation of an immigrant was inconsistent with Article 17 of the ICCPR (prohibiting arbitrary interference with privacy, family, or home), considered whether the threatened impact on the family would be disproportionate to the state's effectuation of immigration policies. Factors to be examined include the length of residence; the age of the children and the impact of expulsion of a parent; the conduct of the parent; and the state's interests in protecting public safety and promoting compliance with immigration laws. As in the admissions context, however, it has been recognized that expulsion does not necessarily destroy family unity; it may simply cause relocation of the entire family to another state.

The Convention on the Rights of the Child appears to apply a stricter standard, permitting family separation only when it is in the best interests of the child.[67] Thus, where expulsion would in fact result in family separation – because of practical relocation and adaptation difficulties – states would have an obligation under the CRC to hear from the child (or his or her representative) and determine whether the expulsion of the parent is in the child's best interest.

---

[65] Less significant today is the denial of exit permission for a person seeking to join family members outside his or her state of origin.

[66] Art. 10(1). See also EU directive on family unity/TP; Convention on Migrant Workers (states shall take measures they deem appropriate to facilitate reunification); Final Act of the Conference of Plenipotentiaries, 1951 Convention Relating to the Status of Refugees; Additional Protocol I, 1977, Art. 74; see also Protocol II, 1977, Art. 4(3)(b).

[67] Art. 9 states "shall ensure that a child shall not be separated from his or her parents against their will, except when ... such separation is necessary for the best interests of the child."

Rights Relating to Immigration Proceedings

Human rights norms limit both the substantive and procedural scope of a state's power to regulate immigration. In managing the movement of persons over its borders, a state necessarily has authority to adopt policies that pertain solely to non-citizens. Non-discrimination norms, however, may check state power to draw lines among non-citizens. For example, immigration policies based on race – once a fixture of some states' legal regimes – are not sustainable under current human rights principles.[68] Gender-based distinctions would also require special justification.[69]

Immigration proceedings must comply with general principles of due process. The ICCPR devotes a specific article, Article 13, to expulsion proceedings:

> "An alien lawfully in the territory of a State Party to the present Covenant may be expelled therefrom only in pursuance of a decision reached in accordance with law and shall, except where compelling reasons of national security otherwise require, be allowed to submit the reasons against his expulsion and to have his case reviewed by, and be represented for the purpose before, the competent authority or a person or persons especially designated by the competent authority."[70]

The somewhat limited scope of this norm is worth noting. First, it applies only to non-citizens "lawfully in territory" – thus, presumably, not to undocumented entrants. The term, however, poses a conundrum because expulsion proceedings normally are held to determine whether or not a person is lawfully in the country. Accordingly, the Human Rights Committee has stated that "if the legality of an alien's entry or stay is in dispute, any decision of this point leading to his expulsion or deportation ought to be taken in accordance with Article 13."[71] Second, the exception for "compelling reasons" of national security might justify *ex parte* or *in camera* proceedings in terrorist cases. Third, the procedural rights guaranteed under the ICCPR are less stringent than those guaranteed in criminal proceedings. It should be noted, however, that many states go significantly beyond the protections identified in Article 13, such as entitling aliens in expulsion proceedings access to a court independent of the initial decision-maker, the right to be represented by counsel, and the right to present evidence and examine evidence used against him.

A number of human rights instruments condemn mass deportations (that is, the summary removal of a large group of persons from a state).[72] Relatedly, the Human Rights Committee has interpreted the ICCPR as entitling "each alien a decision in his own case."[73]

---

[68] See, CERD, Art. 1(2). Policies based on a person's national origin (meant in the sense of citizenship, not ethnicity) do not generally constitute discrimination based on race.

[69] J. Fitzpatrick, this volume.

[70] Art. 13.

[71] General Comment No. 15, para. 9 (1986).

[72] E.g., Protocol No. 4 to the Convention for the Protection of Human Rights and Fundamental Freedoms, securing certain rights and freedoms other than those already included in the Convention and in the first Protocol thereto, 16 September 1963, Art. 4; American Convention on Human Rights, Art. 22(9), November 1969.

[73] General Comment No. 15, para. 19 (1986).

The detention of immigrants in the course of immigration proceedings is also subject to human rights norms that prohibit "arbitrary arrest or detention." Thus, the ICCPR provides that "[a]nyone who is deprived of his liberty by arrest or detention shall be entitled to take proceedings before a court, in order that the court may decide without delay on the lawfulness of his detention and order his release if detention is not lawful."[74] Detention and migrant interdiction policies may impose particular burdens on asylum-seekers, undercutting their rights to seek asylum and to be protected against *non-refoulement*.

INTEGRATION OF IMMIGRANTS

Millions of persons seek not only to cross international borders, but also to take up residence in the foreign state to which they travel. It might be argued that if there is no general duty to admit a non-national, then there can be no duty to foster an admitted non-national's integration into the receiving state. Furthermore, rules establishing the terms and conditions under which migrants could become settled residents would fall primarily within the domestic authority of the receiving state. This has been the traditional position of international law. Part and parcel of the accepted authority to determine admission policies is the authority of a state to establish opportunities (or not) for the integration and membership of immigrants as it sees fit. One cannot speak, then, of an internationally recognized right of immigrants to integrate or to be provided with the means to do so. Concomitantly immigrants do not have a duty to naturalize.

These rather broad conclusions, however, must be supplemented by discussion of other topics that relate to integration and assimilation. Non-discrimination norms prohibit discrimination against non-citizens that both hinders material integration and sends a stigmatizing message to immigrants that they do not belong. Guarantees of political rights – such as freedom of speech and assembly – may also facilitate integration by providing immigrants a means to participate in the country and to provide information about policies that affect them, by training them in the political institutions and norms of their country of residence, and by giving them a sense of stake in the society.

Furthermore, as noted above, there is a trend toward recognizing that in some circumstances a non-national's ties (including family ties) to a state of residence may restrict state authority to expel him or her.[75] Here, integration serves not as a goal of state policy, but rather as a limitation on state power; it represents a set of attachments that should be taken into account in determining whether enforcement of a state's immigration law is arbitrary and is proportional to the harm imposed on the immigrant and his or her family.[76]

---

[74] Art. 9(4). See also J. Fitzpatrick, this volume.

[75] The right to family life is expressly protected in international and regional conventions. ICCPR Arts. 17 and 23; CRC Arts. 3, 9, 10, and 16; ECHR Art. 8; ACHR Arts. 17 and 19; African Charter, Art. 18. See *Winata* v. *Australia*, U.N. Doc. CCPR/C/72/D/930/2000 (16 August 2001). See D. Martin, this volume; K. Jastram, this volume.

[76] Other aspects of the right to family unity also have a pertinent impact on integration.

Integration concerns are also implicated by citizenship rules and by state tolerance of difference or promotion of assimilation.

Citizenship (Nationality) and Naturalization

Citizenship (or nationality) is commonly understood as membership in a state. In today's world, citizenship plays a vital role – both for states and individuals. Thus, the Universal Declaration on Human Rights (UDHR) provides that "[e]veryone has the right to a nationality," and that no one shall be arbitrarily deprived of his nationality or denied the right to change his nationality. (The UDHR does not by itself establish legally binding norms, although many of its guarantes may have attained the status of customary international law.) The international legal community has also recognized that statelessness leaves persons particularly vulnerable.[77] Accordingly, the 1961 Convention on the Reduction of Statelessness mandates, *inter alia*, that States Parties grant nationality to persons born in their territories who would otherwise be stateless and not deprive a person of his or her nationality if it would render him stateless.[78] The importance of possessing citizenship in a state is expressly recognized in the Convention relating to the Status of Refugees, which provides that states "shall as far as possible facilitate the assimilation and naturalization of refugees."[79]

For an immigrant, or an immigrant's children, acquisition of citizenship is likely to be an important measure of integration. This is not to say that integration cannot occur without acquisition of citizenship, nor that citizenship always and everywhere demonstrates integration. Nonetheless, citizenship generally connotes full membership, typically endowing its holder with the full range of domestic rights recognized by the state.

Citizenship is acquired either at birth or by naturalization. In the past, states could be fruitfully categorized as embracing notions of *jus soli* (citizenship based on birth within national territories) or *jus sanguinis* (citizenship based on descent). But more recently this distinction has broken down. Formerly *jus sanguinis* states that have experienced significant immigration have tended to adopt *jus soli* rules in order to avoid multiple non-citizen generations born in the state. And some *jus soli* states have adopted requirements permitting birthright citizenship only if one or both of the immigrant parents was in a lawful immigrant status at time of the child's birth.[80]

While there is thus a growing convergence toward birthright citizenship rules among major immigrant countries, it has not been the product of conventional or customary international law norms. There are no international conventions significantly regulating acquisition of citizenship; and under customary international law, states are generally free to decide upon whom to confer citizenship.[81]

---

[77] Convention relating to the Status of Stateless Persons, 28 September 1954 (entry into force 6 June 1960).

[78] Note, however, that only twenty-six states are parties to the Convention.

[79] Art. 34.

[80] T.A. Aleinikoff and D. Klusmeyer, *Citizenship Policies for an Age of Migration* (2002).

[81] See Hailbronner, "Nationality," this volume. The 1997 European Convention on Nationality states

Immigration is linked to citizenship in another way. Virtually all states provide routes to formal state membership via naturalization laws. Although policies vary from state to state, states generally condition naturalization upon lawful residence on state territory for a certain number of years and non-criminal behavior; and most also require demonstration of ability in an official state language. Some states require evidence of knowledge of the history or culture the country. A number of states also require that persons attaining citizenship through naturalization renounce prior citizenships; this practice is far from universal, and it is neither required nor prohibited by principles of international law.

The exercise of a state's power to grant citizenship is, perforce, limited by overriding human rights norms – such as non-discrimination norms and requirements of procedural fairness. Thus, laws denying citizenship based on race or gender, or permitting termination of citizenship without regular procedures, would be difficult to justify under general human rights norms.

Multiple nationalities are an increasingly common occurrence. In the past, plural nationalities were seen as an irritant in international relations – a status to be discouraged or prohibited in order to avoid attendant issues of loyalty and diplomatic protection. More recently, however, states have shown greater tolerance for multiple nationalities, recognizing that persons can maintain links to more than one state without major interstate conflicts ensuing. The relationship of plural nationalities and integration is not clear; in some cases it may advance integration, in others it may undermine it. Accordingly, the sorting out of rights and duties for dual nationals would be an appropriate area for interstate deliberation and cooperation.

Difference and Assimilation

The term "integration" connotes a level of economic and social functioning within a society. Immigrants are fully integrated when they can find jobs, take care of their families, join in community life, and negotiate every day living in a society. Assimilation has a cultural sense. An immigrant is assimilated when he or she shares the common values of the society, speaks the language, and adopts dominant cultural practices.

As Professor Kälin notes, the issue of cultural assimilation of migrants

"is complex because of a deep tension between two basic principles. On the one hand human rights such as the freedoms of religion, association, expression of opinion, and marriage or the right to privacy and to protection of one's own family life guarantee cultural autonomy. [T]he respect for human beings requires a recognition of their identity as, other-

that "each State shall determine under its own law who are its nationals (Art. 3(1)); however, the Convention requires states to provide nationality to children born or found in their territory who would otherwise be stateless, and to children born on state territory whose parents possesses state nationality. (Art. 6(1), (2)) The Convention also mandates that states facilitate the acquisition of nationality for spouses and children of nationals, and persons (including stateless persons and refugees) who lawfully and habitually reside on state territory. (Art. 6(4))

wise, individuals are degraded. ... On the other hand, a certain basis of commonly accepted values is necessary, in every State and every society, for a minimal degree of cohesion."[82]

International law does not speak directly to these issues, but its protection of individual rights necessarily implies some degree of tolerance of difference (of religion, language, opinion). Furthermore, groups may enjoy rights that give them space from dominant social practices. Thus, Article 27 of ICCPR protects persons belonging to an ethnic, religious, or linguistic minority against denials of their right "in a community with other members of their group, to enjoy their own culture, to profess and practise their own religion, or to use their own language."[83]

States are free to promote assimilation, through educational, social, and immigration policies. But compelled assimilation – such as a requirement that a person practice a particular religion or espouse a particular political opinion – would violate internationally recognized freedoms. Non-discrimination norms also cast doubt on policies that restrict state benefits, institutions, and programs to members of particular groups, or that penalize certain group identities or practices. Indeed, it is likely that some degree of tolerance of difference will advance, rather than retard, the integration of immigrants – as immigrants come to see themselves as equal and valued members of society. Requirements for tolerance would be strongest in the private sphere, as state interests recede and privacy and associational interests grow.[84]

LABOR MIGRATION

People have forever crossed borders in search of work. Today, millions of persons are employed outside their countries of origin, in highly skilled, skilled, and unskilled jobs, as permanent settlers and temporary workers, lawfully admitted and unlawfully present. Both sending states and receiving states benefit from migration for employment purposes; and, not surprisingly, states – at least on a regional and bilateral basis – have sought to regularize the flow in their mutual self-interest and in the interests of the workers.

The migration of workers is sometimes secured by regional agreements that generally permit freedom of movement and settlement for citizens of Member States. Examples include the instruments establishing the European Union, the Treaty of the Economic Community of West African States, and the Agreement of the Council of Arab Economic Unity. Some states have special relations with former colonies that also permit largely unrestricted entry and residence and account for significant

---

[82] W. Kälin, "Human Rights and the Integration of Migrants," this volume at 282-293.

[83] See also CRC, Art. 29(1)(c) (stating that the education of children should be directed both at the national values of the country in which he or she is living and his or her own cultural identity, language, and values and the country from which he or she may originate).

[84] There will be situations where the public/private distinction will prove problematic – for example, cases involving domestic arrangements or practices that are consistent with cultural norms but may violate human rights norms.

labor flows. Other states have established bilateral relationships with neighboring states that specifically authorize the entry of temporary workers.[85]

Major international trade agreements include limited – but important – provisions supporting the temporary movement of persons between trading partners. The General Agreement on Trade in Services (GATS) encourages governments, in the course of multilateral trade negotiations, to commit to opening markets to foreign service-providers. GATS Article I recognizes four modes of trade in services; the fourth mode is the movement of natural persons to provide services in a foreign country. Commitments made by governments under the GATS are enforceable in the World Trade Organization (WTO).[86] Regional trade agreements also have implications for the movement of persons. For example, under the North American Free Trade Agreement, persons engaged in "trade in goods, the provision of services or the conduct of investment activities" are entitled to enter Member States temporarily for business purposes.[87]

International law plays another role regarding non-citizens in the labor force, establishing rights and protections for migrants in three ways. First, the non-discrimination principles of major human rights conventions generally ensure that non-citizen workers benefit from protections afforded to citizen workers – such as minimum wage-maximum hour rules, prohibitions on child labor, rights to establish unions, and collective bargaining.[88] Second, international instruments specifically guaranteeing workers' rights generally apply to non-citizen as well as citizen workers.[89] Third, several international instruments are directly concerned with the rights of non-citizen workers.[90] For example, the International Convention on the Protection of the Rights of All Migrant Workers and Members of Their Families (adopted by a UN General Assembly Resolution in 1990, it will come into force in 2003), secures for migrant workers many of the rights guaranteed by human rights treaties – such as protections against discrimination, torture and forced labor, and the rights to life, freedom of thought, and religion. In provisions specifically related to employment, it provides that migrant workers shall "enjoy treatment not less favourable than that which applies to nationals of the State of employment" in respect of remuneration, conditions, and hours of work; and further, that migrant

---

[85] See examples in IOM, "Inter-state Cooperation on Migration – Significant Bilateral and Multilateral Agreements," this volume.

[86] See S. Charnovitz, "WTO Norms on International Migration," this volume.

[87] North American Free Trade Agreement, ch. 16 and annex 1603.

[88] See J. Fitzpatrick, this volume.

[89] See V. Leary, "The Paradox of Worker's Rights as Human Rights," in L.A. Compa and S.F. Diamond (eds.), Human Rights, Labor Rights and International Trade (1996), pp. 22-47, detailing international conventions pertaining to workers' rights.

[90] See ILO Conventions 97 (Migration for Employment Convention) (1949) (42 ratifications) and 143 (Convention concerning Migrations in Abusive Conditions and the Promotion of Equality of Opportunity and Treatment of Migrant Workers) (1975) (18 ratifications) ("Each Member for which the Convention is in force undertakes to declare and pursue a national policy designed to promote and to guarantee, by methods appropriate to national conditions and practice, equality of opportunity and treatment in respect of employment and occupation, of social security, of trade union and cultural rights and of individual and collective freedoms for persons who as migrant workers or as members of their families are lawfully within its territory").

workers have the right to join and take part in the activities of trade unions and other associations "with a view to protecting their economic, social, cultural and other interests."[91]

MIGRATION AND DEVELOPMENT

Migration and development are linked in a number of important ways. Underdevelopment is a major cause of migration – lawful and unlawful[92] – as persons seek work opportunities outside their countries of origin. But development may equally contribute to migration, as individuals gain the skills and resources that permit them to find employment in other states. Furthermore, the remittances of migrants frequently constitute a large source of foreign capital in developing states. Despite these obvious interstate relationships, there is little international law linking migration and development.

A number of international instruments declare a right to development.[93] Importantly, the ICESCR – which mandates that states "recognize the right of everyone to an adequate standard of living for himself and his family, including adequate food, clothing and housing, and to the continuous improvement of living conditions"[94] – puts stress on "international assistance and cooperation" in achieving realization of the rights secured in the Covenant.[95]

Whether or not a duty of international assistance for developing states has fully crystallized, it is clear that development aid could have a material affect on immigration. It is therefore an important potential topic for interstate cooperation on migration. Thus, the 1994 Cairo Declaration on Population and Development invites states to "aid developing countries and countries with economies in transition in addressing the impact of international migration" and calls on states "to address the root causes of migration, especially those related to poverty."[96]

Developed states may also assist developing states by making employment opportunities available to their nationals. Again, the Cairo Declaration "invites" countries of destination "to consider the use of certain forms of temporary migration, such as short-term and project-related migration, as a means of improving the skills

---

[91] Arts. 26 and 27.

[92] See Programme of Action adopted at the International Conference on Population and Development, Cairo, 10.1 (1994); Bangkok Declaration on Irregular Migration, para. 5 (1999) ("the causes of irregular migration are closely related to the issue of development").

[93] E.g., Declaration on the Right to Development, 41 U.N. GAOR Supp. 53, 186 (1986). Other resolutions and conclusions by scholars to the same affect are reported in B.S. Chimni, "Development and Migration", this volume.

[94] Art. 11(1).

[95] Arts. 11(1) ("The States Parties will take appropriate steps to ensure the realization of this right, recognizing to this effect the essential importance of international co-operation based on free consent"); 2(1). See Committee on Economic, Social and Cultural Rights, Comment 3 (1990).

[96] Report of the International Conference on Population and Development, paras. 10.2(a), 10.6 (September 1994), available at http://www.cnie.org/pop/icpd/poa10.htm.

of nationals of countries of origin, especially developing countries and countries with economies in transition." [97]

CONCLUSION

This study makes clear that a fairly detailed set of international law norms is implicated in the regulation of international migration and migrants. In saying this, it is important to stress that international law does not establish a comprehensive international migration regime. It does not command that certain numbers of persons be permitted to travel between states each year; it does not supply a universal rule for the attribution of citizenship; it does not structure an international system for labor flows; and it does not mandate particular enforcement regimes or the return undocumented migrants. Moreover, in some areas in which international law applies, the norms are not precise or are just emerging. International law, in many respects, channels, influences, and supplies limits on state-to-state and state-to-individual relationships.

It is perhaps best, then, to view the international norms as providing a framework – a background set of principles – for state cooperation on migration matters and for the protection of migrant human rights. That is, existing international legal norms both establish a *space* and a *need* for new initiatives in this age of migration.

The papers in this study disclose numerous areas where state-to-state cooperation is advisable. To mention but a few salient examples:

1. development of arrangements on skilled and unskilled labor flows;
2. further negotiation of readmission agreements;
3. promotion of common definitions and procedures in refugee law;
4. consideration of the impact of measures against unlawful migration on asylum-seekers;
5. coordination of anti-trafficking efforts;
6. clarification of procedures to be followed regarding persons rescued at sea;
7. provision of development assistance to sending states;
8. further promotion of anti-discrimination norms as relate to non-citizens;
9. cooperation in the re-uniting of separated families;
10. consideration of migration issues in multilateral trade negotiations.

States have been most active in adopting domestic regulations for the admission of wanted immigration. Further steps are needed on how to manage both lawful and unlawful flows at the international level, in ways that redound to the benefit of states and migrants and that respect the human rights of migrants. These steps, if they are

---

[97] Id. at para. 10.5. See also Bangkok Declaration, para. 7; ILO Recommendation No. 86 Concerning Migration for Employment (rev'd 1949), Art. 4(1) ("It should be the general policy of members to develop and utilize all possibilities for employment and for this purpose to facilitate the international distribution of manpower and in particular the movement of manpower from countries which have a surplus of manpower to those countries that have a deficiency.")

to be successful, must view international migration in a broader context of global in-equality and insecurity – the main causes of migratory flows. Thus, the effective and humane management of international migration that international law can help to provide will require attention to the needs and interests of sending states, receiving states, and migrants as well as recognition of the root causes of migration.

STATE AUTHORITY AND RESPONSIBILITY

Chapter 2
THE AUTHORITY AND RESPONSIBILITY OF STATES

David A. Martin*

THE STARTING POINT: BROAD STATE AUTHORITY

States possess broad discretion in deciding on the admission and sojourn of non-citizens. A typical judicial pronouncement states:

> "It is an accepted maxim of international law that every sovereign nation has the power, as inherent in sovereignty, and essential to self-preservation, to forbid the entrance of foreigners within its dominions, or to admit them only in such cases and upon such conditions as it may see fit to prescribe."[1]

This underlying principle reflects the basic assumptions of an international system built on nation-states as the foundational units. Classically states have been considered to have complete sovereign authority over a defined territory and population. International human rights law and other treaty obligations, both bilateral and multilateral, have made inroads into the sweep of this sovereign authority-inroads

---

* Doherty Professor of Law and Weber Research Professor of Civil Liberties and Human Rights, University of Virginia. I would like to thank Xinh Luu of the Law Library at the University of Virginia, for excellent work in compiling information on the treaties cited here, and Azish Filabi, for consistently helpful research assistance.

[1] *Nishimura Ekiu* v. *United States*, 142 U.S. 651, 658 (1892); compare *Musgrove* v. *Chun Teeong Toy*, 1891 AC 272. This highly permissive view of broad state authority dates most solidly to the late nineteenth century. Before that time, some classic writers, including Grotius, Vitoria, and Wolff, indicated a somewhat wider set of circumstances in which states might be obligated to admit aliens, or suggested a baseline rule of free movement, subject to specified exceptions within the discretion of states. These views, often set forth cryptically or without elaboration in the classic texts, are summarized and explained in J. Nafziger, "The General Admission of Aliens under International Law," 77 *AJIL* (1983) p. 804. Nafziger argues that the nineteenth century view represents a misreading of the earlier precedents and commentary; thus the baseline, he contends, still should be considered free movement subject to exceptions that states must justify. He does acknowledge, however, broad discretion in states to apply or give precise content to the exceptions (which include public safety, security, public welfare, or threat to essential institutions). In my view, whatever the initial correctness of the nineteenth century readings, their affirmation of sweeping state authority to control migration became so deeply rooted in state practice and popular understanding, at a critical historical moment when exploration, conquest, and settlement were reaching the limits of the frontiers, as to displace any earlier framework and to provide the appropriate starting point for modern legal analysis.

T.A. Aleinikoff and V. Chetail (Eds.), Migration and International Legal Norms
© 2003, T.M.C. Asser Press, The Hague, The Netherlands, et al.

which are sketched below and in the other papers in this study.[2]

The underlying principle or default rule remains, and the restrictions on state authority arise by way of exception. Moreover, national populations, particularly in times of economic stress or security threat, tend to show strong devotion to the principle of broad state authority, and may frame demands for state action in response to such difficulties on the assumption of wide national discretion over the entry and residence of foreigners.

As a corollary to the organization of a global order wherein nation-states serve as the principal building blocks, states carry primary responsibility for securing the health, safety, security, and economic well-being of their populations, which consist in overwhelming proportions of their citizens. Although international law was classically indifferent to how a state treated its own citizens,[3] the development of modern human rights law over the past half-century has significantly changed this situation. International law now requires the observance of a range of civil and political rights, as well as (through norms of less precise content) basic economic, social, and cultural rights.[4] Importantly, most of these obligations extend to all persons, citizen or alien, within the jurisdiction of the state, but the norms do not significantly affect the ongoing authority of the state to set its own criteria for deciding who may enter or stay – and therefore who may remain within the circle of beneficiaries of the state's primary human rights obligations. That is, most of the human rights norms affect the rights of migrants after entry, not rights respecting migration itself. The Declaration on the Human Rights of Individuals Who are not Nationals of the Country in Which They Live, adopted by the UN General Assembly in 1985, reflects this division:

"Nothing in this Declaration shall be interpreted as legitimizing any alien's illegal entry into and presence in a State, nor shall any provision be interpreted as restricting the right of any State to promulgate laws and regulations concerning the entry of aliens and the terms and conditions of their stay or to establish differences between nationals and aliens. However, such laws and regulations shall not be incompatible with the international legal obligations of that State, including those in the field of human rights."[5]

---

[2] See, in particular, the contributions of Joan Fitzpatrick, Vincent Chetail, and Walter Kälin in the present volume.

[3] L. Oppenheim, *International Law: A Treatise*, vol. I (8th edn. 1955) p. 640 ("a State is entitled to treat both its own nationals and stateless persons at discretion and ... the manner in which it treats them is not a matter with which International Law, as a rule, concerns itself"). In contrast, classical international law imposed responsibility on states for the treatment of nonstateless aliens – conceptually based on obligations owed to the state of nationality, not to the individual. A long-standing debate over whether the obligation was to assure treatment of aliens on a par with nationals or instead was to meet an international minimum standard, a debate that became intertwined with the struggle against colonial domination, has faded in importance with the development of more demanding minimum treatment standards under general international human rights law. See I. Brownlie, *Principles of Public International Law* (4th edn. 1990) pp. 518-528.

[4] See International Covenant on Civil and Political Rights (ICCPR), 16 December 1996, 99 *UNTS* 171; International Covenant on Economic, Social and Cultural Rights (ICESCR), 16 December 1966, 993 *UNTS* 3.

[5] Declaration on the Human Rights of Individuals Who are not Nationals of the Country in Which They Live, UNGA Res. 40/114, Art. 2(1), 13 December 1985.

Even before international human rights law dictated certain requirements for a state's stewardship of the rights and economic security of its nationals, states, of course, still based much of their migration policy calculations about how best to advance the health, safety, security, and economic well-being of their own citizens. Nothing in international law significantly undercuts such an assignment of priorities. On these grounds, at least since the early twentieth, century most states have tended to restrict the admission of foreigners and to require review of qualifications to enter, both through visas issued or denied by their consular officers posted in a foreign territory and through inquiry at the border. But it has been exceedingly rare for any state to exercise the maximum of its theoretical power by halting virtually all migration. The regime of broad state discretion has coexisted, as a result of policy choices by states, with a high and rising volume of cross-border travel. For well over a century, states have also frequently entered into international agreements that limit their discretion over migration but also have provided for transnational cooperation in both shaping and implementing immigration rules.

ADMISSION AND EXPULSION

Grounds for Admission and Exclusion

States enjoy wide authority in setting the standards for admission to and exclusion from national territory, absent conflicting treaty obligations. Grounds for denial of a visa or of admission at the border are typically based on such factors as disease, past criminal convictions or activity, earlier violations of immigration laws (including fraud), national security or *ordre public* concerns[6] (including indications of possible terrorist connections), and economic grounds. With respect to the latter, states typically restrict migration to protect a favored position for their own citizens within the internal labor market, and they often insist that a prospective migrant show ability to support himself or herself throughout the stay. States may also set numerical ceilings on admissions or on particular categories of admission.

States may decide that the interests of their citizens call for fairly generous admission policies, at least for temporary purposes – a trend that has accelerated with the expansion of global trade and tourism. State practice has allowed temporary admissions for purposes of study, tourism, business dealings, and employment. Permission for permanent immigration is commonly based on family connections (including cross-national marriages), specified employment skills or particular job offers, and humanitarian grounds. But the patterns and exact criteria vary enormously, and no significant general restrictions on state discretion to set the qualifying grounds apply as a result of general international norms. In contrast, bilateral treaties, especially consular treaties, investment treaties, and friendship, commerce and navigation (FCN) treaties have often been used to set particular procedures, rules,

---

[6] For a comprehensive discussion, see the contribution of David Fisher, Susan Martin, and Andrew Schoenholtz in this volume.

restrictions, or protections, covering migrants from the contracting states – relating both to permission to migrate and treatment of migrants after they enter the other state. Increasingly, regional treaties impose transnational regulation of these matters. The European Union treaties may be the best known and most extensive, but other regional treaties, such as the North American Free Trade Agreement, or the 1975 Treaty Establishing the West African Economic Community, also exemplify this trend.[7] These focus primarily on business- or work-related grounds of admission.

Expulsion

States also have wide discretion in establishing grounds for deportation or expulsion of those who have made an entry into national territory. As a matter of practice, the grounds for expulsion are typically more limited than grounds for barring entry. Contracting a contagious disease while on national territory is less likely to be *per se* a ground for deportation, for example, even though the same illness might well have blocked initial admission if the disease had developed before entry. Moreover, the list of criminal convictions that might bar entry is typically more expansive than the list of later criminal acts that might result in deportation of a resident alien. Human rights norms, such as those protecting family life, have found more of a foothold in restricting expulsion than in constraining admission decisions, as reflected in other papers in this volume.

States typically provide for deportation if the person entered the territory in violation of the law, failed to comply with the terms of admission (for example, working without authorization or overstaying the permitted period), or has been involved in criminal activities. States may also employ grounds relating to national security or foreign policy reasons. Other grounds are not necessarily forbidden, and wide variety in the details of state practice exists. Municipal law in many states requires authorities to balance the interests of individuals, particularly those who have been longtime lawful residents, against the state's interest in deporting, before decreeing expulsion. Other states either observe no such limitation, or provide for such balancing only in narrowly defined circumstances. This diversity indicates that general international law cannot be seen as requiring such individualized balancing.

The Anti-discrimination Norm

The general norm against discrimination[8] may provide some restrictions on state action in the immigration realm, but it has not been applied to impose close scrutiny in

---

[7] North American Free Trade Agreement Between the Government of Canada, the Government of the United Mexican States, and the Government of the United States, 8-17 December 1992, H. Doc. 103-159, vol. 1 (pp. 3-449), 103d Cong., 1st Sess., 4 November 1993, reprinted *in* 32 *ILM* (1993) 289; Treaty Establishing the West African Economic Community, 28 May 1975, 1010 *UNTS* 17, reprinted *in* 14 *ILM* 1200.

[8] The norm appears prominently in the United Nations Charter's human rights provisions (Art. 1(3), 55(c)), and is reinforced and expanded in the International Convention on the Elimination of all Forms of Racial Discrimination, Arts. 2, 3, and 26 of the ICCPR, and Arts. 2 and 3 of the ICESCR, as well as in a host of other universal and regional human rights treaties.

evaluating the widely varied distinctions that states use for admission and expulsion grounds. In this field, the norm serves primarily to place a modest burden on the state to come forward with a plausible justification for any distinctions drawn in law or practice. Some scholars describe the test as requiring reasonableness and proportionality in judging a state's distinctions[9] – a standard that implies a somewhat more demanding inquiry into the state's case, and thereby results in broader authority for the court, international committee, or body of scholars to second-guess the state's distinction. But the American Society of International Law's project on "The Movement of Persons Across International Borders," headed by Professors Louis Sohn and Thomas Buergenthal, states that the government's burden is to put forward "some rational basis for the differentiation relevant to the purpose that is sought to be achieved."[10] This formulation better reflects the real-world application of the anti-discrimination norm to immigration laws and restrictions, because domestic and international tribunals in fact tend to apply highly deferential review to such distinctions.

However the anti-discrimination test is understood, explicit racial distinctions would not today be judged to meet it. Distinctions applied on the basis of the migrant's nationality, in contrast, are quite common and are generally accepted without quarrel. Often such distinctions reflect a state's variant treaty obligations toward different countries. Traditional historical or cultural ties may also give rise to eased rules of admission in comparison with those imposed on citizens of other countries. Nationality-based distinctions may also be validly deployed in response to specific foreign-policy developments, such as the country-specific imposition or lifting of visa requirements, or even the suspension of visa processing or of migration altogether in response to foreign policy developments. (In some circumstances, Article 8 of the Convention relating to the Status of Refugees[11] requires exemption of refugees who formally hold the nationality of their country of origin from such measures directed at that country).

Other Constraints on Exclusion and Expulsion

In some settings, other human rights norms may be seen as placing substantive limits on a state's normally expansive powers to expel or exclude aliens. For example, several human rights instruments bar the collective expulsion of aliens.[12] Furthermore, as a matter of practice that predates modern human rights instruments, most states privilege immigration by family members of citizens (especially spouses and minor children) and often relatives of persons with durable residence rights as well.

---

[9] See, e.g., Joan Fitzpatrick in this volume.

[10] L.B. Sohn and T. Buergenthal (eds.), *The Movement of Persons Across Borders* (1992) p. 18. Significantly, the "reasonable and proportionate" test does not appear in the UN Human Rights Committee's General Comment No. 18, Non-discrimination, U.N. Doc. HRI/GEN/1/Rev.1 at 26 (1994).

[11] Convention Relating to the Status of Refugees, 28 July 1951, 189 *UNTS* 137.

[12] See, e.g., Protocol No. 4 to the Convention for the Protection of Human Rights and Fundamental Freedoms, securing certain rights and freedoms other than those already included in the Convention and in the first Protocol thereto, 16 September 1963, Art. 4, 1469 *UNTS* 263, *ETS* No. 46; American Convention on Human Rights (ACHR), Art. 22(9), 22 November 1969, 1144 *UNTS* 123.

In the deportation setting, states have typically considered family connections before decreeing expulsion. Recent years have seen rapid development of case law considering whether or to what extent explicit human rights norms relating to the family now constrain admission and expulsion decisions. The most extensive protections of this sort have developed under Article 8 of the European Convention for Human Rights (ECHR), which protects a person's right to privacy, home, and family life.[13] Several decisions of the European Court of Human Rights have applied this provision to forbid the expulsion of longtime alien residents (usually, but not always, individuals who first took up residence as children), even though the basis for the proposed expulsion was the commission of serious crimes.[14] State practice outside Europe, however, is far more accepting of the expulsion of longtime residents on the basis of crimes, even over objections based on family rights; and the UN Human Rights Committee has upheld such expulsions over claims based on the comparable provisions of the International Covenant on Civil and Political Rights (ICCPR).[15] Later trends in the Human Rights Committee, however, may reflect a less deferential application of Covenant norms to expulsion.[16] But the Committee's practice remains rather undeveloped – it has had only a limited number of communications in this realm[17] – and, in any event, the Committee has not been given the authority to provide binding interpretations of the Covenant. The ultimate test may prove to be the actual practice of states that are party to the Covenant. It remains far from certain that, outside Europe, state practice will yield so substantially to family protections in such cases.

---

[13] European Convention for the Protection of Human Rights and Fundamental Freedoms (ECHR), Art. 8, 4 November 1950, 213 *UNTS* 221, *ETS* No. 5.

[14] See, e.g., *Beldjoudi* v. *France*, 234 Eur. Ct. H.R. (ser. A) (1992); *Moustaquim* v. *Belgium*, 193 Eur. Ct. H.R. (ser. A) (1991); *Berrehab* v. *Netherlands*, 138 Eur. Ct. H.R. (ser. A) (1988). Other rulings have sometimes sustained deportation despite family ties. For a helpful overview, see K. Groenendijk, et al., *Security of Residence of Long-Term Migrants* (1998) 8-16. More recent ECHR cases have found that in certain highly specific circumstances an obligation to admit, and not solely an obligation to avoid expulsion, may derive from family rights and interests. See *Sen* v. *Netherlands*, Application No. 31465/96 (21 December 2001); *Boultif* v. *Switzerland*, Application No. 54273/00 (2 August 2001).

[15] ICCPR, Arts. 17, 23. See *Stewart* v. *Canada*, 538/1993, 1 November 1996, para. 12.6, (UN Human Rights Committee) (commenting that the expulsion based on the criminal record was not arbitrary in part because "this disability was of his own making"); *Canepa* v. *Canada*, 558/1993, 3 April 1997 (UN Human Rights Committee). A later decision by the Human Rights Committee, however, found a violation of family-related provisions of the Covenant in a situation where Australia proposed to remove the parents (themselves resident for fourteen years, most of it after the expiration of temporary visas) of a thirteen-year-old who had been born in Australia and had acquired Australian citizenship. *Winata* v. *Australia*, 930/2000, 27 July 2001 (UN Human Rights Committee). A more expansive view than my own of the weight of the family reunification norm in the context of admission and expulsion is presented in the conctribution of Kate Jastram in the present volume.

[16] See W. Kälin, "Limits to Expulsion under the International Covenant on Civil and Political Rights" (manuscript 2000).

[17] Id. at 2.

Non-refoulement

A highly significant limitation on expulsion derives (initially) from the *non-refoulement* obligation in Article 33 of the widely accepted 1951 Convention relating to the Status of Refugees.[18] Article 33 bans return or expulsion to a state where the refugee's "life or freedom would be threatened on account of his race, religion, nationality, membership of a particular social group or political opinion." Exceptions are permitted when the person may reasonably be regarded as a danger to the host state's security or upon conviction of a "particularly serious crime." This obligation may now be considered part of customary international law, and it trumps other normal grounds for expulsion, when the individual has shown that she comes within its field of application by demonstrating that she meets the refugee definition. *Non-refoulement* does not automatically lead to asylum, permanent residence, or other durable status – classifications which are generally considered to be within the discretionary prerogative of states. Nonetheless, most countries in the developed world have tended to grant asylum to those who met the refugee definition and therefore were protected by the *non-refoulement* obligation. (Although they could technically be sent to a third country consistently with the *non-refoulement* norm, well-to-do haven states found few such opportunities. Granting asylum or durable status was therefore both compassionate and sensible, helping the beneficiaries to resume a productive life in the territory where they were likely to stay for a considerable period.) Some departure from that trend, however, could be seen in the response to the Yugoslav crisis of the early 1990s. Many European states explicitly provided only temporary protection to those who fled the former Yugoslavia, even in a context where they were willing to concede that most of those so protected would meet the refugee definition.

Comparable non-return obligations have since developed under other treaty regimes. For example, the Convention Against Torture (CAT) bars return of a person "where there are substantial grounds for believing that he would be in danger of being subjected to torture."[19] Article 3 of the European Convention of Human Rights, which bars torture or cruel, inhuman, or degrading treatment, has long been interpreted to bar return to another country if there is a "real risk" of torture or inhuman treatment there.[20] Comparable provisions in other human rights treaties are beginning to be read to impose similar non-return obligations. How far such a non-return obligation extends, however, remains unclear.[21] State practice also reflects frequent national decisions to avoid expelling people (who do not meet the 1951 Convention refugee definition) to countries in the midst of severe armed conflict, often through

---

[18] Convention Relating to the Status of Refugees, Art. 33, 28 July 1951, 189 *UNTS* 137.

[19] Convention Against Torture and Other Cruel, Inhuman or Degrading Treatment or Punishment (CAT), Art. 3, 10 December 1984, 1468 *UNTS* 85.

[20] See M. Pellonpää, "ECHR Case-Law on Refugees and Asylum Seekers and Protection under the 1951 Refugee Convention: Similarities and Differences," *in* International Association of Refugee Law Judges, *The Changing Nature of Persecution* (2000).

[21] An insightful discussion of the practice of the Human Rights Committee in this respect, along with reflections on the extent of the state obligation and its conceptual foundations, appears *in* Kälin, *supra* note 16, at 8-14.

the use of some form of "temporary protection." But the practice varies, and debate persists over whether most states involved see this abstention as a matter of legal obligation or instead as a sound use of their discretionary powers.[22]

Non-refoulement and Admission Obligations

Each version of the *non-refoulement* norm applies with clarity only in the setting of expulsion. Whether *non-refoulement* also mandates non-rejection at the frontiers of those who appear or claim to be refugees has long been contested. That it was not seen, through the 1960s at least, to encompass an absolute obligation of non-rejection is evidenced by the UN Declaration on Territorial Asylum, adopted by the General Assembly in 1967.[23] Article 3(1) generally forbids rejection at the frontier, but Article 3(2) allows exception to that principle "for overriding reasons of national security or in order to safeguard the population, as in the case of a mass influx of persons." There have been significant examples of pushbacks at the frontier, for example by Thailand and Malaysia during the peak years of the Vietnamese refugee exodus, but these usually drew international condemnation. The United States has employed Coast Guard interdiction to prevent the arrival of vessels bearing likely asylum-seekers – a mechanism that typically operates on the high seas before the vessel gets near to national frontiers. Most of the time the U.S interdiction program has made provisions for some sort of refugee screening before returning interdicted passengers. However, for a period in the early 1990s, the instructions were changed to mandate immediate return to Haiti without such screening. The U.S. Supreme Court rejected a challenge to such returns, founded on Article 33 of the Refugee Convention and its implementing provisions in U.S. law, after a lengthy review of the treaty's language and drafting history.[24]

That decision remains controversial, but practice clearly establishes that the *non-refoulement* norm does not forbid the use of various procedural barriers and hurdles that operate beyond a state's frontiers – particularly the use of visa regimes and their enforcement through the use of carrier sanctions. Though some observers have strongly criticized these mechanisms, states have consistently used them, even in settings where there are serious problems of persecution in the source country involved. Indeed, states have commonly toughened visa requirements precisely when they begin to receive increased numbers of asylum-seekers from the source state at issue. Although this practice is hard to reconcile conceptually with the protective premises of the refugee treaties, such barriers may meet a practical need to reconcile the potentially broad coverage of the refugee definition with the political limits to the tolerance of growing numbers of asylum-seekers by the populace in receiving states. The *travaux préparatoires* of the 1951 Convention reveal a shared aversion

---

[22] Compare, e.g., K. Hailbronner, "*Non-refoulement* and 'Humanitarian' Refugees: Customary International Law or Wishful Legal Thinking?," 26 *Virginia Journal of International Law* (1986) p. 857, with D. Perluss and J. Fitzpatrick Hartman, "Temporary Refuge: Emergency of a Customary Norm," 26 *Virginia Journal of International Law* (1986) p. 551.

[23] Declaration on Territorial Asylum, UNGA Res. 2312 (XXII), 14 December 1967.

[24] *Sale* v. *Haitian Centers Council, Inc.*, 509 U.S. 155 (1993).

voiced by many state representatives to granting a "blank cheque" for future migration through refugee guarantees.[25] The use of visa regimes and other barriers to arrival appears to help meet that concern.

Procedural Requirements

International law imposes few procedural requirements on decisions regarding admission at the border or on the issuance and refusal of visas. States typically do provide procedural protections, however, and sometimes full adjudicative hearings, particularly with respect to exclusion decisions covering persons at a port of entry (as distinguished from decisions on visas). International human rights law does impose procedural requirements on expulsion decisions, but the careful limits placed on these obligations reveal the wide margin of discretion states retain even in this realm. Illustrative is Article 13 of the ICCPR, which provides:

> "An alien lawfully in the territory ... may be expelled therefrom only in pursuance of a decision reached in accordance with law and shall, except where compelling reasons of national security otherwise require, be allowed to submit the reasons against his expulsion and to have his case reviewed by, and be represented for the purpose before, the competent authority or a person or persons especially designated by the competent authority."[26]

Note that this procedural guarantee applies only to those lawfully in the territory and does not in terms cover clandestine entrants or those at the border applying for admission.[27] Moreover, the procedural protections under Article 13, although important, are far more modest than those that apply under ICCPR Article 14 to criminal trials. Article 13 requires only a procedure established by law and some opportunity to "submit the reasons against expulsion," with a modest requirement for review by and representation before the competent authority. Even these limited guarantees may be overridden if there are "compelling reasons of national security" – a provision which may make room for *ex parte in camera* procedures in terrorist cases. Other relevant provisions, such as the basic requirement to respect the "inherent dignity of the human person" whenever someone is deprived of liberty, or the right to an effective remedy,[28] may call forth some additional procedural protections. And most developed nations in fact apply procedures that go far beyond these minimums.

---

[25] See D. Martin, "Strategies for a Resistant World: Human Rights Initiatives and the Need for Alternatives to Refugee Interdiction," 26 *Cornell International Law Journal* (1993) p. 753, pp. 756-757.

[26] ICCPR, Art. 13. See *Hammel* v. *Madagascar*, 155/1983, 3 April 1987 (UN Human Rights Committee).

[27] In *Maroufidou* v. *Sweden,* 58/1979, 9 April 1981 (UN Human Rights Committee), the Human Rights Committee held that a woman granted a residency permit for the duration of her asylum proceedings was lawfully present for purposes of Art. 13 and therefore entitled to its procedural protections regarding expulsion proceedings.

[28] ICCPR, Arts. 2(3), 10(1).

ACTION AGAINST SMUGGLING AND TRAFFICKING

States enforce their migration controls through civil and criminal sanctions imposed on unlawful migrants, but increasing emphasis has been placed on criminal prosecution of those who organize or facilitate illegal migration. In keeping with this trend, states are turning to transnational efforts to thwart unauthorized migration, primarily through enhanced cooperation against human smuggling and trafficking. This is a salutary and logical development, because such criminal activity has proliferated and grown in sophistication, and the criminal organizations have benefited from their own transnational character and their ability to take advantage of locations where laws are lax or enforcement ineffective.[29] Although there are some ongoing debates over definitions, in general one can say that smuggling involves the organized movement of persons into a national territory against the law of the receiving state. Trafficking is a subset of smuggling that further involves the use of force, fraud, coercion, or exploitation directed against the migrants. The growing international effort against traffickers partakes of both law enforcement and human rights motivations. Recent international action against trafficking has been energized by the movements to protect the rights of women and children, because women and children are the primary victims, particularly in connection with the sex trade.[30]

Bilateral cooperation against smugglers and traffickers, sometimes embodied in agreements of varying degrees of formality, is increasingly a feature of international practice. Receiving states now often assist in training the law enforcement or carrier personnel of transit or origin states, and may provide direct assistance to foreign governments who wish to modify their laws in order to establish or increase penalties for smuggling and trafficking. In December 2000, the UN General Assembly adopted the UN Convention Against Transnational Organized Crime. The Convention has two Protocols, one to suppress trafficking in persons and the second to suppress the smuggling of migrants. Both provisions require states to criminalize certain acts and to cooperate in prosecuting or extraditing violators. These instruments have not yet entered into force, but when opened for signature in December 2000, the trafficking protocol received eighty-one signatures and the smuggling protocol seventy-nine.[31] Modest antecedents (of limited effectiveness) for these international efforts can be found in old treaties against the so-called white slave traffic and in the 1950 Convention for the Suppression of the Traffic in Persons.[32]

---

[29] R. Koslowski, "Economic Globalization, Human Smuggling, and Global Governance," *in* D. Kyle and R. Koslowski (eds.), *Global Human Smuggling: Comparative Perspectives* (2001) pp. 337-358.

[30] See the presentation of Vitit Muntarbhorn in this volume.

[31] S. Murphy, "International Trafficking in Persons, Especially Women and Children," 95 *AJIL* (2001) p. 407.

[32] Convention for the Suppression of Traffic in Persons and of the Exploitation of Prostitution of Others, 21 March 1950, 96 *UNTS* 27. For other brief provisions requiring action against trafficking, see Convention on the Elimination of All Forms of Discrimination Against Women (CEDAW), 18 December 1979, Art. 6, 1249 *UNTS* 13; Convention on the Rights of the Child, 20 November 1989, Art. 35, 1577 *UNTS* 3.

OBLIGATIONS REGARDING READMISSION

Consistent with the basic organization of international society into nation-states, states retain primary responsibility for their own nationals. This means that they ordinarily may not refuse entry to their nationals, nor may they expel or deport them.[33] The Universal Declaration on Human Rights provides, in Article 13(2), that "Everyone has the right to leave any country, including his own, and to return to his country."[34] ICCPR Article 12(4), seems to permit somewhat greater discretion to the state: "No one shall be arbitrarily deprived of the right to enter his own country."[35]

But whatever discretion states may have under these human rights norms *vis-à-vis* the individual involved, they still owe a separate obligation to other states to accept return, which appears to be of wider application.[36] This norm, requiring that a state accept return of its nationals when demanded by another state on whose territory they are found, is of more ancient lineage than the comparable human rights norm, and may be applicable even if the individual resists return (on grounds that do not give rise to a valid individual claim, such as a well-founded fear of persecution in the country of nationality, that would trump the host state's authority to expel). Some states have attempted to manipulate the application of their nationality laws in order to defeat repatriation of nationals through denationalization, but such measures have usually been condemned by the international community, sometimes under the doctrine of "abuse of rights."

Some have argued that these readmission or non-expulsion obligations may extend beyond the realm of nationals to encompass aliens who have been lawfully resident for a lengthy period, either on the basis of an asserted doctrine of "acquired rights" or "legitimate expectations,"[37] or on the claim that the phrase "his own country" in Article 12(4) of the ICCPR covers such residents and is not limited to citi-

---

[33] International law allows distinctions between nationals of a state, who owe it allegiance and are entitled to certain protections, and citizens, a subset of nationals who typically also enjoy the full range of political rights in the state and may have more extensive personal rights, such as the right to travel throughout all the state's dominions. Oppenheim, *supra* note 3, at 644-645. Natives of a colonial possession, if considered nationals, but not full citizens, of the colonial power, might well lack the right to settle in the central territory of the colonial power. Even so, they would typically have a right of re-admission to the territory of the possession from whence they came, particularly if return was sought by a third state wishing to expel the individual. The citizen-national distinction is of greatly reduced significance with the end of colonialism.

[34] Universal Declaration on Human Rights (UDHR), UNGA Res. 217(III), 10 December 1948.

[35] For generally comparable norms see European Convention for the Protection of Human Rights and Fundamental Freedoms (ECHR), 4 November 1950, prot. 4, Art. 3(2), 213 *UNTS* 221, *ETS* No. 5; see also American Convention on Human Rights (ACHR), 22 November 1969, Art. 22(5), 1144 *UNTS* 123; African Charter on Human and Peoples Rights, 26 June 1981, Art. 12(2), OAU Doc. CAB/LEG/67/3/Rev. 5 (1981), reprinted in 31 *ILM* 58 (1982). For a commentary of these provisions, see the contribution of Vincent Chetail in the present volume.

[36] Oppenheim, *supra* note 3, at 645-646. For a comprehensive discussion, see the paper of Gregor Noll in this volume.

[37] G. S. Goodwin-Gill, *International Law and the Movement of Persons Between States* (1978) pp. 256-259.

zens.[38] State practice generally does not support such a claim. The UN Human Rights Committee rejected the latter argument in *Stewart* v. *Canada*, at least in the context of an individual claimant who had not naturalized even though the state imposed no unreasonable barriers to naturalization.[39]

In any event, it is clear that a country of transit (as distinguished from a country where the individual had enjoyed a significant period of lawful residence) is not obligated by general international law to accept return of someone who passed through that territory, or even who remained for a fairly lengthy period. Nonetheless, in recent decades states have increasingly negotiated bilateral or regional readmission treaties applicable to such transit situations, often in connection with broader regimes determining the state responsible for considering an asylum application. An important example is the Dublin Convention of 1990.[40] Sometimes these arrangements are viewed as helping to enforce an asserted principle of the country of first asylum, but no clear principle of this type is supported by state practice. Nonetheless, even in the absence of a readmission agreement, a state may take an asylum applicant's prior stay in a third state into account in deciding whether to grant asylum (such grant decisions are ultimately discretionary). That is, State C, asked to provide asylum to a national who is at risk of persecution in State A, might properly take into account that person's sojourn and apparent protection in State B, and could deny asylum on that ground. But in these circumstances, State B is under no obligation, absent some other specific readmission pledge, to accept return. The principle of *non-refoulement*, as embodied in Article 33 of the Convention relating to the Status of Refugees, would not permit State C to return the individual to State A. He may well wind up remaining indefinitely on the territory of C, despite the refusal of asylum.

---

[38] J., S., and J. Schultz, and M. Castan, *The International Covenant on Civil and Political Rights: Cases, Materials, and Commentary* (2000) pp. 264-267.

[39] *Stewart* v. *Canada*, 538/1993, paras. 12.2-12.9, 1 November 1996 (UN Human Rights Committee); see also *Canepa* v. *Canada*, 558/1993, para. 11.3, 3 April 1997 (UN Human Rights Committee). Some observers suggest that the Human Rights Committee, in the subsequently adopted General Comment No. 27, Freedom of Movement, U.N. Doc. CCPR/C/21/Rev.1/Add.9, para. 20 (1999), has taken a broader view than that reflected in *Stewart* and *Canepa* of when resident aliens may count the country of residence as their "own country" for purposes of Art. 12(4). In fact, the General Comment's language on this point, while modestly suggestive, is quite cautious, largely inviting states to include additional information on state practice in this regard in future periodic reports.

[40] Convention determining the State responsible for examining applications for asylum lodged in one of the Member States of the European Communities (Dublin Convention), 15 June 1990, *Official Journal C.* 254/1 (1997), reprinted *in* 30 *ILM* 425 (1991). See O. Reermann, "Readmission Agreements," *in* K. Hailbronner, D.A. Martin, and H. Motomura (eds.), *Immigration Admissions: The Search for Workable Policies in Germany and the United States* (1997) pp. 121-145.

STATE RESPONSIBILITIES ASSOCIATED WITH CITIZENSHIP

The Grant or Recognition of Citizenship

States have broad discretion to establish their own rules governing the acquisition of citizenship. Article 1 of the 1930 Hague Convention on Certain Questions Relating to the Conflict of Nationality Laws contains the following provision, which is generally considered to reflect customary international law:

> "It is for each State to determine under its own laws who are its nationals. This law shall be recognized by other States in so far as it is consistent with international conventions, international custom, and the principles of law generally recognized with regard to nationality."[41]

Those other sources of law impose few restrictions on recognition of citizenship decisions, so long as there is a genuine link between the state and the individual.[42] In particular, states may decide whether to adopt *jus soli* or *jus sanguinis* (or more often, a distinctive combination) as the basis for attribution of citizenship at birth. Naturalization regimes may be generous or restrictive, as the state chooses. A state is not required to extend citizenship, even to the second or third generation born on its territory. There is a nascent trend in state practice, however, toward cutting back on rules that may perpetuate such a situation, because of host states' desires to promote the integration of long-resident "alien" populations. The 1999 amendments to Germany's citizenship laws, introducing a modest element of *jus soli* into a system that had been wholly weighted toward *jus sanguinis*, are emblematic.

In a few circumstances, general international law may say something more about acquisition of citizenship, but the norms are modest in scope or soft in character. For example, with regard to recognized refugees lawfully settled in a country of refuge, Article 34 of the Convention relating to the Status of Refugees contains the following provision: "The Contracting States shall as far as possible facilitate the assimilation and naturalization of refugees. They shall in particular make every effort to expedite naturalization proceedings and to reduce as far as possible the charges and costs of such proceedings."[43] The 1961 Convention on the Reduction of Statelessness intrudes more deeply into national authority over citizenship, requiring the bestowal of citizenship in a variety of circumstances if the person would otherwise be left stateless, but only twenty-six states are parties.[44]

---

[41] Hague Convention on Certain Questions Relating to the Conflict of Nationality Laws, 12 April 1930, Art. 1, 179 *LNTS* 89.

[42] Nottebohm Case, 1955 ICJ Reports 4, 23. See the contribution of Kay Hailbronner in this volume.

[43] A nearly identical provision, substituting "stateless persons" for "refugees," appears in the Convention relating to the Status of Stateless Persons, 28 September 1945, Art. 32., 360 *UNTS* 117.

[44] Convention on the Reduction of Statelessness, 30 August 1961, 989 *UNTS* 175. Cf., ICCPR, Art. 24(4) ("Every child has the right to acquire a nationality").

Loss of Citizenship

States have fairly wide discretion in setting their own rules for the loss of citizenship, although Article 15(2) of the Universal Declaration on Human Rights does provide that "No one shall be arbitrarily deprived of his nationality nor denied the right to change his nationality."[45] This norm may well be considered to have become part of customary international law, but concrete standards for assessing arbitrariness in this context have not been clearly defined.

CONCLUSION

Perceived ineffectiveness of immigration control often fuels political movements that support draconian limits on migration and even on refugee protections. The United States went through one such round in 1996, and the success of anti-immigrant parties in Europe in 2000-2002 reflects this phenomenon. If states could manage more effective deployment of existing controls − for example by more systematically using their authority to remove persons who have been adjudged deportable after a full opportunity to put forward any defenses or claims, including refugee claims − then negative popular reactions against aliens might be reduced. States tend to stop short of full use of the deportation authority they have − for lack of resources or because individual violators of immigration rules present appealing cases when viewed in isolation. Immigration systems should build in the capacity to take measured accounts of those sympathetic human factors. But such account must not disable the visible continuation of genuine controls and of meaningful sanctions for violation. A balanced and comprehensive migration management regime must include a resolute commitment to enforce its provisions, fairly but firmly, against violators. Effective international cooperation, involving both source states and receiving states, to help assure effective enforcement of well-designed and humane migration controls, would go far toward diminishing such anti-foreigner backlash.

Selected Bibliography

BROWNLIE, IAN − *Principles of Public International Law* (1990).
GOODWIN-GILL, GUY S. − *International Law and the Movement of Persons Between States* (1978).
GROENENDIJK, KEES, ET AL. − *Security of Residence of Long-Term Migrants* (1998): 8-16.
HAILBRONNER, KAY − "*Non-refoulement* and "Humanitarian" Refugees: Customary International Law or Wishful Legal Thinking?", 26 *Virginia Journal of International Law* (1986): 857.
JOSEPH, SARAH, JENNY SCHULTZ, AND MELISSA CASTAN − *The International Covenant on Civil and Political Rights: Cases Materials, and Commentary* (2000).

---

[45] UDHR, Art. 15(2).

KÄLIN, WALTER – "Limits to Expulsion under the International Covenant on Civil and Political Rights" (manuscript 2000).

KOSLOWSKI, REY – "Economic Globalization, Human Smuggling, and Global Governance," in David Kyle and Rey Koslowski (eds.), *Global Human Smuggling: Comparative Perspectives* (2001): 357-358.

MARTIN, DAVID A. – "Strategies for a Resistant World: Human Rights Initiatives and the Need for Alternatives to Refugee Interdiction," 26 *Cornell International Law Journal* (1993): 753.

MURPHY, SEAN D. – "International Trafficking in Persons, Especially Women and Children," 95 *American Journal of International Law* (2001): 407.

NAFZIGER, JAMES A.R. – "The General Admission of Aliens under International Law," 77 *American Journal of International Law* (1983): 804.

OPPENHEIM, L. – *International Law: A Treatise*, vol. I (1955).

PELLONPÄÄ, MATTI – "ECHR Case-Law on Refugees and Asylum Seekers and Protection under the 1951 Refugee Convention: Similarities and Differences," in International Association of Refugee Law Judges, *The Changing Nature of Persecution* (2000).

PERLUSS, DEBORAH AND JOAN FITZPATRICK HARTMAN – "Temporary Refuge: Emergency of a Customary Norm," 26 *Virginia Journal of International Law* (1986): 551.

REERMANN, OLAF – "Readmission Agreements," in Kay Hailbronner, David A. Martin, and Hiroshi Motomura (eds.), *Immigration Admissions: The Search for Workable Policies in Germany and the United States* (1997): 121-145.

SOHN, LOUIS B. AND THOMAS BUERGENTHAL (EDS.) – *The Movement of Persons Across Borders* (1992).

Chapter 3
FREEDOM OF MOVEMENT AND TRANSNATIONAL
MIGRATIONS: A HUMAN RIGHTS PERSPECTIVE

Vincent Chetail*

We live at a time of unprecedented international movement. The social manifestations of globalization are an explosion of cheap and fast means of communication
and some convergence of the values and expectations held by people. Goods and
capital now circulate with greater ease than ever before, and people increasingly
move across borders. In contrast, control over migration remains one of the last bas-
tions of the truly sovereign state. The rapid changes associated with globalization
have exacerbated this growing discrepancy between the social reality of migration
and its legal regulation. The challenges posed by migratory movements to the international community call for a comprehensive understanding of the normative framework and the legal content of the freedom of movement.

LEGAL FRAMEWORK OF FREEDOM OF MOVEMENT

Freedom of movement across borders as a right cannot be found in international human rights instruments. The general concept of freedom of movement finds its normative expression through the right to leave any country and to return to one's own
country. This latter right is embodied in numerous multilateral instruments relating
to human rights both at the universal and regional level.

Universal Instruments Relating to the Right to Leave and to Return

The Universal Declaration on Human Rights of 10 December 1948 (UDHR) was the
first international instrument to lay down *expressis verbis* the right to leave and return. Article 13(2) acknowledges that:

> "Everyone has the right to leave any country, including his own, and to return to his coun-
> try."[1]

---

* Graduate Institute of International Studies (Geneva).
[1] For a commentary, see notably A. Grahl-Madsen, "Article 13," *in* A. Eide, G. Alfredsson, G.
Melander, L.A. Rehof, and A. Rosas (eds.), *The Universal Declaration of Human Rights: A Commentary*
(1993) pp. 203-214.

T.A. Aleinikoff and V. Chetail (Eds.), Migration and International Legal Norms
© *2003, T.M.C. ASSER PRESS, The Hague, The Netherlands, et al.*

The UDHR proclaims the right to leave and return in absolute terms without mentioning any limitations. However, the general provision of the Universal Declaration was set forth in greater detail in the International Covenant of Civil and Political Rights which gives the right to leave and return a firm and broad conventional basis ratified by 144 states. According to Article 12(2) and (4)

"Everyone shall be free to leave any country, including his own. [...]
No one shall be arbitrarily deprived of the right to enter his own country."[2]

Nevertheless, paragraph 3 provides certain restrictions:

"The above-mentioned rights [in Article 12(2)] shall not be subject to any restrictions except those which are provided by law, are necessary to protect national security, public order (ordre public), public health or morals or the rights and freedoms of others, and are consistent with the other rights recognized in the present Covenant."

Various specialized universal instruments adopted under the auspices of the United Nations specify the provisions of the Covenant in different contexts. Article 5 of the 1965 International Convention on the Elimination of All Forms of Racial Discrimination imposes on states parties the obligation

"to prohibit and to eliminate racial discrimination in all its forms and to guarantee the right of everyone, without distinction as to race, color, or national or ethnic origin, to equality before the law, notably in the enjoyment of the following rights [including notably]: [...] (ii) The right to leave any country, including one's own, and to return to one's country."[3]

The 1973 Convention on the Suppression and Punishment of the Crime of Apartheid,[4] the 1989 Convention on the Rights of the Child,[5] and the 1990 International

---

[2] For a commentary of Art. 12, see R. Higgins, "The Right in International Law of an Individual to Enter, Stay In and Leave a Country," 49 *International Affairs* (1973) pp. 341-357; S. Jagerskiold, "The Freedom of Movement," *in* L. Henkin (ed.), *The International Bill of Rights. The Covenant on Civil and Political Rights* (1981) pp. 166-184; R.B. Lillich, "Civil Rights," *in* Th. Meron (ed.), *Human Rights in International Law: Legal and Policy Issues* (1984) pp. 149-152; H. Hannum, *The Right to Leave and Return in International Law and Practice* (1987); M. Nowak, *U.N. Covenant on Civil and Political Rights CCPR Commentary* (1993) pp. 197-221.

[3] The Convention on the Elimination of All Forms of Racial Discrimination entered into force 4 January 1969 and is presently ratified by 155 states.

[4] Art. 2:

"For the purpose of the present Convention, the term 'the crime of apartheid', which shall include similar policies and practices of racial segregation and discrimination as practiced in southern Africa, shall apply to the following inhuman acts committed for the purpose of establishing and maintaining domination by one racial group of persons over any other racial group of persons and systematically oppressing them: [...]

(c) Any legislative measures and other measures calculated to prevent a racial group or groups from participation in the political, social, economic and cultural life of the country and the deliberate creation of conditions preventing the full development of such a group or groups, in particular by denying to members of a racial group or groups basic human rights and freedoms, including the right to work, the

Convention on the Protection of the Rights of All Migrant Workers and Members of their Families[6] endorse the right to leave and return within their own fields of application. Moreover, a number of universal international agreements establish recognized standards relating to the application of the right to leave a country and return to it without referring to that right expressly. Thus, for example, Article 28 of the Geneva Convention Relating to the Status of Refugees provides for travel documents to be issued to refugees wishing to go abroad.[7] In a completely different area, Article 44 of the Vienna Convention on Diplomatic Relations States provide facilities for departure of persons enjoying privileges and immunities.[8]

---

right to form recognized trade unions, the right to education, *the right to leave and to return to their country*, the right to a nationality, the right to freedom of movement and residence, the right to freedom of opinion and expression, and the right to freedom of peaceful assembly and association [...]" (emphasis added).

The Convention on the Suppression and Punishment of the Crime of Apartheid entered into force 18 July 1976 and is presently ratified by 101 States Parties.

[5] According to Art. 10(2):

"A child whose parents reside in different States shall have the right to maintain on a regular basis, save in exceptional circumstances personal relations and direct contacts with both parents. Towards that end and in accordance with the obligation of States Parties under Article 9, paragraph 2, States Parties shall respect the right of the child and his or her parents to leave any country, including their own, and to enter their own country. The right to leave any country shall be subject only to such restrictions as are prescribed by law and which are necessary to protect the national security, public order (ordre public), public health or morals or the rights and freedoms of others and are consistent with the other rights recognized in the present Convention."

The Convention on the Rights of the Child entered into force 2 September 1990 and is binding for 191 States.

[6] Art. 8:

" 1. Migrant workers and members of their families shall be free to leave any State, including their State of origin. This right shall not be subject to any restrictions except those that are provided by law, are necessary to protect national security, public order (*ordre public*), public health or morals or the rights and freedoms of others and are consistent with the other rights recognized in this Part of the Convention.

2. Migrant workers and members of their families shall have the right at any time to enter and remain in their State of origin."

The International Convention on the Protection of the Rights of All Migrant Workers and Members of their Families will come into force in 2003.

[7] "(1) The Contracting States shall issue to refugees lawfully staying in their territory travel documents for the purpose of travel outside their territory unless compelling reasons of national security or public order otherwise require, and the provisions of the Schedule to this Convention shall apply with respect to such documents. The Contracting States may issue such a travel document to any other refugee in their territory; they shall in particular give sympathetic consideration to the issue of such a travel document to refugees in their territory who are unable to obtain a travel document from the country of their lawful residence.

(2) Travel documents issued to refugees under previous international agreements by parties thereto shall be recognized and treated by the Contracting States in the same way as if they had been issued pursuant to this article."

The Schedule of the Geneva Convention spells out the detail for the issuance of travel documents. The Geneva Convention entered into force 22 April 1954 and is ratified with its Protocol of 1967 by 142 states.

[8] "The receiving State must, even in case of armed conflict, grant facilities in order to enable persons enjoying privileges and immunities, other than nationals of the receiving State, and members of the

In addition to this widespread conventional recognition, the United Nations has dedicated great attention to the right to leave and return. During the last fifty years, the right to leave and return has been the subject of successive studies with the object of defining that right and of devising a mechanism for its enforcement. In 1953 the Sub-Commission on Prevention of Discrimination and Protection of Minorities of the Human Rights Commission requested a study on discrimination in the freedom of movement. Ten years later, Judge José D. Inglés delivered a comprehensive "Study on Discrimination in Respect of the Right of Everyone to Leave any Country and to Return to His Country."[9] This study was updated in 1988 by the Special Rapporteur C.L.C. Mubanga-Chipoya[10] and, more recently, in 1997 by the Special Rapporteur Volodymyr Boutkevitch.[11]

However, the draft principles proposed by Judge Inglés did not lead the General Assembly to adopt a resolution specifying the content of the right of everyone to leave any country and to return to one's own country.[12] Only the Declaration on the

---

families of such persons, irrespective of their nationality, to leave at the earliest possible moment. It must, in particular, in case of need, place at their disposal the necessary means of transport for themselves and their property."

The Vienna Convention on Diplomatic Relations States entered into force 24 April 1964 and is ratified by 179 states. See also Art. 80 of the Vienna Convention on the Representation of States in Their Relations with International Organizations of a Universal Character.

[9] J.D. Inglés, *Study on Discrimination in Respect of the Right of Everyone to Leave any Country and to Return to His Country*, E/CN.4/Sub.2/220/Rev.1.

[10] C.L.C. Mubanga-Chipoya, *Analysis of the Current Trends and Developments Regarding the Right to Leave any Country Including One's Own, and to Return to One's Own Country, and Some Other Rights or Consideration Arising Therefrom*, E/CN.4/Sub.2/1988/35.

[11] V. Boutkevitch, *Working Paper on the Right to Freedom of Movement and Related Issues*, E/CN.4/Sub.2/1997/22.

[12] The draft principles contained in Annex VI of the study of José D. Inglés are the following:

"I. The right of a national to leave his country

(a) Every national of a country is entitled, without distinction of any kind, such as race, colour, sex, language, religion, political or other opinion, national or social origin, property, birth or other status, to leave his country, temporarily or permanently.

(b) No one shall be forced to renounce his nationality, as a condition for the exercise of the right to leave his country; nor shall he be deprived of his nationality as a consequence of his leaving the country.

(c) The conditions prescribed by law or administrative regulations for the exercise of this right shall be the same for all nationals of a country.

(d) The right of every national to leave his country shall not be subject to any restrictions except those provided by law, which shall be only such as are reasonable and necessary to protect national security, public order, health, or morals, or the rights and freedoms of others.

(e) No deposit or other security shall be required to ensure the repatriation or return of any national.

(f) Currency or other economic controls shall not be used as a means of preventing any national from leaving his country.

(g) Any national prevented from leaving his country because of non-compliance with obligations towards the State, or towards another person, shall be allowed to make reasonable arrangements for satisfying those obligations.

(h) Any national who wishes to leave his country permanently is entitled to sell his property and to take the proceeds thereof as well as his personal effects with him either at the time of his departure or within a reasonable period thereafter, subject only to the satisfaction of his local obligations.

II. The right of a national to return his country

(a) Everyone is entitled, without distinction of any kind, such as race, colour, sex, language, religion,

Human Rights of Individuals Who are not Nationals of the Country in which They Live, adopted by the General Assembly on 13 December 1985, contains a general reference to the right to leave without mentioning the right to return.[13] Nevertheless, several attempts have been made to elaborate a declaration specifically devoted to the right to leave and return. In particular, two declarations address the issue in a

political or other opinion, national or social origin, property, birth or other status, to return to his country.

(b) No one shall be arbitrarily deprived of his nationality or forced to renounce his nationality as a means of divesting him of the right to return to his country.

(c) The right of everyone to return to his country shall not be subject to any arbitrary restrictions.

III. The right of a foreigner to leave the country

(a) Every foreigner, without distinction of any kind, such as race, colour, sex, language, religion, political or other opinion, national or social origin, property, birth or other status, has the right to leave the country of his sojourn.

(b) Every foreigner, legally within the territory of a country shall not be accorded lesser rights than a national in the exercise of his right to leave that country.

(c) The right of every foreigner to leave the country of his sojourn shall not be subject to any arbitrary restrictions.

(d) No foreigner shall be prevented from seeking the diplomatic assistance of his own country in order to ensure the enjoyment of his right to leave the country of his sojourn.

IV. Travel documents

(a) Every national of a country is entitled, without distinction of any kind, such as race, colour, sex, language, religion, political or other opinion, national or social origin, property, birth or other status, to apply for and receive such travel documents as passport, identity card, visa or other certificate as he may require to leave his country or to return to his country.

(b) The formalities for the issuance of any travel document, including the grounds for its denial, withdrawal or cancellation, shall be provided by law. Regulations implementing the law shall also be published or communicated to the applicant.

(c) The issuance of any travel document shall not be subject to unreasonable costs or taxes.

V. Fair hearing and recourse to independent tribunals

(a) Everyone denied a travel document or permission to leave the country or to return to his country is entitled to a fair hearing. In particular, he shall have the possibility of presenting evidence on his own behalf, of disputing evidence against him and of having witnesses examined. The hearing shall be public except when compelling reasons of national security or the personal interests of the applicant require otherwise.

(b) The decision of the competent authorities to grant, deny, withdraw or cancel the required permission or travel document shall be made and communicated to the individual concerned within a reasonable and specified period of time.

(c) If the required travel document or permission is denied, withdrawn or cancelled, the reasons for the decision shall be clearly stated to the individual concerned.

(d) In case of denial, withdrawal or cancellation of the required permission or travel document, the aggrieved individual shall have the right of appeal to an independent and impartial tribunal."

[13] According to Art. 5 (2):

"Subject to such restrictions as are prescribed by law and which are necessary in a democratic society to protect national security, public safety, public order, public health or morals or the rights and freedoms of others, and which are consistent with the other rights recognized in the relevant international instruments and those set forth in this Declaration, aliens shall enjoy the following rights:

(a) The right to leave the country […]".

This Declaration was the result of the Sub-Commission's study on the rights of non-citizens. See E. Baroness, *International Provisions Protecting the Human Rights of Non-Citizens*, United Nations publications, Sales No.E.80.XIV.2. For a more recent appraisal, see D. Weissbrodt, *The Rights of Non-citizens*, E/CN.4/Sub.2/2001/20 (preliminary report).

University of Ulster LIBRARY

more comprehensive fashion: the Declaration on the Right to Leave and the Right to Return adopted by a colloquium held in Uppsala, Sweden, in 1972[14] and the Strasbourg Declaration on the Right to Leave and Return adopted by a 1986 meeting of Experts.[15] Although they have not been adopted under the auspices of the United Nations, these Declarations – the later one in particular – identify and clarify the legal content of the right to leave and return in the provisions set forth in the different United Nations instruments. In 1999, the Human Rights Committee adopted General Comment No. 27 on Freedom of Movement[16] and provided an authoritative interpretation of the relevant provisions of the International Covenant on Civil and Political Rights.

Regional Instruments Relating to the Right to Leave and to Return

At the regional level, the right to leave and return is reinforced by all of the instruments relating to human rights.

In Europe, Protocol No. 4 to the European Convention for the Protection of Human Rights and Fundamental Freedoms adopted in 1963 recalls in Article 2(2) and (3):

"Everyone shall be free to leave any country, including his own. […]
No restrictions shall be placed on the exercise of these rights other than such as are in accordance with law and are necessary in a democratic society in the interests of national security or public safety, for the maintenance of *'ordre public,'* for the prevention of crime, for the protection of health or morals, or for the protection of the rights and freedoms of others."[17]

Article 3(2) adds that:

"No one shall be deprived of the right to enter the territory of the State of which he is a national."

The right to leave and return has been recalled in more specific treaties, for example, the 1961 European Social Charter[18] and the 1977 European Convention on Legal Status of Migrant Workers.[19]

---

[14] For the text and a commentary of the Uppsala Declaration, see "The Uppsala Declaration on The Right to Leave and to Return," 4 *Israel Yearbook on Human Rights* (1974) pp. 432-435; K. Vasak and S. Liskovsky (eds.), *The Right to Leave and to Return* (1976).

[15] For the text and a commentary of the Strasbourg Declaration, see R. Hofmann, "The Right to Leave and to Return to One's Own Country, The Strasbourg Declaration on the Right to Leave and to Return: Results of the Meeting of Experts Held in Strasbourg in November 1986," 8 *Human Rights Law Journal* (1987) pp. 478-484; H. Hannum, "The Strasbourg Declaration on the Right to Leave and Return," 81 *AJIL* (1987) pp. 432-438.

[16] CCPR/C/21/Rev.1/Add.9 (2 November 1999).

[17] Protocol No. 4 entered into force 2 May 1968 and is presently ratified by thirty-five states.

[18] Art. 18(4) of the European Social Charter:
"The Right to Engage in a Gainful Occupation in the Territory of other Contracting Parties
With a view to ensuring the effective exercise of the right to engage in a gainful occupation in the territory of any other Contracting Party, the Contracting Parties […] recognize […] the right of their na-

In a broader context, the Final Act of the Conference on Security and Cooperation in Europe, adopted in 1975, recalls that "the participating States [...] make it their aim to facilitate freer movement and contacts, individually and collectively, whether privately or officially, among persons, institutions and organizations of the participating States" and provides specific measures concerning travel for family, personal, or professional reasons.[20] Although the Helsinki Final Act is not legally binding, the fact that the traditional opponents to the right to leave and return – namely the Soviet Union and the Communist countries – were signatories provided a stimulus for a broader recognition of that right. This normative movement toward a firmer acceptance of that right was accelerated after the collapse of the Berlin Wall.[21] The concluding documents of the subsequent Conferences on Security and Cooperation in Europe recalls in unambiguous terms that the participating states undertake to implement and respect the principle "that everyone shall be free to leave any country, including his own, and to return to his country."[22] This formal endorsement enlarges and consolidates the already widespread recognition in other parts of the world.

In the Americas, the principles set forth in the 1948 American Declaration of the Rights and Duties of Man[23] were confirmed in 1969 by the American Convention on

---

tionals to leave the country to engage in a gainful occupation in the territories of the other Contracting Parties".

The Europe Social Charter entered into force 26 February 1965 and is presently ratified by 25 states.

[19] Art. 4 of the European Convention on Legal Status of Migrant Workers:

"Right of exit-Right to admission-Administrative formalities

1. Each Contracting Party shall guarantee the following rights to migrant workers: – the right to leave the territory of the Contracting Party of which they are nationals; – the right to admission to the territory of a Contracting Party in order to take up paid employment after being authorized to do so and obtaining the necessary papers.

2. These rights shall be subject to such limitations as are prescribed by legislation and are necessary for the protection of national security, public order, public health or morals.

3. The papers required of the migrant worker for emigration and immigration shall be issued as expeditiously as possible free of charge or on payment of an amount not exceeding their administrative cost."

The Convention entered into force 1 May 1983 and is presently ratified by eight states.

[20] All of the thirty-one European States, excluding Albania, plus Canada and the United States, signed the Helsinki Final Act, reprinted *in* 14 *ILM* (1975) p. 1293.

[21] For an overview of the changes of the State's practice in the Central and Eastern Countries, see F.A. Gabor, "Reflections on the Freedom of Movement in Light of the Dismantled 'Iron Curtain'," 65 *Tulane Law Review* (1991) pp. 849-881; D.C. Turack, "The Movement of Persons: The Practice of States in Central and Eastern Europe Since the 1989 Vienna CSCE," 12 *Denver Journal of International Law and Policy* (1993) pp. 289-309.

[22] See the Concluding Document of the Vienna Conference on Security and Cooperation in Europe held in 1989, reprinted *in* 10 *Human Rights Law Journal* (1989) p. 270; and the Document of the Copenhagen Meeting of the Conference on the Human Dimension of the CSCE, reprinted *in* 29 *ILM* (1990) p. 1035. See also the 1991 Charter of Paris for a New Europe, reprinted in 30 *ILM* 193 (1991) pp. 193-194, 199-200.

[23] Article VIII. Right to residence and movement.

"Every person has the right to fix his residence within the territory of the state of which he is a national, to move about freely within such territory, and not to leave it except by his own will."

Human Rights. Article 22 states the right to leave and return in similar terms as Protocol No. 4 of the European Convention on Human Rights.[24]

The 1981 African Charter on Human and Peoples' Rights proclaims in Article 12(2) that:

> "Every individual shall have the right to leave any country including his own, and to return to his country. This right may only be subject to restrictions, provided for by law for the protection of national security, law and order, public health or morality."[25]

More recently, in 1994, the right to leave and return was reiterated in the Arab Charter on Human Rights.[26]

Nevertheless, this widespread regional and universal recognition of the right to leave and return does not reflect the practical difficulties in applying that right.

LEGAL CONTENT OF THE FREEDOM OF MOVEMENT

Freedom of movement is composed of two interdependent rights: the right to leave and the right to return.

The Right to Leave

The legal content of the right to leave calls for four main remarks. First, all the universal and regional instruments set forth the basic right to leave without distinguishing between citizens and non-citizens. Freedom to leave is available to everyone, i.e., to nationals and aliens alike. The legal status of aliens is irrelevant and the benefit of this right is not conditioned on lawful residency within the territory of a State Party.

Second, the right to leave covers both temporary stays abroad (right to travel) and long-term departure from a country (right to emigrate). The Human Rights Committee notices in its General Comment No. 27:

---

[24] According to Art. 22(2) and (3) of the American Convention on Human Rights:

"Every person has the right to leave any country freely, including his own.

The exercise of the foregoing rights may be restricted only pursuant to a law to the extent necessary in a democratic society to prevent crime or to protect national security, public safety, public order, public morals, public health, or the rights or freedoms of others." Para. 5 adds that: "No one can be expelled from the territory of the state of which he is a national or be deprived of the right to enter it."

The American Convention entered into force 18 July 1978 and is presently ratified by twenty-five states.

[25] The African Charter entered into force 21 October 1986 and is presently ratified by fifty-three states.

[26] According to Art. 21 of the Arab Charter on Human Rights:

"Citizens shall not be arbitrarily or illegally deprived from leaving any Arab country, including their own, or their residency restricted to a particular place, or forced to live in any area of their country."

Art. 22 adds that: "No citizen can be expelled from his own country, or deprived of the right to return to it."

However, the Arab Charter adopted in 1994 by twenty-two states is not yet enforced.

"Freedom to leave the territory of a State may not be made dependent on any specific purpose or on the period of time the individual chooses to stay outside the country. Thus traveling abroad is covered, as well as departure for permanent emigration. Likewise, the right of the individual to determine the State of destination is part of the legal guarantee."[27]

Third, the right to leave implies a twofold obligation for a state: a negative obligation to not impede departure from its territory and a positive obligation to issue travel documents. The Human Rights Committee has made it clear, in several cases where Uruguay denied passports to some of its nationals residing outside of the country, that the right to issuance of travel document is an integral part of the right to leave and return, as it ensure the effective guarantee of this right.[28] Its General Comment states that:

"Since international travel usually requires appropriate documents, in particular a passport, the right to leave a country must include the right to obtain the necessary travel documents. The issuing of passports is normally incumbent on the State of nationality of the individual. The refusal by a State to issue a passport or prolong its validity for a national residing abroad may deprive this person of the right to leave the country of residence and to travel elsewhere."[29]

Fourth, the right to leave is not an absolute right. Except for the general provisions expressed in the Universal Declaration, the American Declaration, and the Arab Charter on Human Rights, all other conventions provide for restrictions under certain circumstances. As with many other human rights, restrictions are permissible when they are:

- provided by law;
- purported to protect the legitimate state interests and the other rights and freedoms recognized in human rights treaties; and
- necessary for achieving this purpose.

During the long discussions on restrictions in Article 12(3) of the International Covenant, it was agreed that "the right to leave the country could not be claimed in order to escape legal proceedings or to avoid such obligations as national service, and the payment of fines, taxes or maintenance allowances."[30] Besides the great diversity of

---

[27] General Comment No. 27, para. 8.

[28] See, e.g., communication No.57/1979, *Vidal Martins* v. *Uruguay, Report of the Human Rights Committee*, 37 UN GAOR, Supp. 40 (1982) p. 157; communication No. 108/1981, *Varela Nunez* v. *Uruguay, Report of the Human Rights Committee*, 38 UN GAOR, Supp. 40 (1983), p. 225.

[29] General Comment No. 27, para. 9. See also Art. 9 of the Strasbourg Declaration on the Right to Leave and to Return: "Everyone has the right to obtain such travel or other documents as may be necessary to leave any country or to enter one's own country."

[30] UN Doc. A/2929, *Annotations on the Text of the Draft International Covenants on Human Rights* (1955) p. 39. For other examples of the subsequent states' practice, see also Y. Dinstein, "Freedom of Emigration and Soviet Jewry," 4 *Israel Yearbook on Human Rights* (1974) pp. 266-274; S. Jagerskiold, note 2, at 178-179; M. Nowak, *supra* note 2, at 206-217.

the states' practice, the General Comment provides detailed guidelines regarding the application of the permissible limitations of Article 12(3):

"12. The law itself has to establish the conditions under which the rights may be limited. [...] Restrictions which are not provided for in the law or are not in conformity with the requirements of Article 12, paragraph 3, would violate the rights guaranteed by paragraphs 1 and 2.

13. In adopting laws providing for restrictions permitted by Article 12, paragraph 3, States should always be guided by the principle that the restrictions must not impair the essence of the right [...]; the relation between right and restriction, between norm and exception, must not be reversed. The laws authorizing the application of restrictions should use precise criteria and may not confer unfettered discretion on those charged with their execution.

14. Article 12, paragraph 3, clearly indicates that it is not sufficient that the restrictions serve the permissible purposes; they must also be necessary to protect them. Restrictive measures must conform to the principle of proportionality; they must be appropriate to achieve their protective function; they must be the least intrusive instrument amongst those which might achieve the desired result; and they must be proportionate to the interest to be protected.

15. The principle of proportionality has to be respected not only in the law that frames the restrictions, but also by the administrative and judicial authorities in applying the law. States should ensure that any proceedings relating to the exercise or restriction of these rights are expeditious and that reasons for the application of restrictive measures are provided.

16. [...] The application of restrictions in any individual case must be based on clear legal grounds and meet the test of necessity and the requirements of proportionality [...]".[31]

Despite the universal recognition of the right to leave, the bureaucratic and legal barriers imposed by the state practice remain a source of concern.[32] The exceptions

---

[31] See also Art. 4 of the Strasbourg Declaration on the Right to Leave and to Return.

[32] The Human Rights Committee noticed in its General Comment that: "17. A major source of concern is the manifold legal and bureaucratic barriers unnecessarily affecting the full enjoyment of the rights of the individuals [...] to leave a country, including their own [...]. States' practice presents a [...] rich [...] array of obstacles making it more difficult to leave the country, in particular for their own nationals. These rules and practices include, *inter alia*, lack of access for applicants to the competent authorities and lack of information regarding requirements; the requirement to apply for special forms through which the proper application documents for the issuance of a passport can be obtained; the need for supportive statements from employers or family members; exact description of the travel route; issuance of passports only on payment of high fees substantially exceeding the cost of the service rendered by the administration; unreasonable delays in the issuance of travel documents; restrictions on family members traveling together; requirement of a repatriation deposit or a return ticket; requirement of an invitation from the State of destination or from people living there; harassment of applicants, for example by physical intimidation, arrest, loss of employment or expulsion of their children from school or university; refusal to issue a passport because the applicant is said to harm the good name of the country. In the light of these practices, States parties should make sure that all restrictions imposed by them are in full compliance with Article 12, paragraph 3".

of the right to leave still need to be defined more precisely and applied in a more restrictive sense.[33]

The Right to Return

From a theoretical point of view, the right to leave is an incomplete right, without the guarantee to be accepted abroad after the departure from one's own country. The effective exercise of the right to leave is therefore directly dependent on the ability to enter a country. However, under international law, there is no general right of entry into another country of which one is not a national.[34] As in regional conventions, the International Covenant on Civil and Political Rights does not ensure a general human right to enter the sovereign territory of the States Parties, but it does guarantee a right to enter one's own country. The right of return was originally considered as a means for strengthening the right to leave. According to the statement by the representative of Lebanon, who proposed the amendment during the drafting of the Universal Declaration on Human Rights:

> "The ideal would be that any person should be able to enter any country he might choose, but account had to be taken of actual facts. The minimum requirement was that any person should be able to return to his country. If that right were recognized, the right to leave a country, already sanctioned in the article, would be strengthened by the assurance of the right to return."[35]

The question remains open as to what link must exist between an individual and a state for a right to return to apply. Both the European Convention and the American Convention expressly limit the right of return to the state of which the person is a national.[36] On the other hand, the Universal Declaration, the International Covenant, and the African Charter speak of "his country" or "his own country" without specifying that there must be a nationality link. It is commonly argued that this broad and somewhat ambiguous expression covers both nationals and permanent residents of the territory of States Parties.[37] According to the General Comment No. 27:

---

[33] See notably V. Boutkevitch, *supra* note 11, at 20.

[34] However, this does not mean that States are completely free to refuse entry to foreigners, especially when they are refugees. The principle of *non-refoulement* is in this regard the main limit to the traditional sovereign right to decide on the admission of foreigners. See on this question V. Chetail, "Le principe de non-refoulement et le statut de réfugié en droit international," *in* V. Chetail (ed.), *La Convention de Genève du 28 juillet 1951 relative au statut des réfugiés – 50 ans après: bilan et perspectives* (2001) pp. 3-61.

[35] UN Doc. A/777, Third Committee of the General Assembly (September-December 1948).

[36] See also the not yet binding Arab Charter on Human Rights.

[37] See notably R. Higgins, *supra* note 2, at 349-350; S. Jagerskiold, *supra* note 2, at 180-181; H. Hannum, *supra* note 2, at 56-60; M. Nowak, *supra* note 2, at 219-220. For a contrary opinion, see however J.D. Inglés, *supra* note 9, at 60; R.B. Lillich, *supra* note 2, at 151; R. Lapidoth, "The Right of Return in International Law, With Special Reference to the Palestinian Refugees," 16 *Israel Yearbook on Human Rights* (1986) p. 108.

"The wording of Article 12, paragraph 4, does not distinguish between nationals and aliens ('no one'). Thus, the persons entitled to exercise this right can be identified only by interpreting the meaning of the phrase 'his own country.' The scope of 'his own country' is broader than the concept 'country of his nationality.' It is not limited to nationality in a formal sense, that is, nationality acquired at birth or by conferral; it embraces, at the very least, an individual who, because of his or her special ties to or claims in relation to a given country, cannot be considered to be a mere alien. This would be the case, for example, of nationals of a country who have there been stripped of their nationality in violation of international law, and of individuals whose country of nationality has been incorporated in or transferred to another national entity, whose nationality is being denied them. The language of Article 12, paragraph 4, moreover, permits a broader interpretation that might embrace other categories of long-term residents, including but not limited to stateless persons arbitrarily deprived of the right to acquire the nationality of the country of such residence."[38]

The second difference with the right to leave is the absolute character of the right to return. The various regional and universal instruments do not envisage restrictions to its application. However, the term "arbitrarily" contained in the Covenant may imply some possible limits to its benefit.[39] According to the General Comment No. 27:

"The reference to the concept of arbitrariness in this context is intended to emphasize that it applies to all State action, legislative, administrative and judicial; it guarantees that even interference provided for by law should be in accordance with the provisions, aims and objectives of the Covenant and should be, in any event, reasonable in the particular circumstances. The Committee considers that there are few, if any, circumstances in which deprivation of the right to enter one's own country could be reasonable."[40]

States practice remains relatively sparse with regard to the concrete standards for assessing arbitrariness.[41] Moreover, all of the other international instruments do not refer to the term "arbitrarily" and guarantee an unrestricted right to return.

---

[38] General Comment No. 27, para. 20. For an illustration, see communication No. 538/1993, *Stewart* v. *Canada* and Communication No. 558/1993, *Canepa* v. *Canada*. See also Art. 7 of the Strasbourg Declaration on the Right to Leave and to Return: "Permanent legal residents who temporarily leave their country of residence shall not be arbitrarily denied the right to return to that country."

[39] S. Jagerskiold, *supra* note 2, at 181; R.B. Lillich, *supra* note 2, at 151.

[40] General Comment No. 27, para. 21. In this sense, Professor Nowak considers that "in light of the historical background, there can be no doubt that the limitation on the right to entry expressed with the word *'arbitrarily'* ('arbitrairement') is to relate exclusively to cases of *lawful exile as punishment* for a crime, whether this is accompanied by loss of nationality or not." M. Nowak, *supra* note 2, at 219.

[41] See the paper of David Martin in the present volume. For an example of one of the most controversial issue, concerning the right to return of Palestinians, see R. Lapidoth, *supra* note 37; K.R. Radley, "The Palestinian Refugees: The Right to Return in International Law," 72 *AJIL* (1978) pp. 586-614; Y. Tadmor, "The Palestinian Refugees of 1948: The Right to Compensation and Return," 8 *Temple International Comparative Law Journal* (1994) pp. 403-434; J. Quigley, "Displaced Palestinians and a Right of Return," 39 *Harvard International Law Journal* (1998) pp. 171-229.

CONCLUSION

This brief survey of the legal dimensions of the freedom of movement highlights the intrinsic ambiguity of the social reality of migration and its legal regulation. The right to leave any country and to return to one's own country are expressly guaranteed in a series of regional and universal multilateral treaties ratified by the great majority of the international community. It is therefore beyond dispute that this right exists in international law. After the collapse of the Soviet empire, there has been a growing recognition of the right to leave and return, which nowadays may be considered as customary norm with the above-mentioned restrictions.[42]

However, freedom of movement does not guarantee that an individual will have a place to go. Public international law does recognize both an individual's right to leave a country and a right to return one's own country. However, there is no correlative duty of the state to admit foreigners. The prospect for a solution in terms of individual rights is not realistic. States are increasingly reluctant to enter into new legal obligations restricting their sovereign rights to decide on the admission of foreigners.

This phenomenon explains the divorce between the *concept of freedom of movement* and its *legal implications*. The right to leave and return is primarily conceived of as a right concentrated on the state of origin. However, by its very nature the concept of freedom of movement implies relationships between two states: the state of origin and the state of reception. Accordingly, the regulation of migration movements must occur through cooperation among all of the states concerned. The contemporary challenges of the legal regulation of migration calls for a large and comprehensive approach through a more intensive cooperation between the states of immigration and the states of emigration.

Selected Bibliography

CASSESE, A. – "International Protection of the Right to Leave and to Return," *Studi in onore di Manlio Udina* (1975): 219-229.

DINSTEIN, Y. – "Freedom of Emigration and Soviet Jewry," 4 *Israel Yearbook on Human Rights* (1974): 266-274.

FLORY, M. AND R. HIGGINS (EDS.) – *Liberté de Circulation des Personnes en Droit International* (1988).

GABOR, F.A. – "Reflections on the Freedom of Movement in Light of the Dismantled 'Iron Curtain,'" 65 *Tulane Law Review* (1991): 849-881.

GOODWIN-GILL, GUY S. – "The Right to Leave, the Right to Return and the Question of a Right to Remain," in Vera Gowlland-Debbas (ed.), *The Problem of Refugees in the Light of Contemporary International Law issues* (1995): 93-108.

GRAHL-MADSEN, A. – "Article 13," in A. Eide, G. Alfredsson, G. Melander, L.A. Rehof and A. Rosas (eds.), *The Universal Declaration of Human Rights: A Commentary* (1993): 203-214.

---

[42] See notably: R. Plender, *International Migration Law* (1988) p. 119. See however: G.S. Goodwin-Gill, "The Right to Leave, the Right to Return and the Question of a Right to Remain," *in* Vera Gowlland-Debbas (ed.), *The Problem of Refugees in the Light of Contemporary International Law issues* (1995) p. 97.

HAILBRONNER, K. – "Comments On: The Right to Return and the Question of a Right to Remain," in Vera Gowlland-Debbas (ed.), *The Problem of Refugees in the Light of Contemporary International Law issues* (1995): 109-119.

HANNUM, H. – *The Right to Leave and Return in International Law and Practice* (1987).

—."The Strasbourg Declaration on the Right to Leave and Return," 81 *American Journal of International Law* (1987): 432-438.

HIGGINS, R. – "The Right in International Law of an Individual to Enter, Stay In and Leave a Country," 49 *International Affairs* (1973): 341-357.

HOFMANN, R. – "The Right to Leave and to Return to One's Own Country, The Strasbourg Declaration on the Right to Leave and to Return: Results of the Meeting of Experts Held in Strasbourg in November 1986," 8 *Human Rights Law Journal* (1987): 478-484.

JAGERSKIOLD, S. – "The Freedom of Movement," in L. Henkin (ed.), *The International Bill of Rights. The Covenant on Civil and Political Rights* (1981): 166-184.

LAPIDOTH, R. – "The Right of Return in International Law, With Special Reference to the Palestinian Refugees," 16 *Israel Yearbook on Human Rights* (1986): 103-125.

LILLICH, R.B. – "Civil Rights," in Th. Meron (ed.), *Human Rights in International Law: Legal and Policy Issues* (1984): 149-152.

NOWAK, M. – *U.N. Covenant on Civil and Political Rights CCPR Commentary* (1993): 197-221.

PLENDER, R. – *International Migration Law* (1988).

TURACK, D.C. – "The Movement of Persons: The Practice of States in Central and Eastern Europe Since the 1989 Vienna CSCE," 12 *Denver Journal of International Law and Policy* (1993): 289-309.

VASAK, K. AND S. LISKOVSKY (EDS.) – *The Right to Leave and to Return* (1976).

WEIS, P. – "Emigration," *Encyclopedia of Public International Law* (1995): 74-78.

Chapter 4
RETURN OF PERSONS TO STATES OF ORIGIN AND THIRD STATES

Gregor Noll*

INTRODUCTION

As emigration has become cheaper and less controlled, and global economic deregu-
lation progresses, liberal welfare states have been increasingly faced with the dilemma of defending the delimitation of their populations. One step – arguably a
central one – is the formulation and implementation of stringent return policies:
those who are not or are no longer permitted to stay, shall be returned to their country of origins or turned over to another country prepared to accept them. From the
perspective of remittance economies, and less affluent states in general, this increased emphasis on return has been perceived as threatening, as returns could reduce the amounts migrants transfer back to their countries of origin and could create
or exacerbate socio-political tensions within them. Undocumented migrants who
cannot be returned are costly for welfare states: they are denied access to labor markets and will inevitably draw on public subsidies. In addition, detention and forcible
return result in important expenses. For many countries in the South, remittances are
the largest single source of income, bypassing foreign direct investment and development aid. The economic interests for states at both ends of the return spectrum are
considerable, which perhaps explains why return practices are fraught with tensions,
frictions, and ambiguities, in spite of allegedly clear-cut international norms.

While the North has emphasized the duty to readmit one's citizens and attempted
to conclude an ever-tighter mesh of readmission agreements both with countries of
origin and with third states to make return effective, the South has countered with
conditionality demands (e.g., readmission swapped for economic aid) or dragged its
feet when faced with actual readmission requests. Furthermore, there is an urgent
problem of how to deal with undocumented migrants whose nationality cannot be
assessed with sufficient certainty, which leaves states without a reliable allocative
criterion.[1]

---

* Faculty of Law, University of Lund.

[1] A very real risk is that a dumping market will develop, where unscrupulous officials of northern
countries simply buy readmission from corrupt officials of southern countries, regardless of any objective substantiation of citizenship.

T.A. Aleinikoff and V. Chetail (Eds.), Migration and International Legal Norms
© 2003, T.M.C. ASSER PRESS, *The Hague, The Netherlands, et al.*

This chapter seeks to answer the question of how international law regulates the return of persons to either their countries of origin or to third countries. The first section distinguishes three relationships relevant for understanding norms on return. The second section discusses the efforts of doctrinal writers to identify a customary obligation to readmit citizens in international law. The next section argues that this norm, to the extent it exists, is insufficiently precise. The fourth section addresses why human rights exacerbate rather than mitigate the ambiguity of interstate norms on return. The following section discusses the nexus between state and population, and its impact on interstate relationships. Against the backdrop of previously developed arguments, the question of return to third states is dealt with rather briefly. The last section illustrates why international law cannot sever the Gordian knot in a coherent fashion; it also offers a choice between two readings (weak claims and obligations *erga omnes* or strong claims and obligations *inter partes*).

THREE RELATIONSHIPS

The return of aliens cuts across the state-individual divide in international law, opening up the risk of fallacious analogies and unwarranted conclusions. Legally, the issue can be broken down into three different relationships:[2] the relationship between the two states involved, the relationship between the returning state and the individual, and the relationship between the receiving state (country of origin or third country) and the individual. International lawyers shuttle back and forth over the limits of these three relations in a quest for unambiguous norms. Disregarding the limits has a price, and much of the ostensibly clear-cut arguments will crumble when subjected to closer scrutiny.

The discussion that follows will deal largely with the question whether a country is obliged under international law to admit a person expelled from another state. This suggests an overriding importance of the first relationship. However, doctrine usually draws on the other two relations as well, and thus involves the individual in this interstate dimension.

The term *return* should be properly reserved for the turning over of aliens to their country of origin. Indeed, and in spite of their generic name, some readmission agreements do not presuppose that an alien had territorial contact with the third country to which she is turned over by the destination state – hence, it would be linguistically inappropriate to speak of return in such cases. With this caveat in mind, we will use the term return in a less precise sense for the turning over of an alien to both categories of countries.[3] Methodologically, it makes sense to deal with return to

---

[2] Much of the doctrine in this area attempts to sever the interstate relationship from the relationship between individual and state. R. Plender, *International Migration Law* (1988) [hereinafter Plender] p. 134, with further references to earlier doctrinal texts; L.B. Sohn and T. Buergenthal (eds.), *The Movements of Persons Across Borders* (1992) p. 2; K. Hailbronner, *Rückübernahme Eigener und Fremder Staatsangehöriger. Völkerrechtliche Verpflichtungen der Staaten* (1996) [hereinafter Hailbronner] pp. 6-12.

[3] In the bulk of cases, an alien turned over to a third country has actually been in contact with the territory of that state.

the country of origin first, and to address the return to third countries thereafter, to the extent this is warranted.

A further complication is whether the allocative criterion linking state and individual should be that of citizenship or nationality. While citizenship is formally circumscribed, nationality reverberates with essentialist overtones and comprises a wider group that could be ethnically defined. Certainly, this choice plays a role in the practice of return and readmission. However, it will not be addressed in this text, which uses the term citizen as a minimum common denominator.

THE INTERSTATE DIMENSION

Which norms govern the interstate relationship in matters of return? The standard account from doctrinal writers goes as follows: as a corollary flowing from their personal and territorial sovereignty, states possess a qualified right to expel aliens from their territory. In order for this right to be effectively exercised, another state has to receive the person expelled. It is generally held that the obligation to receive rests upon the state of which the expelled person is a citizen.[4] Thus, the returning state's right of removal corresponds to a duty on the part of the country of origin to readmit the incumbent. Citizenship is the decisive factor that links two countries in this relationship of entitlement and duty. Citizenship (and, to a certain extent, habitual residence) is the allocative principle for responsibility in a world divided into nation-states. This justifies a distinction between states of origin and third states. Following this allocative logic, third states are not obliged to receive an alien turned away by her destination state, unless such an obligation has been specifically created on a bilateral or multilateral level (e.g., through a readmission agreement).

On which sources of international law may we rely when professing the existence of a state right to return a non-citizen and a duty to readmit her? Both are surprisingly difficult to document. There is no universal treaty obligation laying down the normative couplet of return and readmission, and the occasional attempts to codify states' rights and duties fail to address this issue.[5]

Doctrinal writers go to some length to show that a duty to readmit constitutes a norm of general international law. They begin by demonstrating the existence of a customary right to expel, followed by the duty to readmit as its logical correlate.[6]

---

[4] See *supra* note 2. Kay Hailbronner's monograph in particular offers a rich array of further references.

[5] To be considered a person of international law, a state must also possess a permanent population, a government, and the capacity to enter into relations with other states. The quoted provision is generally regarded as reflecting customary international law. Neither the Montevideo Convention (Convention of the Rights and Duties of States, Montevideo, 26 December 1933, 165 *LNTS* 19) nor the abortive ILC attempts to codify basic rights and duties of states contain a pertinent rule. To underpin a general duty to readmit, Hailbronner adduces the Convention on the Status of Aliens, Havana, 20 February 1928, which requires states "to receive their nationals expelled from foreign soil who seek to enter their territory." This is inconclusive, as the formulation clearly contains a voluntaristic element ("who seek to enter"), which brings us back to the post-war discussion on a "right not to return" implied in Art. 12(4) ICCPR and dealt with Hailbronner, *supra* note 2, at 30.

[6] "The principle that every State must admit its own nationals to its territory ... is often implied by

There are no serious attempts to show the existence of an interstate obligation to re-admit as a customary norm not using this inductive method. Perhaps the induction argument appears intuitively convincing, or rather, the difficulties of documenting state practice overwhelming. The viability of the argument however, is doubtful. Before explaining why this is the case, we need to assess whether customary international law contains a duty to readmit citizens, independent of the induction argument. If such an obligation can be tracked independently, it would be superfluous to challenge the induction argument.

THE CUSTOMARY OBLIGATION TO READMIT CITIZENS

The party invoking a norm of customary international law bears the onus of demonstrating its existence. This puts the ball in the court of the North, if the South would confront it on this count. However, the strategy of the South seems to be evasion rather than confrontation, conditionality rather than denial.

The North could argue that it returns thousands of undocumented migrants each year. Together with the absence of claims that a duty to readmit does not exist, such practice might be said to have crystallized into a custom. However, to allow for the construction of custom, state practice needs to be extensive and uniform.[7] The numbers of undocumented migrants returned globally would need to be broken down. The number of voluntary returns and returns based on readmission agreements must be subtracted, as treaty law can be invoked to support those returns. Of interest is how many persons are forcibly sent back and accepted in the absence of treaty law. How does the number of the latter category compare to the number of undocumented migrants who cannot be sent back due to action or omission on behalf of the country of origin?

The absence of detailed statistics allowing for precise answers illustrate why the distribution of the argumentative burden under international law is quite important. Ultimately, the North would be at pains to show that accepted returns indeed dominate state practice even beyond the realm of treaty regulation.[8] To illustrate the problem, let us resort to statistics from three EU Member States, which are among the few countries making such information publicly available.[9]

---

those who assert that each State has the right to deny admission to aliens [footnote omitted]." Plender, *supra* note 2, at 133. See also Hailbronner, *supra* note 2, at 28-34, with further references to doctrinal writings of the last century, mainly relying on the logic of correlates.

[7] "State practice [...] should have been both extensive and virtually uniform in the sense of the provision invoked." *North Sea Continental Shelf* case *ICJ Reports* 1969: 44.

[8] Apart from those states outright denying readmission to non-voluntary returnees, others obstruct return by administrative measures. By way of example, the returnee is declared not to be a citizen of the requested state, or return is denied due to lacking travel or identity documents. See G. Noll, "Unsuccessful Asylum Seekers – The Problem of Return," 37 *International Migration* 267 (1999) pp. 274-275.

[9] Return has been difficult to research because many states in the north have either not collected statistics and relevant information, or kept them secret for various reasons. The IGC continuously compiles reports on return policies and practices in its participating states. Those reports are not in the public domain, although it is understood that they contain highly relevant information on the reluctance of

The United Kingdom initiated enforcement action against 43,460 rejected asylum-seekers in 2000, while merely 8,980 rejected asylum-seekers were removed from UK territory during the same year. The lack of travel documents is a significant reason why the number of deportations is limited.[10] Spain served 6,576 persons with expulsion orders in 2000, while 1,226 expulsions were actually carried out that year. Among the impediments to deportation, the Spanish government names "identification, lack of cooperation of countries of origin, documentation, no direct flights."[11] Belgium also names difficulties in identification and the lack of diplomatic cooperation as impediments to deportation; its authorities issued 13,563 deportation orders in 2000, and carried out 3,002 expulsions.[12] If the 2000 numbers could be extrapolated, roughly one in five persons served with an expulsion order is actually removed. The remainder could move voluntarily, abscond, or remain due to such impediments as uncooperative countries of origin. This raises more questions: who is to blame for problems with identification and travel document procurement: the individual or her country of origin, or both? As a number of EU Member States cite the behavior of countries of origin as an impediment to deportation,[13] a significant fraction of unimplemented expulsion orders appear to be linked with that factor. This then casts doubt on whether the requirement of state practice being extensive as well as uniform can be satisfied. Nothing indicates that Belgium, Spain, and the United Kingdom are isolated cases among destination countries in the North.

Further differentiation is necessary. Issuing travel documents becomes protracted because less affluent countries cannot fall back on a well-functioning domestic infrastructure when it comes to determining who is a citizen and who is not. Such factual impossibility of performance would not disaffirm the existence of a duty to readmit. It is doubtful, however, whether poverty is the bottom line. This brings us to factors motivating state behavior, and thus the issue of *opinio juris*.

Tracking *opinio juris* leaves an ambiguous outcome. The non-binding 1994 Cairo Program of Action is one of the few instruments directly alluding to a responsibility to readmit borne by countries of origin: "Governments of countries of origin of undocumented migrants and persons whose asylum claims have been rejected have the responsibility to accept the return and reintegration of those persons, and should not penalize such persons on their return."[14] It may still be asked to whose benefit this responsibility works – that of the individual, that of the destination state, or that of both?

Passages on state responsibility can be found in the General Assembly's yearly endorsement of the United Nations High Commissioner for Refugees' (UNHCR)

---

countries of origin to readmit its citizens. The present paragraph draws on a public domain study commissioned by the European Refugee Fund (ICMPD), *Study on Comprehensive EU Return Policies and Practices for Displaced Persons under Temporary Protection, Other Persons whose International Protection has Ended, and Rejected Asylum Seekers*, January 2002 (hereinafter ICMPD).

[10] Id. at 147.

[11] Id. at 123.

[12] Id. at 69, 70.

[13] Id. at Annex III.

[14] Programme of Action, International Conference on Population and Development, Cairo, 5-13 September 1994, UN Doc. No. A/CONF.171/13, 18 October 1994, para. 10.20.

activities. Thus, in 1992, it was stated that the General Assembly "[u]nderlines strongly State responsibility, particularly as it relates to the countries of origin, including addressing root causes, facilitating voluntary repatriation of refugees and the return, in accordance with international practice, of their nationals who are not refugees."[15] This raises the additional question of what exactly international practice is, or rather, should be. In 2001, it is noted that the General Assembly "[e]mphasizes the obligation of all States to accept the return of their nationals, calls upon all States to facilitate the return of their nationals who have been determined not to be in need of international protection, and affirms the need for the return of persons to be undertaken in a safe and humane manner and with full respect for their human rights and dignity, irrespective of the status of the persons concerned."[16] This is perhaps the closest one can get to an affirmation of readmission duties, but still lacks specification of its beneficiary. To the North, it could mean an obligation to readmit whomever states wish to return, while the South can read an obligation to readmit those wishing to return into it.

Bilateral arrangements of states demonstrate greater precision, but they are regularly covered by a veil of diplomatic discretion. Often, the conclusion of a readmission agreement is adduced as an element further corroborating the existence of an unqualified customary law obligation to readmit citizens. But if an obligation to receive is already part and parcel of customary law, why do states conclude agreements on the readmission of their own citizens? One answer is that such arrangements both confirm the obligation and flesh it out.[17] Yet why does a customary obligation, the existence of which is allegedly beyond doubt, need reconfirmation in a treaty, and why are negotiations of these agreements complicated and protracted affairs? The preludes to readmission agreements provide interesting insights. In December 1997, the Swedish Minister for Immigration and the Scandinavian Ambassadors met the Ethiopian Minister of Foreign Affairs and a number of officials from the Ministry to discuss readmission matters. While the Ethiopian side affirmed the existence of an obligation to readmit, it was willing to receive only such persons returning voluntarily. Moreover, the Ethiopian Government preferred bilateral negotiations. The Ethiopian delegation referred explicitly to the readmission agreement between the Netherlands and Ethiopia, of which development contributions were an essential element.[18] At the time of writing, the readmission agreement between Sweden and Ethiopia is still under negotiation.[19]

---

[15] UNGA Res. of 16 December 1992, UN Doc. No. A/RES/47/105, para. 10. An identical formulation can be found in UNGA Res. of 16 December 1991, UN Doc. No. A/RES/46/106.

[16] UNGA Res. of 19 December 2001, UN Doc. No. A/RES/56/137, para. 10.

[17] In a number of bilateral readmission agreements regulating the return of citizens to their country of origin, the state obligation to readmit is merely reaffirmed. See, e.g., the preamble of the 1992 German-Romanian readmission agreement, reaffirming the international obligation to readmit citizens. Vereinbarung zwischen dem Bundesminister des Innern der Bundesrepublik Deutschland und dem Innenministerium von Rumänien über die Rückübernahme von deutschen und rumänischen Staatsangehörigen [Agreement between the Minister of the Interior of the Federal Republic of Germany and the Interior Ministry of Romania on the Readmission of German and Romanian citizens], 1 November 1992, *ILM,* vol. 31 (1992), pp. 1296-1300.

[18] Information provided by a Swedish governmental source.

[19] ICMPD, *supra* note 9, Annex II.

If the Ethiopian case is not a singular one, it would mean that some countries in the South indeed see their customary obligation to readmit as limited to voluntarily returning citizens, while readmission agreements are needed to create readmission obligations for citizens to be forcibly removed. An increasing number of readmission agreements would merely illustrate that a stand-alone customary duty to readmit forcible removals has not existed in the view of those states. Or, in the words of a 1997 memorandum on repatriation by the Dutch Minister of Justice: "Although the authorities in the countries of origin do occasionally recognize their obligation to admit their own subjects, they will then also often call attention to the socio-economic consequences of large-scale repatriation."[20] This seems to reflect the general state of affairs: if an obligation to readmit forcibly returned citizens is accepted by relevant states of the South, it is usually conditioned on development aid or other benefits for the country of origin. Provided this is the root of the problem, tracking customary international law is not helpful. The details of a norm on return-in-exchange-for-aid would have to be worked out in a treaty document.[21] An equally undesirable result would be if customary international law indeed held an abstract obligation to readmit forcibly returned citizens, but gave countries of origin the prerogative of pegging the required level of proof for corroborating citizenship. Again, this kind of evasion strategy could only be overcome in treaty law.

This scrutiny has brought only limited clarity. There are strong indications that states accept an unconditional obligation to readmit their citizens returning voluntarily as a norm of customary international law. Additional conclusions would appear dubious until a systematic mapping of positions taken by states in the South is made. A duty to readmit voluntary returns is somewhat helpful to the North, as would be a conditional duty to readmit forcible returns once a form of compensation has been delivered or a norm putting the determination of citizenship to the discretion of the country of origin. This brings us back to the doctrinal writings professing that an obligation to readmit can be induced from other norms of international law, in particular the state right to expel non-citizens and the human rights to enter one's country.

THE HUMAN RIGHTS DIMENSION

It is striking to see that much of the evidence on the state right to expel is found in documents dealing with individual rights. Article 2(1) of the 1985 Declaration on

---

[20] Ministry of Justice of the Netherlands, Repatriation Policy, June 1997.

[21] It is indicative that the European Commission deplores the absence of "leverage" to convince countries of origin of the necessity to conclude readmission agreements with the EU: "As readmission agreements are solely in the interest of the Community, their successful conclusion depends very much of the 'leverage' at the Commission's disposal. In that context it is important to note that, in the field of JHA, there is little that can be offered in return. In particular visa facilitation or the lifting of visa requirement can be a realistic option in exceptional cases only (e.g., Hong Kong, Macao); in most cases it is not." European Commission, Green Paper on a Community Return Policy on Illegal Residents, COM (2002) 175 final, Brussels, 10 April 2002, p. 23.

the Human Rights of Individuals Who are not Nationals of the Country in which They Live[22] might serve as an example:

"Nothing in this Declaration shall be interpreted as legitimising the illegal entry into and presence in a State of any alien, nor shall any provision be interpreted as restricting the right of any State to promulgate laws and regulations concerning the entry of aliens and the terms and conditions of their stay or to establish differences between nationals and aliens. However, such laws and regulations shall not be incompatible with the international legal obligations of that State, including those in the field of human rights."

Reverting to the induction argument discussed above, it is perfectly legitimate to infer a correlative obligation to readmit from a right to expel. The question itself is, however, whether this has been done with due respect to the complications flowing from the individual-state divide in international law. Before responding, it appears justified to explore the relevance of the international law of human rights for this issue in greater depth.

The individual is not merely an object of interstate relations. A number of human rights instruments gives individuals the right to leave and to return to one's own country.[23] Article 13(2) of the Universal Declaration on Human Rights (UDHR) states:

"Everyone has the right to leave any country, including his own, and to return to his country."

Formulations of this right can also be found in the International Covenant on Civil and Political Rights (ICCPR) Article 12(2), (3), and (4),[24] and in a number of other human rights instruments,[25] as well as in the case law of the European Court of Justice.[26] Thus, there are two rights to return. One is expressed in a claim one state has on another state; the other right is expressed in the individual's claim against the country of nationality. The individual right to return concurrently reinforces and weakens the interstate claim. In cases where an individual wishes to return to his country of origin, the latter's obligation to readmit is owed not only to the returning state, but also to the individual. In cases where the individual chooses not to make use of the right to return, this individual right cannot be invoked by the returning

---

[22] Declaration on the Human Rights of Individuals who are not Nationals of the Country in which They Live, G.A. Res. 40/144 of 13 December 1985.

[23] See Vincent Chetail, this volume.

[24] International Covenant on Civil and Political Rights, 16 December 1966, 999 *UNTS* 171 [hereinafter ICCPR].

[25] The following instruments contain provisions relating to the right to leave and the right to return: International Convention on the Elimination of Racial Discrimination, Art. 5(d)(ii) (21 December 1965, 660 *UNTS* 195); African Charter on Human and Peoples' Rights, Art. 12 (Addis Ababa, June 1981, 21 *ILM* 58 (1992)); American Convention of Human Rights, Art. 22 (22 November 1969, *OASTS* 36). A right to enter the country of which one is a national is enshrined in ECHR Protocol No. 4 securing certain Rights and Freedoms other than those already included in the Convention and in the First Protocol thereto, Strasbourg, Art. 3 (16 September 1963, *ETS* 46).

[26] Case 41/74, *Van Duyn* v. *Home Office* [1974] *ECR* 1337, at 1351.

state to reinforce its claim against the country of origin. The question remains, does the individual's unwillingness to repatriate translate into a right not to return[27] with respect to all other states?[28] Indeed, the right to leave one's country would be nullified in a situation where no other state was prepared to receive the individual making use of this right. An interpretation along the lines of Articles 31 and 32 of the Vienna Treaty Convention[29] leaves us with an indeterminate result.[30]

The ideal to be realized by the right to leave and the right to return is the free movement of persons. The actual problem has shifted since these rights were conceived. During the Cold War, the Soviet Union and its satellites regarded emigration as undesirable and penalized persons who left the country without permission by, *inter alia*, blocking their return.[31] Now, the number of states inhibiting their citizens to leave or prohibiting their return is clearly decreasing.[32] Instead, free movement is hampered by a parallel emergence of immigration restrictions. In this context, it should be noted that the right to leave could be interpreted as a simple entitlement in regard to the country of origin or as an entitlement in regard to all states.[33] The wording of the various texts enshrining the right to leave does not restrict it to be a claim only against the country of origin. Structurally, the latter reading would be a symmetric mirroring of Richard Plender's attempt to construct a state duty to readmit citizens as an obligation *erga omnes*, i.e., an obligation of a state towards the international community as a whole.[34]

---

[27] Hailbronner observes this complication: "Als ausschließlich menschenrechtliche Garantie wäre das Recht auf Rückkehr in den Heimatstaat wesensmäßig vom Entschluß des Rückkehrwilligen abhängig." ["As a guarantee exclusively of a human rights character, the right to return to a country of origin would be essentially dependent on the decision of the person willing to return." Translation by this author.] Hailbronner, *supra* note 2, at 10. He attempts to disarm this potential of Art. 12 of the ICCPR by pointing to the fact that it cannot be logically reconciled with a state right to expel (id. at 11). Technically, this remains unconvincing, and it reveals his axiomatic assumption of a normative hierarchy putting state rights above human rights.

[28] In practice, countries of origin have denied readmission on the grounds that the individual was not willing to repatriate.

[29] Vienna Convention on the Law of Treaties, 24 May 1969, 1155 *UNTS* 331 [hereinafter VTC].

[30] See G. Noll, *Negotiating Asylum. The EU Acquis, Extraterritorial Protection and the Common Market of Deflection* (2000) pp. 416-423.

[31] It should be recalled that the content of legal norms must not be identified by resorting to their historical context, unless the primary means of interpretation cannot yield clarity (Arts. 31 and 32 VTC, *supra* note 29). Therefore, the historical changes of the return problem do not in themselves affect Art. 12(4) ICCPR, unless these changes condense into a modified state practice and *opino juris* (or simply spawn treaties shedding new light on the content of old norms). Moreover, had Art. 12(4) of the ICCPR merely been an instrument to embarrass the east and discredit its population policies, it would never have seen the light of the day.

[32] Hailbronner, *supra* note 2, at 6.

[33] Goodwin-Gill observes that the Soviet Union's proposal that the right to leave should be recognized as exercisable *only* in accordance with the laws of the state was rejected as a matter of principle when negotiating the wording of the 1948 UDHR. Nonetheless, he concludes that only the rights of the "national" government were involved in the right to leave, and no correlative obligations beyond the particular nation state. G. Goodwin-Gill, "The Right to Leave, the Right to Return and the Question of a Right to Remain," in V. Gowlland-Debbas (ed.), *The Problem of Refugees in the Light of Contemporary International Law Issues* (1996) p. 98.

[34] Plender, *supra* note 2, at 138.

As noted earlier, a state's right to remove aliens from its territory has been extrapolated to induce a duty owed by the country of origin to readmit that person. Assume, for a moment, that the requirements of a sufficiently consistent practice and the requirement of *opinio juris* are satisfied. This would prove that interstate international law accepts the deduction of a correlative duty from a right, indeed, that the logic of correlates is an inseparable element of law.[35] If the same argumentative technique of constructing a duty as a correlate to a right is applied in the field of human rights, the right to leave produces a duty to admit. In order for the former to be effective, one has to construct the latter. This line of argument entails an all-or-nothing outcome. Either it is accepted that the logic of correlates is part of customary international law, thus validating both an interstate duty to readmit citizens and a human right to immigration, or it is denied that customary international law embraces the logic of correlates. In that case, a human right to immigration would fail, thereby undermining the interstate duty to readmit citizens. Much seems to depend on whether we choose to formulate weak correlates, merely commanding passive respect, or strong correlates, commanding positive obligations to assist in implementation.

The point is not that the individual right to leave should override the state's right to return, thus letting contemporary forms of migration control appear as simply illegal. Rather, it should be made clear that the resolution in the conflict of rights hinges on our initial assumptions about international law. Do state interests trump individual interests, since international law is ultimately conceived by states, not individuals? Or is the liberal-protective content of human rights law, once unleashed, placed above the logic of state interest?

SOVEREIGNTY AND THE ADDRESSEE OF RETURN OBLIGATIONS

The discussion has shown that it is difficult to reconcile the interstate narrative with the human rights narrative to produce a single, determinate outcome. Beyond specific treaty provisions, the precise legal foundation of an individual right not to return or a state's duty to readmit citizens remains dubious. This is no surprise – shuttling back and forth between the state-individual and the state-state relationships cannot be done without causing damage to coherence. Let us revert to the state's right to expel aliens to illustrate this foundational fallacy of migration law. It is correctly asserted that this right is a corollary of a state's personal and territorial sovereignty.[36] The organizational delimitation of the state community would be impossible without this right, and the very idea of a state would be denied by an un-

---

[35] It might be objected that international law does not necessarily seek to maximize its own logical coherence. At the very least, there is a duty on states to interpret treaty norms in a manner maximizing coherence. This is precisely the function of contextual interpretation, as prescribed by Art. 31 of the VTC. Indeed, to the extent the general rule of interpretation in the quoted article is applicable to other sources of international law, it would inform the interpretation of customary law as well, which is at stake here.

[36] Hailbronner, *supra* note 2, at 29, with further references.

qualified right to become part of a state population and to enjoy the protection inherent in such membership. It is plausible to claim a state right to exclude an alien from the state community and its resource-base, i.e., state territory.

So, correctly understood, the right to expel is a corollary of a state's personal sovereignty – territorial sovereignty plays but a subordinate role.[37] It must be underscored that such a right is situated in the relationship between a country of destination and the individual alien. Stipulating a concurrent duty for a third actor – the country of origin – is simply a non sequitur. Lamentably, it is precisely this error that is repeatedly – and sometimes consciously[38] – committed by doctrinal writers. To the extent the state prerogative to expel aliens unfolds powers on the interstate level, it merely commands a weak duty of other states to respect the exercise of that right. A duty to respect means to refrain from interfering with the domestic admission policies made by destination states, provided these policies do not transgress international human rights law, and to not regard such policies as an unfriendly act toward the country of origin.[39] Theoretically, any farther-reaching induction remains untenable, which could explain practical difficulties in implementing the duty to readmit.

The induction of a state duty to readmit not only confuses two different relationships, it also begs the question why one state's personal self-determination should be more important than that of another state. After all, state sovereignty is to be exercised without infringing into the sovereignty of other states and what could be called the sovereignty of the individual, as expressed in internationally recognized human rights. Both delimitations merit further explanation.

A state duty to readmit a person expelled by another state would mean the subordination of one states' personal delimitation to that of another one. Given the sovereign equality of states, such subordination would be doctrinally untenable. Regulation of the state prerogative to exclude aliens takes place in domestic law, and the enforcement of such law is a domestic matter (again, with reservation made for human rights obligations and specific treaty obligations). If we choose to regard migration legislation as a matter of predominantly domestic concern, it will be hard, if not impossible, to argue the existence of international obligations for *other* states to enable or facilitate its enforcement. The practice of some sending states in the

---

[37] "Ein Staat ist aber in erster Linie ein Personenverband und basiert insofern auf einer "persönlichen" Grundlage, als er ein Treueverhältnis zwischen dem Staat und seinem Staatsvolk voraussetzt." ["However, a state is primarily a conjunction of persons, and rests on a 'personal' basis, as it presupposes loyalty between state and state population." Translation by this author.] K. Ipsen, *Völkerrecht* (1990) p. 298.

[38] Hailbronner, *supra* note 2, at 29, stating that the duty to admit one's own citizens is a correlate of a right to expel directed against aliens.

[39] This understanding corresponds well with the original understanding of the "right to seek and enjoy asylum from persecution" laid down in Art. 14 of the UDHR, which, in spite of its lip-service to the individual, merely obliges states not to regard the grant of asylum by another state as an unfriendly act. Åke Holmbäck, "Förenta nationerna och asylrätten" ["The United Nations and the right to asylum"], in 1949 års utlänningskommitté, SOU 1951:42. Betänkande med förslag till Utlänningslag m.m., 1951 [Report of the Swedish Parliamentary Committee on a new aliens act].

South appears to reflect this perspective, as their dependence on remittances turns large-scale readmission of citizens into a considerable loss for their economies. Arguing with citizenship or the human right to return to overcome this obstacle is, again, only helpful in cases where the individual *wishes* to avail herself of the protection flowing from her nationality, and, indeed, *wants* to return. In cases of involuntary removal, it is arbitrary – one might as well argue that the right to leave would be nullified by readmission to the country of origin, and thus reverse the subordination of individual to state rights.

If, however, we focus on the fact that restrictions on migration through domestic law have been on the rise during the last decades, we might wish to hypostasize an abstract international norm of migration control, obliging all states to assist in the enforcement of one state's migration control norms. Such a norm reflects the perspective of the North. Ultimately, do we believe that *lacunae* in law are filled out by a principle of free movement of persons or rather by a principle of population control? The indeterminacy of citizenship and human rights arguments in the area of state obligations to readmit illustrate again that right-duty correlates cannot straddle the divide between the three relationships described in the outset of this chapter.

THE RETURN TO THIRD STATES AS A SPECIAL CASE

Under general international law, a third state is not obliged to admit aliens expelled by their destination state.[40] Such obligation must be created by treaty. In the nineties, the number of agreements covering the readmission of non-nationals increased worldwide. However, there is no basis for the conclusion that the practice of concluding such agreements in itself allows for the inference of a customary obligation to readmit non-citizens.[41]

CONCLUDING REMARKS

There is a state right to expel aliens that corresponds to an individual obligation under domestic law to obey an expulsion order. There is an individual right under international law to return to one's country, and a corresponding international duty to readmit citizens making voluntary use of that right. From a regulatory perspective, this layer of norms is too thin, and the ensuing unpredictability of outcomes potentially strikes against states as well as individuals.

Choices have to be made beyond these two statements. In our earlier explorations, we have shown that the logic of correlates cannot be reserved to apply exclusively to the interstate domain, but perforce affects the interpretation of human rights as well. Also, it matters whether a right is construed to apply only between two parties (creating obligations *inter partes*), or among a wider circle of parties

---

[40] Hailbronner, *supra* note 2, at 71.
[41] Hailbronner, *supra* note 2, at 72.

(creating obligations *erga omnes*). We may now conclude what happens if we construe migration-related norms in the narrower or wider sense.

Table 1 below maps the two versions – a strong claim, drawing on the logic of correlates and assuming *erga omnes* obligations crossing the limits of the three relationships; and a weak claim, keeping obligations strictly within the limits of the three relationships. For those professing a maximalist version of individual rights, it should be worrying that even the strong claim merely allows for a temporary stay in a destination country and leaves that state's right to expel unfettered. Conversely, the weak claim makes an alien's access to a destination state more difficult, but does the same for her removal. Neither of the interpretations gives much hope to the practitioner.

Table 1 – Two Versions of Migration-Related Rights

	Individual	**Destination State**	**State of Origin**	**Third State**
Strong claim, obligations erga omnes	Human right to leave opposable to all states	Duty to admit and right to expel opposable to the alien	Duty to readmit owed to the citizen	Duty to facilitate transit owed to alien
		Right to expel opposable to all states of origin	Duty to readmit owed to all destination states	Duty to facilitate readmission owed to all states
Weak claim, obligations inter partes	Human right to leave opposable only to the country of origin	Duty to respect the exercise of this right, but no duty to admit owed to the alien	Duty to readmit owed to the citizen	Duty to respect the exercise of the right to leave, but no duty to facilitate transit
		Right to expel opposable to the alien	Duty to respect the exercise of the destination state's right, but no duty to readmit owed to that state	Duty to respect the exercise of the destination state's right, but no duty to readmit owed to that state

Faced with this dilemma, one may feel tempted to resort to taking quite disparate positions. First, one could merge the two models into one, and suggest that interstate obligations and human rights obligations have developed differently and must be seen as pertaining to separate legal spheres, each commanded by their own logic, and not necessarily coherent with each other.[42] The price of taking this position is rather high – it splits up the unity of international law, and begs a new theoretical framework, explaining how an identical doctrine of sources and interpretation can

---

[42] I am indebted to Aleksandra Popovic for pointing out this line of argument to me. Goodwin-Gill's attempt to explain the right to leave as non-correlative, and the right to return as correlative could be read as a reflection of such an approach. Goodwin-Gill, *supra* note 22, at 98, 100.

spawn different logics in application. Second, one may wish to deny that international law is logical at all, which would devaluate the reasoning on correlates. However, one would still need to show that a strong obligation to readmit, covering forcibly returned citizens, is unambiguously part of contemporary custom. This meets considerable difficulties, as we have shown in above, implying that the second position does little more than to throw out the baby with the bathwater.

If general international law does not appear to contain sufficiently determinate norms, these can – and should – be created by treaty. The augmenting number of readmission agreements reflects a need for greater clarity. For the North, professing the preexistence of readmission duties in customary law lowers the price of readmission agreements with less affluent countries. For the South, it will typically pay off to deny such duties, and to insist on voluntary return as a precondition for readmission. The South can also point to earlier precedents, where readmission of citizens and development aid or other side payments were combined in a treaty package. Either way, the risk is that human beings are reified as pawns in a game played by welfare states against remittance economies.

Selected Bibliography

CASTRÉN, ERIK – "Die gegenseitigen Pflichten der Staaten in Bezug auf den Aufenthalt und die Aufnahme ihrer Staatsangehörigen und der Staatenlosen," 11 *Zeitschrift für ausländisches öffentliches Recht und Völkerrecht* (1942-1943): 325.

GOODWIN-GILL, GUY – "The Right to Leave, the Right to Return and the Question of a Right to Remain," in V. Gowlland-Debbas (ed.), *The Problem of Refugees in the Light of Contemporary International Law Issues* (1996): 93-108.

HAILBRONNER, KAY – *Rückübernahme Eigener und Fremder Staatsangehöriger. Völkerrechtliche Verpflichtungen der Staaten* (1996).

HIGGINS, ROSALYNN – "The Right in International Law of an Individual to Enter, Stay In and Leave a Country," 49 *International Affairs* (1973): 341.

HUNNUM, HURST – *The Right to Leave and Return in International Law and Practice* (1987).

NOLL, GREGOR – "Unsuccessful Asylum Seekers – The Problem of Return," 37 *International Migration* (1993): 267.

RICHARD PLENDER – *International Migration Law* (1988).

SOHN, LOUIS B. AND THOMAS BUERGENTHAL (EDS.) – *The Movements of Persons Across Borders* (1992).

VASAK K. AND S. LISKOVSKY (EDS.) – *The Right to Leave and to Return: Papers and Recommendations of the International Colloquium held in Upssala*, Sweden, 19-21 June 1972 (1976).

WEIS, PAUL – *Nationality and Statelessness in International Law* (1979).

Chapter 5
NATIONALITY

Kay Hailbronner*

THE CONCEPT OF NATIONALITY

The concept of nationality[1] is inseparably connected with the notion of a sovereign state. The sovereignty of states, though under permanent challenge, and sometimes described as a dying concept, is still an essential element of public international law. Yet, nationality has changed, as did the notion of sovereignty. Permeability of borders, a globalized, interdependent economy and the approximation of political and social systems make the delimitating function of nationality less important, if not partially obsolete. Claims for observance of human rights are no longer dependent upon a person's nationality. Within the European Union, the concept of Union citizenship is gradually substituting important elements of the nationality of the Member States. Nevertheless, there are as yet no indications for a "post-national" or "transnational" nationality. Nationality still determines the scope of application of basic rights and obligations of states *vis-à-vis* other states and the international community, such as personal jurisdiction, application of treaties, and claims of protection. The individual nationality is a fundamental requirement for the exercise of political rights. It has also an important bearing on a person's legal status.

It is not surprising, therefore, that the frequently described decline of the notion of sovereignty has not led to a decline of the concept of nationality. It seems that, on the contrary, nationality issues are gaining importance. The European Convention on Nationality of 6 November 1997 (ECN), ratified by eight states, indicates the request of states for a comprehensive code of nationality embracing not only issues of conflict but also questions of acquisition of nationality, general principles relating to nationality, procedures, state succession, and cooperation between States Parties.

It is one of the main features of more recent nationality legislation that the traditional distinction between ethno-cultural nationality laws based upon *jus sanguinis* and more politically orientated nationality laws based upon *jus soli* has been blurred by substantial changes related to the acquisition of nationality of migrants in all major immigration countries. The rapidly increasing number of persons with multiple

---

* Dr. Kay Hailbronner, Professor of Law at the University of Konstanz/Germany, Director of the Center for International and European Law on Immigration and Asylum.
[1] The term "nationality" is used here in the sense of the European Convention on Nationality to describe the legal bond between an individual and the state.

T.A. Aleinikoff and V. Chetail (Eds.), Migration and International Legal Norms
© 2003, T.M.C. ASSER PRESS, The Hague, The Netherlands, et al.

nationalities has attracted the attention of international law makers. The issue of the human rights implications of nationality is also closely related to migration and refugee problems. There is an increasing debate as to a right to a specific nationality and the role that public international law has to play in determining questions of substance and loss of nationality. Many of these issues have arisen in the process of the dissolution of the Soviet Union and the formation of new states in Eastern Europe.

Under customary international law states are generally free to determine who their own nationals are.[2] It is sometimes asserted that there must be a genuine and effective link between an individual and a state in order to establish a nationality that must be accepted by other states. It is doubtful, however, whether the genuine and effective link requirement, used by the International Court of Justice in the Nottebohm Case to deny Liechtenstein's claim to exercise protection, can be considered as a relevant element for international recognition of nationality or as a requirement of a valid naturalization under public international law. State practice shows a wide variety of criteria for attributing nationality, going beyond the traditional criteria of descent, residence, or particular services for a country. It is frequently argued that in the absence of any recognized criteria the attribution of nationality must be considered as arbitrary[3] and that there must be some kind of a personal and territorial link,[4] but there is little state practice providing clear limits on the states' discretion to grant nationality. In any event, states have a large discretion to attribute their nationality to nationals of another state, if there are some links traditionally recognised as a justification for naturalization. It follows that simultaneous application of different criteria may lead to multiple nationality.

Limits under public international law to the sovereign right of the states to determine their own rules on the acquisition and loss of nationality are broadly derived from human rights considerations and the principle of non-intervention into the internal affairs of another state. The laws of nationality, therefore, shall be accepted in so far as they are consistent with international treaties, customary international law, and the principles of law generally recognized with regard to nationality.[5]

Articles 4 and 5 of the ECN list some principles that can be considered as generally recognized. The right of everyone to a nationality[6] is already enshrined in Article 15 of the Universal Declaration on Human Rights (UDHR). The right to a nationality can be interpreted as a positive formulation of the duty to avoid statelessness.[7] The duty to avoid statelessness is laid down in various international instruments, in particular in the 1961 Convention on the Reduction of Statelessness. A duty to extend birthright citizenship in order to avoid statelessness could also be inferred from a largely unanimous state practice as well as from the conventions on

---

[2] See ECN, Art. 3 para. 1; Tunis and Morocco Nationality Decrees, *PCIJ-Reports* (1923), Series B No. 4; Art. 1 Hague Convention of 1930 on certain questions relating to the conflict of nationalities.

[3] *Decisions of the German Federal Court,* vol. 5, 230; 9, 175, 178.

[4] *Decisions of the German Federal Constitutional Court,* vol. 1, 322, 329.

[5] See ECN, Art. 3 para. 2.

[6] ECN, Art. 4a.

[7] See Explanatory Report to the European Convention on Nationality, Council of Europe, *Achievements in the Field of Law* (2000) pp. 168, 174.

nationality reaffirming the principle of avoidance of statelessness. The term state-lessness refers to the "*de jure* stateless persons" rather than "*de facto* stateless per-sons." Some of the rules of Article 6 of the ECN relating to the acquisition of nationality to avoid statelessness have received almost uniform acceptance and may therefore be considered as a codification of customary international law. This is true for instance for foundlings found or children born in the territory who otherwise would be stateless.[8] Whether there is already a general obligation under customary international law to grant nationality in case of statelessness or whether the relevant rules derive exclusively from treaty obligations may be questionable.[9]

ACQUISITION OF NATIONALITY FOR MIGRANTS

The right to a nationality as a human rights concept raises a number of issues with regard to acquisition of nationality by second or third generation migrants.[10] The In-ter-American Court of Human Rights, in an advisory opinion, proclaimed that the right to nationality must be considered as an inherent human right and that the pow-ers of states to regulate matters relating to nationality are determined by the states' obligations to ensure the full protection of human rights.[11] Under customary interna-tional law there is no right to a specific nationality or a right to change nationality to acquire an additional nationality. One may raise the question whether the rule of un-limited discretion of states in deciding on the acquisition of nationality adequately reflects the human rights implications of second and third generation migrants and recognised refugees. As to refugees, Article 34 of the Geneva Convention provides for a duty of states to facilitate – as far as possible – the naturalization of refugees. According to the wording and purpose of Article 34, there is no individual right for naturalization although the duty to facilitate must be taken into account in the exer-cise of administrative discretion.

There has been no similar treaty provision for migrant workers and their families. Recent European state practice, however, shows a clear tendency to grant certain categories of migrants a right to acquire nationality either *ex lege* or on the basis of an application. Article 6, paragraph 3 of the ECN provides that internal law shall contain rules that make it possible for foreigners lawfully and habitually resident in the territory of a State Party to be naturalized. The maximum period of residence that can be required for naturalization is fixed to a maximum of ten years. This cor-responds to a common standard in Europe, most countries requiring between five to ten years of residence. There are, in addition, other justifiable conditions for natural-ization, in particular, language, absence of a criminal record, and the possibility to earn a living may be required.[12]

---

[8] See also Art. 7 of the Convention of the Rights of the Child.

[9] See K. Hailbronner and G. Renner, *Staatsangehörigkeitsrecht*, Introduction Chapter I, No. 42 f (3rd edn.).

[10] Cf., Chan, *Human Rights Law Journal* (1991), vol. 12, p. 1.

[11] See Amendments to the Naturalization Provisions of the Constitution of Costa Rica, OC-4/84, *Human Rights Law Journal* (1984), vol. 5, p. 14.

[12] Cf., ECN, Explanatory Report, p. 177.

There are other categories of foreigners, who generally receive preferential treatment in acquiring nationality by, for example, an easier procedure, a reduction of the length of required residence, and less integration requirements. Article 6, paragraph 4 of the ECN lists in particular foreign spouses[13] and adopted children, as well as second and third generation migrants who may generally be considered as more apt to integrate into the society of the host state.[14] Article 3 of the 1957 Convention on the Nationality of Married Women also provides for a duty to facilitate the acquisition of nationality of the husband, without, however, excluding a requirement to give up a previous nationality.

The rules on acquisition of nationality cannot yet be considered as customary international law even within the European countries. In spite of an approximation of nationality legislation between *jus soli* and *jus sanguinis* countries, there is still a considerable divergence as to the cultural, social, and historic basis of nationality.[15] Nationality is a product of historic evolution of each state and therefore cannot easily be codified without taking into account the complexities and particularities of every country.

This, however, does not exclude the emergence of certain principles as nationality concerns not only sovereignty, but individual rights as well. Therefore, the acquisition of nationality by foreigners whose habitual and lawful residence is in the "host state," must be enabled, provided certain reasonable requirements are met. One could also add that full political participation follows from the concept of democratic government. It is hardly tolerable for any state if a large number of its population stays outside the political community over decades and is excluded from the citizens' rights and obligations *vis-à-vis* the state. Democracy requires a congruence between the holders of democratic political rights and the resident population permanently subject to the public rule.[16]

There are other implications of a more human rights oriented approach to nationality. In some countries decisions on nationality are treated like issues of sovereign prerogative, either wholly or partly excluded from review even if a decision may be considered as arbitrary. The general non-discrimination clauses of human rights treaties, in particular the 1966 International Convention on the Elimination of all Forms of National Discrimination, apply. Caution, however, is required concerning the scope of the application of human rights treaties. Discrimination clauses may not be applicable to nationality issues. Thus, for instance, Article 14 of the ECHR applies only to the human rights enshrined in the Convention. In addition, there may be legitimate reasons to give preferential treatment to nationals of certain states. Article 5 of the ECN prohibits only distinctions amounting to discrimination on the

---

[13] See Council of Europe Res. (77), p. 12.

[14] See also Second Protocol Amending the 1963 European Convention on Reduction of Dual Nationality.

[15] See M. Autem, "The European Convention on Nationality: Is a European Code on Nationality Possible?," *in Trends and Developments* (2000) p. 19.

[16] Schnapauff, in: Martin/Hailbronner (eds.), *Rights and Duties of Dual Nationals, Referring to the Legal History of the Draft Act to Reform the German Nationality Law.*

grounds of sex, religion, race, color, or national or ethnic origin. Social origin has been deliberately omitted as being too vague.[17]

Article 5, paragraph 2 of the ECN also provides that each State Party "shall be guided" by the principle of non-discrimination, whether they are nationals by birth or have acquired its nationality subsequently. It should be noted, however, that this provision may raise difficulties. The principle that nationals must be treated equally can be considered as generally accepted. It follows that there can be no difference in the substance of political, economic, and social rights connected with nationality. This, however, does not exclude distinctions relating to the loss of nationality. The German law on nationality contains a duty to opt for one nationality at the age of eighteen for only specified categories of second-generation migrants born on German territory who have acquired both German nationality and the nationality of their parents. Children of mixed marriages do not have to opt for one nationality at the age of eighteen.

Under public international law the administrative procedure and judicial remedies are within each state's domain, unless human rights treaties are applicable. Nevertheless, the recognition of the human rights aspects of nationality implies procedural fairness and independent review. State practice shows a tendency to submit nationality disputes to the ordinary administrative and judicial process. This is reflected in the provisions of Articles 10 through 12 of the ECN that provide for an obligation to give reasons in writing and administrative or judicial review of nationality decisions.

Facilitation of access to nationality for migrants has resulted in a growing concern of states that a more open access to nationality may be misused to evade immigration restrictions or to escape expulsion or deportation. Misuse of nationality laws, therefore, has also become an issue of international cooperation. Thus, for instance, nationality law has been renounced in order to escape deportation by acquiring a status of statelessness. States permitting such renunciation are generally acting in violation of public international law. A state's duty to respect the sovereignty of other states and their sovereign right to decide on the admission of foreigners implies a duty to accept a responsibility for a states' own citizens, including an obligation to allow their return. This obligation could be easily overcome by a renunciation of nationality in order to prevent the return of a state's own citizens. In addition, state practice supports the rule of avoidance of statelessness. Establishing statelessness for the main purpose of restricting a state's sovereign right to decide on the admission and residence of foreign nationals means acting against the Committee of Nations. Such renunciation may, therefore, be considered invalid for the purpose of execution of immigration laws.

Marriages of convenience qualify either for automatic entitlement to nationality or facilitated access to naturalization. There are new problems of misuse of nationality law related to the recognition of registered partnerships entitled under national law to preferential access to nationality. Misuse may also occur from state legislation that allows a person claiming to be the father to recognize a child by a simple

---

[17] See Explanatory Report, *supra* note 2, at 176.

declaration, thereby establishing the parenthood relationship and transmitting nationality to a child.[18]

It is generally up to the states to prevent misuse. International law does not exclude appropriate measures against the misuse of nationality laws. There may, however, be scope for increased international cooperation, particularly in order to exchange information about techniques of fraught, presentation of false documents, and registering of renunciation and acquisition of nationality.

MULTIPLE NATIONALITY

There is an increasing number of persons holding multiple nationalities, despite efforts to the contrary. The principle that can be found in the European Convention of 1963 on Reduction of Cases of Multiple Nationality and Military Obligations in Case of Multiple Nationals, whereby multiple nationalities are generally undesirable, has been abandoned by subsequent legal instruments, in particular the Second Protocol Amending the 1963 Convention and the European Convention on Nationality of 1977. The present state of public international law is correctly reflected in Article 15 of the ECN. The Convention does not limit the right of states to determine, in their internal law, whether their nationals who acquire or possess the nationality of another state retain its nationality or lose it, or whether the acquisition or retention of its nationality is subject to the renunciation or loss of another nationality.

Article 15 of the ECN clearly marks a shift in the attitude of states towards multiple nationality, although no general principle against or in favor of multiple nationality can be derived from the Convention. The 1963 Convention already provided for a limited category of persons. It covered the special case of voluntary acquisition of another nationality obliging states to provide for the renunciation or loss of their previous nationality.

A major reason for the change has been the recognition of the interests of immigrants to maintain connection with their country of origin, while attribution of the host state's nationality was also considered as an essential requirement for full integration. On the other hand, there is no general consensus on whether multiple nationality is an adequate tool for promoting integration or whether it may obstruct integration by facilitating the formation of separate cultural and political interest groups, identifying with their country of origin rather than with the country of residence.

Although there is no evidence that problems of failed integration are linked to the issue of multiple nationality, Giovanni Kojanec's conclusion is correct, that the stance of international law in relation to the problem of multiple nationality is the result of historical, philosophical, and social factures that lay at the basis of the legislative approach in each state and determine its finalities.[19]

Nevertheless, there is a clear tendency for a more liberal toleration of multiple nationalities. A large number of European states have changed their legislation to

---

[18] See A. Walmsley, "Misuse of Nationality law," in *Trends and Developments* (2000) p. 63 f.

[19] G. Kojanec, "Multiple Nationality," *in Trends and Developments* (2000) pp. 35-47.

accept multiple nationalities for certain categories of immigrants, thereby taking account of the connections of an immigrant with his or her country of origin. Even those countries maintaining the principle of avoidance of dual nationality, like Germany, have largely facilitated the maintenance of a previous nationality if renunciation of nationality meets serious obstacles or must be considered as unreasonable for other reasons. Article 14 of the ECN provides for multiple nationalities in cases in which children have different nationalities acquired automatically at birth and where individuals automatically acquire a nationality due to marriage. In addition, multiple nationalities are, under Article 16, accepted when renunciation or loss is not possible or cannot reasonably be expected.

An increasing number of persons with multiple nationalities may give rise to more international disputes resulting from conflicting rights and obligations. A traditional rule of customary international law, set forth in Article 4 of the Hague Convention of 1930, provides that a state may not afford diplomatic protection to one of its nationals against the state whose nationality the individual also possesses. The rule, although maintained in state practice, has been gradually diminished in importance due to a number of exceptions.

One exception concerns claims of human rights violations, although the development of human rights has not made the institution of diplomatic protection of a state in favor of its nationals obsolete.[20] Another exception relates to the application of the genuine and effective link theory for multiple nationals. Although the theory is doubtful if interpreted as a general requirement for acquisition of nationality or even diplomatic protection, it has gained acceptance in the context of multiple nationality. International tribunals have frequently accepted a claim of diplomatic protection even in case of dual nationals if the nationality of the state raising a claim can be considered as the genuine and effective one in contrast to a more formal nationality of the other state.[21] The rule, that in case of multiple nationals conflicting claims may be solved by recourse to the more effective connection test, may well be considered as an emerging principle in spite of the somewhat reluctant attitude of the ECN to provide for exceptions to the traditional rules.[22]

Multiple nationals in general are accorded the same rights and obligations as any other national holding only one nationality. Conflicting obligations or loyalties may create difficulties if there are no special agreements providing for a mutual recognition of military service.[23] Article 21 of the ECN states that multiple nationals shall fulfil their military obligations in relation to one of the States Parties. Normally, that State Party will be the state of habitual residence. The Convention, however, leaves it to the person concerned to submit voluntarily to military obligations in relation to any other state of which they are also a national.

---

[20] See J. Dugard, *First Report on Diplomatic Protection*, UN CN. 4/506, at p. 10.

[21] For further references see K. Hailbronner, *in* Graf Vitzthum, *Völkerrecht* (2nd edn. 2001) p. 204; see also Dugard, *supra* note 20, at 42.

[22] See Hailbronner, *supra* note 21, at 204, 205.

[23] Cf., The European Convention of 1963 on Reduction of Multiple Nationality; see S. Legomsky, "Dual Nationality and Military Service," *in* D. Martin and K. Hailbronner, *Rights and Duties of Dual Nationals* (2003) p. 79 ff.

It is doubtful whether a principle of free choice adequately reflects a proper balance of the interests of the individual and the society. Recognition of multiple nationality should not undermine legitimate integration concerns of states. Voluntary military service in a state other than the state of residence is hardly suitable to promote integration and may even be considered by internal legislation as a reason for loss of nationality.

Larger numbers of multiple nationals may also create difficulties and conflicts in connection with the exercise of political rights of non-residents and the potential interference of external interests in the political process. Political rights should be attached to the state of permanent residence; permanent residence should also be the decisive factor in deciding conflicts of law issues rather than relying exclusively upon nationality of the forum state.[24]

Although multiple nationality in general does not imply problems of conflicting loyalty, there may be situations in which such conflicts, at least in the public perception, cannot be excluded. It is a legitimate concern of states to require that such nationals surrender their other nationality before taking high official functions in the government or in the public domain. Experience with multiple nationals does not indicate any need to exclude multiple nationalities from the lower end of civil service jobs.

Since public international law is largely silent on the question of solving conflicts arising from the exercise of multiple nationalities, it is up to the states concerned to conclude special agreements on issues of conflict of laws, exercise of political rights, and military and other obligations. A guiding principle should be that primary obligations of dual nationals are with the state of residence, and that state should serve as a primary protector of the individual. Consequently, in the case of dual nationalities, issues of civil status and conflicts of laws should be resolved by reference to the laws of the country of habitual residence. It would be advisable to devote some effort on the conclusion of international agreements that would facilitate management of multiple nationality and effectively deal with the issues related to the exercise of multiple rights and obligations.[25]

LOSS AND DEPRIVATION

Like acquisition of nationality, loss and deprivation is generally considered a matter of state discretion. Since loss and deprivation affects existing rights, however, it is subject to stricter limits as determined in international instruments. Article 15 of the Universal Declaration on Human Rights[26] provides that nobody may be arbitrarily deprived of nationality or refused the right to change his or her nationality. It follows that there is a duty of states not to refuse arbitrarily voluntary renunciation of nationality. This duty must be taken into account when interpreting bilateral agreements providing for a right of states to veto their national's naturalization.

---

[24] See D. Martin and K. Hailbronner, *supra* note 23, at 383.

[25] See D. Martin and K. Hailbronner, *supra* note 23, at 383 ff.

[26] See also Art. 12 International Covenant on Civil and Political Rights.

Of greater practical significance is the prohibition of arbitrary loss of nationality. Although international jurisprudence does not provide very clear rules as to when expatriation must be considered as arbitrary, it is recognized that discriminatory individual or collective expatriation constitutes a violation of public international law.[27] Article 8 and 9 of the ECN provide for a wide range of exceptions under which a loss of nationality is accepted including

- voluntary acquisition of another nationality;
- acquisition of the nationality of the State Party by means of fraudulent conduct, false information, or concealment of any relevant fact attributable to the applicant;
- voluntary service in a foreign military force;
- conduct seriously prejudicial to the vital interest of the State Party;
- lack of a genuine link of the State Party and a national habitually residing abroad;
- where it is established during the minority of a child that the preconditions set forth by international law that led to the *ex lege* acquisition of the nationality of the State Party are no longer fulfilled; and
- adoption of a child if the child acquires or possesses the foreign nationality of one or both of the adopting parents.

The catalogue of exceptions reflects to some extent a rising concern of states about the acquisition of a mere "formal" nationality. Increasing tolerance towards multiple nationalities carries a larger risk that such multiple nationalities will be transmitted without a corresponding genuine link. States have generally encouraged the maintenance of nationality of their nationals even in case of permanent emigration on ethnic or cultural reasons. However, as nationality concepts change, such considerations are losing momentum. Generally speaking, facilitation of acquisition of nationality, particularly where it occasions multiple nationality, supports measures that seek to limit traditional criteria for nationality – like descent – that can permit the indefinite transmission of nationality without a genuine and effective connection to the state concerned. International law does not restrict the competence of states to provide for expatriation of those nationals who do not have a continuing link and who dispose of a different nationality in the country of habitual residence.

The rights and obligations attached to nationality are determined by internal law. With the exception of the principle of equal treatment (Article 17 of the ECN), few international rules restrict the right of states to prescribe additional requirements like habitual residence for the exercise of rights that are usually attached to nationality, provided that nationals are not discriminated against.

Article 3 of Protocol 4 of the ECHR provides that no one shall be expelled by means of an individual or a collective measure, from the territory of the state, of which he is a national. In addition, Article 3, paragraph 2 states that no one shall be deprived of the right to enter the territory of the state to which he is a national. The duty of states to admit their own nationals for entry and residence, particularly if

---

[27] For an example of the German legislation between 1933 and 1945 on depriving Jews of their German nationality, see *Decision of the Federal Constitutional Court,* vol. 23, 58, 105.

they are expelled from other states, is a general principle of customary international law set forth in many bilateral and multilateral treaties on readmission.[28] Although originally conceived as a mere interstate obligation, the rule must now be interpreted as implying an individual right to be granted admission. There is, however, no corresponding right not to be admitted in order to avoid expulsion.[29]

The question has been raised as to what extent Article 3 of Protocol 4 of the ECHR limits the rights of states to deprive a person of a nationality where a person can avail himself of another nationality.[30] The delicate issue of the legitimacy of measures depriving individuals of nationality, however, has deliberately not been dealt with in Protocol 4.[31]

With the exception of the special case of state succession, there is very little international guidance on the limits of states to deprive multiple nationals of their nationality. The refusal to renounce one of two nationalities acquired *ex lege* on reaching the age of adulthood can be considered as a legitimate reason for expatriation, provided that such renunciation is legally accepted by the former home state and does not face unacceptable difficulties.

There are no generally recognized rules on nationality in cases of state succession. The rules contained in Articles 18 through 20 of the ECN on state succession and nationality reflect experience and recommendations in Eastern Europe after the dissolution of the Soviet empire and may therefore be considered as an important element in the formation of future international law.[32] Article 18 obliges states, in deciding on the granting or the retention of nationality, to take into account the genuine and effective link of the person concerned with the state, the habitual residence of the person concerned, the will of the person concerned, and the territorial origin of the person concerned. The Convention, in Article 19, provides for a duty to regulate matters by agreement. In such agreements parties should respect the principle that nationals of a predecessor state habitually resident in the territory of which sovereignty is transferred to a successor state and who have not acquired its nationality shall have the right to remain in that state and that such persons shall enjoy equal treatment with the nationals of the successor state in relation to social and economic rights. Similar principles are contained in the recommendation of principles on citizenship legislation concerning the parties to the peace agreements on Bosnia and Herzegovina[33] and the declaration on the consequences of state succession for the nationality of natural persons adopted by the European Commission for Democracy through law.[34]

It is premature to say whether these principles will eventually emerge into cus-

---

[28] See K. Hailbronner, *ZaöRV*, vol. 57 (1957), 51; idem, *Rückübernahme eigener und fremder Staatsangehöriger, völkerrechtliche Verpflichtungen der Staaten* (1996) p. 5 f.

[29] See for instance ECR, No. 41/74, Van Duyn/Home Office, 1974, 1337, 1351.

[30] N. Mole, *Challenges to National and International Law on Nationality at the Beginning of the New Millennium, Multiple Nationality and the European Convention on Human Rights*, Second European Conference on Nationality, Strasbourg, 13 September 2001.

[31] Explanatory Report to the 2.-5. Protocol, 1971, at p. 48.

[32] For a survey see Galicky, "State Succession," *in Trends and Developments* p. 81 f.

[33] Council of Europe Achievements in the Field of Law (2000) p. 193.

[34] Council of Europe Achievements in the Field of Law (2000) p. 197.

tomary international law. It is clear, however, that public international law requires at least that a balance between the legitimate interests of individuals and the interests of states has to be drawn and that human rights aspects of nationality legislation be taken into account.

Selected Bibliography

ALEINIKOFF, T. ALEXANDER AND DOUGLAS KLUSMEYER (EDS.) – *Citizenship Today – Global Perspectives and Practices* (2000).

COUNCIL OF EUROPE, *Challenges to National and International Law at the Beginning of the New Millennium* Conf/Nat (2001) PRO.

— . *First European Conference on Nationality, Trend and Developments in National and International Law* (2000).

—. *Council of Europe Achievements in the Field of Law, Nationality* DIR/JUR (2000).

DUGARD, JOHN – *First Report on Diplomatic Protection*, A/CN 4/506 (2000).

HAILBRONNER, KAY AND GÜNTER RENNER – *Staatsangehörigkeitsrecht* (3rd edn. 2001).

KOSTAKOPOULOU, D. (ED.) – *From Migrants to Citizens, Membership in a Changing World* (2001).

—. *Citizenship, Identity and Immigration in the European Union – Between Past and Future* (2001).

MARTIN, DAVID AND KAY HAILBRONNER – *Rights and Duties of Dual Nationals, Evolution and Prospects* (2003).

MYKOLA, RUDKO – *Challenges to National and International Law on Nationality at the Beginning of the New Millennium, Second European Conference on Nationality* (2001).

NUALA, MOLE – *Challenges to National and International Law on Nationality at the Beginning of the New Millennium, Multiple Nationality and the European Convention on Human Rights, Second European Conference on Nationality* (2001).

SCHUCK, PETER – *Citizens, Strangers and In-Betweens* (1998).

Chapter 6
MIGRATION AND SECURITY IN INTERNATIONAL LAW

David Fisher, Susan Martin, and Andrew Schoenholtz*

INTRODUCTION

There are no comprehensive instruments or sets of rules specifically devoted to migration and security at the international level. For the most part, security serves simply as a check on rules governing migration, particularly in the domain of human rights. As two commentators have recently noted, "[n]ational security is the Achilles' heel of international law[;] [w]henever international law is created, the issue of national security gives rise to some sort of loophole, often in the form of an explicit national security exception."[1] Such "loopholes" are usually (although, as discussed below, not always) essential prerequisites for states to agree to bind themselves to international commitments, including those relating to migration. These loopholes exist because states consider the power to protect their own security to be the core of their sovereignty.

Nevertheless, international law facilitates state security measures with regard to migration through criminalizing acts such as trafficking and smuggling of aliens, requiring information sharing for purposes of border control, enforcing extradition rules, and regulating extraterritorial enforcement of immigration controls (i.e., carrier sanctions agreements and interdiction at sea). Historically, international law on terrorism has only tangentially impacted migration. This may be changing, however, as recent Security Council resolutions and a proposed antiterrorism convention explicitly address border control as a means of combating terrorism.

This chapter begins with a brief definition of the scope of security in the context of international law and then surveys the existing international law facilitating cooperation in the area of migration and security. The numerous areas in which security appears in international instruments as an exception to rules concerning migration is then discussed. The inquiry is divided into four modes of state response to migration: control of entry, control of exit, internal regulation, and expulsion.

* Georgetown University, Institute for the Study of International Migration, Washington, DC.

[1] See H.L. Schloemann and S. Ohlhoff, "Constitutionalization and Dispute Settlement in the WTO: National Security as an Issue of Competence," 93 *AJIL* (1999) pp. 424, 426.

T.A. Aleinikoff and V. Chetail (Eds.), Migration and International Legal Norms
© 2003, T.M.C. ASSER PRESS, The Hague, The Netherlands, et al.

THE SCOPE OF SECURITY FOR PURPOSES OF THIS CHAPTER

This chapter addresses international law affecting national security as traditionally defined, i.e., the protection of the state from external foes.[2] The international law concerning state efforts to halt infiltration by (or in the case of exit, the escape of) military foes (e.g., spies or saboteurs) and terrorists will be examined, as will the states' attempts to block the entry or escape of common criminals, particularly those engaged in smuggling and trafficking.[3] Moreover, as Professor Myron Weiner has noted, "[m]igration can be perceived as threatening by governments of either population-sending or population-receiving communities."[4] This question will be addressed from both ends.[5]

INTERNATIONAL LAW FACILITATING STATE SECURITY MEASURES WITH REGARD TO MIGRATION

Border Security Controls and Extradition

A number of international conventions address crimes frequently associated with the movement of peoples across borders, such as terrorism,[6] narcotics trafficking,[7]

---

[2] See, e.g., N. Poku and D. Graham, "Redefining Security for a New Millennium," *in* N. Poku and D. Graham (eds.), *Redefining Security: Population Movements and National Security* (1998) p. 4 (describing the traditional notion of national security).

[3] This is arguably an element of "human security" as opposed to "national security" because it seeks to protect individuals from criminal depredations rather than the state as a whole. See W. Tow and R.l. Trood, "Linkages Between Traditional Security and Human Security," *in* W. Tow, R. Thakur, and I. Hyun (eds.), *Asia's Emerging Regional Order: Reconciling Traditional and Human Security* (2000) p. 16; M.E. Beare, "Illegal Migration: Personal Tragedies, Social Problems or National Security Threats?," 3 *Transnational Organized Crime* (1997) pp. 11, 13-15. But see R. Day, "National Security Implications of Immigration," 38 *Oklahoma Law Review* (1985) pp. 845, 845 (discussing "two ways that immigration can affect national security": (1) "the entry of agents of foreign states seeking to harm the U.S. or to advance their own interests," or (2) "the entry of criminals").

[4] M. Weiner, "Introduction: Security, Stability and International Migration," *in* M. Weiner (ed.), *International Migration and Security* (1993) p. 9.

[5] In addition to the foregoing types of threats, both population-sending and population-receiving states are frequently concerned about : (1) foreign policy complications, (2) domestic political destabilization, (3) cultural or ethnic dilution, and (4) economic loss (for example, from loss of jobs or the necessity to care for new wards by the receiving state, or loss of productive capacity and "brain drain" from the sending state). See Weiner, *supra* note 4, at 11; P.J. Smith, "Military Responses to the Global Migration Crisis: A Glimpse of Things to Come," 23 *Fletcher Forum of World Affairs* (1999) pp. 77, 79-80; see also C. Keely, "The Effects of International Migration on U.S. Foreign Policy," *in* M. Teitelbaum and M. Weiner (eds.), *Threatened Peoples, Threatened Borders* (1995) (describing these types of perceived threats as "soft security issues"). Whether these concerns can fairly be deemed "security" concerns, (e.g., "economic security" or "cultural security") is subject to debate. See I. Cameron, *National Security and the European Convention on Human Rights* (2000) pp. 40-49; Beare, *supra* note 3, at 14. We do not address them herein.

[6] See Convention on Offenses and Certain Other Acts Committed on Board Aircraft, 14 September 1963, 20 *UST* 2941, 704 *UNTS* 219; Convention for Suppression of Unlawful Seizure of Aircraft, 16 December 1970, 22 *UST* 1641, 860 *UNTS* 105; Convention for Suppression of Unlawful Acts Against

transnational organized crime,[8] migrant smuggling,[9] and trafficking in persons.[10] These treaties obligate Member States to criminalize the conduct in question, to act to prevent its preparation within their borders, to prosecute persons responsible for such crimes, and/or to cooperate with intended target states through extradition of perpetrators and mutual legal assistance.

Traditionally, international law has not focused specifically on measures to prevent the interstate movements of would-be criminals and terrorists. This is beginning to change. The Protocol Against the Smuggling of Migrants by Land, Sea and Air, Supplementing the United Nations Convention Against Transnational Organized Crime ("Migrant Smuggling Protocol"),[11] the Protocol to Prevent, Suppress and Punish Trafficking in Persons, Especially Women and Children, Supplementing the United Nations Convention against Transnational Organized Crime ("Trafficking Protocol")[12] and the Inter-American Convention Against Terrorism ("Inter-American Convention")[13] will require State Parties to establish effective domestic controls on travel and identity documents.[14] Likewise, in 1999, a number of Asian states pledged in the Bangkok Declaration to coordinate on issues of "irregular migration" and to address human trafficking and smuggling.[15]

---

the Safety of Civil Aviation, 23 September 1971, 24 *UST* 565, 974 *UNTS* 177; Convention to Prevent and Punish the Acts of Terrorism Taking the Form of Crimes Against Persons and Related Extortion That Are of International Significance, 2 February 1971, 27 *UST* 3949, *TIAS* No. 8413; International Convention Against the Taking of Hostages, 17 December 1979, *TIAS* No. 11,081, 1316 *UNTS* 205 (hereinafter "Hostages Convention"); International Convention for the Suppression of Terrorist Bombing, GA Res. 52/164, annex (15 December 1997), 37 *ILM* 249 (1998) (not yet in force) (hereinafter "Bombings Convention"); International Convention for the Suppression of the Financing of Terrorism GA Res. 54/109 (9 December 1999), 39 *ILM* 270 (2000) (not yet in force).

[7] See, e.g., United Nations Convention Against Illicit Traffic in Narcotic Drugs and Psychotropic Substances, 19 December 1988, U.N. Doc. E/CONF.82/15 (1988), 28 *ILM* 493 (1989).

[8] United Nations Convention Against Transnational Organized Crime (hereinafter, "Transnational Crime Convention"), 9 January 2001, GAOR 55th session, U.N. Doc. A/Res/55/25, 40 *ILM* 335 (2001) (not yet in force).

[9] See Protocol Against the Smuggling of Migrants by Land, Sea and Air Supplementing the United Nations Convention Against Transnational Crime (hereinafter, "Migrant Smuggling Protocol"), 15 November 2000, ch. II, U.N. Doc. A/55/383 (2000), 40 *ILM* 335 (2001) (not yet in force).

[10] See Protocol to Prevent, Suppress and Punish Trafficking in Persons, Especially Women and Children, Supplementing the United Nations Convention against Transnational Organized Crime (hereinafter "Trafficking Protocol"), 15 November 2000, UN Doc. A/55/383 p. 53, 40 *ILM* 335 (2001) (not yet in force).

[11] See Migrant Smuggling Protocol, *supra* note 9, at Art. 12.

[12] See Trafficking Protocol, *supra* note 10, at Art. 12.

[13] Inter-American Convention Against Terrorism (hereinafter "Inter-American Convention"), 3 June 2002, OAS Doc. AG/Res. 1840 (XXXII-O/02) (not yet in force).

[14] Interestingly, such provisions do not (yet) appear in drafts of the Comprehensive Convention on Terrorism still being discussed by an ad hoc committee of the United Nations General Assembly. See Report of the Ad Hoc Committee Established by General Assembly Resolution 51/210 of 17 December 1996, U.N. GAOR, 6th Sess., Supp. No. 37, U.N. Doc. A/57/37 (2002).

[15] See Bangkok Declaration on Irregular Migration (23 April 1999), available at www.iom.int/DOCUMENTS/OFFICIALTXT/EN/Bangkok_decl.htm. As noted by Vitit Muntarbhorn in this volume, the South Asian Association for Regional Cooperation also adopted the Convention on Preventing and Combating Trafficking in Women and Children for Prostitution in 2002.

While the Protocols and the Inter-American Convention are not yet in force, and the Bangkok Declaration is non-binding, the requirement that states improve their border controls has already entered international law by way of United Nations Security Council Resolution 1373. That resolution, passed in response to the 11 September 2001 attacks on the United States, requires states to "[p]revent the movement of terrorists or terrorist groups by effective border controls and controls on issuance of identity papers and travel documents, and through measures for preventing counterfeiting, forgery or fraudulent use of identity papers and travel documents[.]"[16]

The Protocols and the Inter-American Convention further require State Parties to exchange information with each other for purposes of border control.[17] Article 7 of the Inter-American Convention provides, in relevant part, that "[t]he states parties, consistent with their respective domestic legal and administrative regimes, shall promote cooperation and the exchange of information in order to improve border and customs measures[.]"

The breadth of states' duty to extradite accused criminals is growing with the greater international willingness to enter into regional[18] and multilateral treaties addressing transnational crime.[19] The United Nations Convention Against Transnational Organized Crime, for instance, is a milestone in defining transnational crime and requiring states to extradite or prosecute members of transnational criminal organizations.[20]

Historically, provision for the prosecution and extradition of terrorists in multilateral conventions has been piecemeal,[21] in large part because of the international community's failure to agree on a comprehensive definition of terrorism.[22] However, the recently adopted International Convention for the Suppression of Terrorist Bombing and International Convention for the Suppression of the Financing of Terrorism will fill important gaps. Furthermore, the effort to create a comprehensive convention on terrorism has been revived since 11 September 2001.[23] Such specific

---

[16] See S.C. Res. 1373, U.N. SCOR, 4385th meeting, 28 September 2001, U.N. Doc. No. S/RES/ 1373 (2001).

[17] See Migrant Smuggling Protocol, *supra* note 9, at Art. 10; Trafficking Protocol, *supra* note 10, at Art. 10; Inter-American Convention, *supra* note 13, at Art. 7.

[18] The most extensive regional extradition mechanisms are in Europe. See G. Gilbert, *Transnational Fugitive Offenders in International Law: Extradition and Others Mechanisms* (1998) p. 36. However, both the Inter-American system and the League of Arab States have a number of regional extradition agreements. Id. at 34-35.

[19] Although most extradition treaties are bilateral, see Gilbert, *supra* note 18, at 32, regional and multilateral agreements play an important part in creating a uniform and efficient international system of rendition, either by directly modifying, or by charging Member States to modify, their bilateral agreements to bring them into conformity with new standards.

[20] See Transnational Crime Convention, *supra* note 8.

[21] See J. Murphy, "The Future of Multilateralism and Efforts to Combat International Terrorism," 25 *Columbia Journal of Transnational Law* (1986) p. 35.

[22] See C. Bassiouni, *Legal Responses to International Terrorism: US Procedural Aspects* (1988) p. xvi .

[23] However, this effort may well founder on the same definitional disagreements that doomed the United States' Draft Convention on Terrorism proposed after the kidnapping and killing of eleven Israeli Olympic competitors by terrorists in Munich. See J. Murphy, "Control of International Terrorism," *in* J. Moore, F. Tipson and R. Turner (eds.), *National Security Law* (1990) pp. 459-461.

agreements concerning prosecution and extradition of terrorists are particularly important because of the customary law "political offense" doctrine, which normally bars extraditing people for crimes committed for a "political purpose."[24]

Extraterritorial Application of Migration Controls

In addition to extending the reach of criminal and terrorism law, states are increasingly seeking to enforce their domestic immigration laws beyond their own borders.[25] These immigration laws directly promote state security by barring entry of suspected terrorists, spies, saboteurs, and criminals.[26] However, the doctrine of state sovereignty generally precludes a state from enforcing its laws on the territory, or within the exclusive jurisdiction, of another.[27] There are two emerging areas of exception from this rule.

Carrier Sanctions and Departure Site Inspections

Although originally conceived as a means of controlling illegal immigration, carrier sanctions and departure site inspection policies have recently been promoted as national security measures, especially since the attacks of 11 September 2001.[28] Both types of policies are also emerging from the sphere of domestic law to the international level.

Domestic law in a number of states requires common carriers (including, in various combinations, sea, air, and land carriers) servicing their territories internationally to verify travel documents of all boarding passengers.[29] Sanctions are imposed upon carriers that fail to comply.[30] In 1985, members of the Schengen Convention in Europe agreed to impose such sanctions on their domestic carriers on behalf of other

---

[24] See Gilbert *supra* note 18, at 251-261; R. Stuart Phillips, "The Political Offense Exception and Terrorism: Its Place in the Current Extradition Scheme and Proposals for Its Future," 15 *Dickinson Journal of International Law* (1997) p. 337.

[25] See United Nations High Commission for Refugees Executive Committee, Interception of Asylum-Seekers and Refugees: The International Framework and Recommendations for a Comprehensive Approach (hereinafter, "UNHCR Executive Committee Note on Interception"), 9 June 2000, EC/5/SC/CRP.17.

[26] See, e.g., 8 U.S.C. 1182(a)(2) (2001) (providing, *inter alia*, that criminals and suspected spies, saboteurs, and terrorists are ineligible for entry into the United States); Ordonnance No. 45-2658 of 2 November 1945, Art. 5 (providing that access to French territory may be refused to any foreigner whose presence may constitute a threat to public order ("*ordre public*")).

[27] See UNHCR Executive Committee Note on Interception, *supra* note 25, at 3.

[28] See, e.g., Second Stage Debate on Immigration Bill 2002, 169 *Seanad Deb.* Col. 1332 (27 March 2002) (statement of Irish Minister of Justice, Equality and Law Reform John O'Donoghue) (asserting, with regard to carrier sanctions, that "document checks are an important measure in combating and preventing acts of terrorism"); Enhanced Border Security and Visa Entry Reform Act of 2002, Pub. L. No. 107-173 (HR 3525) para. 401 (mandating a study of expansion of preinspection as an anti-terrorism measure).

[29] See, e.g., European Council on Refugees and Exiles, *Carriers' Liability: Country Up-Date on the Application of Carriers' Liability in European States* (1999), www.ecre.org/research/carrier.doc.

[30] Id.

Member States receiving the undocumented persons and to require their carriers to take responsibility for returning any passengers delivered to a State Party without proper documentation.[31] The provisions of the Schengen Convention were later incorporated into the Treaties of the European Union and the European Community and now apply to all members of the European Union except the United Kingdom and Ireland.[32] A 2000 European Council Directive reinforces the Schengen requirements, adding that the required sanctions must be "dissuasive, effective and proportionate," with a minimum fine of 3,000 euros per inadmissible passenger.[33]

The Convention on International Civil Aviation ("Chicago Convention"),[34] with 188 Member States,[35] has much wider application. While the Chicago Convention does not expressly require[36] states to implement carrier sanctions policies, annex 9 to the Convention provides that "[o]perators shall take precautions at the point of embarkation to the end that passengers are in possession of the documents prescribed by the States of transit and destination for control purposes" and that "Contracting States and operators shall cooperate, where practicable, in establishing the validity and authenticity of passports and visas that are presented by embarking passengers."[37] If they choose to implement a domestic carrier sanction regime, annex 9 prohibits Member States from imposing such sanctions on carriers who deliver inadmissible passengers unless there is evidence showing the carrier to be negligent in its inspection of documents.[38]

When they enter into force, the Migrant Smuggling Protocol and the Trafficking Protocol will take an approach akin to the Schengen Convention, although their

---

[31] Agreement Between the Governments of the States of the Benelux Economic Union, the Federal Republic of Germany and the French Republic on the Gradual Abolition of Controls at the Common Frontiers, 14 June 1985, Art. 26, 30 *ILM* 73. This agreement was updated in 1990. See Convention Applying the Schengen Agreement of 14 June 1985 Between the Governments of the States of the Benelux Economic Union, the Federal Republic of Germany and the French Republic, on the Gradual Abolition of Checks at their Common Borders, 19 June 1990, 30 *ILM* 84.

[32] See Treaty of Amsterdam Amending the Treaty on European Union, the Treaties Establishing the European Communities and Certain Related Acts, Annex B Protocol Integrating the Schengen Acquis into the Framework of the European Union (hereinafter, "Treaty of Amsterdam"), 2 October 1997, 1997 *Official Journal* (C 340) 1, 37 *ILM* 56 (1998) (entered into force 1 May 1999). Denmark is in the process of ratifying its accession to the Treaty of Rome. See European Union, Amsterdam: Questions and Answers – Are Checks on People at the European Union's Internal Borders Finally Going to Be Abolished?, at http://europa.eu.int/abc/obj/amst/en/qa.htm. Norway and Iceland, non-EU members, are bound to the same provisions through parallel agreements.

[33] See Council Directive 2001/51/EC, Art. 4, 2002 *Official Journal* (L187) 45.

[34] 7 December 1944, 61 Stat. 1180, 15 *UNTS* 295.

[35] For ratification information, see International Civil Aviation Organization website at http://www.icao.int/cgi/goto_leb.pl?icao/en/leb/treaty.htm.

[36] In fact, Annex 9 appears to recommend a more cooperative approach, urging states as a "recommended practice" to enter into memoranda of agreement with operators "setting out guidelines for their mutual support and co-operation in countering the abuses associated with travel document fraud." See Annex 9 to the Convention on International Civil Aviation, Art. 3.40.1 (10th edn. 1997).

[37] Id. at Arts. 3.39, 3.40. In this regard, Annex 9 recommends that states adopt standardized machine-readable passports and "advance passenger information systems" allowing passenger identification data to be transmitted to the destination state before the flight arrives. See id. at Arts. 3.4.1, 3.14.2.

[38] Id. at Art. 3.41.

reach (in terms of number of State Parties) will likely be more comparable to the Chicago Convention. Both protocols will require State Parties to "establish[] the obligation of commercial carriers ... to ascertain that all passengers are in possession of the travel documents required for entry into the receiving State."[39]

States have also begun to allow departure site inspections by destination-state personnel. In 1996, the European Union adopted a policy allowing states to post "Airline Liaison Officers" (ALOs) abroad for purposes of advising air carriers about the authenticity of specific travel documents.[40] The United Kingdom, the Netherlands, Germany, and Denmark have all posted such officers in their embassies in refugee-producing countries.[41]

Similarly, the United States has established "preinspection stations" through bilateral agreement in several other countries, allowing Immigration and Naturalization Service staff to inspect persons prior to departure to the United States.[42] In recently enacted legislation on border security, the United States Congress directed the federal government to study both expanding such preinspection to other sites and instituting voluntary "preclearance" programs (for persons wishing to avoid extended security checks during travel).[43]

Human rights organizations are concerned that forcing carriers to verify travel documents at the point of departure impinges upon the rights of refugees trying to flee persecution[44] because airline employees are neither qualified nor mandated to perform screening for any other protected status. Similar concerns have been voiced about ALOs[45] and preinspection officers,[46] who are reportedly not trained to solicit or respond to asylum requests. Without measures to ensure responsibility for the protection of persons seeking to flee, extraterritorial screening methods may conflict with states' responsibilities under human rights and refugee law (discussed in greater detail below).

---

[39] See Migrant Smuggling Protocol, *supra* note 9, at Art. 11(3); Trafficking Protocol *supra* note 10, at Art. 11(3).

[40] See Joint Position of 25 October 1996 Defined by the Council on Pre-Frontier Assistance and Training Assignments, 1996 *Official Journal* L281/1. Annex 9 to the Chicago Convention approves and recommends this practice. See Annex 9, *supra* note 36, at Art. 3.40.2.

[41] See Human Rights Watch, "Special Issue – Refugees, Asylum-Seekers and Displaced Persons," in *World Report 2000*, http://www.hrw.org/wr2k1/special/refugees2.html.

[42] See, e.g., Agreement Between the United States of America and Ireland on Preinspection, 25 June 1986, *TIAS* No. 11379; Agreement on Preinspection Between the United States of America and the Netherlands in Respect of Aruba, 16 June 1987, *TIAS* No. 11275.

[43] See Enhanced Border Security and Visa Entry Reform Act of 2002, *supra* note 28, at para. 401.

[44] See, e.g., Amnesty International, *No Flights to Safety – Carrier Sanctions: Airline Employees and the Rights of Refugees* (1997), www.amnesy.org.

[45] See J. Morrison, *The Trafficking and Smuggling of Refugees: The End Game in European Asylum Policy* (July 2000) p. 41 (www.unhcr.ch).

[46] See Testimony of AILA Member Kathleen Campbell Walker Before the Senate Immigration Subcommittee on Enhanced Border Security, AILA InfoNet, Doc. No. 02041234 (23 April 2002), at http://www.aila.org (noting the need for training of officers "to assure that legitimate asylum-seekers are afforded a meaningful opportunity to seek protection").

Maritime Enforcement

In addition to formalizing carriers' responsibilities, states are increasing their cooperation with each other in guarding against unauthorized entry by sea. In the 1990s, maritime smuggling and trafficking of migrants rose to the fore of international interest. Since 11 September 2001, interdiction of terrorists at sea has gained equal prominence. However, the international law in this area remains less developed.

Under the United Nations Convention on the Law of the Sea (UNCLOS) and customary maritime law, states are entitled to enforce domestic laws, including immigration and criminal laws, on ships bearing their own flags, stateless ships, and any ships in their territorial seas, subject to the right of innocent passage.[47] UNCLOS extends the right to enforce certain types of domestic law, including immigration controls, to ships in "contiguous zones" (which extend an additional twelve nautical miles from the end of the territorial sea).[48] In these circumstances, therefore, states may interdict ships in order to search for illegal migrants, including persons deemed security threats, such as criminals and terrorists.

On all other waters (including the high seas, "exclusive economic zones," and "continental shelf" zones as defined by the UNCLOS), maritime law generally forbids states from interfering with foreign flag vessels unless the flag state consents.[49] A number of states interdict ships bearing illegal migrants on the high seas as a matter of regular policy, either by seeking ad hoc consent from the flag states (if any) of offending vessels or by invoking standing bilateral treaties or memoranda of understanding allowing such actions.[50] The resulting patchwork of such agreements cannot, however, guarantee security where flag states refuse to cooperate.

The Migrant Smuggling Protocol sets out a framework among State Parties for seeking permission to board and search vessels suspected of smuggling migrants.[51] While it does not expressly provide that such permission must be granted, the Protocol will require that parties respond to any such requests "expeditiously" and that parties generally "cooperate to the fullest extent possible to prevent and suppress the smuggling of migrants by sea."[52]

The United States is currently studying a proposal to "regularly board and search suspicious vessels on the high seas around the world even when permission is not

---

[47] See United Nations Convention on the Law of the Sea (hereinafter "UNCLOS"), 10 December 1982, Art. 2, 1833 *UNTS* 397; Restatement (Third) of Foreign Relations (hereinafter, "Restatement") paras. 511-12, 522(2)(b) and n. 7 (1987). Warships and ships owned or operated by states for non-commercial purposes are immune from arrest, attachment, or execution. See Restatement, *supra*, at para. 512, n. 6.

[48] See UNCLOS, *supra* note 47, at Arts. 2 (territorial sea), and 33(1) (contiguous zone).

[49] See Restatement, *supra* note 47, at para. 522 cmt. e; UNCLOS *supra* note 47, Art. 92; Convention on the High Seas, 29 April 1958, Art. 6, 13 *UST* 2312, *TIAS* 5200, 450 *UNTS*; Gary W. Palmer, "Guarding the Coast: Alien Migrant Interdiction Operations at Sea," 29 *Connecticut Law Review* (1997) pp. 1565, 1567-1568.

[50] See, e.g., Palmer, *supra* note 49, at 1568; United States Executive Order No. 4685 (29 September 1981) (authorizing the interdiction of vessels carrying illegal aliens to the United States) and Order No. 12807 (24 May 1982) (same).

[51] See Migrant Smuggling Protocol, *supra* note 9, at ch. II.

[52] Id. at Arts. 7, 8.

granted" as part of its "war on terrorism."[53] Although the parameters of the proposal are not yet publicly available as of the writing of this chapter, it is safe to assume that at least one motivating force is the desire to halt terrorists from reaching American shores by sea. It is also safe to assume that if the United States undertakes such a policy, other states will follow suit.[54]

Legal authority for such a policy is unclear. In 1992, the Convention for the Suppression of Unlawful Acts Against the Safety of Maritime Navigation, pertaining to terrorist acts committed at sea, entered into force.[55] However, that treaty was not meant to address the question of interdiction of ships ferrying terrorists to coastal states.[56] Thus, any state pursuing a policy for interdicting vessels on the high seas would have to rely on customary international law or, potentially, the laws of war.

According to the Restatement of the Law of Foreign Relations (a basic reference in the area of customary international law), warships and law enforcement vessels may board and inspect a ship not owned or operated by a foreign state on the high seas if "there is reason to suspect" that the ship is stateless, of the same nationality as the warship, or engaged in piracy, slave trading, or unauthorized broadcasting.[57] The Restatement suggests that these exceptions arise from their status as "*jus cogens* norms*" (which means that they have been so widely accepted as crimes that they have become international in character, overriding any contrary law, and subject to "universal jurisdiction").[58] The Restatement further notes that "the present international law is unclear" as to whether there is a right to interdict ships carrying "escaping terrorists."[59] Some scholars have argued that terrorism has been so universally condemned that it too has reached the level of *jus cogens* and universal jurisdiction.[60] By extension, a state might assert a right to intercept ships suspected of carrying terrorists to its borders. However, this is far from settled law.

Further legal grounds for intercepting terrorists at sea may be derived from the laws of war and the doctrine of self-defense recognized by the United Nations Charter. Article 51 of the United Nations Charter recognizes states' inherent right to defend themselves against an "armed attack" ("*agression armée*") by other states.[61] The United States has asserted that the events of 11 September 2001 constituted such an attack, even though it was carried out by a terrorist organization rather than directly by a state. Precedent from the International Court of Justice suggests that

---

[53] See T.E. Ricks, "Aggressive New Tactics Proposed for Terror War," *Washington Post*, 3 August 2002, at A1.

[54] Cf., *Refugees Clear*, The Mercury, 20 September 2001 (reporting on fears by an Australian member of parliament that Al Quaeda terrorists posing as asylum-seekers may be entering Australia by sea).

[55] 10 March 1988, 1678 *UNTS* 201, 27 *ILM* 668 (1988).

[56] See id. at Art. 9 ("Nothing in this Convention shall affect in any way the rules of international law pertaining to the competence of States to exercise investigative or enforcement jurisdiction on board ships not flying their flag.").

[57] See Restatement, *supra* note 47, at para. 522.

[58] See id. at para. 522 cmt. d.

[59] Id. at para. 522, n. 6.

[60] See, e.g., M. Ermolaeva, "Crimes Without Punishment," 23 *Southern Ilinois University Law Journal* (1999) pp. 755, 777.

[61] See U.N. Charter Art. 51.

attacks by such independent networks may not trigger the right to self-defense under the Charter.[62] However, recent practice, including U.N. Security Council Resolution 1368 accepting the United States' assertion of the right of self-defense against Afghanistan in response to attacks by the al Quaeda network,[63] and the North Atlantic Treaty Organization (NATO),[64] the Organization of American States (OAS),[65] and the Security Treaty Between Australia, New Zealand, and the United States of America (ANZUS)[66] invocations of Member States' duty to collective defense in response to the attacks on the United States, indicate that a contrary consensus is forming. As a lawful belligerent, the United States would have the right under the laws of naval warfare to intercept vessels – even those under neutral state flags – suspected of carrying "enemy" personnel.[67] Other states that have not been the object of such terrorist attacks might have to rely on the controversial doctrine of "anticipatory self-defense"[68] to justify similar interdictions.

However, because of the paucity of international legal precedent in this area and the potential for substantial conflict between flag states and states wishing to interdict ships thought to be carrying terrorists, coastal states may benefit from new guidelines similar to those discussed above in the Migrant Smuggling Protocol. Moreover, the same concerns about the rights of refugees that arise in the context of carrier sanctions and preinspection would also arise in interdiction at sea and could be addressed in such guidelines.

---

[62] See Military and Paramilitary Activities (*Nicaragua* v. *U.S.*), 1986 I.C.J. 14 (27 June) (holding that armed groups can only be considered an "armed attack" from a state if that state controls their actions).

[63] See S.C. Res. 1368, U.N. SCOR, 56th Sess., 4730th mtg. at 1, U.N. Doc. S/RES/1368 (2001). See also Letter Dated 7 October 2001 from the Permanent Representative of the United States of America to the President of the Security Council, S/2001/1946 (2001) (notifying the Security Council of the United States' intention to act in self defense against al Quaeda and the Taliban); S.C. Res. 1373, U.N. SCOR, 56th Sess., 4385th mtg. At 1, U.N. Doc. S/RES/1373 (2001) (reaffirming that the right to self-defense applies to terrorist attacks).

[64] See Statement of the Ministerial Meeting of the North Atlantic Council, 6 December 2001, M-NAC-2 (2001) p. 159.

[65] See *Terrorist Threat to the Americas*, Res. 1, Twenty-Fourth Meeting of Consultation of Ministers of Foreign Affairs Acting as Organ of Consultation in Application of the Inter-American Treaty of Reciprocal Assistance, OAS Doc. OEA/Ser.F/II.24/RC.24/RES.1/01 (21 September 2001).

[66] See Prime Minister Media Release, *Application of ANZUS Treaty to Terrorist Attacks on the United States*, 14 September 2001, http://www.pm.gov.au/news/media_releases/2001/media_release1241.htm.

[67] See, e.g., L. Donald-Beck (ed.), *San Remo Manual on International Law Applicable to Armed Conflicts at Sea* (1995) p. 67(f), available at www.icrc.org (allowing for attacks of neutral vessels being effectively used as a means of warfare by an enemy power).

[68] See generally I. Dieter, *The Law of War* (2nd edn. 2001) pp. 86-87 (noting that although the doctrine of anticipatory self-defense is legally "difficult to tackle" it has become more acceptable in practice in recent years).

SECURITY AS A LIMIT ON INTERNATIONAL LAW CONCERNING MIGRANTS

Just as the rights of migrants sometimes limit how states secure their borders against dangerous migrants, security limits the rights migrants enjoy under international law. Security exceptions appear in human rights law, refugee law, trade law, and regional integration law pertaining to migrants, and limit rights in fundamental ways. In a broader sense, security also limits the rights of migrants in times of armed conflict under the laws of war.

Security exceptions can be implied, such as prohibitions on arbitrary infringement of a particular right, or can be explicit. In trade law and regional law, the exceptions appear as straightforward escape clauses allowing states to back away from certain commitments for purposes of security. In human rights and refugee law, the explicit security exceptions take two forms: limitation clauses or – clawbacks – and derogation clauses.

Limitation clauses are called clawbacks because they restrict, or take back from, a particular right. Clawbacks appear immediately after the phrase guaranteeing the right. The International Covenant on Civil and Political Rights (ICCPR) is typical in allowing certain rights to be subjected to restrictions so long as the restrictions are "provided by law, are necessary to protect national security, public order (*ordre public*), public health or morals or the rights and freedoms of others, and are consistent with the other rights recognized in the present Covenant."[69]

The Human Rights Committee (the monitoring body for the ICCPR) and most scholars considering clawbacks have asserted that they should be narrowly construed. Thus, it is widely agreed that to be "provided by law," a restriction may not be purely administrative or executive, but rather must have clear legislative origin.[70] To be "necessary," a restriction must be narrowly tailored and proportional to the interest addressed.[71] National security in this context is reduced to protection of territorial integrity against foreign threats of force concerning the entire nation.[72] How-

---

[69] See, e.g., International Covenant on Civil and Political Rights (hereinafter "ICCPR"), 16 December 1966, Art. 12(3), 999 *UNTS* 171. Similarly worded clawbacks appear in the African Charter on Human and Peoples' Rights (hereinafter, "African Charter"), 26 June 1981, 21 *ILM* 59 (1981), American Convention on Human Rights (hereinafter "American Convention"), 22 November 1969, 1144 *UNTS* 123; Convention on the Rights of the Child (hereinafter "CRC"), 20 November 1989, U.N. Doc. A/RES/44/25 (1989), 28 *ILM* 1457 (1989); and the European Convention for the Protection of Human Rights and Fundamental Freedoms (hereinafter "ECHR"), 4 November 1950, 213 *UNTS* 22. The proposed Arab Charter on Human Rights would subject all of the rights it recognizes to such a clawback. See Arab Charter on Human Rights, 15 September 1994, Art. 4(a), *reprinted in La Charte Arabe des Droits de l'Homme*, 7 *Revue universelle des droits de l'homme* 212 (1995), available at http://www1.umn.edu/humanrts/instree/arabhrcharter.html (not yet ratified by any state).

[70] See D. Jordanger, "Note, Alien Departure Control – A Safeguard for Both the Exercise of Fundamental Human Rights and National Security," 28 *Virginia Journal of International Law* (1987) pp. 159, 168; S. Jagerskiold, "The Freedom of Movement," *in* L. Henkin (ed.), *The International Bill of Rights* (1981) pp. 172-173.

[71] See H. Hannum, *The Right to Leave and Return in International Law and Practice* (1987) pp. 26-27.

[72] See Siracusa Principles on the Limitation and Derogation Provisions in the International Cove-

ever, public order, derived from the French doctrine of *"ordre public,"* is much broader, encompassing the full police powers of the state to ensure the orderly functioning of society.[73]

The ICCPR, the European Convention for the Protection of Human Rights and Fundamental Freedoms (ECHR) and the American Convention on Human Rights (American Convention) additionally include derogation clauses allowing many of the rights they protect to be abrogated in exceptional circumstances.[74] Derogation requires an officially proclaimed public emergency that threatens the life of the nation.[75]

None of the human rights instruments or treaty monitoring bodies has developed a catalog of the types of situations that qualify as a public emergency.[76] A number of circumstances can provoke the declaration of a state of emergency in domestic law, including war, rebellion, civil unrest, terrorist attacks, natural disasters, and even economic crises.[77] However, none of these situations is considered a "per se" public emergency at the international level; rather, the determination of the gravity of the situation must be made on a case-by-case basis based on the criteria noted above.[78]

ICCPR Article 4 requires that any derogation be applied (1) only "to the extent strictly required by the exigencies of the situation," (2) consistent with a state's other obligations under international law, and (3) without discrimination on protected grounds.[79] Derogation under Article 4 must be temporary, subject to some sort of parliamentary and judicial control, and responsive to an apparent, violent situation that cannot otherwise be controlled, above and beyond mere social unrest.[80] Thus,

---

nant on Civil and Political Rights ("Siracusa Principles") pp. 29-32; 7 *Human Rights Quarterly* (1985) pp. 1, 6; Hannum *supra* note 71, at 27-28; Nowak, *U.N. Covenant on Civil and Political Rights CCPR Commentary* (1993) p. 212; A. Kiss, "Permissible Limitations on Rights," L. Henkin (ed.), *The International Bill of Rights* (1981) pp. 295-297.

[73] See Siracusa Principles, *supra* note 72, at 22-24; Hannum, *supra* note 71, at 29-40.

[74] ICCPR, *supra* note 69, at Art. 4, ECHR, *supra* note 69, at Art. 15, American Convention, *supra* note 69, at Art. 27.

[75] See ICCPR, *supra* note 69, Art. 4, ECHR, *supra* note 69, at Art. 15, American Convention, *supra* note 69, at Art. 27. The American Convention phrases the requirement differently, stating that rights may be "suspended" "in time of war, public danger, or other emergency" if "the independence or security" of the state is threatened. See American Convention, *supra* note 69, at Art. 27. Notwithstanding the different language, however, the Inter-American Court of Human Rights has interpreted the provision in a manner similar to the construction of the corresponding provisions in the ICCPR and the ECHR by their treaty bodies. See J. Oraa, *Human Rights in States of Emergency in International Law* (1992) p. 27.

[76] The drafters of the ICCPR expressly rejected early drafts of Art. 4 which would have laid out qualifying situations. See Oraa, *supra* note 75, at 27. In a 1982 study of the question, the International Law Association asserted that it would be "neither desirable nor possible to stipulate *in abstracto* what particular types of events will automatically constitute a public emergency; each case has to be judged on its own merits taking into account the overriding concern for the continuance of a democratic society." See id. at 31 (citing ILA Paris Report (1984) p. 599(1)).

[77] See Oraa, *supra* note 75, at 30-31.

[78] See, e.g., Human Rights Committee, General Comment No. 29, States of Emergency (Art. 4), at 5, 11 August 2001, U.N. Doc. No. CCPR/C/21/Rev.1/Add.11.

[79] See also American Convention, *supra* note 69, at Art. 27(1); ECHR, *supra* note 69, at Art. 15(1).

[80] See A. Svensson-McCarthy, *The International Law of Human Rights and States of Exception* (1998) pp. 239-241.

even if it is apparent that there is an emergency threatening the life of the nation, a state must still demonstrate that any derogation of a particular right is justified in scope and duration by the specific circumstances facing it.

These different kinds of security exceptions are discussed below within four modes of state response to migration.

Control of Entry

Human Rights

None of the international or regional human rights instruments expressly grants aliens the right to enter a foreign state.[81] Nevertheless, several of these instruments suggest limitations on a state's refusal to allow entry when the circumstances implicate respect for family life, the best interests of the child, and prohibitions on non-discrimination.[82] State security arguably trumps each of these rights in the appropriate circumstances. Moreover, states' needs for security-related information about aliens applying for admission generally trumps aliens' rights to privacy with regard to transborder sharing of such information. On the other hand, the right of a person to enter his own country is expressly protected and is generally not limited in the international instruments by state security interests.[83]

---

[81] See the contribution of Joan Fitzpatrick in this volume.

[82] See Human Rights Committee, General Comment No. 15 5, 27th Sess. (1986), reprinted *in* Compilation of General Comments and General Recommendations Adopted by the Human Rights Bodies, U.N. Doc. HRI/GEN/1/Rev.1/ at 8 (1994) (noting that the "Covenant does not recognize the right of aliens to enter or reside in the territory of a State party" but that "in certain circumstances an alien may enjoy the protection of the Covenant even in relation to entry or residence, for example, when considerations of non-discrimination, prohibition of inhuman treatment and respect for family life arise"). The European Commission and European Court of Human Rights have come to similar conclusions under the European Convention on Human Rights. See G. Goodwin-Gill, "Migration: International Law and Human Rights," *in* B. Ghosh (ed.), *Managing Migration. Time for a New International Regime?* (2000) pp. 172-173; R. Lillich, *Human Rights of Aliens in Contemporary International Law* (1984) pp. 95-96. The issue of torture is dealt with separately below.

[83] See Universal Declaration on Human Rights ("UDHR"), Art. 13(2); G.A. Res. 217A, U.N. GAOR, 3rd Sess., Supp. No. 3, at 71; U.N. Doc. A/810 (1948); ICCPR, *supra* note 69, at Art. 12(4); Convention on the Elimination of All Forms of Racial Discrimination (hereinafter "CERD"), 21 December 1965, Art. 5(D)(ii), 660 *UNTS* 195 (providing for equal protection in the exercise of this right), American Declaration on the Rights and Duties of Man (hereinafter, "American Declaration"); O.A.S. Res. XXX, O.A.S. Off. Rec. OEA/Ser.L/V/I.4, Art. 8 (1965) (not expressly providing for a right to return, but providing a right of residence which might imply the former right); American Convention, *supra* note 69, at Art. 22(5); African Charter, *supra* note 69, at Art. 12(2); Protocol (No. 4) to the European Convention for the Protection of Human Rights and Fundamental Freedoms, Securing Certain Rights and Freedoms Other Than Those Already Included in the Convention and in the Protocol Thereto (hereinafter "ECHR protocol 4"), 16 September 1963, Arts. 2-3, *ETS* 46, 7 *ILM* 978 (1986), 58 *AJIL* 334 (1964).

Respect for Family Life

The separation of family members through denial of entry may implicate the right to respect for family life.[84] However, this right is not absolute. The ICCPR protects family life from "arbitrary or unlawful interference."[85] The American Convention on Human Rights (American Convention) likewise prohibits "arbitrary or abusive interference" with the family.[86] Thus, exclusion of family members for national security or public order reasons should be permissible under these instruments so long as it is performed according to law and in a non-arbitrary (i.e., appropriate and just[87]) fashion. The ECHR expressly conditions the right to respect for family life with a clawback for purposes of "national security, public safety or the economic well-being of the country, for the prevention of disorder or crime, for the protection of health or morals, or for the protection of the rights and freedoms of others."[88] The court has construed the scope of this clawback and the proper balance between the right and the state's security interests, but only in the context of expulsion.[89]

Best Interests of the Child

Article 9(1) of the Convention on the Rights of the Child (CRC) appears to assert an absolute obligation on states not to separate children from their parents against their will "except when competent authorities subject to judicial review determine, in accordance with applicable law and procedures, that such separation is necessary for the best interests of the child." However, the drafting history indicates disagreement among the drafters as to whether this provision should even apply to immigration enforcement.[90] Moreover, CRC Article 10, which covers family reunification, merely calls upon states to deal with reunification requests in a "positive, expeditious and humane manner."

---

[84] See the contribution of Kate Jastram in this volume.

[85] See ICCPR, *supra* note 69, at Art. 17.

[86] See American Convention, *supra* note 69, at Art. 11(2). The African Charter more vaguely requires the state to "assist the family." See African Charter, *supra* note 69, at Art. 18(2).

[87] The Human Rights Committee notes that "the notion of 'arbitrariness' must not be equated with 'against the law' but be interpreted more broadly to include such elements as inappropriateness and injustice." *A. v. Australia*, Comm. No. 560/1993, Views of 3 April 1997, at 9.2; U.N. Doc. CCPR/C/59/D/560/1993 (1997).

[88] See ECHR, *supra* note 69, at Art. 8(2).

[89] See *infra* p. 117.

[90] In 1989, the chairman of the working group drafting the Convention made a declaration on behalf of the group indicating that Art. 9 should not apply to immigration proceedings: "It is the understanding of the Working Group that [Article 9] of this Convention is intended to apply to separations that arise in domestic situations, whereas [Article 10] is intended to apply to separations involving different countries and relating to cases of family reunification. [Article 10] is not intended to affect the general right of States to establish and regulate their respective immigration laws in accordance with their international obligations." E/CN.4/1989/49 at 203, reprinted in *The United Nations Convention on the Rights of the Child* (S. Dietrick (ed.) 1998) pp. 181-182. However, state representatives from Portugal, Sweden, Italy, and Germany promptly demurred on the record. Id. at 205-207.

The comments of the Committee on the Rights of the Child indicate that it believes that Article 9 does apply to immigration proceedings, but that the best interests of the child do not have to trump other state interests.[91] A United States district court recently came to a similar conclusion, applying the CRC "best interests" standard as a principle of customary international law.[92] Thus, it may be argued that the "best interests of the child" can be balanced against a state's security interests under the CRC as the right to respect for family is under the ECHR.

Non-Discrimination

Most of the major human rights conventions include prohibitions against discrimination in the exercise of the other rights guaranteed by those conventions.[93] These provisions might be implicated, for instance, if a state allowed family reunification for male resident aliens but not for females, thus discriminating in the effect given to the right to respect family life.[94] In addition, the African Charter on Human and Peoples Rights (African Charter), the American Convention, the Convention on the Elimination of All Forms of Racial Discrimination (CERD), the Convention on the Elimination of All Forms of Discrimination Against Women (CEDAW), the CRC, and the ICCPR include broader prohibitions against other discriminatory actions by states.[95]

The non-discrimination provisions are not subject to specific clawbacks for purposes of security, and derogation clauses prohibit a suspension of rights in a dis-

---

[91] See Concluding Observations of the Committee on the Rights of the Child: Norway, U.N. Doc. CRC/C/15/Add.126 (28 June 2000) at 31 (noting that where deportation will result in the separation of parents and children, the best interests of the child should be "taken into consideration"); Summary Record of the 216th Meeting: Canada, U.N. Doc. No. CRC/C/SR.216 (1 June 1995) at 55 (noting that the best interests of the child "must be taken into account" in determination of requests for family reunification).

[92] See *Beharry v. Reno*, 181 F. Supp. 2d 584, 603-605 (E.D.N.Y. 2002) (holding that an American immigration statute must be construed, consistent with customary and conventional human rights law, to require a hearing where a potential deportee may raise the interests of his deportation on his children).

[93] See African Charter, *supra* note 69, at Art. 2; American Convention, *supra* note 69, at Art. 1; CRC, *supra* note 69, at Art. 2; ECHR, *supra* note 69, at Art. 14; ICCPR, *supra* note 69, at Art. 2; International Convention of the Rights of All Migrant Workers and their Families (hereinafter "ICMW"), 18 December 1990, Art. 7, U.N. Doc. A/RES/45/158, 30 *ILM* 1517 (1991) (not yet in force).

[94] See *Abdulaziz, Babales, and Balkandi v. UK*, (1985) 7 E.H.R.R. 471,71-86); J. Madureira, *Aliens' Admission to and Departure from National Territory: Case-Law of the Organs of the European Convention on Human Rights and the European Social Charter* (1989) p. 13.

[95] See African Charter, *supra* note 69, at Art. 18 (discrimination against women); American Convention, *supra* note 69, at Art. 24 (equal protection); Convention on the Elimination of All Forms of Discrimination Against Women, 18 December 1979, 19 *ILM* 33 (1980) (passim); CERD, *supra* note 83 (passim); CRC, *supra* note 69, at Art. 2(2); ICCPR, *supra* note 69, at Art. 26. The ECHR has no such broad antidiscrimination provision. However, if discrimination in admission of aliens is particularly "severe" it might amount to "degrading treatment" under ECHR Art. 3. See Madureira, *supra* note 94, at 16-17 (citing European Commission on Human Rights, Application No. 4626/70, 13 Decisions and Reports 5 (8)).

criminatory manner.[96] However, these instruments permit discrimination if it is based on "reasonable and objective criteria" and the discriminatory means are proportional to the reasonable end.[97] This requirement would be met if a state can make out a "reasonable and objective" case that differing treatment of applicants for entry of a particular national origin is required for its security.[98]

Privacy

As noted above, international law is increasing the requirements of information sharing between states for purposes of border control. Presumably, this will include information concerning criminal records, terrorist connections, and other security-related issues. Western states, and in particular the United States, are becoming increasingly enthusiastic about receiving this and other identification information about migrants. For example, as of 2004, the United States will require any visitors arriving under its visa-waiver program to present passports including microchips containing biometric information.[99] The degree to which migrants can affect the content and use of such information is controlled by the right to privacy.

Aliens' right to privacy is protected under the major human rights instruments.[100] The Human Rights Committee and the European Court of Human Rights have made clear that the right extends to controlling the "gathering and holding of personal information on computers, databanks and other devices" as well as the sharing of that information.[101]

---

[96] See American Convention, *supra* note 69, at Art. 27(1); ICCPR, *supra* note 69, at Art. 4(1). The derogation clause in ECHR Art. 15 does not expressly mention discrimination and the antidiscrimination provisions of Art. 14 are not listed as non-derogable. However, given the overlapping international obligations of ECHR Member States, including the ICCPR, the UN Charter, and the Geneva Conventions of 1948, all of which contain anti-discrimination provisions, abuse of this loophole appears unlikely. See Svensson-McCarthy, *supra* note 8o; Nowak, *supra* note 72, at 658-660.

[97] See *S.W.J. Broeks* v. *The Netherlands*, Comm. No. 172/1984, GAOR A/42/40, 13 (1987); Inter-American Court of Human Rights, Proposed Amendments to the Naturalization Provisions of the Constitution of Costa Rica, Advisory Opinion OC-4/84 of 19 January 1984, Series A, No. 4 p. 80 para. 82; European Court of Human Rights, *Judgment in the Belgian Linguistic Case*, Series A., No. 6 p. 34 para. 10.

[98] See the contribution of David Martin in this volume. Although not relying on security, the parliament of the United Kingdom recently granted the Home Office special powers to target certain ethnic groups for particularly "tough questioning" at border entry points based on claims that these groups tend to pose greater risks of illegal migration. See M. Clarke, "Immigration Go-Ahead to Target Key Ethnic Groups," *Daily Mail*, 3 May 2001, at 39, available at www.unhcr.ch.

[99] See Enhanced Border Security and Visa Entry Reform Act of 2002, *supra* note 28, at para. 303.

[100] See American Convention, *supra* note 69, at Art. 11 (prohibiting "arbitrary or abusive interference with [a person's] private life" as well as "unlawful attacks on his honor or reputation"); CRC, *supra* note 69, at Art. 16; ECHR, *supra* note 69, at Art. 8; ICCPR, *supra* note 69, at Art. 17; UDHR, *supra* note 83, at Art. 12. The African Charter is a notable exception in failing to provide for a right to privacy.

[101] See Human Rights Committee, General Comment No. 16, at 10 (1988), reprinted *in* Compilation of General Comments and General Recommendations Adopted by Human Rights Treaty Bodies, U.N. Doc. HRI/GEN/1/Rev.1 at 21 (1994). See also *Rotaru* v. *Romania*, 8 B.H.R.C. 449 at 46 (2000) (noting that "both the storing by a public authority of information relating to an individual's private life

The scope of these rights has also been interpreted in a number of international instruments dealing with transborder information flows, including the Council of Europe's Convention for the Protection of Individuals with Regard to Automatic Processing of Personal Data (COE Privacy Convention),[102] the Organization for Economic Cooperation and Development's Guidelines on the Protection of Privacy and Transborder Flows of Personal Data (OECD Guidelines),[103] as well as a United Nations General Assembly resolution (UN Guidelines)[104] and EU directives and regulations.[105] The OECD Guidelines and the EU initiatives were designed primarily to prevent states from invoking privacy interests in an effort to create non-tariff barriers to the flow of information.[106] However, they also address data transfers by and for governmental entities.[107]

With regard to data storage and transfer, the right to privacy in the human rights and in the privacy-specific instruments requires that: (1) data only be collected by lawful means with consent and knowledge of the subject; (2) data will be accurate, complete, and current; (3) data will only be used for a previously specified purpose; (4) data will be kept safe from inadvertent disclosure; (5) the purposes and use of the data will be disclosed to the public; and (6) subjects will have the right to review data about themselves and to make corrections to any inaccuracies.[108] Some of these rights may prove problematic for states, especially for information gathered as a result of covert intelligence. In such circumstances, states would have to rely on security exceptions.

All of the human rights instruments prohibit "arbitrary"[109] interference with the right to privacy, except for the ECHR, which specifically qualifies the right with a clawback concerning "national security, public safety [and] prevention of disorder or crime."[110] Even though they are meant to be non-binding, the OECD and the UN Guidelines include similar clawback clauses for "national sovereignty, national security and public policy ('*ordre public*')[.]"[111] The Guidelines urge, however, that exceptions for these purposes should be "(a) as few as possible and (b) made known

---

and the use of it and the refusal to allow an opportunity for it to be refuted amount to inference with the right to respect for private life secured in Art. 8(1) of the [ECHR]").

[102] 28 January 1981, *ETS* 108 ("Coe Privacy Convention").

[103] 1980 O.E.C.D. Doc. (C 58 final), 20 *ILM* 422 (1981).

[104] See Guidelines for the Regulation of Computerized Personal Data Files, G.A. Res. 44/132, 44 U.N. GAOR Supp. (No. 49) at 211, U.N. Doc. A/44/49 (1989).

[105] See, e.g., Council and Parliament Directive 95/46/E, 1995 *Official Journal* (L 281) 31; Council and Parliament Regulation 45/2001, 2001 *Official Journal* (L 8) 1.

[106] See "Introduction to the International Regulations," *in* J. Holvast, W. Madsen, and P. Roth (eds.), *The Global Encyclopedia of Data Protection Regulation* (Supp. No. 1/2000) (2001) p. 2; see also COE Privacy Convention, *supra* note 102, at Art. 12(2).

[107] See OECD Guidelines, *supra* note 103, at Art. 2.

[108] See id. at Arts. 7-13; COE Privacy Convention, *supra* note 102, at Arts. 5-15; Council and Parliament Regulation 45/2001, *supra* note 105, at Arts. 4-9.

[109] See *supra* note 87 and accompanying text.

[110] Id.

[111] OECD Guidelines, *supra* note 103, at Art. 4. See also UN Guidelines Concerning Computerized Personal Data Files, Art. 6, U.N. Doc. E/CN.4/1990/72 (1990).

to the public."[112] Similarly, the COE Privacy Convention allows for "derogation" of individual privacy rights:

> "when such derogation is provided for by the law of the Party and constitutes a necessary measure in a democratic society in the interests of:
> (a) protecting State security, public safety, the monetary interests of the State or the suppression of criminal offenses;
> (b) protecting the data subject or the rights and freedoms of others."[113]

Each of these instruments requires an objectively demonstrated security need for departing from personal data privacy rights. In cases involving suspected terrorists and criminals seeking entry, it is difficult to imagine that states would not normally be able to make this showing.

To the extent that an information-requesting state does not require such an objective showing in its domestic law, however, the human rights instruments and, to a lesser degree, privacy-specific law may prevent Member States from sharing immigration-related data with it, even for purposes of border control.[114] Moreover, in 1987, the Council of Europe issued a Recommendation concerning the use of personal data in the police sector.[115] The Recommendation urges that data gathered for police purposes that is communicated to foreign authorities "should be restricted to police bodies," and only if "there exists a clear legal provision under national or international law" or if required to prevent a serious and imminent danger or to suppress a serious criminal offense.[116]

Entry into One's "Own Country"

The major human rights treaties specifically provide that persons have the right to re-enter their own country.[117] Of the major instruments, only the African Charter conditions this right with a clawback in favor of national security or public order.[118]

---

[112] Id.

[113] COE Privacy Convention, *supra* note 102, at Art. 9.

[114] See Council and Parliament Directive 95/46/EC, *supra* note 105, at Art. 25; J. Michael, *Privacy and Human Rights: An International and Comparative Study, with Special Reference to Developments in Information Technology* (1994) pp. 45-50.

[115] Council Recommendation No. R(87) 15, 17 September 1987, available at www.humanrights.coe.int.

[116] Id. at Art. 54.

[117] See UDHR, *supra* note 83, at Art. 13(2); ICCPR, *supra* note 69, at Art. 12(4); CERD, *supra* note 83, at Art. 5(D)(ii) (providing for equal protection in the exercise of this right); American Declaration, *supra* note 83, at Art. 8 (not expressly providing for a right to return, but providing a right of residence which might imply the former right); American Convention, *supra* note 69, at Art. 22(5); African Charter, *supra* note 69, at Art. 12(2); ECHR protocol 4, *supra* note 83, at Arts. 2-3. See the contributions of Vincent Chetail and Gregor Noll in this volume.

[118] Cf., African Charter, *supra* note 69, at Art. 12(2) (conditioning the right to re-entry on national security interests) *with* American Convention, *supra* note 69, at Art. 22(5); ICCPR, *supra* note 69, at Art. 12(4); ECHR protocol 4, *supra* note 83, at Art. 5; CRC, *supra* note 69, at Art. 10(2). See also Convention on the Nationality of Married Women, 309 *UNTS* 65, entered in to force 11 August 1958 (requiring Member States to allow the alien wife of one of its nationals to naturalize "subject to such limitations as may be imposed in the interests of national security or public policy.").

The ICCPR instead provides that the right to re-enter may not be arbitrarily denied.[119] The Human Rights Committee noted that this qualifier "guarantees that even interference provided for by law should be in accordance with the provisions, aims and objectives of the [ICCPR] and should be, in any event, reasonable in the particular circumstances."[120] The Committee added that "there are few, if any, circumstances in which deprivation of the right to enter one's own country could be reasonable."[121] It appears, therefore, that states wishing to exclude their own nationals (and any aliens who might also qualify for the right of re-entry)[122] for security reasons must rely on general derogation clauses (discussed below).

Non-Refoulement in Refugee and Torture Law

The Convention Relating to the Status of Refugees (Refugee Convention), the Convention on the Specific Aspects of Refugee Problems in Africa (OAU Refugee Convention) and the Convention Against Torture and Other Cruel, Inhuman or Degrading Treatment or Punishment (Torture Convention) all guarantee the right of *non-refoulement*, the right not to be returned to a state where the migrant faces persecution and/or torture.[123] Theoretically, the prohibition on *refoulement* does not guarantee a right to entry; the receiving state may send the applicant to a safe third state.[124] In

---

[119] See ICCPR, *supra* note 69, at Art. 12(4).

[120] See Human Rights Committee, General Comment No. 27, "Freedom of Movement (Art. 12)," 21, U.N. Doc. CCPR/C/21/Rev.1/Add.9 (1999).

[121] Id.

[122] Neither the UDHR nor the ICCPR phrase the right as one limited to nationals. See UDHR, *supra* note 78, at Art. 13(2); ICCPR, *supra* note 69, at Art. 12(4); but cf., ECHR protocol 4, *supra* note 83, at Art. 3(2) (expressly limiting the right to nationals). According to the Human Rights Committee, therefore, the right includes, in addition to nationals, "at the very least, an individual, who because of his or her special ties to or claims in relation to a given country, cannot be considered a mere alien." Human Rights Committee, General Comment No. 27, *supra* note 120, at 20. Thus, the right (1) applies to residents (a) arbitrarily stripped of their nationality, or (b) whose country of nationality has been transferred to another entity, and (2) "might embrace" stateless persons or other aliens who have been arbitrarily denied the right to naturalize in their country of residence. Id. at 20. The right does not extend to long-time resident aliens who fail to take advantage of reasonable opportunities to naturalize in their state of residence. See *Stewart* v. *Canada,* Comm. No. 538/1993 at 12.5, 2 BHRC 235 (1996). Moreover, the right applies to non-residents, even those who have never resided in the country, if they hold that country's citizenship or nationality (for example through a rule of jus sanguinis). See Hannum, *supra* note 71, at 56. Some scholars read the phrase "his own country" much more broadly. For instance, those supporting the Palestinian right to return to Israel argue that the phrase should be read to include those with historical, religious, and other ties to a country. See T. Kramer, "Note, The Controversy of a Palestinian Right to Return to Israel," 18 *Arizona Journal of International and Comparative Law* (2000) pp. 1979, 1009-1010.

[123] See Convention Relating to the Status of Refugees, 28 July 1951, Art. 33, 189 *UNTS* 150 and Protocol Relating to the Status of Refugees, 31 January 1967, 606 *UNTS* 267 (collectively hereinafter "Refugee Convention"); Convention Against Torture and Other Cruel, Inhuman or Degrading Treatment or Punishment (hereinafter, "Torture Convention"), Art. 3, 10 December 1984, GA Res. 39/46/ Annex, UN Doc. No. A/39/15.

[124] See *Aemi* v. *Switzerland*, Comm. No. 34/1995, ¶ 11, U.N. Doc. CAT/C/18/D/34/1995 (1998)

practice, however, the right of *non-refoulement* amounts to a right to enter, at least for the time necessary to find an alternative state of refuge.

Refugee Law

The Refugee Convention expressly limits the right to *non-refoulement* in favor of states' national security interests. Article 33(2) of the Refugee Convention provides that the right to *non-refoulement* does not apply to any refugee "whom there are reasonable grounds for regarding as a danger to the security of the country in which he is, or who, having been convicted of a final judgment of a particularly serious crime, constitutes a danger to the community of that country."[125] This provision was originally intended to address communist infiltration, and the determination as to who falls within its parameters was to be in the discretion of the receiving state.[126] The scope and type of the requisite "danger" involved has, unsurprisingly, subsequently been subject to varying interpretations.[127]

In contrast, the OAU Refugee Convention creates an absolute right of *non-refoulement* for refugees, without reference to any exception for national security.[128] However, state practice under the convention has not demonstrated absolute adherence to this principle.[129]

UNHCR and other advocates have additionally pointed to the exclusion clause of the Refugee Convention, Article 1(F), as a means of ensuring state security within the framework of refugee law.[130] That clause excludes from the definition of "refugee" any person about whom there are serious reasons for considering that (a) he or she has committed a war crime, a crime against humanity, or genocide; (b) he or she has committed a serious non-political crime outside the receiving country; or (c) he or she has been "guilty of acts contrary to the purposes and principles of the

---

(noting that states may, consistent with Article 3, "find a third State willing to admit the applicant to its territory and undertaking in its turn not to return or expel him").

[125] See also Declaration on Territorial Asylum, G.A. Res. 2312 (XXII), Art. 3(2), 22 U.N. GAOR Supp. (No. 16) at 81, U.N. Doc. A/6716 (1967) (providing an exception for the right of *non-refoulement* "for overriding reasons of national security or in order to safeguard the population, as in the case of a mass influx of persons").

[126] See J. Hathaway and C.J. Harvey, "Framing Refugee Protection in the New World Disorder," 34 *Cornell International Law Journal* (2001) pp. 257, 289; G. Goodwin-Gill, *The Refugee in International Law* (2nd edn. 1996) pp.139-140 and n.104

[127] See Hathaway & Harvey, *supra* note 126, at 290 (comparing *Suresh* v. *Minister of Citizenship and Immigration*, 183 DLR (4th) 629, 671 (Can. Fed. Ct. 2000) [holding that the danger of a terrorist activity in the non-host state may suffice], with *Home Secretary* v. *Rehman* [2000] 3 WLR 1240 (Eng. C.A.). [holding that there must be a "real possibility" of adverse consequences in the host state]).

[128] See OAU Refugee Convention *supra* note 123, at Art. 2(3), 1001 *UNTS* 45, 8 *ILM* 1288 (1969); Goodwin-Gill, *supra* note 126, at 140.

[129] See Lawyers Committee for Human Rights, *African Exodus: Refugee Crisis, Human Rights and the 1969 OAU Convention* (1995).

[130] See *UNHCR Makes Proposals to Enhance the Security of Asylum Systems*, UNHCR Press Release, 2 August 2002, at www.unhcr.ch.

United Nations."[131] The OAU Refugee convention includes a similar provision.[132]

Although the exclusion clause does not specifically mention terrorism as a basis for exclusion, there is ample support for the argument that terrorist acts should be considered "contrary to the purposes and principles of the United Nations."[133] However, the exclusion clause was not designed to provide security to states, but rather to withhold aid from undeserving persons, and it can offer only imperfect protection because it only applies to persons who have already committed the prohibited acts.[134]

Torture Law

The Torture Convention expressly prohibits Member States from returning an alien to a state that would torture him.[135] Similar injunctions have been inferred from the less explicit provisions of the ICCPR[136] and the ECHR[137] and the principle has been identified as part of customary international law.[138]

---

[131] Refugee Convention, *supra* note 123, at Art. 1(F).

[132] See OAU Refugee Convention, *supra* note 123, at Art. 1.

[133] The drafters took differing views as to what might constitute acts contrary to the purposes and principles of the United Nations, with some pointing to war criminals or violators of human rights, and others additionally positing wartime collaboration with the Nazis. See N. Robinson, *Convention Relating to the Status of Refugees: Its History, Components and Interpretation* (1953) p. 69. However, there are numerous United Nations treaties condemning various types of terrorism, *see supra* note 6, and the Security Council has expressly declared that such acts are contrary to the United Nations' purposes and principles. See U.N. SCOR Res. 13773 5, 28 September 2001, U.N. Doc. No. S/Res/1373.

[134] See Robinson, *supra* note 133, at 66 (noting that "Section F treats persons who fulfill the conditions [for refugee status] but are not deemed to be worthy of international protection"); Hathaway and Harvey, *supra* note 126, at 296 (noting that "Article 1(F) and Article 33(2) of the Refugee Convention are intended to further two distinct goals ... [s]pecifically, the duty of peremptory exclusion under Article 1(F)(b) applies only to persons who are fugitives from domestic justice – their crimes must have been committed outside the asylum state, remain justiciable, and justify a grant of extradition. The right of particularized refoulement under Article 33(2), on the other hand, entitles state parties to defend their most basic interests in safety and security."); N. Yakoob, "Note: Political Offender or Serious Criminal? Challenging the Interpretation of 'Serious, Nonpolitical Crimes,' *in INS* v. *Aguirre-Aguirre*," 14 *Georgetown Immigration Law Journal* (2000) pp. 545, 567 (noting that "it is important to clarify ... the different functions of the exclusion clauses ... and the exceptions to the *non-refoulement* provision. In the broader context of state discretion, the exclusion clauses, including the serious nonpolitical crimes exception, establish categories of individuals undeserving of refugee protection. The exceptions to the bar on *refoulement*, however, recognize situations where concerns for state sovereignty override the state's obligation to prevent the return of individuals to areas where they would suffer persecution.").

[135] Torture Convention, *supra* note 123, at Art. 3.

[136] See Human Rights Committee, General Comment 20 (Art. 7), at 9 (1992), reproduced in Compilation of General Comments and General Recommendations Adopted by Human Rights Treaty Bodies, U.N. Doc. HRI\GEN\1\Rev.1 at 30 (1994) (concluding that "States parties must not expose individuals to the danger of torture or cruel, inhuman or degrading treatment or punishment upon return to another country by way of their extradition, expulsion or *refoulement*").

[137] Although the European Court of Human Rights has not yet directly addressed the effect of Art. 3 of the ECHR on the admission of aliens, it has made clear that expulsion or extradition to states where the alien faces torture is absolutely prohibited. See *Soering* v. *United Kingdom* (1989) 11 *EHRR* 439 88. It may be presumed, therefore, that a similar rule would apply to the question of initial entry.

[138] See Nowak, *supra* note 72, at 137.

There is no security limitation on the right of *non-refoulement* in the Torture Convention and the treaty expressly disavows any possibility of derogation.[139] The Committee Against Torture (the monitoring body for the Torture Convention) has criticized the laws of several states that provide for such an exception.[140] The Committee has also made clear that the bases for exclusion from refugee status enumerated in Article 1(F) of the Convention Relating to the Status of Refugees are inapplicable to the Torture Convention, insisting that "[t]he test of Article 3 of the [Torture Convention] is absolute."[141]

Similarly, the European Court of Human Rights has expressly rejected the argument that the security of the host state limits an alien's right not to be sent to a state where he will be subject to torture.[142] On the other hand, the Court has also made clear that the right of *non-refoulement* does not prohibit the state from taking other actions otherwise permissible under human rights law, such as detention or other restrictions on movement under appropriate circumstances, to protect itself from security threats who cannot be sent home.[143]

Trade Law

At the Uruguay Round in 1994, participating states promulgated the General Agreement on Trade in Services (GATS),[144] the first multilateral agreement governing international trade in services. One of the modes of the trade in services covered by the GATS is the temporary movement of natural persons across borders for the purpose of providing services.[145] Member States committed themselves through individual schedules to allow entry of business visitors, intra-corporate transferees, and certain types of foreign professionals.[146]

Article XIV bis of GATS provides in relevant part that "[n]othing in this Agreement shall be construed ... to prevent any Member from taking any action which it

---

[139] See Torture Convention, *supra* note 123, at Art. 2(2).

[140] See CAT/C/SR.12 21 and 27; CAT/C/SR.13 27, available at www1.umn.edu/humanrts; Summary of the 126th Session: New Zealand, at 51, 30 September 1993, UN Doc. No. CAT/C/SR.126; CAT/C/24/8 8 and 22. See also *Chahal* v. *United Kingdom*, 1996-V Eur. Ct. H.R. 1831 (holding that national security cannot justify expulsion where torture is likely in the receiving state).

[141] See *Paez* v. *Sweden*, CAT Comm. No. 39/96 14.4. and 14.5, available at www1.umn.edu/humanrts/cat/decisions/39-1996.html. For a general discussion of Committee Against Torture "jurisprudence" in this area, see B. Gorlick, "The Convention and the Committee Against Torture: A Complementary Protection Regime for Refugees," 11 *International Journal of Refugee Law* (2000) p. 479.

[142] See *Chahal, supra* note 140, at 80.

[143] See discussion of detention and internal movement, *infra*.

[144] Marrakesh Agreement Establishing the World Trade Organization, Annex 1B, Legal Instruments – Results of the Uruguay Round, 33 *ILM* 1168 (1994).

[145] See General Agreement on Trade in Services (hereinafter "GATS"), 15 April 1994, Art. I(2)(d), 33 *ILM* 1167 (1994). The GATS does not apply to persons crossing a border to seek employment and/or permanent residence. See Annex on Movement of Natural Persons Supplying Services Under the Agreement, Art. 2.

[146] This area of the GATS has undergone continuous negotiation since 1994. In 1995, the Third Protocol to the General Agreement on Trade in Services was promulgated updating the previously published schedules.

considers necessary for the protection of its essential security interests" relating to provisioning of the military, relating to fissionable and fusionable materials, or "taken in time of war or other emergency in international relations."[147] This language was drawn verbatim from Article XXI of the General Agreement on Tariffs and Trade of 1947 (GATT).[148]

Article XIV bis of GATS has not yet been formally invoked. Its counterpart in the GATT, albeit much older, has only infrequently arisen, and its scope has not been defined by the dispute resolution body.[149] Some states have asserted that each nation is the sole judge of its national security interests and that assertions of national security under the GATT are therefore non-justiciable by the GATT dispute resolution body.[150] Other states dispute this interpretation, but the GATT as a whole has not yet decisively determined the issue.[151] Thus, although the language of the exception appears to be somewhat restrictive, its application might become quite broad.

The North American Free Trade Agreement (NAFTA) signed in 1992 between the United States, Canada, and Mexico contains a provision obligating parties to allow "temporary entry" to certain types of "business persons."[152] However, this obligation is directly qualified by the requirement that such persons must be "otherwise qualified" under "applicable measures relating to – national security[.]"[153] NAFTA also includes a general security exception using language similar to GATS Article XIV bis and GATT Article XXI.[154]

Regional Integration Law

The European Union boasts the world's most ambitious regional agreements concerning the free movement of persons across international borders. Yet, even here, national security may trump the right to enter. Article 48 of the Treaty of Rome pro-

---

[147] GATS, *supra* note 145, at Art. XIV bis (1)(b). Likewise, the Annex on Movement of Natural Persons Supplying Services Under the Agreement provides that "[t]he Agreement shall not prevent a Member from applying measures to regulate the entry of natural persons into, or their temporary stay in, its territory, including those measures necessary to protect the integrity of, and to ensure the orderly movement of natural persons across its borders."

[148] 30 October 1947, 61 Stat. A-11, *TIAS* 1700, 55 *UNTS* 194.

[149] See J.H. Jackson, W.J. Davey, and A. O. Sykes Jr., *Legal Problems of International Economic Relations* (4th edn. 2002) p. 1046; R. Bhala, "National Security and International Trade Law: What the GATT Says and What the United States Does," 19 *University of Pennsylvania Journal of International Economic Law* (1998) p. 263. See also Unpublished Panel Report on United States – Trade Measures Affecting Nicaragua, 1986 WL 363154 K/6053, pp. 5.2, 5.15 (13 October 1986) (unadopted).

[150] See W.A. Cann, Jr., "Creating Standards and Accountability for the Use of the WTO Security Exception: Reducing the Role of Power-Based Relations and Establishing a New Balance Between Sovereignty and Multilateralism," 26 *Yale Journal of International Law* (2001) p. 413 (citing the United States, Canada, Japan, New Zealand, Australia, and the European Union).

[151] Id.

[152] North American Free Trade Agreement (hereinafter, "NAFTA"), 17 December 1992, Art. 1603, 32 *ILM* 289 (1993).

[153] Id. Art. 1601 of NAFTA makes clear that "the need for border security" is one of the agreement's primary objectives.

[154] See NAFTA, *supra* note 152, at Art. 2012.

vided for free movement of European nationals within Europe without discrimination as to employment.[155] Article 48(3) provided that this freedom may be infringed for reasons of "public policy, public security, or public health."[156] The European Court of Justice has interpreted these provisions to require a "genuine and sufficiently serious" threat to the "fundamental interests of society" before a European national's freedom of movement may be infringed.[157] Moreover, EU citizens may only be barred from entry for their personal conduct.[158] A prior criminal record is not a ground for exclusion unless it is indicative of a current threat.[159] While there is a margin of appreciation as to the scope of the exceptions, the overriding importance of the right of free movement requires strict interpretation.[160] The 1997 Treaty of Amsterdam, which incorporates the Treaty of Rome, the 1985 and 1990 Schengen Agreements (eliminating internal borders within Member States), and the 1992 Treaty of Maastricht, recodifies the provisions of Article 48 of the Treaty of Rome, including the provisions concerning "public security."[161]

The Americas, Mercosur, the Andean Community, and the Caribbean Community are all taking steps toward free movement areas. For example, in 2001, the Andean Council of Foreign Ministers reached Decision No. 503 allowing nationals and permanent residents of Member States to visit other Member States as tourists (without employment rights) using only national identification (rather than externally issued visas). Article 2 provides that such persons "shall enjoy the same rights as the citizens of the Member Country in which they find themselves, without prejudice to domestic provisions on immigration, the domestic order, *national security*, and public health" (emphasis added).

In Africa, the Economic Community of West African States (ECOWAS) agreed to permit the free movement of persons within the Member States in both the Treaty of Lagos 1975 and its 1979 Protocol.[162] However, the Protocol provides that any member may refuse to admit a person based solely on local law.[163] Thus, a state need merely pass a local law concerning security to avoid its obligations with regard to ECOWAS migration.

---

[155] Treaty Establishing the European Economic Community, Art. 48, 298 *UNTS* 3 (1957).

[156] Id. See also Council Directive 64/221.

[157] See *Rutili* v. *Minister for the Interior* (1982) 62 *ILR* 390 at 28.

[158] See id.; Case 41/74 *Van Duyn* v. *Home Office* [1974] *ECHR* 1337, see also S. Peers, "Towards Equality: Actual and Potential Rights of Third-Country Nationals in the European Union," *in* S. Goulbourne (ed.), *Law and Migration* (1998) p. 46.

[159] See D. Pollard, "Rights of Free Movement," *in* N. Neuwahl and A. Rosas (eds.), *The European Union and Human Rights* (1995) p. 112 (citing Directive 64/221, Art. 3; Case 30/77, *Regina* v. *Bouchereau* [1977] ECR 1999; Case 131/79, *Regina* v. *Secretary of State for Home Affairs* [1980] ECR 1585; and Case 67/74, *Bonsignore* v. *Stadt Köln* [1975] ECR 297). See also *Proll* v. *Entry Clearance Officer, Dusseldorf* [1988] 2 *CMLR* 387 (holding that a German national's prior conviction could not serve as a per se basis for her exclusion from the United Kingdom in light of the freedom of movement of EU workers).

[160] See Pollard, *supra* note 159, at 114 (citing *Van Duyn*, *Rutili*, and *Bouchereau*).

[161] See Treaty of Amsterdam, *supra* note 32, at Art. 39.

[162] See C. Beyani, *Human Rights Standards and the Free Movement of Peoples Within States* (2000) pp. 52-53.

[163] Id.

The South African Development Community (SADC) has adopted two protocols designed to remove barriers to movement within the region. In 1995, the SADC approved a Draft Protocol on the Free Movement of Persons in the Southern African Development Community that called for the eventual elimination of internal borders.[164] The Protocol contained no specific exception for security, although it allowed for members to apply for exemptions to the SADC as a whole for a limited time period.[165] In 1997, the much less ambitious Draft Protocol on the Facilitation of Movement of Persons in the Southern African Development Community was adopted. The Draft Protocol provides for cooperation between members, *inter alia*, in border controls. Neither of these protocols has entered into force.

Control of Exit

Human Rights and Refugee Law

The right to leave a country is provided for in a number of the major human rights and refugee instruments and applies to both nationals and aliens.[166] In all of the binding instruments, however, the right to leave is subject to a clawback for restrictions that are provided by law, and necessary for the maintenance of public order (*ordre public*), public safety, or national security.[167]

Limitations on the right to leave have been successfully justified in the Human Rights Committee on national security grounds for military personnel, persons subject to a mandatory national service requirement, and persons subject to criminal proceedings or sentences.[168] In contrast, the Human Rights Committee has criticized states prohibiting individuals with access to state secrets from leaving on a national security rationale.[169] Some scholars maintain that limitations on the right to leave under the rubric of "public order" may include "minors, paupers, persons under legal disability, fugitives from justice, persons under court restraining orders, habitual

---

[164] See H. Solomon, *Toward the Free Movement of People in Southern Africa?*, Institute for Security Studies Occasional Paper No. 18 (1997), available at http://www.iss.co.za/Pubs/PAPERS/18/Paper18.html.

[165] See Beyani, *supra* note 162, at 55.

[166] See African Charter, *supra* note 69, at Art. 12; American Declaration, *supra* note 83, at Art. 8; American Convention, *supra* note 69, at Art. 22; CERD, *supra* note 83, at Art. 5(d)(ii); ECHR protocol 4, *supra* note 83, at Art. 2; ICCPR, *supra* note 69, at Art. 12; ICMW, *supra* note 93, at Art. 8; UDHR, *supra* note 78, at Art. 13(2); see also Refugee Convention, *supra* note 123, at Art. 28. For a commentary, see the paper of Vincent Chetail in this volume.

[167] See African Charter, *supra* note 69, at Art. 12(2); American Convention, *supra* note 69, at Art. 22(3); ECHR protocol 4, *supra* note 83, at Art. 2(3); ICCPR, *supra* note 69, at Art. 12(3). Each of these instruments has slightly different additional requirements.

[168] See Jagerskiold, *supra* note 70, at 178; A. Grahl-Madsen, G. Melander, and R. Ring, "Article 13," *in* G. Alfredsson and A. Eide (eds.), *The Universal Declaration of Human Rights* (1999) p. 274); *Gonzalez del Rio* v. *Peru*, Comm. No. 263/1987 (noting that a state may legitimately withhold a passport to a national subject to criminal proceedings, but not if those proceedings are unreasonably delayed); *Peltonen* v. *Finland*, Communication No. 492/1992 (concluding that a state may withhold a passport to a citizen who has failed to complete national military service).

[169] See General Comment No. 27, *supra* note 120, at 16.

criminals, and persons whose conduct is prejudicial to orderly conduct of the internal affairs of the State."[170]

In practice, many states continue to restrain the right to leave, most notably through restrictions on the issuance or scope of passports.[171] For example, prior to 1978, the United States frequently imposed geographic area restrictions on its passports.[172] The law was amended in 1978 to allow such restrictions only for "countr[ies] with which the United States is at war, where armed hostilities are in progress, or where there is imminent danger to the public health or the physical safety of United States travelers."[173] However, the United States has subsequently acted more indirectly to restrain travel, by, for example, severely limiting financial transactions incident to travel to and from Cuba, Iraq, and Libya by its own citizens and permanent residents.[174]

Humanitarian Law

In international armed conflicts, the Fourth Geneva Convention requires belligerents to allow alien civilians to leave their territories unless doing so would be "contrary to the national interests of the State."[175] Under the Third Geneva Convention, certain gravely injured prisoners of war must be directly repatriated to their home countries after receiving care – even during active hostilities – so long as the prisoners are willing.[176] Others who are less grievously wounded may be interned in neutral countries.[177] Upon termination of hostilities, all prisoners of war must be repatriated "without delay" to their home countries.[178]

Internal Regulation of Migrants

Human Rights

Like all other persons, migrants are guaranteed basic rights by international and regional human rights instruments.[179] Moreover, the International Labor Organization has adopted several instruments specifically pertaining to the rights of migrants[180]

---

[170] See Beyani, *supra* note 162, at 26 (citing J. Ingles, Study of the Right of Everyone to Leave Any Country, Including His Own, and to Return to His Country, E/CN.4/Sub.2/220 (1963), at 49).

[171] See Goodwin-Gill, *supra* note 82, at 170-173.

[172] See *Zemel* v. *Rusk*, 381 U.S. 1. 8-12 (1965) (describing the history of such area restrictions).

[173] See Passport Act, 22 U.S.C. para. 211a (2000).

[174] See 31 C.F.R. paras. 515.560 (Cuba); 550.207 (Libya); 575.207 (Iraq) (2001); see also *Regan* v. *Wald*, 468 U.S. 222 (1984) (upholding the U.S. rule from constitutional attack).

[175] See Geneva Convention Relative to the Protection of Civilian Persons in Time of War (hereinafter "GC IV"), 12 August 1949, Art. 35, 75 *UNTS* 287.

[176] Geneva Convention Relative to the Treatment of Prisoners of War (hereinafter "GC III"), Arts. 109-110, 12 August 1949, 75 *UNTS* 135.

[177] Id.

[178] Id. at Art. 118.

[179] See generally the contribution of Joan Fitzpatrick in this volume.

[180] See, e.g., Migration for Employment Convention (Revised) (ILO No. 97) of 1949; Recommendation No. 86 concerning Migration for Employment (revised) of 1949, and the Migrant Workers Convention (ILO No. 143) of 1975.

and, in 1990, the United Nations adopted the International Convention on the Protection of the Rights of All Migrant Workers and Members of their Families (ICMW) (which has recently obtained enough ratifications to enter into force).[181]

As noted above, a number of the basic rights provided by the major human rights instruments are subject to clawbacks for national security and public order ("*ordre public*"). The rights so limited are the right to a public trial;[182] the right to manifest religious beliefs;[183] the right to freedom of expression;[184] the right to peaceful assembly;[185] the right to freedom of association;[186] and the right of freedom of movement.[187] The ECHR additionally limits the right to respect for private and family life for security purposes.[188]

Most rights provided by the ICCPR, the American Convention, and the ECHR are subject to derogation.[189] However, these conventions reserve some rights as "non-derogable," even in time of emergency.[190] The number and type of such rights differ in the various instruments. The ECHR provides for four non-derogable rights: the right to life; the right to be free of torture; the right to be free of slavery; and the right not to be convicted of violation of any ex post facto law.[191] The ICCPR additionally prohibits derogation of the right to be free of medical experimentation; the right to be free of imprisonment for a contractual obligation; the right to recognition as a person before the law; and the right to freedom of thought, conscience, and religion.[192] The Human Rights Committee concluded that the right to procedural guarantees, "including, often, judicial guarantees" and an adequate remedy are inherent in the explicitly listed non-derogable rights.[193] The American Convention has the longest list of non-derogable rights. In addition to those noted above, the American Convention lists the rights of the family; the right to a name; the rights of the child; the right to nationality; the right to participate in government; and the right to judicial guarantees essential for the protection of all non-derogable rights.[194]

Migrants' rights with respect to detention and internal movement are of particular concern after 11 September. The major human rights instruments protecting civil

---

[181] U.N. Doc. A/RES/45/158, 30 *ILM* 1517 (1991).

[182] ICCPR, *supra* note 69, at Art. 14(1); ECHR, *supra* note 69, at Art. 6(1).

[183] American Convention, *supra* note 69, at Art. 12(3); ICCPR, *supra* note 69, at Art. 18(3); ECHR, *supra* note 69, at Art. 9(2).

[184] ICCPR, *supra* note 69, at Art. 19(3); ECHR, *supra* note 69, at Art. 10.

[185] American Convention, *supra* note 69, at Art. 15; ICCPR, *supra* note 69, at Art. 21; ECHR, *supra* note 69, at Art. 11.

[186] American Convention, *supra* note 69, at Art. 16(2); ICCPR, *supra* note 69, at Art. 22(2); ECHR, *supra* note 69, at Art. 11.

[187] American Convention, *supra* note 69, at Art. 22(3); ICCPR, *supra* note 69, at Art. 12(3); ECHR protocol 4, *supra* note 83, at Art. 2(3).

[188] ECHR, *supra* note 88, at Art. 8(2).

[189] See *supra* note 74.

[190] See American Convention, *supra* note 69, at Art. 27(2); ECHR, *supra* note 69, at Art. 15(2); ICCPR, *supra* note 69, at Art. 4(2).

[191] See ECHR, *supra* note 69, at Art. 12(2).

[192] See ICCPR, *supra* note 69, at Art. 4(2).

[193] See General Comment No. 29, *supra* note 78, at 14-16.

[194] See American Convention, *supra* note 69, at Art. 27(2).

rights uniformly prohibit arbitrary detention of anyone, including legal and illegal aliens.[195] Detention of aliens incident to the enforcement of immigration laws is expressly permitted by the ECHR,[196] and has been accepted under the other instruments.[197] However, in order to be considered non-arbitrary, such detention may only be for a reasonable amount of time necessary for adjudication of the alien's status[198] and any alien so detained must be informed of the reasons of his detention, allowed access to counsel, consular officers, and relatives, and afforded access to a court.[199]

Although no specific clawback for security is included in the detention provisions, states have claimed, and been accorded, somewhat greater leeway in the detention of migrants deemed security threats.[200] The American Convention, the ECHR, and the ICCPR do not make clear whether security-related "administrative detention" (i.e., detention of security threats by order of the executive, without charge or trial) is permissible.[201] Many states' domestic law permits such detention, even outside of times of emergency.[202] However, the Human Rights Committee and other commentators have asserted that administrative detention should not be allowed absent a public emergency.[203]

The prohibition against arbitrary detention is not included as a non-derogable right in the American Convention, the ECHR, or the ICCPR. However, even in a state of emergency, indefinite detention and detention without any access to judicial review is arguably prohibited. The Inter-American Court of Human Rights has taken this position, as have a number of commentators.[204] Moreover, inasmuch as deroga-

---

[195] See African Charter, *supra* note 69, at Art. 6; American Convention, *supra* note 69, at Art. 7; ICCPR, *supra* note 69, at Art. 9; ECHR, *supra* note 69, at Art. 5; UDHR, *supra* note 78, at Art. 3, ICMW, *supra* note 93, at Art. 16.

[196] See ECHR, *supra* note 88, at Art. 5(1)(f).

[197] See, e.g., *A. v. Australia*, *supra* note 87, at 9.3 (concluding that it is not *per se* arbitrary to detain asylum-seekers).

[198] See id.; Human Rights Committee Concluding Remarks, at 15, UN. Doc. No. CCPR/C/79/Add.70 (1996); *Chahal*, *supra* note 140, at 113.

[199] See United Nations Commission on Human Rights Working Group on Arbitrary Detention, Body of Principles of the Protection of All Persons under Any Form Of Detention or Imprisonment Regarding the Situation of Immigrants and Asylum-Seekers, U.N. Doc. No. E/CN.4/2000/4/Annex 2 (1999) (setting forth "guarantees" relevant to the determination whether detention of an immigrant or asylum-seeker is arbitrary); see also Human Rights Committee General Comment No. 8 at 1 (1982), reprinted *in* Compilation of General Comments and General Recommendations Adopted by Human Rights Treaty Bodies, U.N. Doc. HRI\GEN\1\Rev.1 at 8 (1994) (noting that ICCPR Art. 9's requirement of judicial control applies to immigration-related detention as well as to criminal cases).

[200] See *Chahal*, *supra* note 140, at 120-123, 132 (approving a six-year period of detention while the state attempted to deport a suspected terrorist). See also Cameron, *supra* note 5, at 283 (noting that the "[t]he standards of 'non-arbitrariness' are ... set rather low" and that the *Chahal* decision "indicates ... that very long periods of detention pending deportation can be acceptable under Article 5(1)(f)").

[201] See J. Fitzpatrick, *Human Rights in Crisis: The International System for Protecting Rights During States Emergency* (1994) p. 45.

[202] Id.

[203] See id. at 45-46 (citing the Special Rapporteur on States of Emergency and the International Commission of Jurists); Human Rights Committee, General Comment No. 8, *supra* note 199, at 4 (noting that "so-called preventive detention" is subject to the same requirements as other types of detention).

[204] See Oraa, *supra* note 75, at 110 (citing the Inter-American Court, the Siracusa Principles, the Special Rapporteur on Emergencies, and the ILA).

tion may not be carried out in a discriminatory manner,[205] states may not derogate from migrant's liberty rights without also doing so for their own nationals unless they can produce reasonable and objective criteria justifying the distinction.[206]

In addition to the right of personal liberty, the ICCPR provides for the freedom of internal movement to persons "lawfully within the territory of a State," subject, as noted above, to restrictions based on reasons of national security and public order.[207] The other binding instruments have similar provisions,[208] as does the ICMW.[209] Thus, aliens who are not lawfully within the territory of the state do not enjoy this right, and may have their range of movement restricted to a particular zone.[210] "Legal" aliens may suffer similar restrictions if the requirements of the limitations provisions are met.

Refugee Law

The Refugee Convention does not explicitly address the issue of detention of asylum-seekers. The UNHCR has urged states to make detention of asylum-seekers and refugees "an exception, not the rule," but acknowledges that detention for purposes of national security and public order is permissible.[211] The Refugee Convention expressly protects refugees' right of movement within the host country, but this right

---

[205] See *supra* note 96.

[206] The United Kingdom's Special Commission on Immigration Appeals recently came to such a conclusion in a case involving detention of aliens under the United Kingdom post-September 11 Anti-Terrorism Crime & Security Act. The Commission noted that the United Kingdom had announced its derogation from Art. 5 of the ECHR, but not Art. 14 (concerning discrimination) and that the Anti-Terror law expressly allowed detention of aliens but not of citizens in similar circumstances. Accordingly, the Commission determined that the Act was contrary to the ECHR. See *Nine UK Terror Suspects Win Appeal*, CNN.com (30 July 2002), at www.cnn.com. See also SIAC Press Release, available at www.statewatch.org. The UK plans to appeal the ruling to a higher national court.

[207] See ICCPR, *supra* note 69, at Art. 12(1).

[208] See African Charter, *supra* note 69, at art 12(1); American Convention, *supra* note 69, at Art. 22(1), (3); CERD, *supra* note 83, at Art. 5(d)(i) (concerning equal enjoyment of the right); ECHR protocol 4, *supra* note 83, at Art. 2(1). See also Convention Relating to the Status of Stateless Persons, Art. 26 (conditioning the right of internal movement for stateless persons on "any regulations applicable to aliens generally in the same circumstances"). Several of the non-binding instruments describe this right but do not expressly condition it on public safety. See American Declaration, *supra* note 83, at Art. 8; UDHR, *supra* note 78, at Art. 13(1).

[209] See ICMW, *supra* note 93, at Art. 3. The ICMW makes clear that the right of internal movement is limited to lawfully-present aliens by placing rights for "all" migrant workers and "documented" migrant workers in separate sections of the treaty.

[210] See *U. v. Sweden,* No. 1334/87, Decision of 5 July 1989 (European Human Rights Commission) (alien under order of deportation may be restricted pending the expulsion) and *Aygün v. Sweden*, No. 14102/88, 63 DR 195 (1989); Cameron, *supra* note 5, at 278-279; *Celepi v. Sweden*, Communication No. 456/91 (Human Rights Committee); see also American Convention, *supra* note 69, at Art. 22(4) (providing that the right of movement "may also be restricted by law in designated zones for reasons of public interest").

[211] See UNHCR Executive Committee, Detention of Asylum-Seekers and Refugees: The Framework, the Problem and the Recommended Practice, 4 June 1999, at 7, 14, U.N. Doc. EC/49/SC/CRP.13.

can likewise be denied for "compelling reasons of national security or public order[.]"[212]

The Refugee Convention also requires Member States to accord refugees access to the courts;[213] identification and travel documents[214] and protection against discrimination;[215] the same treatment as nationals in the enjoyment of certain rights (such as the rights of freedom of religion,[216] artistic expression,[217] and access to rationed items[218]); and the same treatment as other aliens in the enjoyment of certain other rights (such as the rights to own property,[219] to associate with others,[220] and to seek employment[221]). With the exception of the right to travel documents, none of these rights are directly conditioned by the state's interest in national security or public order. However, Article 9 of the Refugee Convention allows states to take "provisional measures" in "time or war or other grave and exceptional circumstances" for purposes of safeguarding national security.

Humanitarian Law

The Fourth Geneva Convention provides that during international armed conflicts in belligerent states, aliens must be given not only the same rights as aliens in peacetime, but certain additional rights, such as the ability to find alternative employment if they lose their jobs due to the war.[222] However, if the security of the state "makes it absolutely necessary" aliens may be interned or "placed in assigned residence."[223] In this regard, however, stateless persons and refugees are not to be considered enemy nationals if they no longer enjoy the protection of their home countries, and they may not be returned (*refoulé*) to those countries against their will.[224]

The Third Geneva Convention allows for prolonged detention of combatants pending hostilities.[225] The extent to which these provisions might apply to suspected terrorists, and the issue whether the provisions of the human rights treaties have some overlapping control in such circumstances, is currently the subject of intense debate.[226]

---

[212] See Refugee Convention, *supra* note 123, at Art. 26.

[213] Id. at Art. 16.

[214] Id. at Arts. 27-28.

[215] Id. at Art. 3.

[216] Id. at Art. 4.

[217] Id. at Art. 14.

[218] Id. at Art. 20.

[219] Id. at Art. 13.

[220] Id. at Art. 15.

[221] Id. at Art. 17.

[222] See GC IV, *supra* note 175, at Arts. 38-39.

[223] See id. at Art. 42.

[224] See id. at Art. 44; Protocol I Art. 73.

[225] GC III, *supra* note 176, at Art. 118.

[226] See, e.g., "Agora: Military Commissions," 96 *AJIL* (2002) p. 320 (collecting opposing views on this and related issues).

Expulsion

Human Rights

Procedural Protections

Under Article 13 of the ICCPR and Protocol 7 of the ECHR, aliens lawfully present in a state are entitled to procedural protections prior to being expelled, including review by a competent authority and the opportunity to submit reasons against the expulsion.[227] These procedural rights, however, may be denied if national security so requires.[228] Although the Human Rights Committee has repeatedly indicated that it will not "test a sovereign State's evaluation of an alien's security rating,"[229] it has rejected national security justifications for summary expulsion where the state failed to make any showing as to why extreme measures were required.[230] The European Court of Human Rights has offered little guidance on the national security exception in this context; scholars, however, have urged that an objective showing of the security need should be required.[231]

Substantive Bars on Expulsion

As with denial of entry, expulsion may implicate the right to respect for family life, the best interests of the child, and the prohibition against discrimination. In fact, most of the commentary and case law from the treaty bodies in this area concerns deportation or extradition.[232]

---

[227] See ICCPR, *supra* note 69, at Art. 13; Protocol No. 7 to the Convention for the Protection of Human Rights and Fundamental Freedoms (hereinafter "ECHR protocol 7"), 22 November 1984, Art. 12(4), 24 *ILM* 435, 436. Compare African Charter, *supra* note 69, at Art. 12(4) (providing merely that an alien may be expelled only pursuant to law); American Convention, *supra* note 69, at art 22(6) (same).

[228] See ICCPR, *supra* note 69, at Art. 13 (requiring "compelling reasons"); ECHR protocol 7, *supra* note 227, at Art. 1(2).

[229] See *V.M.R.B.* v. *Canada*, Comm. No. 236/1987, U.N. Doc. CCPR/C/33/236/1987 (1987) at 6.3; *J.R.C.* v. *Costa Rica* 296/1988 at 8.4, available at www1.umn.edu.

[230] In *Giry* v. *Dominican Republic*, Comm. No. 193/1985, 95 *ILR* 321 (1990), the Dominican Republic intercepted the author at the airport as he attempted to buy a ticket for Saint-Bartholemy and unceremoniously forced him onto a flight to Puerto Rico where he was apprehended by American agents on drug charges. The Committee dismissed the Dominican Republic's argument that summary expulsion was necessary for security reasons, noting that "it was the author's very intention to leave the Dominican Republic at his own volition for another destination." Id. at 5.5. Similarly, in *Hammel* v. *Madagascar,* Comm. No. 155/11983, 3 April 1987, U.N. Doc. Supp. No. 40 (A/42/40), the Committee concluded that the state had violated Art. 13 in expelling an attorney apparently because he had represented clients in prior cases before the Human Rights Committee, and that the state had failed to make any showing of security requiring summary expulsion.

[231] See Cameron, *supra* note 5, at 430-432.

[232] The Human Rights Committee has noted that "[e]xtradition as such is outside the scope of application of the Covenant," but that if an person's rights under the ICCPR are foreseeably violated as a result of a decision to extradite, the state may be in violation of its obligations. See *Charles Chitat Ng* v. *Canada*, Comm. No. 469/1991 U.N. Doc. CCPR/C/49/D/469/1991 (1994) (holding that it violated Canada's obligations under ICCPR Art. 7 to extradite a person to the United States where he

With regard to respect for family life, the European Court of Human Rights has indicated that it will not accept at face value a state's assertion of the danger posed by a particular family member.[233] Moreover, in order for the expulsion of a family member to be justified, it must be "necessary," meaning that the states' interest (for example, in preventing crime and disorder) must be motivated by a "pressing social need" that outweighs, on balance, the affected persons' interest in family unity.[234] Thus, the mere fact that an alien has been convicted of a crime may not be sufficient to justify deportation if the circumstances render the alien's interests in remaining particularly strong and/or the prior conviction does not necessarily demonstrate a criminal propensity.[235]

With regard to discrimination among aliens in deportation proceedings, however, the European Court has afforded states a fairly wide "margin of appreciation." For example, in *Moustaquim* v. *Belgium*, the Court rejected the argument by a Moroccan resident of Belgium that his deportation after conviction of a crime was discriminatory because a citizen of an EU country would not have been subject to deportation on the same basis, noting that there was "[an] objective and reasonable justification ... as Belgium belongs, together with those States, to a special legal order."[236]

The Human Rights Committee has taken a similarly restricted approach, rejecting claims of discrimination by persons deported for security reasons.[237] As noted above, the Committee has indicated that it will not "test a sovereign State's evaluation of an alien's security rating."[238] However, approval of the states' action by the Committee has not been inevitable; the state wishing to discriminate for security purposes must still make a convincing showing as to the reason for the discrimination.[239]

---

might be subject to execution by gas asphyxiation). The European Court of Human Rights has come to a similar conclusion with regard to the ECHR. See, e.g., *Soering* v. *United Kingdom*, 11 Eur. Ct. H.R. 439 (1989) (holding that the United Kingdom would violate Art. 3 of the ECHR if it extradited to the United States to face the "inhumanly" long delays associated with death penalty jurisprudence in that country).

[233] See *Moustaquim* v. *Belgium* (1991) 13 *EHRR* 802 (holding that Belgium had failed to demonstrate that a deportee's years-old juvenile infractions demonstrated a present propensity to crime).

[234] See *Beldjoudi* v. *France* (1992) 14 *EHRR* 801 at 74.

[235] See id. at 75-80; *Moustaquim*, *supra* note 233; *Nasri* v. *France* (1996), 21 *EHRR* 458 at 46; but see *Boughanemi* v. *France* (1996) 22 *EHRR* 228 (holding on balance that conviction carrying a sentence of four years imprisonment was sufficiently serious to outweigh a deportees' right to respect for family); Madureira, *supra* note 94, at 12 (discussing an unpublished European Commission on Human Rights decision upholding the denial of entry of an alien with a criminal record notwithstanding his claim for family unity).

[236] See *Moustaquim, supra* note 233. The Court held, however, that his deportation was in violation of the ECHR on other grounds.

[237] See, e.g., *Celepi* v. *Sweden*, Comm. No. 456/1991, 2 August 1994, U.N. Doc. CCPR/C/51/D/456/1991 (rejecting the authors claim that his deportation for security reasons constituted discrimination); *V.M.R.B, supra* note 229 (concluding that "the author ha[d] failed to establish how the deportation of an alien on national security grounds constitutes discrimination").

[238] See *V.M.R.B.*, *supra* note 229, at 3.

[239] See *Aumeeruddy-Cziffra* v. *Mauritius*, Comm. No. 35/1978, 9 April 1981, U.N. Doc. No. CCPR/C/12/D/35/1978 at 9.2(b)2(ii)3 (noting that "[t]hough it might be justified for Mauritius to restrict the access of aliens to their [sic] territory and to expel them therefrom for security reasons, the Committee is of the view that the legislation which only subjects foreign spouses of Mauritian women to those restrictions, but not foreign spouses of Mauritian men, is discriminatory with respect to Mauritian women and cannot be justified by security requirements").

Refugee and Torture Law

In addition to prohibiting *refoulement* of persons facing persecution, the Refugee Convention, the Torture Convention, and comparable provisions of some regional instruments prohibit states from deporting or extraditing persons in such circumstances. However, under Article 32 of the Refugee Convention, aliens may be expelled for reasons of national security and public order, and such expulsions may be ordered without a hearing for the refugee if "compelling reasons of national security" so require. No such exception exists in the African Refugee Convention. Likewise, under the Torture Convention and the ECHR, no one may be sent to any country where they would be subject to torture.[240] There is no exception for national security.[241]

Humanitarian Law

In situations of both internal and international armed conflict, armed factions are forbidden to engage in deportations or transfers (i.e., internal displacement) of civilians "regardless of their motive" for reasons other than immediate military necessity and/or to protect the safety of those civilians.[242] In the event of justified evacuations, the civilians must be allowed to return to their homes as soon as practicable.[243]

CONCLUSION

The effects of globalization and the events of 11 September 2001 highlighted the need for states to enhance cooperation with each other in law enforcement and immigration control activities. New law in both areas, which should soon be coming into force, will bind states to criminalize acts inimical to border security, such as migrant smuggling and trafficking, and require states to act affirmatively in the collective interest of the international community by ensuring the integrity of their own travel documents and border controls. States are also becoming more willing to allow each other to screen incoming migrants at the point of embarkation, through carrier sanctions, preinspection regimes, and agreements concerning the interdiction of vessels.

States' interests in protecting themselves must be balanced against their interests in participating in the global labor market and in protecting the rights of migrants themselves. This balance has been written directly into international law concerning human rights, refugee rights, labor integration, trade law, and humanitarian law through security exceptions and other qualifications of migration-related rights. For the most part, international courts and monitoring institutions have accorded states

---

[240] See Torture Convention, *supra* note 123, at Art. 3; ECHR, *supra* note 69, at Art. 3.

[241] See, e.g., *Chahal, supra* note 140, at 79-80.

[242] See GC IV, *supra* note 175, at Art. 3, 49; Protocol II Additional to the Geneva Conventions of 12 August 1949, 8 June 1977, Art. 17, 1125 *UNTS* 17512, 16 *ILM* 1391 (1977).

[243] Id.

substantial leeway in identifying their security interests as protected by the various instruments and taking appropriate measures to protect them. However, the balance does not and cannot always tilt in favor of states' security, especially where fundamental human rights are at stake.

Selected Bibliography

AMNESTY INTERNATIONAL – *No Flights to Safety – Carrier Sanctions: Airline Employees and the Rights of Refugees* (1997).

BASSIOUNI, CHERIF – *Legal Responses to International Terrorism: US Procedural Aspects* (1988).

BEYANI, CHELOKA – *Human Rights Standards and the Free Movement of Peoples Within States* (2000).

CAMERON, IAIN – *National Security and the European Convention on Human Rights* (2000).

DIETER, INGRID – *The Law of War* (2nd edn. 2001).

DIETRICK, SHARON (ED.) – *The United Nations Convention on the Rights of the Child* (1998).

DONALD-BECK, LOUISE (ED.) – *San Remo Manual on International Law Applicable to Armed Conflicts at Sea* (1995).

EUROPEAN COUNCIL ON REFUGEES AND EXILES – *Carriers' Liability: Country Up-Date on the Application of Carriers' Liability in European States* (1999).

FITZPATRICK, JOAN – *Human Rights in Crisis: The International System for Protecting Rights During States of Emergency* (1994).

GILBERT, GEOFFREY – *Transnational Fugitive Offenders in International Law: Extradition and Other Mechanisms* (1998).

GOODWIN-GILL, GUY – "Migration: International Law and Human Rights," in Bimal Gosh (ed.), *Managing Migration: Time for a New International Regime?* (2000).

—. *The Refugee in International Law* (2nd edn. 1996).

HATHAWAY, JAMES AND COLIN HARVEY – "Framing Refugee Protection in the New World Disorder," 34 *Cornell International Law Journal* (2001): 257.

JOSEPH, SARAH, JENNY SCHULTZ AND MELISSA CASTAN – *The International Covenant on Civil and Political Rights: Cases, Materials, and Commentary* (2000).

LILLICH, ROBERT – *Human Rights of Aliens in Contemporary International Law* (1984).

MADUREIRA, JOAO – "Aliens' Admission to and Departure from National Territory: Case-Law of the Organs of the European Convention on Human Rights and the European Social Charter," Council of Europe Doc. No. H89.4E (7 December 1989).

MICHAEL, JAMES – *Privacy and Human Rights: An International and Comparative Study, with Special Reference to Developments in Information Technology* (1994).

MURPHY, JOHN – "The Future of Multilateralism and Efforts to Combat International Terrorism," 25 *Columbia Journal of Transnational Law* 35 (1986): 35.

NOWAK, MANFRED – *UN Covenant on Civil and Political Rights: CCPR Commentary* (1993).

ORAÁ, JAIME – *Human Rights in States of Emergency in International Law* (1992).

PHILLIPS, STUART R. – "The Political Offense Exception and Terrorism: Its Place in the Current Extradition Scheme and Proposals for Its Future," 15 *Dickinson Journal of International Law* (1997): 337.

POKU, NANA AND DAVID GRAHAM (EDS.) – *Redefining Security: Population Movements and National Security* (1998).

SIRACUSA PRINCIPLES of the Limitation and Derogation Provisions in the International Covenant on Civil and Political Rights, 7 *Human Rights Quarterly* (1985): 1.

SVENSSON-MCCARTHY, ANNA – *The International Law of Human Rights and States of Exception* (1998).

WEINER, MYRON (ED.) – *International Migration and Security* (1993).

WILLIAMS, PAUL R. – *Treatment of Detainees* (1990).

FORCED MIGRATION

Chapter 7
FORCED MIGRATION AND INTERNATIONAL LAW

Guy S. Goodwin-Gill* and **Kathleen Newland****

INTRODUCTION[1]

Notwithstanding its attraction as an encompassing shorthand, "forced migration" is not yet a term of art in international law. There is no category of "forced migrant" known to international law, whose status determines rights and obligations, or engages the protection responsibilities of an international agency.

Several bodies of international law, however, constrain the behavior of states toward certain categories of people who have been forced to flee their usual places of residence and cross an international border in search of safety. In particular, international refugee law prohibits the expulsion or forced return ("*refoulement*"[2]) of a refugee to a place "where his life or freedom would be threatened on account of his race, religion, nationality, membership in a particular social group or political opinion." In order to be able to claim this protection, a person must conform to the refugee definition embodied in the 1951 United Nations Convention relating to the Status of Refugees and/or its 1967 Protocol.[3] (CSR) In addition, the 1984 UN Convention Against Torture and Other Cruel, Inhuman and Degrading Treatment or Punishment (CAT) provides that "No State Party shall expel, return ("*refouler*") or extradite a person to another State where there are substantial grounds for believing that he would be in danger of being subjected to torture."[4] International human

---

* Professor of International Refugee Law, University of Oxford.
** Co-Director, Migration Policy Institute, Washington, D.C.
[1] The present paper draws on G.S. Goodwin-Gill, "Migration – International Law and Human Rights," *in* B. Ghosh (ed.), *Managing Migration: Time for a New International Regime?* (2000) pp. 160-189.
[2] The term derives from the French *refouler*, meaning to drive back or repel, as of an enemy who fails to breach one's defences. In the context of immigration law in continental Europe, it is a term of art covering, in particular, summary reconduction to the frontier of those discovered to have entered illegally and summary refusal of admission of those without valid papers. See G.S. Goodwin-Gill, *The Refugee in International Law* (1996) p. 117.
[3] The Convention and Protocol define a refugee as a person who "… owing to well-founded fear of being persecuted for reasons of race, religion, nationality, membership of a particular social group or political opinion, is outside the country of his nationality and is unable or, owing to such fear, is unwilling to avail himself of the protection of that country …".
[4] Art. 3.1.

T.A. Aleinikoff and V. Chetail (Eds.), Migration and International Legal Norms
© 2003, T.M.C. ASSER PRESS, *The Hague, The Netherlands, et al.*

rights law also imposes constraints on the behavior of States toward non-citizen civilians under their control in wartime. Such "protected persons," according to the Fourth Geneva Convention of 1949, "shall not be transferred to a Power which is not a party to the Convention...In no circumstances shall a protected person be transferred to a country where he or she may have reason to fear persecution for his or her political opinions or religious beliefs."[5]

The international system of states is organized in the expectation that every person holds the nationality of at least one country and can rely on that state for protection of his or her rights. International law makes a crucial distinction between migrants who are failed by the state that is expected to protect them – normally the state of their nationality (or, if stateless, their country of habitual residence) – and migrants who are the victim of circumstance, no matter how dire. Thus a crucial part of the refugee definition is that the person with a well-founded fear of persecution is outside his or her own country and is "unable or, owing to such fear, unwilling to avail himself of the protection of that country."[6] Similarly, a state that uses torture fails in its duty of protection, and people who flee such a state are protected in international law against *refoulement*. People who have fallen into the hands of a foreign power during wartime are clearly beyond the protective power of their own state. On the other hand, people who flee their countries owing to desperate poverty, natural disasters, or severe environmental degradation are not protected against involuntary return to their countries. The assumption is often (in the absence of an additional threat of persecution or torture) that such international response to the dangers that may materialize can be channeled through or undertaken with the permission of the state concerned, and that the nature of the response needed is humanitarian rather than legal.

The migrant who is forced to leave home to escape persecution or torture but does not cross an international border cannot be protected against *refoulement* in the formal sense, not having left his or her country of origin. But the protections of international human rights law and humanitarian law apply, and a set of "Guiding Principles" based on these and on analogies with refugee law has been drawn up. The Guiding Principles are widely acknowledged as a basis for protecting and assisting internally displaced persons.[7]

INSTITUTIONAL ARRANGEMENTS

In 1950, the UN General Assembly established the office of the United Nations High Commissioner for Refugees (UNHCR), with a mandate to protect refugees and to seek solutions to their disconnection from national protection. A year later, the Convention relating to the Status of Refugees provided that "[t]he Contracting

---

[5] Art. 45, Geneva Convention Relative to the Protection of Civilian Persons in Time of War (Fourth Convention of 12 August 1949).

[6] Art. IA, 1951 Convention relating to the Status of Refugees.

[7] UN Commission on Human Rights, Guiding Principles on Internal Displacement, UN Doc. E/CN.4/1998/Add.2, 11 February 1998.

States undertake to cooperate with the Office of the United Nations High Commissioner for Refugees ... in the exercise of its functions and shall in particular facilitate its duty of supervising the application of the provisions of this Convention."[8] UNHCR's supervisory mandate is carried out primarily through diplomatic means, in cooperation with states. This structure differs from the UN human rights machinery, such as the Human Rights Commission, and the treaty bodies associated with human rights treaties, such as the CAT, in that there is in UNHCR no mechanism for a refugee to file an individual petition, or for the Office publicly to examine and pass judgment on the legality of specific actions of states.

Dr. Chaloka Beyani, of the London School of Economics Law Faculty, attributes the inadequate protection of refugees' rights to the lack of a mechanism to hold states accountable for the implementation of their obligations under the Convention. He writes that "it has also led to the fragmentation of the application of those obligations by subjective processes determined chiefly by domestic legal systems instead of the international legal system. ... This is, of course, unavoidable to a large extent given the predominance of domestic law in the field of refugee protection and entry into state territory. However, it has had the undesirable effect of subjecting the application of an international standard to domestic interpretations, thus isolating the wide potential for refugee protection from human rights at the international level."[9]

One of the most striking examples of this phenomenon can be found in the decision of the U.S. Supreme Court that United States interdiction and summary return of Haitian asylum-seekers to Haiti, without screening to determine if any might qualify as refugees, did not violate the United State's obligations under the Refugee Convention or domestic law. The Court reasoned that domestic law provisions incorporating *non-refoulement* did not apply outside United States territory. This is contrary to most other interpretations holding that the essence of the obligation is the prohibition of return "in any manner whatsoever" of refugees to a country where they may face persecution.[10] This obligation is triggered whenever a refugee or asylum-seeker comes under the control or jurisdiction of a State Party to the CSR, the CAT, or the Geneva Conventions, whether or not he or she is physically in the territory of that state.[11]

SAFEGUARDS

The growing tendency of states to interpret narrowly their obligations to refugees and other forced migrants or to evade them altogether underscores the importance of legal safeguards against *refoulement* or further violations of the rights of refugees.

---

[8] CSR, Art. 35(1).

[9] C. Beyani, "Human Rights and the Protection of Refugees" in *Interights Bulletin*, Vol. 11, No. 2 (1997) pp. 39-40.

[10] See G.S. Goodwin-Gill, *The Refugee in International Law* (1996) pp. 141-145.

[11] See, for example, Sir Elihu Lauterpacht and D. Bethlehem, "Opinion: The Scope and Content of the Principle of Non-refoulement," 20 June 2001. Prepared for the UNHCR Global Consultations on Refugee Protection, Expert Roundtable, Cambridge, England, 9-10 July 2001.

The Refugee Convention itself contains an important safeguard in Article 31, which says that "[t]he Contracting States shall not impose penalties, on account of their illegal entry of presence, on refugees who, coming directly from a territory where their life or freedom was threatened in the sense of Article 1, enter or are present in their territory without authorization, provided they present themselves without delay to the authorities and show good cause for their illegal entry or presence."[12] These and other safeguards are necessary to make meaningful the obligation of *non-refoulement* because the right to seek asylum is not matched with a right to be admitted to the territory of a state where a refugee or forced migrant may pursue an asylum claim. A person seeking protection may therefore resort to illegal entry in order to engage the obligation of a state not to return him or her to a place where he/she may face danger. The increasingly common practice of prolonged detention of asylum-seekers, often under harsh conditions, is seen by many as a violation of Article 31.

Many of the measures that States have adopted to deter or apprehend unauthorized migrants have no way of distinguishing between a refugee and a migrant with no claim to international protection. These measures include interdiction, visa requirements, carrier sanctions, summary exclusion at borders, and so forth. Without safeguards aimed at identifying people who may be in need of protection, policies aimed at combating unauthorized migration may make it impossible for a person at risk of persecution, torture, or deprivation of life and liberty to seek asylum. Thus, interceptions at sea or procedures to deny boarding to undocumented air passengers, for example, should include standard procedures to identify and accommodate those who need to claim asylum.

It has become increasingly common for states to return or try to return refugees and asylum-seekers, not to their countries of origin, but to third countries through which they have traveled en route to the country where they ultimately wish to file their asylum claims. Nothing in the Refugee Convention requires an asylum-seeker to seek protection in the first possible place of potential refuge, but neither does the Convention require any state to admit refugees unless their rejection at the frontier would return them to a place where they would be in danger. Thus, return to a "safe third country" may not amount to *refoulement* if the asylum-seeker can find effective protection in the third country. (Returns to third countries raise other concerns, such as burden-sharing, international solidarity, the absorptive capacities of third countries, and so forth.) An expert roundtable in December 2002 enumerated a substantial list of legal safeguards that must be satisfied before return to a third country can be regarded as acceptable.[13] In addition to the assurance that the person concerned does not have a well-founded fear of persecution in the third country and would enjoy respect for his or her fundamental human rights there, other critical considerations included:

---

[12] CSR, Art. 31.

[13] See "Summary Conclusions on the Concept of Effective Protection in the Context of Secondary Movements of Refugees and Asylum-Seekers," from the Expert Roundtable on Effective Protection organized by the UNHCR and the Migration Policy Institute, 9-10 December 2002.

- the absence of risk that the third country would remove the person to yet another country from which he or she might be refouled;
- access to adequate means of subsistence and prospects of self-reliance;
- access to fair and efficient refugee determination procedures;
- agreement from the third country to admit the person as an asylum-seeker (if the person so wishes); and
- the availability of effective protection to persons who are recognized as refugees until a durable solution can be found for them.

In addition to such assurances (and a commitment not to return an asylum-seeker to a country that cannot satisfy them), certain procedural safeguards were also thought to be needed, such as notifying a third country that the person being returned has not has his or her asylum claim rejected, but is still in need of a substantive consideration of the claim.

HUMAN RIGHTS LAW AND FORCED MIGRANTS

To a certain extent, international human rights law avoids many of the distinctions among refugees, internally displaced people, other forced migrants, and migrants in general.[14] Even from this perspective, however, the category of "forced migration" is too large and covers too many disparate issues, insofar as it purports to include both refugees and internally displaced people. From a human rights perspective, these would include the substantive responsibilities of the state towards its citizens at large (civil and political rights, economic, social and cultural rights, rights to development, and so forth) and its obligation to provide protection (remedies, law and order). Beyond guaranteeing rights "in the community," the state also has obligations towards citizens on the move, whether internally, or crossing borders, or returning home. In refugee and related cross-border movements, other states also have clear international responsibilities – for example, to admit, to provide protection, to ensure human rights, to facilitate return, to cooperate in pursuit of solutions.

International human rights law has developed with little direct regard for forced migrants, including refugees and others involuntarily displaced, yet it is clearly and necessarily relevant, in regard to both causes and solutions. This lack of focus is partly due to notions of state sovereignty, which lead non-nationals to be seen as standing outside both the community and the substantive and procedural entitlements normally accorded to members; or to the systemic, sometimes deliberate, failure of governments to provide protection to sections of their own population who are compelled to uproot themselves in search of safety. The present paper reviews only a small portion of the rights dimension to forced migration.[15]

---

[14] See Joan Fitzpatrick, in this volume.

[15] See further and in particular, C. Beyani, *Human Rights Standards and the Movement of People within State* (2000). On the human rights of internally displaced persons, see the "Guiding Principles on Internal Displacement," together with an introduction by Walter Kälin: 10 *International Journal of Refugee Law* (1998) pp. 557-572; W. Kälin, *Guiding Principles on Internal Displacement – Annotations*

Where refugees and asylum-seekers are concerned, gaps still exist in both formal and informal systems of protection; these include matters of refugee definition, admission, sharing of responsibility between states, standards of treatment, and solutions. The situation of internally displaced persons is further complicated as a putative subject of international concern by the juridically relevant fact of sovereignty over territory, the reserved domain of domestic jurisdiction, and the absence of agreed international institutional mechanisms.

In principle, human rights law would seem to offer an important system of protection. However, its extension into the broad field of forced migration is not fully effective, as it must also meet "new" challenges thrown up by the "war on terrorism," the challenges of national security, the HIV/AIDS pandemic, and the negative impact of globalization. On the other hand, the forced migrant is located squarely within the human rights context, possessing a particular interest in liberty and personal integrity rights, whether they relate to movement, admission, due process, family, employment, personal and social security, freedom of expression, or culture and language. At the same time, these rights and the rules behind these interests operate in a context of ever-changing national priorities and sensitivities. It ought to be clear that the very nature of the phenomenon of people moving between states demands a significant measure of international agreement if problematic issues are to be resolved satisfactorily. Yet a number of recent incidents have underlined once again the short-term attractions of unilateralist measures unrelated to principle or foresight.

The body of applicable international principles is solidly established. Article 1 of the 1948 Universal Declaration on Human Rights (UDHR) opens with the affirmative, "All human beings are born *free and equal* in dignity and rights." The Preamble to the Charter of the United Nations proclaims the determination "to reaffirm faith in fundamental human rights, in the *dignity and worth* of the human person." The Annex to the ILO Constitution affirms that "all human beings, irrespective of race, creed or sex, have the right to pursue both their material well-being and their spiritual development in conditions of freedom and dignity, of economic security and equal opportunity."[16]

Yet the doctrine of inalienable rights, inherent in the individual, has frequently had to give way to sovereignty, considered in its high positivist sense, as an absolute assertion of right and power in a society of competing nation-states. The factual situation within which rules operate, change, and develop must therefore be taken into account, together with the interests and entitlements of national or host communities and the frequently conditional or qualified nature of many human rights. Moreover, states have long practiced discrimination in immigration,[17] and have attempted to re-

---

(2000). But see also UN General Assembly Resolution 55/74, 4 December 2000, Office of the United Nations High Commissioner for Refugees, Operative Paragraph 20 – Note by the Editor-in-Chief: 13 *International Journal of Refugee Law* (2001) pp. 251, 255.

[16] All texts in I. Brownlie, *Basic Documents in International Law* (2002).

[17] And it still continues; see comments by the representative of Mexico *in* Report of the Working Group of Intergovernmental Experts on the Human Rights of Migrants Submitted in Accordance with Commission on Human Rights Resolution 1997/ 15, UN Doc. E/CN.4/1998/76, 10 March 1998.

late their policies and choices to rational or defensible bases, such as social and economic grounds. The challenge for international law is to provide principled guidance to states in the exercise of sovereign powers and to international organizations in the promotion of policies and practices oriented towards human welfare.

Migratory and refugee flows are now interwoven, perhaps inextricably, and are assisted by the booming business in the traffic of human beings. And the rights of those who move are increasingly a matter of concern to the international community, irrespective of their status in municipal law (even as some states attempt to reduce the opportunities for legal challenge to migration-related decisions, such as detention or summary removal). The United Nations Commission on Human Rights now regularly focuses on the situation of migrants, refugees, and the displaced, and on thematic issues, such as violence against migrant women.[18] Treaty-monitoring bodies and individual complaints procedures are also developing a coherent body of jurisprudence affecting the sovereign rights of states to regulate admission to their territory.

The movement of persons between states is an area in which competing and conflicting interests arise, engaging communities, individuals, and states.[19] There clearly *are* human rights aspects to traditionally sovereign questions about the admission, treatment, and removal of non-nationals. The failure so far to manage these disparate elements argues strongly for more highly developed institutional arrangements competent to pursue strategic goals on behalf of the international community, in cooperation with states and in furtherance of the promotion and protection of the human rights of migrants and refugees.

States have a margin of appreciation, or discretion, in determining whether and what restrictions may be called for in the light of local circumstances. They may exclude from refugee protection those who have persecuted others, committed serious crimes, or constitute threats to national security or public order. The standard of compliance, nonetheless, remains an international one, involving elements of necessity and proportionality. Some rights, however, may not be derogated from, even in exceptional circumstances; they benefit everyone, nationals, foreigners, migrants, and refugees, whether lawfully or unlawfully in the state, and regardless of any situation of emergency. Such non-derogable rights traditionally include:

- the prohibition of genocide;
- the prohibition of slavery;
- the prohibition of racial discrimination;
- the right to life, so far as the individual is guaranteed against arbitrary deprivation;
- freedom from torture or inhuman treatment;
- the right not to be convicted or punished under retroactive laws;

---

[18] See, among recent examples, Commission on Human Rights, Resolution 2001/52, Human Rights of Migrants, 24 April 2001; Commission on Human Rights, Resolution 2001/54, Internally Displaced Persons, 24 April 2001; Commission on Human Rights, Resolution 2001/56, Protection of Migrants and Their Families, 24 April 2001.

[19] See UN General Assembly Resolution 55/92, Protection of Migrants, 4 December 2000.

- the right to recognition as a person before the law;
- the right to freedom of conscience, thought, and religion.

FORCED MIGRATION AND FREEDOM OF MOVEMENT

The paradox of the forced migrant is that he or she is obliged to exercise a right generally considered a matter of free choice, namely, the right to freedom of movement. Depending on the particular circumstances, exercise of that right may lead to internal or external displacement.

The right to leave any country, including one's own, features in most international human rights instruments, beginning with the 1948 Universal Declaration on Human Rights. Article 13(2) declares the right, immediately after the right to freedom of movement and residence within the borders of each state, set out in the first paragraph.[20]

Together with its universal and regional treaty counterparts, Article 13 of the UDHR proclaims a general right to freedom of movement for everyone, including the right to leave any country, including their own, and to return to their country.[21] So far as the *right to leave* any country, including one's own, may be relatively well accepted, the right to enter or to return to a particular country, as a matter of law, generally depends on possessing its nationality.

In regard to entry and removal, a protected right will thus be engaged by the international law provisions on children, family, and refugees. Thus, for example, no state may return a refugee in any manner whatsoever to a country in which he or she may be persecuted. This prohibition extends to measures such as rejection at the frontier, where the effect is to compel the individual to return to or remain in a territory where his or her life, physical integrity, or liberty would be threatened for relevant reasons.[22] Moreover, the 1989 Convention on the Rights of the Child endorses the standard of the "best interests" of the child which, in principle and in appropriate circumstances, is capable of prevailing over other considerations, including the legally recognized but competing interests of the state. In a wide range of other universal and regional instruments, states have also recognized that the family should receive "protection by society and the State," and that "special measures of protection and assistance should be taken on behalf of all children and young persons."[23] Together with the principle of the best interests of the child as a primary consideration,[24] this puts in question any state action with respect to children that might

---

[20] See further Beyani, *supra* note 9. Freedom of movement, of course, has both internal and external aspects; human rights treaties also speak to the right of everyone to move freely *within* the territory of the State of which they are citizens or residents.

[21] See also Art. 12 ICCPR; Art. 2, Protocol 4, ECHR; Art. 12 ACHR. See the contribution of Vincent Chetail in the present volume.

[22] Art. II(4), 1969 OAU Convention; Art. 3, 1966 AALCC Principles Concerning Treatment of Refugees.

[23] Art. 23(1) ICCPR; Art. 10(3) ICESCR.

[24] Art. 3(1) CRC89; see also Art. 4, 1990 African Charter on the Rights and Welfare of the Child.

either "officially" remove the child from the family environment, or have the effect of leaving the child without care and support.[25]

The right to leave one's country can be considered completed in one particular context, namely, as the right to seek asylum from persecution. Here the correlative duty of states combines the principle of *non-refoulement* with a duty not to impede exercise of the right where it would leave individuals exposed to persecution, torture, or other serious violations of human rights.[26]

FORCED MIGRATION AND FORCED REMOVAL

State practice over many decades has established a number of limitations on the sovereign power of removal (expulsion or deportation) – for example, to the effect that it should not be exercised arbitrarily, that it should respect acquired rights, be implemented in accordance with due process, and carried out with full regard for the dignity and integrity of the individual. The collective or mass expulsion of non-citizens has also been condemned, in particular, for its necessarily arbitrary and discriminatory character.[27]

Article 13 of the ICCPR, Articles 32 and 33 of the CSR, and Article 3 of the CAT, all mention expulsion specifically when laying down protection standards for non-citizens generally, in favor of refugees, or against return to torture. The Human Rights Committee has considered the lawfulness of expulsion against the requirements of Article 13 of the ICCPR (entitlement to a remedy for the purpose of challenging an order of removal) in a number of cases,[28] while the European human rights institutions have reviewed the exercise of the competence to expel non-citizens more broadly, against a range of the ECHR rights including Article 3 (prohibition against torture, inhuman and degrading treatment), Article 8 (freedom from interference with private or family life), and Article 14 (non-discrimination).[29]

---

[25] Australia's so-called temporary protection visa, which is issued to refugees recognized by Australia who arrived "without invitation," does not permit the holder to be reunited with spouse or minor children. Its effect is thus mandatory denial of family life, and a clear violation of international legal obligations.

[26] See G.S. Goodwin-Gill, "The Right to Leave, the Right to Return and the Question of a Right to Remain," *in* V. Gowlland-Debbas (ed.), *The Problem of Refugees in the Light of Contemporary International Law Issues* (1995) pp. 95-106.

[27] See J. Henckaerts, *Mass Expulsion in Modern International Law and Practice* (1995) pp. 8-49, on the prohibition of mass expulsion; pp. 50-77 on mass expulsion of migrant workers. See also ECHR, Protocol No. 4, Art. 4.

[28] See, for example, *Mafroufidou* v. *Sweden*, No. 58/ 1979: *Selected Decisions of the Human Rights Committee*, vol. 1: UN Doc. ICCPR/C/CP/1, 80; *Hammel* v. *Madagascar*, No. 155/ 1983: id., vol. 2, 11; *M.F.* v. *The Netherlands*, No. 173/ 1984: id., vol. 2, 179, cited by O. Andrysek, "Gaps in International Protection and the Potential for Redress through Individual Complaints Procedures," 9 *International Journal of Refugee Law* (1997) pp. 392, 402.

[29] *Abdulaziz, Cabales and Balkandali* (15/1983/71/107-109), 28 May 1985.

FORCED MIGRATION AND THE RIGHT TO RETURN

By contrast to the right to leave as understood in the practice of states, the right to return has a clear *international* dimension. At the level of state to state relations, the state's obligation to admit its nationals is the correlative to the absence of duty on any other state to allow foreign citizens to remain and of such other state's right of expulsion. Considered from another perspective, the state's right of protection over its citizens abroad is matched by its duty to receive those of its citizens who are not allowed to remain on the territory of other states. To the reciprocal relationship of rights and duties is now added a human rights dimension: the individual's right to enter or return to the state of which he or she is a national. As an incident of nationality, the duty to admit thus encompasses both the rights of other states, and the right of the individual to access his or her own country. The human right to return to one's own country is implied in Article 9 of the 1948 Universal Declaration on Human Rights, prohibiting "arbitrary arrest, detention or exile," and in the prohibitions on the expulsion of nationals. It is expressly recognized in Article 13(2). The only restriction or limitation with respect to the right to return is that the beneficiaries must be *citizens*.[30] Both the American and European Conventions provide that citizens shall not be deprived of the right to enter their own country.[31]

The relevance and importance of the human rights dimension for those forcibly displaced beyond the borders of their own state is obvious, for the primary solution of voluntary repatriation is premised upon their basic human right to return to their own country in conditions of security. From time to time, the state of origin may seek to "write off" those who have fled, and to ignore the link of nationality, but this potentially involves a breach of obligation to the state of refuge, even though in the prevailing conditions the actual return of refugees may be prohibited by the principle of *non-refoulement*. How those competing responsibilities may be resolved in the best interests of the displaced is a constant challenge in the political context linking state of origin, state of refuge, and the international community.

FORCED MIGRATION AND THE "RIGHT NOT TO TAKE FLIGHT"

At an early stage of the conflict in former Yugoslavia, the Special Rapporteur, Tadeusz Mazowiecki concluded that, "[a] large number of displaced persons would not have to seek refuge abroad if their security could be guaranteed and if they could be provided with both sufficient food supplies and adequate medical care."[32] The provision of security and the basic necessities of life reflects a somewhat narrow idea of the essential elements in a "right to remain." At the same time, however, the prevention of movements, in particular where the emphasis is on stopping flight rather than removing causes, is no solution and, so far as it follows from the actions

---

[30] This does *not* exclude the possibility that re-admission obligations may also be owed to permanent residents, refugees, and stateless persons.

[31] Art. 3, Protocol 4, ECHR; Art. 22(5) ACHR.

[32] Report on Human Rights in former Yugoslavia, UN Doc. E/CN.4/1992/S-1/10 (1992), para. 2(b).

of other states, will often amount to an abuse of rights, particularly if no *effective protection* of their human rights is provided to those, including the internally displaced, who would otherwise flee across an international frontier. Full protection further implies measures to guarantee the integrity of the principle of return: "The argument that providing refuge ... is to conform to the policy of ethnic cleansing cannot override the imperative of saving their lives. ... In order to ensure that providing refuge will not contribute to ethnic cleansing, it is essential to reaffirm and provide lasting protection for the right to return."[33]

In short, the right to remain comprises the common sense of not having to become a refugee, not having to flee, and not being displaced by force or want with the felt security that comes with being protected. It is another way of expressing, in concrete terms, the connection between individual, community, and territory, but its effective realization depends upon human rights and development considerations that pose a considerable challenge.

THE PROTECTION OF FORCED MIGRANTS

Refugees are a class known to enjoy the protection of general international law.[34] The principle of asylum has been consistently endorsed by the United Nations, both in the resolutions adopted by the General Assembly and in the practice of Member States individually and at the regional level. Article 14 of the 1948 UDHR, for example, provides that "Everyone has the right to seek and to enjoy in other countries asylum from persecution." The main international instruments have been widely ratified.[35] By 1 January 2003, 145 states had agreed to be bound by the CSR and its 1967 Protocol, including the definition of a refugee in Article 1, and by the fundamental principle of *non-refoulement* in Article 33.[36] This rule, which requires that states parties not return a refugee to a country in which he or she may face persecution on grounds of race, religion, nationality, membership of a particular group or political opinion, now extends to the protection of those who, if returned to a particular country, would face a substantial risk of torture.[37] Lawfully resident refugees are also protected against expulsion, save on the most serious grounds and subject to lawful procedures and the opportunity for challenge.[38]

At the regional level, in the 1969 Organization of African Unity Convention on the Specific Aspects of Refugee Problems in Africa[39] and in the 1984 Cartagena Declaration on the Problems of Refugees and the Displaced in Central America,[40]

---

[33] Id. at para. 25(a).

[34] Goodwin-Gill, *supra* note 2.

[35] For ratifications at 31 January 2002, see I. Brownlie and G.S. Goodwin-Gill, *Basic Documents on Human Rights,* xiii-xix, Table of Ratifications and Sources.

[36] 1951 Convention (CSR51): 189 *UNTS* 150; 1967 Protocol (CSRP67): 606 *UNTS* 267.

[37] Art. 3, 1984 Convention against Torture and Other Cruel, Inhuman or Degrading Treatment or Punishment (CAT): 1465 *UNTS* 85 (No. 24841).

[38] Art. 32, CSR.

[39] 1000 *UNTS* 46.

[40] OAS/ Ser. L/V/II.66, Doc. 10, rev. 1; text *in* Goodwin-Gill, *supra* note 2, at 444.

states have developed the content of refugee protection, either directly, by way of treaty obligations, or indirectly, through statements of principle backed by concerted practice.

That refugee protection also engages a human rights responsibility has been recognized by a number of treaty supervisory bodies. The Human Rights Committee, for example, considers that the principle of *non-refoulement* is effectively included within Article 7 of the ICCPR:

> "In the view of the Committee, States parties must not expose individuals to the danger of torture or cruel, inhuman or degrading treatment or punishment upon return to another country by way of their extradition, expulsion or *refoulement* ... "[41]

While the 1966 Covenant does not recognize the right of non-citizens to enter or reside in the territory of a State Party, "in certain circumstances an alien may enjoy the protection of the Covenant even in [such matters], for example, when considerations of non-discrimination, [or] prohibition of inhuman treatment ... arise."[42] The Committee against Torture has indicated that "non-admission to a country engages the responsibility of the State Party [to CAT] under Article 3 if returning a person would result in exposure to torture." In several "Views," the Committee has confirmed the protection due to the non-citizen at risk on expulsion or return.[43]

CONCLUSION

International legal standards of treatment for forced migrants extend into such areas of sovereign competence as control over admission and expulsion, and are all well-founded in treaty and general international law. The existing international systems of legal guarantees for forced migrants are far from complete, however. Compliance is still a problem, and even where the principles seem clear, their effective implementation depends upon levels of official action that are not always forthcoming. Recent years have once again seen mass expulsions, the forced repatriation of refugees, xenophobic and violent attacks upon established migrant minorities and asy-

---

[41] Human Rights Committee, General Comment No. 20, "Replaces General Comment 7 concerning prohibition of torture or cruel treatment or punishment (Art. 7)," 10 April 1992, para. 9.

[42] Human Rights Committee, General Comment No. 15, "The position of aliens under the Covenant," para. 5, 11 April 1986.

[43] *Mutombo* v. *Switzerland,* Communication No. 13/1993, Committee against Torture, 27 April 1994: 7 *International Journal of Refugee Law* (1995) p. 332; *Alan* v. *Switzerland,* Communication No. 21/1995, Committee against Torture, 8 May 1996: 8 *International Journal of Refugee Law* (1996) p. 440; *Kisoki* v. *Sweden,* Communication No. 41/1996, Committee against Torture, 8 May 1996: 8 *International Journal of Refugee Law* (1996) p. 651. See also, O. Andrysek, "Gaps in International Protection and the Potential for Redress through Individual Complaints Procedures," 9 *International Journal of Refugee Law* (1997) p. 392. In particularly striking fashion, the European Court of Human Rights has ruled that there are no exceptions to the protection required under Art. 3 of the ECHR; see *Chahal* v. *United Kingdom* No. 70/1995/576/662, Judgment of 15 November 1996, paras. 79, 80 (individual whom the UK wished to expel on national security grounds).

lum-seekers, and arbitrary and unprincipled policies implemented outside the rule of law.

Compliance with international human rights obligations in the migration field is thus patchy at best, and the reasons for this failing call for serious attention. States are disinclined to legislate on family reunion, for example, or to incorporate international standards into policy guidelines or best practice statements. The traditional conception of sovereign state rights to control entry, removal, and membership still carries weight, but it is rather the incompleteness and lack of balance in the present regime that militates against effectiveness.

The movement of persons between states is a matter of international relations and raises international human rights issues; it also brings state responsibilities clearly into the picture. At a certain level of generality, states are responsible not only for protecting the human rights of all those within a territory and a jurisdiction, but also between themselves, for "operationalizing" the duties that attach to the fact of nationality and for making the migration bridge a truly two-way, reciprocal process. The better protection of the rights of forced migrants must be based on international human rights law, the essentials of which are obligations *erga omnes* and much of which draws its authority from peremptory rules of international law (*jus cogens*). But it must also promote effective cooperation to these ends by institutionalizing mechanisms whereby states are able to fulfil their responsibilities, such as that of sending states or states of origin towards their citizens; this is a matter both of individual rights, and of responsibility in and towards the international community. The sovereignty of the state exists within a community of principle; given the manifestly international dimensions to migratory and refugee movements, a significantly higher degree of cooperation among states is now called for if these are to be effectively dealt with.

The broad field of forced migration contains nothing comparable to the existing regime of international protection of refugees which, with all its evident deficiencies, nonetheless provides principles, institutions, and mechanisms that permit the solution of problems of concern to the community of nations. A comparable protection and management regime is required for the wider context, which also now combines matters of international concern and issues of individual rights and claims. The confrontational response to the phenomenon of forced migration, based on unilateralist and almost nineteenth-century conceptions of sovereignty and isolation, has proven its inadequacy.

The internationalist or collective duty with respect to the protection of persons displaced internally or moving across borders and the obligation to cooperate derive, in part at least, from the character *erga omnes* of human rights obligations, considered within the cooperative framework established by the United Nations Charter and general international law. They extend through the general structure of international organization to cover measures to prevent the necessity for flight, to regulate and humanize the natural phenomenon of migration, in both directions, and to protect the common interest of the international community in the protection of individual human rights and the preservation of international public order – a challenging agenda for decades to come.

Selected Bibliography

ANDRYSEK, O – "Gaps in International Protection and the Potential for Redress through Individual Complaints Procedures," 9 *International Journal of Refugee Law* (1997): 392-414.

BEYANI, CHALOKA – *Human Rights Standards and the Movement of People within States* (2000).

—. "The International Protection of Human Rights in the Context of Refugees," unpublished manuscript.

BROWNLIE, IAN (ED.) – *Basic Documents in International Law* (2002).

BROWNLIE, IAN AND GUY GOODWIN-GILL (EDS.) – *Basic Documents on Human Rights* (2002).

GOODWIN-GILL, GUY – *The Refugee in International Law* (1996).

—. "Migration: International Law and Human Rights," in Bimal Ghosh (ed.), *Managing Migration: Time for a New International Regime?* (2000): 160-189.

—. "The Right to Leave, the Right to Return and the Question of a Right to Remain," in V. Gowlland-Debbas (ed.), *The Problem of Refugees in the Light of Contemporary International Law Issues: Papers Presented at the Colloquium Organized by the Graduate Institute of International Studies in Collaboration With the Office of the United Nations High Commissioner for Refugees* (1995): 95-106.

HENCKAERTS, JEAN-MARIE – *Mass Expulsion in Modern International Law and Practice* (1995).

KÄLIN, WALTER – *Guiding Principles on Internal Displacement – Annotations* (2000).

—. "The Guiding Principles on Internal Displacement – Introduction," 10 *International Journal of Refugee Law* (1998): 557-572.

LAUTERPACHT, SIR ELIHU AND DANIEL BETHLEHEM – "Opinion: The Scope and Content of the Principle of Non-Refoulement," 20 June 2001. Paper prepared for the UNHCR Global Consultations on Refugee Protection, Expert Roundtable, Cambridge, England, 9-10 July 2001.

UN COMMISSION ON HUMAN RIGHTS – "Guiding Principles on Internal Displacement," in UN Doc. E/CN.4/1998/Add.2, 11 February 1998.

UNHCR AND THE MIGRATION POLICY INSTITUTE (MPI) – "Summary Conclusions on the Concept of 'Effective Protection' in the Context of Secondary Movements of Refugees and Asylum-Seekers," from the Expert Roundtable on Effective Protection, 9-10 December 2002.

Chapter 8
THE PROTECTION OF ASYLUM-SEEKERS AND REFUGEES RESCUED AT SEA

Office of the United Nations High Commissioner for Refugees*

INTRODUCTION

The phenomenon of people taking to the seas in search of safety, refuge, or simply better economic conditions is not new. The mass exodus of Vietnamese boat people throughout the 1980s was followed in the 1990s by large-scale departures from places such as Albania, Cuba, and Haiti. The term "boat people" has now entered into common parlance, with asylum-seekers and migrants trying to reach the closest destination by boat, in the Mediterranean, the Caribbean and the Pacific regions. Since the vessels used are often overcrowded and unseaworthy, rescue-at-sea, disembarkation, and processing of those rescued has reemerged as an important but difficult issue for states, international organizations, the shipping industry and, of course, the vulnerable boat people themselves. In an effort to stem the flow of boat people, destination states have increasingly resorted to interception measures within the broader context of migratory control measures, albeit that in some instances adequate protection safeguards have not been evident.

This chapter examines provisions from different strands of international law that bear on the rescue-at-sea of asylum-seekers and refugees. It focuses on relevant norms, and highlights areas of law that require clarification. It also looks at institutional collective efforts to tackle this issue in the past and suggests elements that could be explored further to address the current situation more effectively within an international cooperative framework.

GENERAL LEGAL FRAMEWORK

The legal framework governing rescue-at-sea and the treatment of asylum-seekers and refugees rests on the applicable provisions of international maritime law, in conjunction with international refugee law. Aspects of international human rights law

---

* This chapter is adapted from a background note prepared by UNHCR for the purposes of an expert roundtable entitled, Rescue-At-Sea; Specific Aspects relating to the Protection of Refugees and Asylum-Seekers, held in Lisbon, Portugal on 25–26 March 2002. The original paper, including all annexes referred to therein, can be accessed on UNHCR's public webiste at www.unhcr.ch by conducting a search on rescue at sea through the Global Consultations section of the website.

T.A. Aleinikoff and V. Chetail (Eds.), Migration and International Legal Norms
© 2003, T.M.C. ASSER PRESS, The Hague, The Netherlands, et al.

and the emerging regime for combating transnational crime are also relevant. The following paragraphs set out the more pertinent legal provisions and offer an interpretation, which would though benefit from analysis and further elaboration.

International Maritime Law

Aiding those in peril at sea is one of the oldest of maritime obligations. Its importance is attested by numerous references in the codified system of international maritime law as set out in several conventions, namely:

- the United Nations Convention on the Law of the Sea of 1982, (UNCLOS);
- the International Convention for the Safety of Life at Sea of 1974, as amended, (SOLAS);
- the International Convention on Maritime Search and Rescue of 1979, as amended, (SAR);
- the 1958 Convention on the High Seas (to the extent that it has not been superseded by UNCLOS).

Responsibilities of Different Actors

These conventions explicitly contain the obligation to come to the assistance of persons in distress at sea.[1] This obligation is unaffected by the status of the persons in question, their mode of travel, or the numbers involved. The legal framework also foresees different sets of responsibilities that need to be considered both independently and to the degree to which they interrelate.

The responsibility of the shipmaster[2] – The shipmaster is responsible for providing assistance and/or rescue. International maritime law does not, however, elaborate on any continuing responsibility of the master once a rescue has been effected. Indicative of the nature of the responsibility assumed by the master is the fact that he or she may be criminally liable under national law for failing to render assistance while commanding a vessel under the flag of certain states.[3] In addition, the master

---

[1] See for example, para. 2.1.10 of ch. 2 of the Annex to SAR (1979) which states, "Parties shall ensure that assistance be provided to any person in distress at sea. They shall do so regardless of the nationality or status of such a person or the circumstances in which that person is found." Regulation 15 of ch. V of the Annex to SOLAS, obliges each state to "ensure that any necessary arrangements are made for coast watching and for the rescue of persons in distress at sea around its coasts." Art. 98(1) of UNCLOS, 1982, states that every State shall require the master of a ship flying its flag, in so far as he can do so without serious danger to the ship, the crew or the passengers, *inter alia*, to render assistance to any person found at sea and in danger of becoming lost. Some of these provisions have become so universally recognized as to be considered customary international law.

[2] The obligation of shipmasters to provide assistance is repeatedly articulated in international maritime law. First codified in 1910, it is incorporated in Art. 98 of UNCLOS and Art. 10 of the 1989 Salvage Convention. It is also explicitly mentioned in SOLAS (V/7). All three conventions require the master of a ship, so far as he can do without serious danger to his vessel and persons thereon, to render assistance to any person in danger of being lost at sea and to proceed with all possible speed to the rescue of persons in distress. It is again specifically mentioned in SOLAS (V/33) but is not referred to in SAR, the emphasis of which is more on the responsibilities of States Parties to that Convention.

[3] This is the case in the United Kingdom and in Germany, for example.

bears responsibilities not only to those rescued but also for the general safety of his vessel. Effecting a rescue may, under certain circumstances, result in danger to both, for example when the number of persons rescued outnumbers those legally permitted to be aboard and exceeds the availability of lifejackets and other essential safety equipment.

The responsibility of coastal states – Coastal states are obligated to develop adequate search and rescue services. The relevant instruments do not expand on the responsibility of coastal states for disembarkation or landing of those rescued, nor any follow-up actions.[4] Obviously, coastal states with particularly long coastlines, those with a large coverage area for search and rescue operations, and those located on major shipping routes are particularly affected.

The responsibility of flag states – Flag states are bound by the dictates of international maritime law, but, in practice, responsibilities can be difficult to locate given the distinction between those vessels that have a clear relationship to the flag under which they sail and those operating under the open registry system – so-called *flags of convenience*.[5] Flag state responsibility has been invoked partly on the basis of the vessel being considered a "floating extension" of the state in question, which is problematic as regards *flags of convenience*. While this position may not have a firm legal grounding, it seems to have contributed to the practice of attributing certain responsibilities to flag states and/or the commercial vessels operating under their authority. For example, with regard to the treatment of stowaways, a practice has evolved that holds ship owners largely responsible for any stowaways found aboard their vessels.[6]

The distinction between commercial vessels and vessels owned or operated by a

---

[4] The obligation of states to render assistance to persons in distress at sea is an enshrined principle of maritime law. Art. 98 of UNCLOS requires every coastal state to promote the establishment, operation, and maintenance of an adequate and effective search and rescue service regarding safety on and over the sea and, where circumstances so require, by way of mutual regional arrangements, to cooperate with neighbouring states for this purpose. The detail of search and rescue obligations is to be found in SAR, which defines rescue as involving not only the retrieving of persons in distress and the provision of initial medical care but also their *delivery to a place of safety*. The SAR Convention expands further on the technical obligations of States *vis-à-vis* rescue operations but without specifically mentioning the question of disembarkation or landing of those rescued.

[5] In relation to flag states, Art. 6 of the Convention on the High Seas (1958) states: "Ships shall sail under the flag of one State only and save in exceptional cases expressly provided for in international treaties or in these articles, shall be subject to its exclusive jurisdiction on the high seas. A ship may not change its flag during a voyage or while in a port of call, save in the case of a real transfer of ownership or change of registry." In addition and more specifically on the point of non-commercial vessels, Art. 9 of the same Convention states that, "Ships owned or operated by a State and used only on government non commercial service shall, on the high seas, have complete immunity from the jurisdiction of any State other than the flag State."

[6] Despite efforts to promote shared responsibilities for resolving the problem of stowaways, as exemplified by the development of IMO *Guidelines on the Allocation of Responsibilities to Seek the Successful Resolution of Stowaway Cases* (under the auspices of the FAL Committee/Convention of the Facilitation of Maritime Traffic), practice continues to focus on the responsibilities of the shipping companies, to the extent of obliging them to re-assume responsibility for those stowaways disembarked and considered under national asylum systems but whose cases are ultimately rejected. It is worth noting that the Guidelines were developed to fill the gaps resulting from the fact that the 1957 International Convention Relating to Stowaways has yet to enter into force.

government and used only on government non-commercial service affects the nature of flag state responsibility. Such state vessels include, *inter alia*, naval vessels, coast guard vessels, and national lifeboats specifically tasked with search and rescue operations. Where such vessels engage in rescue operations within territorial waters, the responsibility for those rescued would devolve on that state. This may arguably be the case even when rescues occur on the high seas, particularly if the rescue occurs in the context of interception measures.

The roles and responsibilities of international agencies and the international community as a whole – international agencies, such as the International Maritime Organization (IMO), the UNHCR, and the International Organization for Migration (IOM) have specific but differing responsibilities towards persons rescued-at-sea. The IMO has the widest and most direct set of responsibilities. It oversees the development of international maritime law, with emphasis on safety aspects and providing technical advice and assistance to states to ensure that they respect their obligations. The UNHCR has a specific responsibility to guide and assist states and other actors on the treatment of asylum-seekers and refugees found at sea and to monitor compliance with refugee protection responsibilities in such scenarios.[7] The IOM plays a specific role regarding the needs of migrants at sea as part of its broader mandate to address issues related to migration. The international community as a whole has a responsibility in terms of developing appropriate responsibility-sharing mechanisms involving states and other actors in order to ensure appropriate responses to the array of scenarios involving migrants, asylum-seekers, refugees, and others facing difficulties at sea. Responsibilities assumed by the international community extend not only to response measures but also to include preventative actions.[8]

Delivery to a Place of Safety

The obligation to come to the aid of those in peril at sea is beyond doubt. There is however, a lack of clarity, and possibly lacunae, in international maritime law when it comes to determining the steps that follow once a vessel has taken people on board.

The SAR definition of rescue[9] implies disembarkation since the requirement of delivery to a place of safety cannot be considered to be met by maintaining people on board the rescuing vessel indefinitely. Neither SAR nor other international instruments elaborate, however, on the criteria for disembarkation. Recent discussions at IMO fora have also highlighted the lack of clarity on this issue. Faced with this gap

---

[7] For further detail on the competence of UNHCR please refer to Annex 1, *Background Note; Concerning the Competence of the United Nations High Commissioner for Refugees (UNHCR), in relation to rescue-at-sea matters,* as distributed to the participants in COMSAR 6, Working Group 1, during the Committee session held in London, 18-20 February 2002.

[8] See for example the Preamble to the Protocol Against the Smuggling of Migrants by Land, Sea and Air (2000) that acknowledges the need to strengthen international cooperation in order to address the root causes of migration.

[9] Described in the Annex, ch. 1, para. 1.3.2 as, "an operation to retrieve persons in distress, provide for their medical or other needs, and deliver them to a place of safety."

in the law, the UNHCR has consistently argued for prompt disembarkation at the next port of call.[10]

The effectiveness of the international search and rescue regime rests on the swift and predictable action of all actors. This however, poses a particular challenge where it transpires that there are asylum-seekers and refugees among those rescued. In such instances, states have questioned the extent of their responsibilities and have delayed, and even blocked, disembarkation, arguing that this would result in a strain on their asylum systems, encourage irregular movements, and even contribute to smuggling operations. These concerns are valid and need to be fully reflected in the design of an international cooperative framework to deal with the situation of asylum-seekers rescued at sea.

From the perspective of the shipmaster, the security of his vessel and the health and safety of those aboard are of paramount concern. Existing guidelines and procedures rarely take sufficient account of the potential for danger if the ship were prevented from proceeding immediately to the first appropriate port of call.

Health and safety concerns include:

- insufficient water and provisions for the number of people on board;
- insufficient medical care for the number of people on board;
- medical emergencies at sea;
- exceeding the number of persons legally permitted to be on board;
- insufficient life-saving equipment for the number of people on board;
- insufficient accommodation for the number of people on board; and
- risk to the safety of both crew and passengers if the persons taken on board display aggressive or violent behavior or threaten to do so.

From the UNHCR's perspective, the pressing humanitarian challenge in any rescue situation is to ensure an immediate life-saving solution for the plight of severely traumatised persons, without an overemphasis on legal and practical barriers. It is crucial that shipmasters are actively facilitated in their efforts to save lives, confident that safe and timely disembarkation will be guaranteed.

As a result, there are a number of factors that come into play when considering the question of disembarkation or landing of rescued persons and in particular of asylum-seekers and refugees. These include legal obligations; practical, security, and humanitarian concerns; and commercial interests. On occasion, these differing considerations may be perceived as competing or conflicting interests and there is a need for a deeper analysis of the interplay between them. The UNHCR believes that guidance on formulating the most appropriate responses can be found in an analysis of the interaction between international maritime law and other relevant bodies of international law and practice, and in particular the dictates of international refugee law.

---

[10] The term "next port of call" is nowhere mentioned in international maritime law in connection with rescue-at-sea but has been used in this context by UNHCR's Executive Committee in a number of its Conclusions on the subject.

International Refugee Law[11]

International maritime law assumes that the nationality and status of the individual are of no relevance *vis-à-vis* the obligation to rescue.[12] By contrast, international refugee law is premised on the understanding that a person has a well-founded fear of persecution, on specific grounds, before he or she can avail of international protection. Clarification of status is therefore crucial in the refugee context to determine obligations owed to the refugee. It is clear that a shipmaster is not the competent authority to determine the status of those who fall under his temporary care after a rescue operation. Ensuring prompt access to fair and efficient asylum procedures is therefore key to ensuring the adequate protection of asylum-seekers and refugees among those rescued.

State responsibility under international refugee law, and in particular the 1951 Convention Relating to the Status of Refugees, is activated once it becomes clear that there are asylum-seekers among those rescued. Consistent with the object and purpose of the 1951 Convention and its underlying regime, the responsibilities of states to ensure admission, at least on a temporary basis, and to provide for access to asylum procedures have been elaborated upon in a number of Executive Committee Conclusions of UNHCR's Programme (EXCOM Conclusions).

While not exhaustive, these include:

- EXCOM Conclusion No. 22 (1981), Part II A, paragraph 2 states: "In all cases the fundamental principle of *non-refoulement*, including – non-rejection at the frontier – must be scrupulously observed."
- EXCOM Conclusion No. 82 (1997), paragraph d (iii) reiterates: "The need to admit refugees into the territories of States, which includes no rejection at frontiers without fair and effective procedures for determining status and protection needs."
- EXCOM Conclusion No. 85 (1998), paragraph q "… reiterates in this regard the need to admit refugees to the territory of States, which includes no rejection at frontiers without access to fair and effective procedures for determining status and protection needs."

The 1951 Convention defines those on whom it confers protection and establishes key principles such as non-penalization for illegal entry and *non-refoulement*.[13] It

---

[11] The main body of international refugee law, comprised of the 1951 Convention Relating to the Status of Refugees, its 1967 Protocol and numerous Conclusions of the Executive Committee of UNHCR (EXCOM Conclusions), is further complemented by international human rights law. Much of the emphasis of international refugee law is placed on the identification of those who meet the definition of a refugee contained in Art. 1 A(2) of the 1951 Convention and thus benefit from international protection. Please note that Art. 11 of the 1951 Convention makes explicit reference to refugee seamen. See Convention Relating to the Status of Refugees; Its History, Contents, and Interpretation, a Commentary by Nehemiah Robinson, p. 82, republished by UNHCR in 1997, for further information on the rationale behind this provision and the obligations it imposes on flag states. The 1957 Hague Agreement Relating to Refugee Seamen further elaborates on these specific obligations.

[12] As specified for example in the Annex, ch. 2, para. 2.1.10 of the SAR Convention.

[13] 1951 Convention Relating to the Status of Refugees, Arts. 1, 31, and 33.

does not, however, set out specific procedures for the determination of refugee status. Despite this lack of clarity, it is clearly understood and accepted by states that fair and efficient procedures are an essential element in the full and inclusive application of the 1951 Convention.[14] States require such procedures to identify those who should benefit from international protection under the 1951 Convention, and those who should not benefit.

The principle of access to fair and efficient procedures is equally applicable in the case of asylum-seekers and refugees rescued at sea. The reasons motivating their flight and the circumstances of their rescue frequently result in severe trauma for the persons concerned. In the UNHCR's view, this provides added impetus for prompt disembarkation followed by access to procedures to determine their status. Achieving this objective requires clarity on a number of key issues, including the identification of asylum-seekers among those rescued and the determination of the state responsible under international refugee law for admission and processing of the asylum-seekers.

The Identification of Asylum-seekers

At a land border, the *identification of an asylum-seeker* usually occurs through the lodging of an asylum request with the competent state authorities. This may be done by a formal written application or verbally, to the border authorities at the point of entry. In the case of rescue-at-sea, the mechanism of lodging an asylum application is unclear.

While the legal regime applicable on board ship is that of the flag state, this does not mean that *all* administrative procedures of the flag state would be available and applicable in such situations. The shipmaster will not be aware of the nationality or status of the persons in distress and cannot reasonably be expected to assume any responsibilities beyond rescue. The identification of asylum-seekers and the determination of their status is the responsibility of state officials adequately trained for that task.

In the UNHCR's view, the identification and subsequent processing of asylum-seekers is an activity most appropriately carried out on dry land. Onboard processing, both in the form of initial screening and more comprehensive determination, has been attempted in past refugee crises. It proved problematic in various respects, including, *inter alia,* ensuring adequate access to translators, safeguarding the privacy of the interviews carried out under difficult conditions on board ship, ensuring access to appropriate counsel, and providing appropriate appeal mechanisms.

Onboard processing may be appropriate in some limited instances, depending on the number and conditions of the persons involved, the facilities on the vessel, and its physical location. It would, however, be impractical for situations involving large numbers of people or where their physical and mental state is not conducive to im-

---

[14] See EXCOM Conclusion No. 81 (XLVII) 1997, para. (F) (A/AC.96/895, para. 18); EXCOM Conclusion No. 82 (XLVIII) 1997, para. (d)(iii) (A/AC/96/895); EXCOM Conclusion No 85 (XLIX), 1998, para. (q) (A/AC.96/911, para. 21.3). It should be noted that in mass influx situations, access to individual procedures may not prove practicable and other responses may be required.

mediate processing. Onboard processing is inappropriate where the rescued persons are aboard a commercial vessel. The first priority in most instances remains prompt and safe disembarkation followed by access to fair and efficient asylum procedures. An effective response to the challenge of properly identifying asylum-seekers should therefore acknowledge that the status of the rescued persons is best determined by the appropriate authorities after disembarkation.

Determination of the State Responsible under International Refugee Law

This raises the question of *determining the state responsible under international refugee law* for admitting the asylum-seekers (at least on a temporary basis) and ensuring access to asylum procedures. International refugee law, read in conjunction with international maritime law, suggests that this is generally the state where disembarkation or landing occurs. This will normally be a coastal state in the immediate vicinity of the rescue.

The flag state could also have primary responsibility under certain circumstances. Where it is clear that those rescued intended to request asylum from the flag state, that state could be said to be responsible for responding to the request and providing access to its national asylum procedure. In the event that the number of persons rescued is small, it might be reasonable for them to remain on the vessel until they can be disembarked on the territory of the flag state. Alternatively, circumstances might necessitate disembarkation in a third state as a transitional measure without that state assuming any responsibility to receive and process applications. Arguably, and even on the high seas, the responsibility accruing to the flag state would be stronger still, where the rescue operation occurs in the context of interception measures. The cumulative effect of the original intended destination and the deliberate intervention of the state to prevent the asylum-seeker from reaching the final destination underpins such an argument.[15]

The Executive Committee of the UNHCR has formulated a number of Conclusions in relation to rescue-at-sea emphasising the question of disembarkation and admission. These Conclusions reflect the experience of the 1980s, which was characterised by serious concerns that refusals to permit disembarkation, especially if only requested on a temporary basis, would have the effect of discouraging rescue-at-sea and undermining other international obligations. While the current situation is not as acute as that faced during the 1980s, there are similarities and now, as then, lives are at risk. The underlying need to uphold the obligation to rescue in full compliance with the consequent obligations that arise under international refugee law remains paramount.

The most salient guidance from EXCOM Conclusions includes the following:

---

[15] EXCOM Conclusion No. 15 (XXX) of 1979 states, *inter alia*, "The intentions of the asylum-seeker as regards the country in which he wishes to request asylum should as far as possible be taken into account." This does not imply an unfettered right of asylum-seekers to pick and choose at will the country in which they intend to request asylum. Rather the reference is framed in the context of situations involving individual asylum-seekers and is but one of a number of criteria. It does, however, provide guidance as to how to address the problem of refugees without an asylum country.

- EXCOM Conclusion No. 14 (1979), paragraph c notes as a matter of concern "… that refugees had been rejected at the frontier … in disregard of the principle of *non-refoulement* and that refugees, arriving by sea had been refused even temporary asylum with resulting danger to their lives … ."
- EXCOM Conclusion No. 15, (1979) paragraph c states: "It is the humanitarian obligation of all coastal States to allow vessels in distress to seek haven in their waters and to grant asylum, or at least temporary refuge, to persons on board wishing to seek asylum."
- EXCOM Conclusion No. 23, (1981) paragraph 3 states: "In accordance with international practice, supported by the relevant international instruments, persons rescued at sea should normally be disembarked at the next port of call. This practice should also be applied to asylum-seekers rescued at sea. In cases of large-scale influx, asylum-seekers rescued at sea should always be admitted, at least on a temporary basis. States should assist in facilitating their disembarkation by acting in accordance with the principles of international solidarity and burden-sharing in granting resettlement opportunities."

In summary, the Executive Committee pronouncements, taken in conjunction with the obligation under international maritime law to ensure delivery to a place of safety, call upon coastal states to allow disembarkation of rescued asylum-seekers at the *next port of call.*[16]

Next Port of Call

Since the "next port of call" with reference to the disembarkation of rescued persons is nowhere clearly defined, there are a number of possibilities that would need to be further explored to clarify this concept. In many instances, especially when large numbers of rescued persons are involved, the nearest port in terms of geographical proximity will be given the overriding safety concerns. Under certain circumstances, it is also possible to conceive the port of embarkation as the appropriate place to effect disembarkation, arising from the responsibility of the country of embarkation to prevent unseaworthy vessels from leaving its territory. Another option would be the next scheduled port of call. This would be appropriate, for instance, in cases where the number of people rescued is small and the safety of the vessel and those on board is neither endangered nor likely to necessitate a deviation from its intended course. There may be instances where the next port of call may not be the closest one but, rather, the one best equipped for the purposes of receiving traumatized and injured victims and subsequently processing any asylum applications. In other situations involving state vessels intercepting illegal migrants, the nearest port of that state could be regarded as the most appropriate port for disembarkation purposes. From a safety and humanitarian perspective, ensuring the safety and dignity of those rescued and of the crew must be the overriding consideration in determining the point of disembarkation.

---

[16] As previously noted, the term "next port of call" in connection with disembarkation or landing of rescued persons is unknown as such to maritime law but results from EXCOM Conclusions.

With regard to all of these considerations, the development of criteria that help to define the *most appropriate port for disembarkation purposes* will be informed by the following factors:

- the legal obligations of states under international maritime law and international refugee law;
- the pressing safety and humanitarian concerns of those rescued;
- the safety concerns of the rescuing vessel and the crew;
- the number of persons rescued and the consequent need to ensure prompt disembarkation;
- the technical suitability of the port in question to allow for disembarkation;
- the need to avoid disembarkation in the country of origin for those alleging a well founded fear of persecution; and
- the financial implications and liability of shipping companies engaged in undertaking rescue operations.

International Human Rights Law

International human rights law also contains important standards in relation to those in distress and rescued at sea. The safe and humane treatment of all persons rescued regardless of their legal status or the circumstances in which they were rescued is of paramount importance. Basic principles such as the protection of the right to life, freedom from cruel, inhuman or degrading treatment and respect for family unity by not separating those rescued must be upheld at all times.[17]

International Criminal Law

Questions of international criminal law arise where the rescue operation is necessitated as a consequence of smuggling operations. Smugglers frequently place large numbers of persons on poorly equipped and unseaworthy vessels, flouting the basic standards of maritime safety. The scale, scope, and huge profits generated by smuggling makes it a matter of concern for states worldwide.

The 2000 Protocol against the Smuggling of Migrants by Land, Sea and Air, supplementing the United Nations Convention against Transnational Organized Crime, while not yet in force, constitutes the most comprehensive legal instrument to date covering smuggling of persons.[18] Under the Protocol, the fact that migrants, including asylum-seekers and refugees, were smuggled does not deprive them of any

---

[17] For further discussion of the applicable human rights standards please see *Reception of Asylum-Seekers, Including Standards of Treatment, in the Context of Individual Asylum Systems*, EC/GC/01/17, the contents of which can be considered to apply *mutatis mutandis* in rescue situations.

[18] Art. 16(1) obliges States to take "all appropriate measures … to preserve and protect the rights of persons" who have been the object of smuggling, "in particular the right to life and the right not to be subjected to torture or other cruel, inhuman, or degrading treatment, or punishment." In addition, according to Art. 16(3), states should "afford appropriate assistance to migrants whose lives and safety are endangered" by reason of being smuggled. In applying the provisions of Art. 16, states are required in its para. 4 to take into account the special needs of women and children.

rights with respect to access to protection and assistance measures. In the context of rescue-at-sea, it is crucial that the rights of those rescued are not unduly restricted as a result of actions designed to tackle the crime of people smuggling. Criminal liability falls squarely upon the smugglers and not on the unwitting users of their services.

With respect to the special circumstances of asylum-seekers and refugees, it should be noted that the Protocol contains a general saving clause in Article 19 to ensure compatibility with obligations under international refugee law.[19] It is clear from the formulation of Article 19 that there is no inherent conflict between the standards set by the international law to combat crimes and those contained in international refugee law. Combating crime does not mean a diminution of the rights of asylum-seekers and refugees.

THE INTERNATIONAL COOPERATIVE FRAMEWORK

Given the complexity of rescue-at-sea situations, not the least due to the involvement of different actors and sets of responsibilities, there is a need for an effective international cooperative framework in this area. The overriding objective of such a framework is to develop responses defining responsibilities in a manner that can be activated without undue delay.

Past Practice and Current Challenges

A brief examination of past practices provides some guidance as to the type of arrangements that may be required to face current challenges.

- The crisis of the Vietnamese boat people prompted specialized response mechanisms to support rescue efforts and the subsequent search for durable solutions. The most important of these were the Disembarkation Resettlement Offers Scheme (DISERO) and the Rescue-at-Sea Resettlement Offers Scheme (RASRO).[20] Both schemes provide an indication of the level of state cooperation required to secure effective response mechanisms.

- The constituent elements of both schemes included:
  - agreement of the coastal states to allow disembarkation;
  - agreement of the coastal states to provide temporary refuge;

---

[19] Art. 19 states that "nothing in this Protocol shall affect the other rights, obligations and responsibilities of States and individuals under international law, including international humanitarian law, and in particular, where applicable, the 1951 Convention and the 1967 Protocol relating to the Status of Refugees and the principle of *non-refoulement* as contained therein."

[20] Both schemes were developed during the 1980s as part of broad-based cooperation between UNHCR and states. Further detailed information on the operation of the DISERO and RASRO schemes can be found in the attached Annex 2, comprised of documentation of the Sub-Committee on the Whole on International Protection, Sessions 32 to 36 inclusive, dating from 1981 to 1985.

- open-ended guarantees from contributing third states that those rescued would be resettled elsewhere.

Eventually however, both DISERO and RASRO were terminated as the guarantee that any Vietnamese rescued at sea would be resettled within ninety days did not square with the 1989 Comprehensive Plan of Action guidelines. These guidelines required that all new arrivals undergo screening to determine their status. Countries in the region became increasingly unwilling to disembark rescued boat people, fearing that resettlement guarantees would not be forthcoming.

Any consideration of mechanisms akin to DISERO and RASRO in the current context will need to take account of the fact that the vast majority of those rescued were considered *prima facie* refugees, in direct flight from their place of origin. Today's situation is characterized by complex movements and mixed flows where the refugee status of those involved must be carefully determined.[21] The composite nature of today's movements, coupled with more restrictive asylum practices generally, compounds the difficulty of agreeing on policies and standards for the processing of asylum applications of persons rescued at sea.

Elements of an International Framework

Against this background, it is suggested to explore an international framework, the goals of which would generally be the following:

- support for the international search and rescue regime;
- easing the burden on states of disembarkation;
- an equitable responsibility sharing approach to the determination of refugee status and international protection needs of those rescued;[22]
- an equitable responsibility-sharing approach to the realization of durable solutions to meet international protection needs;[23]
- agreed readmission and strengthened assistance, financial and otherwise, to first countries of asylum; and

---

[21] Most of the migratory flows that have given rise to the current debate on rescue-at-sea are characterized as mixed. This should not, however, be taken to exclude the possibility of prima face recognition in the event of a massive outflow by sea directly from a country of origin, similar to that of the Vietnamese in the 1980s. In such a scenario individual refugee status determination would be impractical and response mechanisms would need to be tailored accordingly.

[22] This could, for instance, include *stand-by arrangements* to assist states in processing asylum applications, when the number of rescued asylum-seekers overwhelms the capacity of the individual asylum system at the point of disembarkation. This could mean the dispatch of additional asylum officers from third countries, transfer arrangements for the processing of cases, and capacity-building measures to strengthen protection and assistance. Potential distribution mechanisms in the immediately affected region, based on pre-arranged quotas and criteria, could play a positive role in facilitating such arrangements.

[23] Specific *resettlement pools* for rescue-at-sea situations could, for instance, be created. This would require the activation of emergency mechanisms to deal with especially pressing cases.

- agreement by countries of origin to accept the return of their nationals determined, after access to fair and efficient asylum procedures, not to be in need of international protection.

In order to ensure the effectiveness of an international framework, the roles and responsibilities of numerous actors would have to be clarified. The principal actors involved would include:

- asylum-seekers and refugees;
- countries of origin;
- countries of first asylum;
- countries of transit;
- countries of embarkation;
- countries of disembarkation;
- flag states;
- coastal states;
- resettlement countries;
- donor community; and
- international organizations, notably UNHCR, IMO, and IOM.

From the UNHCR's perspective the main concerns at stake which involve issues of refugee law, include:

- the right to seek and enjoy asylum;
- *non-refoulement;*
- access to fair and efficient asylum procedures;
- conditions of treatment;
- appropriate balance between state responsibilities and that of international organizations;
- safe return to first countries of asylum;
- durable solutions for those recognised as refugees; and
- orderly and humane return of persons determined not to be in need of international protection.

A workable framework will also need to take due account of the broader context, including the following factors:

- the impact on smuggling and irregular movement;
- interception practices;
- the adverse impact of exporting condoned practices;
- appropriate responsibility sharing versus individual state responsibility;
- the impact on resettlement policy; and
- the challenge of dealing with cases found not to be in need of international protection.

In addition, the importance of preventative measures should not be overlooked. Many concrete steps can be taken to discourage people from risking dangerous sea voyages. Public information campaigns, actions to prevent the departure of unseaworthy vessels, and stringent criminal law enforcement measures directed against smugglers are features of such measures.

Finally, certain information needs need to be met. These include measures to fill existing information gaps on the scale and scope of the problem; measures to compile and analyze the existing legislative norms in a more detailed fashion, including recommendations for amendments where these prove necessary; an open and transparent exchange of information on current practices in order to identify good state practice; and the development of a comprehensive information strategy designed to inform public opinion on problems related to rescue-at-sea, especially on the rights and obligations of those involved.

Chapter 9
COMBATING MIGRANT SMUGGLING AND TRAFFICKING IN PERSONS, ESPECIALLY WOMEN: THE NORMATIVE FRAMEWORK RE-APPRAISED

Vitit Muntarbhorn*

The issue of migrant smuggling and trafficking in persons, especially women and children, has come to the fore dramatically in recent years as part of the negative side of globalization. The world is facing a proliferation of crime and criminality – often invisible, abusive, and intractable – that constitutes a modern form of slavery, thus demanding closer cooperation among states in counteracting abuses.

The literature on the subject is copious, thus indicating that the knowledge base for action already exists.[1] The normative framework and responses referred to below relate primarily to the laws, policies, and plans at various levels against the phenomenon of trafficking and smuggling. The normative framework exists to inspire measures to help the victims. The main challenge is the effective implementation of laws and policies in practice, and this depends upon how they help to protect rather than aggravate the plight of the victims.

At the outset, a number of considerations may be highlighted. First, the trafficking in persons is both internal and external, within and across countries. The phenomenon relates primarily to the movement of persons coercively or due to abuse of authority by those having power over the victims, for the purpose of exploitation. By contrast, migrant smuggling is essentially a cross-border situation entailing the procurement of the illegal entry of a person into another country. Whether in relation to

---

* Professor at the Faculty of Law, Chulalongkorn University, Bangkok; formerly UN Special Rapporteur on the Sale of Children (UN Human Rights Commission, Geneva).

The author wishes to thank warmly Phil Marshall, Farooq Azam, Lance Bonneau, Herve Berger, Hans van der Glind, Jahanshah Assadi, Indrika Ratwatte, Khun Jiravudh, G.Balagopal, Anne Gallagher, the International Organization for Migration (IOM), and the Office of the United Nations High Commissioner for Refugees (UNHCR) for some of the information used in this study. All views expressed are the author's personal views.

[1] For general reading, see M. Wijers and Lin Lap Chew, *Trafficking in Women, Forced Labor and Slavery Like Practices in Marriage, Domestic Work and Prostitution* (1997); V. Muntarbhorn, *Extraterritorial Criminal Laws against Child Sexual Exploitation* (1998); S. Farrior, "The International Law on Trafficking in Women and Children for Prostitution: Making It Live Up to Its Potential," 10 *Harvard Human Rights Journal* (1977), pp. 213-255; "Trafficking in Children for Sexual Purposes," background paper of the Second World Congress against Commercial Sexual Exploitation of Children, Yokohama, 17-21 December 2001.

T.A. Aleinikoff and V. Chetail (Eds.), Migration and International Legal Norms
© 2003, T.M.C. ASSER PRESS, *The Hague, The Netherlands, et al.*

trafficking or smuggling, countries are often concurrently source countries, transit countries, and destination countries.

Second, while the trafficking for sexual exploitation – prostitution – is often in the news, the trafficking for other purposes is common as well. For instance, it may relate to forced labor, debt bondage, begging, child adoption, and even possibly the sale of human organs.

Third, the growing transcontinental nature of trafficking and smuggling has put on the map new areas and populations affected by the phenomenon. For example, a few years ago, it would have been rare to hear of Uzbek and Russian women being trafficked or smuggled to Bangkok, boatloads of Afghans and Iraqis en route to Australia, or Chinese nationals being trafficked or smuggled in container lorries to and through Europe. This geographic and ethnic spread results in an understandable sense of insecurity on the part of destination countries. Yet, at times it leads to over-blown fears with draconian actions in breach of human rights.

Fourth, in view of the increasing global preoccupation with the issue of terrorism since the attacks on the United States on 11 September 2001, there is a trend on the part of several states to turn to more stringent migration policies as a weapon against terrorism. A key challenge is how to prevent overreaction with drastic consequences for the rights of migrants, especially victims of trafficking and smuggling. Inter-linked with this is the worrying tide of racism and discrimination against migrants.

Fifth, any consideration of laws and policies would be incomplete unless the call for comprehensive measures is heeded, bolstered by genuine political commitment and adequate resources. Added to this is the challenge of enabling the various stake-holders – not simply states and intergovernmental organizations, but also civil so-ciety actors, such as non-governmental organizations (NGOs), the media, the business sector, and the victims themselves – to cooperate as a vigilant force against the phenomenon.

THE NORMATIVE FRAMEWORK

The framework of laws, policies and plans against trafficking and smuggling exists at three levels: multilateral, regional, and national.

Multilateral

There are age-old treaties on the issue of trafficking. These include the International Agreement for the Suppression of the White Slave Traffic (1904),[2] the International Convention for the Suppression of White Slave Traffic (1910),[3] the International

---

[2] 18 May 1904, I *LNTS* 83. As commented by Farrior, *supra* note 1, at 20, "The title of the instru-ment shows that only the exploitation of white women was of enough concern to prompt treaty protec-tion. The goal of the Agreement was to halt the sale of women into prostitution in Europe at a time when economic conditions were so dire that women were increasingly vulnerable to being forced into prostitution. The provisions of the Agreement were aimed at protecting the victims, not at punishing the procurers. This approach proved ineffective, thereby prompting the adoption in 1910 of the Inter-national Convention for the Suppression of White Slave Traffic."

[3] 4 May 1910, III *LNTS* 278. There were only thirteen signatories to this treaty. This instrument and

Convention for the Suppression of the Traffic in Women and Children (1921),[4] the International Convention for the Suppression of the Traffic in Women in Full Age (1933),[5] and the Convention on the Suppression of Trafficking and the Exploitation of the Prostitution of Others (1949).[6] All of them, to a lesser or greater extent, were aimed at crime prevention and suppression.

These early treaties suffered from the fact that they were not gender-sensitive enough and were not broad enough to cover the range of trafficking situations noted earlier. The 1949 Convention suffered the further fate of being perceived as stigmatizing prostitution, whereas globally, at least in relation to adult prostitution, there are two contra-posed lobbies – one lobby views adult prostitution as exploitation, while the other views it as legitimate work. All of these early instruments were shaped by another defect; they belonged to an era where there did not yet exist adequate monitoring mechanisms at the international level to trace and track human trafficking and the needed countermeasures.

More recently, a variety of treaties tackle the issue of trafficking with increasing emphasis on a human rights perspective from the angle of protection of the victims. These include:

- the Convention on the Elimination of All Forms of Discrimination Against Women (CEDAW) (1979);[7]
- the Convention on the Rights of the Child (CRC) (1989);[8]
- the International Convention on the Protection of the Rights of All Migrant Workers and their Families (1990);[9]
- the Hague Convention on the Protection of Children and Cooperation in respect of Inter-country Adoptions (1993);[10]
- the International Labor Organization's (ILO) Convention No. 182 concerning the Prohibition and Immediate Action for the Elimination of the Worst Forms of Child Labor (1999);[11]
- the Optional Protocol to the CRC on the Sale of Children, Child Prostitution and Child Pornography (2000).[12]

---

the others, which followed until the rise of the United Nations (UN), were particularly concerned with the growing sex trade affecting Europe. However, these treaties were limited in terms of geographic participation, since many developing countries were still colonies at the time such treaties were formulated. Moreover, the emphasis on the "white slave trade" had a racial undertone, more oriented to protecting white women than all women irrespective of race.

[4] 30 September 1921, 9 *LNTS* 431.

[5] 11 October 1933, 150 *LNTS* 431.

[6] 21 March 1950, 96 *UNTS* 271. While nearly eighty countries have signed and or ratified this Convention, it is seen as a flawed treaty, compounded by limited accessions, weak implementation and lack of a specific monitoring mechanism. In terms of impact, arguably it has been superseded by more recent instruments.

[7] G.A. Res. 34/180, U.N. GAOR, 34th Sess., Supp. No. 46 (1979).

[8] G.A. Res. 44/25, U.N. GAOR, 45th Sess., Supp. No. 49, UN Doc. No.A/44/49(1990); 1577 *UNTS* 3. This is the most universally ratified human rights treaty, with 191 State Parties by the year 2002.

[9] G.A. Res. 45/158, reprinted *in* 5 *ILM* 352 (1966).

[10] http://www.hcch.net/e/vconventions.

[11] 38 *ILM* 1207 (1999).

[12] 39 *ILM* 1285 (2000).

There are also a number of other treaties related to the ILO, such as those against forced labor, which have bearing on the issue of trafficking.

Taken together, these human rights instruments advocate a range of actions to respond to the rights of women and children concerning the issue of trafficking and smuggling. For instance, the approach based on human rights calls for effective and woman-and-child sensitive laws, policies, programs, mechanisms, resources, information and education to protect women and children. These instruments also have various monitoring mechanisms such as international committees to oversee the performance of Member States. They imply greater transparency and accountability, as well as the empowerment of women and children in the process. Yet, the key challenge in practice is their implementation, particularly at the national and local levels. Lax implementation or poor enforcement is, in reality, often the order of the day, and it is shaped in several settings by five key C's: Corruption, Collusion, Cronyism, Clientelism, and Crime.

In addition, a range of international declarations and plans of action call for action against trafficking. These include the Plan of Action of the International Conference on Population and Development (1994),[13] the Beijing Platform of the World Conference on Women (1995),[14] and the Declaration and Agenda for Action against Commercial Sexual Exploitation of Children adopted by the Stockholm World Congress (1996) (supplemented by the Yokohama Global Commitment (2001) as the follow-up process for the Stockholm Congress and Declaration).[15] The principles espoused by such instruments pertain to both trafficking and smuggling, although the former is more explicitly targeted. The human rights approach inherent in them calls for responsive laws, policies, programs, practices, mechanisms, resources, monitoring, and joint cooperation. A key tenet is to advocate comprehensive actions – in law and in other fields – to thwart those who abuse the persons concerned, while being victim-sensitive. The issue of individual responsibility for crimes has been given added impetus by the Rome Statute of the International Criminal Court (1998),[16] which confers jurisdiction on this new Court to tackle a number of international crimes such as crimes against humanity and war crimes which may cover elements of trafficking and smuggling directly or indirectly.

The most recent treaties specifically on the issue of trafficking and smuggling are two of the three Protocols attached to the United Nations Convention against Transnational Organized Crime (1998).[17] This Convention covers transnational crimes involving a structured group of three or more persons. Of the three Protocols, the two most pertinent to this study are as follows:

---

[13] http://www.unfpa.org/icpd.

[14] http://www.un.org/womenwatch/daw/beijing/platform.

[15] For Stockholm World Congress documents, see *Report of the World Congress against Commercial Sexual Exploitation of Children*, Stockholm, Sweden, 29-31 August 1996 (1996); for Yokohama World Congress documents, see *Second World Congress against Commercial Sexual Exploitation of Children* (The Yokohama Congress), Yokohama, Japan, 17-20 December 2001 (Tokyo: Ministry of Foreign Affairs, Japan, 2002).

[16] 38 *ILM* 999 (1998).

[17] 40 *ILM* 335 (2001).

- the Protocol to Prevent, Suppress and Punish Trafficking in Persons, especially Women and Children, supplementing the United Nations Convention against Transnational Organized Crime (1998);[18]
- the Protocol against the Smuggling of Migrants by Land, Sea and Air, supplementing the United Nations Convention against Transnational Organized Crime (1998).[19]

By the middle of 2002, none of the three instruments mentioned was yet in force. There were 141 signatories and 8 State Parties to the UN Convention; 104 signatories and 6 State Parties to the anti-trafficking Protocol; and 100 signatories and 6 State Parties to the anti-smuggling Protocol. Each of these instruments needs 40 ratifications (State Parties) to enter into force.

With regard to the anti-trafficking protocol, this definition of "trafficking in persons" is stipulated:

"The recruitment, transportation, transfer, harboring or receipt of persons, by means of the threat or use of force or other forms of coercion, of abduction, of fraud, of deception, of the abuse of power or of a position of vulnerability or of the giving or receiving of payments or benefits to achieve the consent of a person having control over another person, for the purpose of exploitation. Exploitation shall include, at a minimum, the exploitation of the prostitution of others or other forms of sexual exploitation, forced labor or services, slavery or practices similar to slavery, servitude or the removal of organs." (Article 3)

The Protocol provides the following directives for action:

- not only is coercion and force covered but also abuse of authority as a part of the trafficking;
- the exploitation behind the trafficking encompasses sexual exploitation and other forms, e.g., forced labor, slavery, and removal of organs;
- consent on the part of the victim is irrelevant;
- "child" means any person under eighteen years old;
- legislation to criminalize the trafficking is to be adopted by states parties;
- a wide range of measures to protect the human rights of the victims is provided for, e.g., legal assistance, counseling, shelter, and medical help in appropriate cases;
- measures to permit the victims to remain in the territory of the transit and destination country are to be considered in appropriate cases;
- in relation to the State Party of which the victim is a national or has a right of permanent residence, safe return of the victim to that state is to be facilitated;
- measures to prevent the trafficking and to promote cooperation are to be adopted, e.g., media campaigns, information exchange and training, border controls, and security of travel documents; and

---

[18] Id. at. 377-384.
[19] Id. at 384-394.

- monitoring of the implementation of the Protocol is provided for by the Convention against Transnational Organized Crime through periodic conferences of States Parties.

This Protocol endeavors to answer the question concerning the trafficked victim who is a refugee or seeking refugee status as follows:

> "1. Nothing in this Protocol shall affect the rights, obligations and responsibilities of States and individuals under international law, including international humanitarian law and international human rights law and in particular, where applicable, the 1951 Convention and the 1967 Protocol relating to the Status of Refugees and the principle of *non-refoulement* as contained therein." (Article 14)

In practice, this means that the rights of refugees are to be guaranteed, even though such persons may also be victims of trafficking. By implication, refugees are not be sent back to areas of dangers (*non-refoulement*) and those seeking refugee status are to have access to asylum procedures and refugee determination procedures.

NGOs have been critical of some aspects of the UN Convention against Transnational Organized Crime and the anti-trafficking Protocol above (as well as that on smuggling below).[20] In particular, these instruments are seen as anti-crime measures without being sufficiently human rights sensitive. For instance, in the provision in the anti-trafficking Protocol on the assistance to the victims of trafficking, instead of there being a clear commitment from Member States to render effective assistance, such States are only committed to providing assistance "in appropriate cases" (Article 6). This "diluted" style of commitment from governments is also seen in other Articles of the Protocol. For instance, in regard to Article 7 on the status of the victims of trafficking in receiving States, there is the following stipulation:

> "1. In addition to taking measures pursuant to Article 6 of this Protocol, each State Party shall consider adopting legislative or other *appropriate* measures that permit victims of *trafficking* in persons to remain in its territory, temporarily or permanently, in *appropriate* cases.
> 2. In implementing the provision contained in paragraph 1 of this article, each State Party shall give *appropriate* consideration to humanitarian and compassionate factors." (emphasis added by the author)

The anti-smuggling protocol provides this definition of migrant smuggling:

> "The procurement, in order to obtain, directly or indirectly, a financial or other material benefit, of the illegal entry of a person into a State Party of which the person is not a national or permanent resident." (Article 3)

---

[20] For the lead-up to the UN Convention against Transnational Organized Crime and its two Protocols, including the various governmental and non-governmental positions, see *Report of the Ad Hoc Committee on the Elaboration of a Convention against Transnational Organized Crime on the Work of its First till Eleventh Sessions*, UN Doc. A/55/383 (November 2000); http://www/catwinternational.org/.

The Protocol provides the following directives for action:

- migrants are not to be liable to criminal prosecution for the fact of having been smuggled;
- migrant smuggling is to be criminalized;
- a State Party which suspects that a vessel flying the flag or displaying the marks of registry of another State Party is engaged in smuggling of migrants by sea may notify the flag State and request authorization from the flag State to board and search the vessel and take appropriate measures *vis-à-vis* the smuggling;
- where a State Party suspects that a vessel is engaged in migrant smuggling and is without nationality, it may board the vessel, search it, and take appropriate measures;
- measures taken in relation to migrant smuggling at sea are to take account of the need not to interfere with the rights and obligations under the international law of the sea;
- measures to prevent migrant smuggling and to promote cooperation are to be taken, e.g., information exchange, training and information dissemination programs, checks on travel documents, and border measures;
- protection and assistance measures for the victims are to include access to consular help under the relevant international treaty on consular relations;
- return of the smuggled migrants to the country of nationality or country where they have permanent residence is to be facilitated; and
- protection for refugees under international law is ensured with a provision similar to Article 14 of the anti-trafficking Protocol above.

Upon scrutiny, while it is not altogether easy to distinguish between trafficking and smuggling, one difference may be that while trafficking is always exploitative of the victims, those being smuggled may at times be gaining some kind of benefit from the smugglers (e.g., assisted passage to another country). From the angle of the victims, therefore, trafficking is more objectionable than smuggling, although the latter may also be abusive.

Read together with the Convention against Transnational Organized Crime, the anti-trafficking Protocol and the anti-smuggling Protocol advocate at least a three-pronged approach, namely:

- to prevent and combat the trafficking and smuggling, particularly by criminalizing such acts;
- to treat those who are trafficked and smuggled as victims with inherent rights; and
- to promote international cooperation such as through mutual cooperation between law enforcers and extradition of the culprits.

Furthermore, even if the victims enter a country with false documents, this should not *per se* lead to an offence being committed by them as they may have had no option but to use such documents. This is particularly pertinent to those seeking refugee status.

Because the UN Convention against Transnational Organized Crime and its two Protocols are not yet in force, it may be premature to offer a prognosis of their full impact. However, it is apparent that the process leading up to these instruments and their finalization has had substantial impact in a variety of ways, including the following:

- greater public exposure to the issue of trafficking and smuggling, and more extensive media coverage;
- greater political will of and more cooperation between governments to address the issue, especially from the angle of anticrime measures, evident in some of the regional and national actions cited below;
- greater sensibility towards the rights of the victims, exemplified by various new laws on the subject, as seen in the sections below; and
- broader networking among civil society, such as NGOs.

However, implementation of anti-trafficking and anti-smuggling measures remains weak or selective on several fronts. Anti-crime measures are often not victim-sensitive enough. There is a tendency among governments to propose new laws and policies on the issue, without adequate attention to the question of how to promote quality law enforcement. The emphasis on anti-trafficking and anti-smuggling may also undermine the position of those seeking refugee status – the latter may all too easily become "reclassified" from "refugee status" with substantial guarantees – to "trafficked or smuggled status" with fewer guarantees.

Regional

An array of regional initiatives has arisen in recent years against trafficking and smuggling, ranging from treaties to plans of action, dialogue processes, and joint actions. For example, there is the Convention on Preventing and Combating Trafficking in Women and Children for Prostitution adopted by the South Asian Association for Regional Cooperation in 2002.[21] The treaty is more limited in scope that the anti-trafficking Protocol noted above since it only covers trafficking for prostitution and only encompasses protection for women and children. It defines trafficking as "the moving, selling or buying of women and children for prostitution within or outside a country for monetary or other considerations with or without the consent of the person subjected to trafficking" (Article 1). It calls for measures for prevention, interdiction, and suppression of such trafficking, paralleling many of the measures voiced by the anti-trafficking Protocol above, particularly the criminalization of those who traffic in women and children. Protection of the victims is called for; this ranges from information programs to care, protective homes and shelters, counseling, job training, and repatriation of the victims. Measures of cooperation between countries, such as mutual assistance in the legal field, are stipulated. Interestingly, the role of non-governmental organizations is explicitly recognized, particularly in providing care and protection of the victims.

---

[21] htpp://www.saarc.org.

With regard to other parts of Asia and the Pacific, there are various policies and plans of action, and cooperative processes currently at work. The Association of Southeast Asian Nations has a plan of action against transnational organized crimes, which can also be used to counter trafficking, and smuggling.[22] There is the Asia-Pacific Consultations (APC) Process dealing with refugees, displaced persons and migrants; it holds periodic meetings to discuss issues like smuggling and trafficking.[23] Likewise, the Asian Initiative against Trafficking (ARIAT) that has a plan of action ranging from measures of prevention to prosecution of the traffickers, rescue and reintegration of the victims.[24] A regional plan of action against trafficking has also been adopted under the umbrella of the United Nations Economic and Social Commission for Asia and the Pacific (ESCAP).[25] There are various projects on the issue under the United Nations in the Mekong region.

A key declaration preceding both the APC and ARIAT processes was the Bangkok Declaration on Irregular Migration adopted by Asia-Pacific countries in 1999 resulting from the International Symposium on Migration "Towards Regional Cooperation on Irregular/Undocumented Migration."[26] This called for closer cooperation, information exchange and dissemination, criminalization of smuggling and trafficking, and humane treatment of the victims. The Symposium leading to this Declaration was propelled by the escalation of irregular migration in the region and the need felt by governments to come together to cooperate more closely to address the issue. The Symposium was conditioned by the many types of irregular migration – including forced migration interrelated with human trafficking, the search for asylum, and other displacements – needing comprehensive responses. The follow up to this Bangkok Declaration has been linked with the APC and ARIAT mentioned above; it has manifested itself in more consultations and closer cooperation between governments, with emphasis on more legislation and policies to criminalize human trafficking, and related information sharing and dissemination.

The European, American, and African regions all have intergovernmental human rights protection systems in the form of human rights treaties and mechanisms such as regional courts, which can help to protect victims. In recent years, they have been exploring more avenues for policies and plans of action, and cooperation dialogues specifically on the issue of trafficking and smuggling. In Europe, there have been several initiatives from the Council of Europe and the European Union in the form of recommendations and joint actions.[27] The European Charter of Fundamental Rights proclaimed by the European Union in 2000 has a provision related to the traf-

---

[22] htpp://www.aseansec.org.

[23] IOM, "Migrant Trafficking and Trafficking in Persons," background paper of the Conference on People Smuggling, Trafficking in Persons and Related Transnational Crime, Bali, 26-28 February 2002; IOM, "Cooperation in International Migration Management through Regional Consultative Processes on Migration," id.

[24] Id.

[25] 1998 Regional Conference on Trafficking in Women: Bangkok Accord and Plan of Action (Tokyo: Asian Women's Fund, 1998).

[26] IOM, *supra* note 23.

[27] See further F.G. Jacobs and R.C.A. White, *The European Convention on Human Rights* (1996); P. Alston (ed.), *The EU and Human Rights* (1999); see IOM, *supra* note 23.

ficking phenomenon,[28] while the Union itself is moving, through framework decisions, towards increased harmonization of laws on this matter. There are various dialogue processes related to the Baltic Sea States Council and the Black Sea Economic Council on the phenomenon.[29] Central Europe has been involved since 1991 with the Budapest Process, which also counters organized crime and trafficking.[30]

In America, there is the Puebla Process involving North and Central America in information exchange and cooperation on the issue of irregular migration,[31] while South America began a parallel process pursuant to the Lima Declaration of 1999.[32] In Africa, there is the Migration Dialogue for Southern Africa (MIDSA) and a parallel process for West Africa.[33]

In terms of transcontinental dialogue, various cooperation meetings are held periodically between countries of North America, Europe, and Australia under the umbrella of the Inter-governmental Consultations on Asylum, Refugees and Migration Policies (IGC).[34] In relation to the European and Asian countries formerly linked with the Soviet Union, there is the process, which emerged from the Geneva Conference on Refugees, Displaced Person and other forms of involuntary displacement under the umbrella of the Commonwealth of Independent States (CIS) (1995).[35] The Asian-African Legal Consultative Committee has also decided to take up the issue of migration recently, especially the protection of migrant workers.[36] Meanwhile, the Asia-Europe Meetings (ASEM) have been targeting more measures against human trafficking and have set up a computerized data base on laws concerning child sexual exploitation.[37]

The most recent pulse on this issue was felt at the Conference on People Smuggling, Trafficking in Persons and Related Transnational Crime in 2002 in Bali on the initiative of Indonesia and Australia. The conference had transcontinental participation at the ministerial level, involving over fifty countries and key international agencies. While the refugee issue was discussed to some extent, there tended to be a shift of interest towards the trafficking and smuggling issue rather than refugee protection. The message from the Co-Chairpersons' Statement underlines priorities at this point in time, at least from the viewpoint of governments, including the following:[38]

• more information and intelligence sharing arrangements;

---

[28] See further J. Meyer, *The Charter of Fundamental Rights as a First Step Towards a European Constitution* (2000).

[29] See IOM, *supra* note 23.

[30] Id.

[31] Id.

[32] Id.

[33] Id.

[34] Id.

[35] Id.

[36] Id.

[37] ASEM Action for Children (1998).

[38] "Bali Ministerial Conference on People Smuggling, Trafficking in Persons and Related Transnational Crime: Co Chairs' Statement," Bali, 26-28 February 2002.

- more cooperation between law enforcement agencies to enhance deterrence and fight against illegal immigration networks;
- more cooperation on border and visa systems;
- more public awareness programs;
- enhancement of return to the source country as a strategy to deter illegal migration through the conclusion of appropriate arrangements;
- cooperation in verifying the identity and nationality of illegal immigrants; and
- assistance from the international community to tackle to root causes.

Consequently, two working groups have been set up to promote more interchanges; one on information exchange coordinated by New Zealand and the other on laws and law enforcement coordinated by Thailand.

There are various similarities between the regional approach and the multilateral approach above. Both aim for criminalization of smuggling and trafficking. Both recognize the question of victims' rights. Both propound the need for more cooperation. The value added of the regional approach is that precisely because it is smaller in scale, as compared with the multilateral approach, there are more opportunities for more focused activities and closer cooperation between countries in each region. However, in reality, care should be exercised so that the regional preoccupation with deterrence should not be used to deter migration (*vis-à-vis* the migrants) without other humane options. The verbal commitment against trafficking and smuggling still need to be matched by an equally strong commitment to protect victims' rights in practice, and to ensure that those seeking refuge have effective access to asylum procedures and refugee determination procedures, and international protection in the absence of national protection.

National

All countries have some laws that may be used against trafficking and smuggling. The most obvious is the ubiquitous presence of national criminal laws. These are supplemented by various labor laws and other more specific laws, e.g., laws on child protection or violence against women and children, which may indirectly counter trafficking and smuggling.

In recent years, several countries have taken a more focused approach of passing targeted laws, particularly against trafficking. A case in point is the United States, which in 2000 passed the Trafficking Victims Protection Act.[39] The Act takes a strong crime suppression approach while having broader vistas. For instance, in addition to strong penalties of fines and imprisonment for the traffickers, it provides for the possibility of giving temporary visas – T visas – to the victims to stay temporarily in the United States to help prosecute the traffickers. The Act establishes an interagency task force to monitor the trafficking, and offers economic alternatives to source countries to prevent and deter trafficking, such as micro-credit lending programs, programs to promote women's participation in decision-making, educational

---

[39] See further 146 *Cong. Rec. H* 8855 (5 October 2000); htpp://www.state/gov/g/inl/rls/tiprpt/2001.

programs to help children access education, and assistance to non-governmental organizations to help in the development process. It provides for annual reports covering the globe on what actions countries are taking to curb the trafficking, with the possibility of sanctions for those failing to take adequate measures. While there are many positive aspects of this new law, a question remains concerning whether the threat of sanctions is appropriate, especially if it is based upon a degree of unilateralism. There is also a query concerning whether the T visas will undermine the access of asylum-seekers to refugee determination procedures.

Thailand has also adopted a specific law against trafficking in women and children. The 1997 law provides for severe penalties against traffickers.[40] It provides for more victim-friendly procedures and opens the door to taking testimonies by videotape. It allows early depositions to be taken from victims and witnesses so that they will not have to stay in the country too long, pending their return to the country of origin. Interestingly, it provides for the role of non-governmental organizations to provide shelters to the victims. This has been supplemented by a memorandum of understanding between government agencies and non-governmental organizations to treat the victims of trafficking as victims rather than as illegal immigrants where they enter the country in breach of the immigration law. The approach is to shift them to welfare shelters rather than to incarcerate them in an immigration jail, pending their return home. In the return process, safety is to be ensured for the victims. These responses are coupled with various national policies and plans of action against trafficking and child sexual exploitation. These developments are now being coupled with bilateral agreements with neighboring countries to ensure safe return of the victims to the country of origin; potentially the first bilateral agreement will be with Cambodia.

Have these laws and related policies led to a decline in trafficking and smuggling? There are no easy answers. In some countries, there have been huge caseloads of prosecutions of traffickers and smugglers, e.g., in China.[41] Potentially, this may prevent many other cases of trafficking and smuggling from taking place. In other countries, it has been very difficult to prosecute the wrongdoers, precisely because law enforcement is generally poor and corruption is a major hurdle to law enforcement as a whole.

The normative framework also needs to be re-appraised from the angle of how some national laws may regrettably (re)victimize the victims rather than protect them. The stakes include the following:

• National immigration laws. The immigration laws of several countries still have no adequate provision to exempt the victims of trafficking and smuggling from their strictures. In effect, this means that the victims who enter a country without

---

[40] Memorandum of Understanding on Common Guidelines of Practices for Agencies concerned with Cases where Women and Children are Victims of Human Trafficking B.E.2542 (1999) and National Policy, Plan of Action and Legal Measures in the Elimination of Sexual Abuse and Exploitation of Children (1999).

[41] See further *Proceedings of the 1997 Regional Conference on Trafficking in Women and Children*, Bangkok, Thailand (1999).

proper immigration papers are classified as illegals or illegal immigrants subject to fines and imprisonment. Matters are aggravated by those systems that impose upon their nationals the need to acquire exit visas before leaving the country; those failing to do so may be treated as illegals or illegal emigrants. The juridical traumas suffered by the victims may thus be three-fold: as victims of trafficking and smuggling, as illegal immigrants, and as illegal emigrants.

- National Anti-prostitution Laws. Most countries still criminalize prostitution, and those landing up in prostitution – including victims of trafficking and smuggling – may find themselves criminalized as prostitutes. Thus the double stigma of being victims of trafficking and smuggling, and criminals and prostitutes.

- National Juvenile Justice Laws. Several countries still treat children and adolescents who find themselves in various criminal activities as delinquents rather than as victims, including in regard to sexual exploitation. The approach taken by the law is thus punitive rather than child-rights-centered and victim-responsive. The punitive approach may lead to incarcerating the young people rather than treating them as victims and thereby leading to a healing process and social reintegration.

There is, therefore, a need for transparency of the normative responses to ensure that they do not re-traumatize the victims and to ensure that those laws and policies, which fail to meet international standards, are reformed accordingly.

Finally, a caveat may be entered: it does not suffice to promote the normative framework based only upon a crime suppression and punitive approach. There are many other laws and policies beyond the criminal law which need to be promoted. These include, for example, laws promoting people's development and countering poverty so that people will become less gullible to the trafficking and smuggling. Such laws may include a law to promote access to education, a law to foster employment opportunities, a law to provide micro-finance, a law to offer social security, and a law to promote people's participation and freedom of association as a vigilant force against crime.

Collateral to these, labor laws can be used to give incentives to employers so that they do not resort to employing victims of trafficking and smuggling. The laws can also lead to regularization of the status of the victims, e.g., through registration of migrant workers (who initially entered without proper papers or documents) with the authorities, so that the illegal status is transformed into legal status. This helps to prevent an underground situation whereby the victims are manipulated and blackmailed by criminals and their syndicates concerning their illegal status, in a vicious cycle of enslavement.

Above all, there is the pervasive issue of effective implementation with sensibility towards the victims, and this is regrettably lacking in many countries.

The impact of the above has thus to be appraised at least from the angle of quality law enforcement, good governance *vis-à-vis* corruption, non-discrimination, and access to justice for all.

ORIENTATIONS

While the range of initiatives against trafficking and smuggling at the multilateral, regional, and national levels are generally welcome, an assessment of their operationalization reveals various challenges that need to be addressed more concretely.

First, despite the definitions of trafficking and smuggling offered by the normative framework, the overlaps or conflicts in the application of these definitions should not be underestimated in practice. A key concern is that while some authorities may classify a situation as smuggling, others may view that situation as a matter of trafficking, and others may simply view it as an unlawful situation of illegals. The scenario becomes more complex when there are also claims of asylum, opening the door to the possibility of refugee status. Legal technicalities at the national level may regrettably be used to impede rather than promote access to protection and justice for the victims. The optimal result is to ensure that the victims are accorded the highest protection and standard of treatment – and not the lowest.

Second, there is the related challenge of how the victims of trafficking or smuggling are categorized by the legislation of source countries, transit countries, and destination countries. As previously noted, the victims are re-traumatized or re-victimized by various national laws and policies when they are seen as illegals rather than as victims. This exemplifies the situation where the law enforcement itself is counterproductive because it aggravates the plight of the victims, and such enforcement is rendered more reprehensible if it is influenced by corruption. The preferred method of classifying the victims is to regard them as irregulars or irregular migrants, implying that although in strict law, they are illegals, they should not be treated negatively by the law and that other avenues for preventing and solving their dilemmas should be explored. This would imply, for instance, that if they enter a country without proper travel documents, humane options should be explored, e.g., housing them in shelters pending their return home rather than detaining them in an immigration jail.

Third, many responses to the issue of trafficking and smuggling are not yet gender-sensitive enough, and women's rights have not been mainstreamed sufficiently into national legislation and policies. This is compounded by the cult of patriarchy, which exists in many regions, and negative traditional practices that discriminate against women. A parallel situation pertains to child victims whose rights have not been integrated adequately into the national and local framework, compounded by a patriarchal culture.

Fourth, it is important to view the various responses to combat trafficking and smuggling from the angle of how they address both the supply and demand behind the phenomenon. Often, the environment of poverty and underdevelopment is seen as a key factor propelling the supply. By contrast, the demand side interrelates with the spread of crime, related intermediaries, and the pull of the market in terms of clients, customers, and members of the business sector worldwide. Yet, the profiles of those behind the demand side, especially their psychological patterns and distortions, are often not adequately documented or understood, thus weakening the needed counteractions.

Fifth, there is a tendency on the part of several states to deny that migration is a normal rather than an exceptional phenomenon. This is enmeshed in a zero immigration policy that is counterproductive and unrealistic. It also adds fuel to the premise that the less the possibility of legal and orderly immigration channels into a country, the greater the likelihood of clandestine channels being used by those seeking entry who then land up in the trap of trafficking and smuggling into that country.

Finally, while international cooperation is emerging on many fronts against trafficking and smuggling, a persistent challenge is to ensure that it reaches those in need and that there is effective implementation of victim-sensitive norms. International cooperation depends upon effective programming and related monitoring with disaggregated data on a long-term basis; these demand actions beyond by the mere presence of laws and policies.

The preferred orientations for the future include the following:

- there is a need to propagate the message that migration is a natural process and that the better way of dealing with it is through orderly and regular channels giving rise to managed migration rather than clandestine migration, with the realization that the lack of such channels may fuel human trafficking and smuggling;
- it is important to bear in mind the population projections for the future and their interrelationship with migration; the fact that in the next century, population growth will take place primarily in developing countries, especially Asia and Africa, while an ageing society in the north should provide a prognosis for the type of out-migration that will take place towards developed countries;[42]
- the positive features of migration, especially the contributions of the migrants to the destination countries, should be recognized, and there is a need to nurture, from an early age, an appreciation of the diversity of different ethnic groups to prevent racism and discrimination;
- trafficking and smuggling of persons are the negative side of migration; to counter them, criminalization of such conduct is essential and can be done by means of national criminal laws or more specific legislation targeted against trafficking and smuggling, coupled with effective law enforcement; such laws should abide by international standards, especially the two new Protocols and the various human rights instruments mentioned;
- ratification of the two Protocols and related human rights instruments should be fostered, together with effective implementation against the traffickers and smugglers; national actions complying with these instruments should be to the benefit and not to the detriment of the victims – they need to be tested from the angle of how they respect human rights;
- the crime suppression and punitive approach by itself is inadequate; it needs to be coupled with a variety of measures aimed at people's development, countering poverty and promoting livelihood opportunities;
- laws, procedures, policies, and programs countering trafficking and smuggling should be victim friendly, gender-sensitive, and attuned to international human

---

[42] See further IOM, *World Migration Report 2000* (2000).

rights standards; they need to be transparent, open to reforms, and part of a socialization and mobilization process, and educational and awareness campaigns
respectful of human rights, while not impeding people's right to leave and seek
asylum in other countries;

- access to help for the victims needs to be enhanced; this implies a role not only
for state organs and international organizations but also for civil society actors,
including NGOs, the media, the business sector, and survivors of the trafficking
and smuggling to protect and assist the victims, in addition to international protection where national protection is deficient;
- actions against trafficking and smuggling should target both the supply and demand, and the good practices on this front need to be identified and supported,
while overcoming the not-so-good-practices; a systematic monitoring program
and long term data collection and surveys are required; and
- in-country and inter-country cooperation is a key to countering trafficking and
smuggling; and it needs to be bolstered by political will and adequate resources;
it should avoid duplication and wastage, while being targeted to efficacy and
sustainability in implementing the normative framework, with due regard to the
need for empowerment of women and children.

Selected Bibliography

GAATW – *Human Rights and Trafficking in Persons: A Handbook* (2001).
INTERNATIONAL LABOR ORGANIZATION – *Labor Migration and Trafficking within the Greater Mekong Subregion* (2001).
INTERNATIONAL ORGANIZATION FOR MIGRATION – *World Migration Report 2000* (2000).
—. "Migrant Trafficking and Trafficking in Persons", Background Paper of the Conference on People Smuggling, Trafficking in Persons and Related Transnational Crime, Bali, 26-28 February 2002.
—. "Cooperation in International Migration Management through Regional Consultative Processes on Migration," Background Paper of the Conference on People Smuggling, Trafficking in Persons and Related Transnational Crime, Bali, 26-28 February 2002.
LIM, LIN LEAN – *The Sex Sector: The Economic and Social Bases of Prostitution in Southeast Asia* (1998).
MUNTARBHORN, VITIT – *Report of Second World Congress against Commercial Sexual Exploitation of Children, Yokohama, 17-20 December 2001*. htpp://www.ecpat.net.
—. *Extra-territorial Criminal Laws against Child Sexual Exploitation* (1998).
REPORT OF THE AD HOC COMMITTEE on the Elaboration of a Convention against Transnational Organized Crime on the Work of its First to Eleventh Sessions, U.N. Doc. A/55/383 (November 2000).
REPORTS OF THE UNITED NATIONS Special Rapporteur on the Sale of Children, Child Prostitution and Child Pornography (annual). htpp://www.unhchr.
REPORTS OF THE UNITED NATIONS Special Rapporteur on Violence against Women (annual). htpp://www.unhchr.
"TRAFFICKING IN CHILDREN FOR SEXUAL PURPOSES," – Background Paper of the Second World Congress against Commercial Sexual Exploitation of Children, Yokohama, 17-20 December 2001.
UN ECOSOC – *Addendum to the Report of the United Nations High Commissioner for Human Rights to the Economic and Social Council: Recommended Principles and Guidelines on Human Rights and Human Trafficking*, forthcoming (2002).
UNHCR – *The Status of the World's Refugees: Fifty Years of Humanitarian Action* (2000).
WIJERS, M. AND LAP CHEW LIN – *Trafficking in Women, Forced Labor and Slavery Like Practices in Marriage, Domestic Work and Prostitution* (1997).

HUMAN RIGHTS OF MIGRANTS

Chapter 10
THE HUMAN RIGHTS OF MIGRANTS

Joan Fitzpatrick*

The international human rights regime shapes the normative framework in which state activity occurs, and virtually all migration policies affect the enjoyment of recognized human rights. The focus of this chapter is the permissible extent to which states may take alienage into account in policy matters.[1] The vast and varied topic of the human rights of migrants[2] includes such broad issues, important to contemporary migration control, as the following:

- customary law doctrines concerning the rights of aliens;
- non-discrimination norms, including protection from racism and xenophobia;
- human rights of migrant workers;
- rights in the immigration context, including substantive limits on expulsion, procedural protections, and detention;
- economic, social, and cultural rights of non-citizens.

This chapter focuses exclusively on the rights of non-nationals (international migrants); the human rights of internal migrants are not analyzed.

THE RIGHTS OF ALIENS/MIGRANTS

Traditional doctrines of sovereignty emphasized the link to nationality and permitted distinctive treatment of aliens. However, customary norms concerning state responsibility for injuries to aliens became the topic of heated debate. Controversy centered on the property and procedural rights of aliens, especially foreign investors, and a sharp division of opinion existed whether aliens were entitled to national treatment in these matters, or whether there was a higher minimum international standard

---

* Jeffrey and Susan Brotman Professor of Law, University of Washington.
[1] IOM's recent collection of articles on *The Human Rights of Migrants* (2001), also published as *International Migration*, vol. 38(6)(2000)), surveys some of the same issues digested here.
[2] R. Cholewinski, *Migrants Workers in International Human Rights Law* (1997); G. Goodwin-Gill, *International Law and the Movement of Persons between States* (1978); R. Lillich, *The Human Rights of Aliens in Contemporary International Law* (1984); and C. Tiburcio, *The Human Rights of Aliens under International and Comparative Law* (2001), address various aspects of the subject.

T.A. Aleinikoff and V. Chetail (Eds.), Migration and International Legal Norms
© 2003, T.M.C. ASSER PRESS, The Hague, The Netherlands, et al.

of fair treatment. Especially in the Americas, diplomatic protection became a controversial element linked to these customary norms. In a series of drafts written for the International Law Commission (ILC), Francisco V. García-Amador attempted to synthesize competing approaches by using emerging international human rights norms to articulate an international standard to protect nationals and aliens equally.[3] Since García-Amador's approach proved divisive, the ILC's work on state responsibility essentially jettisoned the rights of aliens as a focus and the ILC undertook a separate study on diplomatic protection.[4]

No general codification of the human rights of aliens has been achieved.[5] Concerns over mass expulsions of non-citizens prompted a study by Baroness Elles for the United Nations Sub-Commission on Prevention of Discrimination and Protection of Minorities,[6] which, in 1985, led to a rather compromised and limited General Assembly Declaration on the Human Rights of Individuals Who are not Nationals of the Country in which They Live.[7] The Declaration addressed several aspects of the treatment of lawfully resident non-citizens, such as the right to social security or the right to equal remuneration for work of equal value, but it has apparently had little influence on state practice.

The recent appointments of the UN Special Rapporteur on the Human Rights of Migrants[8] and the Special Rapporteurship on Migrant Workers and Members of Their Families of the Inter-American Commission on Human Rights (IACHR)[9] pro-

---

[3] See F.V. Garcia-Amador, L.B. Sohn, and R.R. Baxter, *Recent Codification of the Law of State Responsibility for Injuries to Aliens* (1974).

[4] Draft Articles on Responsibility of States for Internationally Wrongful Acts, Report of the International Law Commission on the Work of Its Fifty-First Session, UN GAOR 56th Sess., Supp. No. 10, UN Doc. A/56/10 (2001).

[5] "Aliens" is the traditional term for designating non-nationals in customary international law, but it has many negative connotations. This paper uses the term "migrants," but the author wishes to emphasize that in the contemporary human rights context this term may suggest a limitation to migrant workers, which is not intended here. This chapter examines the human rights of persons who are not nationals of the state whose conduct toward them is in question, and the extent to which the alienage of those persons may justify differential treatment as compared to nationals. One further drawback to the term migrants is that it encompasses naturalized citizens, as well as internal migrants; neither meaning is intended in this chapter.

[6] Sub-Commission on Prevention of Discrimination and Protection of Minorities, International Provisions Protecting the Human Rights of Non-Citizens, Study prepared by the Baroness Elles, UN Doc. E/CN.4/Sub.2/392/Rev.1 (1980), UN Sales No. E.80.XIV.2 (1980).

[7] GA Res. 40/144 of 13 December 1985. More recently, David Weissbrodt of the Sub-Commission on Protection and Promotion of Human Rights has noted gaps in the normative framework regarding the human rights of non-citizens. The Rights of Non-citizens, Working paper submitted by David Weissbrodt in accordance with Sub-Commission decision 1998/103, UN Doc. E/CN.4/Sub.2/1999/7 (1999).

[8] The Special Rapporteur was appointed pursuant to UN Commission on Human Rights Resolution 1999/44 of 27 April 1999. The Special Rapporteur replaced a Working Group of intergovernmental experts on the human rights of migrants, which had been convened pursuant to Commission Resolution 1997/15 of 3 April 1997.

[9] The IACHR Special Rapporteurship's mandate is limited to transnational migrant workers and members of their families. Nevertheless, the Special Rapporteurship examines legal developments relating more generally to the human rights of migrants. Annual Report of the Inter-American Commission on Human Rights 2000, OAS Doc. OEA/Ser.L/V/II.111, Doc. 20 rev., ch. VI, Second Progress Report of the Special Rapporteurship on Migrant Workers and Their Families in the Hemisphere, at 1417-1486 (2001).

vide a focal point for clarifying the human rights of migrants.[10] The General Assembly has declared 18 December to be International Migrants Day in order to bring greater visibility to the special situation of migrants, including their grave human rights problems.[11]

Migrants are treated variously by general human rights instruments that do not always explicitly address citizenship status. Certain human rights instruments, especially those concerning migrant workers, deal exclusively with the rights of non-nationals. To a limited extent, migrants are privileged in international law, for example, with respect to the right to diplomatic protection and consular access. These rights, however, can also be seen as compensatory for disadvantages faced by foreigners. Settled, temporary, and undocumented migrants may sometimes enjoy differential rights, although there is no comprehensive codification of these categories and their accompanying rights. With narrow exceptions relating to citizens' rights to political participation and exemption from immigration measures, the denial or limitation of migrants' human rights must be justified as serving legitimate state aims pursuant to measures that are proportionately linked to their migration status.

NON-DISCRIMINATION, INCLUDING RACISM AND XENOPHOBIA

The ancient confusion between strangers and enemies still prevails in some quarters. While racism and xenophobia are distinct concepts, demands for strict migration controls may arise from a linkage of these attitudes. In some states, the manifestation of racism primarily involves intolerance of and violence against migrants, a phenomenon noted at the 2001 World Conference against Racism, Racial Discrimination, Xenophobia and Related Intolerance.[12]

The non-discrimination norm plays a central role in defining the human rights of migrants. The widely ratified human rights treaties are of general application, rather than instruments that specifically define migrants' rights. The major universal and regional human rights treaties prohibit discrimination, and, in general, permit only reasonable and proportionate differences in treatment. Non-discrimination is also notable for being included in the United Nations Charter[13] and, at least as it applies to race, the norm is *jus cogens*.[14]

---

[10] See, for example, the UN Special Rapporteur's description of the legal framework for her monitoring efforts, in Migrant Workers, Report of the Special Rapporteur, Gabriela Rodríguez Pizarro, submitted pursuant to Commission on Human Rights Resolution 2000/48, UN Doc. E/CN.4/2001/83, paras. 16-34 (2001). Though titled "Migrant Workers," the report deals broadly with the human rights of migrants.

[11] UNGA Res. 55/93, 4 December 2000, UN Doc. A/RES/55/93 (2001).

[12] Durban Declaration against Racism, Racial Discrimination, Xenophobia and Related Intolerance, 8 September 2001, paras. 24-33 (addressing the situation of migrants), reprinted *in* 9 *IHRR* 578 (2002).

[13] UN Charter art. 1(3) includes among the purposes of the UN "promoting and encouraging respect for human rights and for fundamental freedoms for all without distinction as to race, sex, language, or religion ... ." Art. 55(c) commits the UN to promote non-discrimination.

[14] International Court of Justice, Case Concerning Barcelona Traction, Light and Power Company,

However, human rights law does not forbid all distinctions between nationals and migrants. International rules concerning discrimination against migrants are nuanced, and require careful delineation. The terminology of the Universal Declaration on Human Rights (UDHR) is notable, with references throughout to "everyone" and "no one."[15] Article 2 of the UDHR expresses an open-ended non-discrimination principle, but neither "nationality" nor "alienage" is specifically listed.[16] The UDHR does not clearly delineate permissible and impermissible discrimination against migrants, and further illumination must be sought from the more precise and binding provisions of universal and regional human rights treaties.

The non-discrimination provisions of three United Nations treaties and three regional treaties are especially relevant: the International Covenant on Civil and Political Rights (ICCPR), the International Covenant on Economic, Social and Cultural Rights (ICESCR), the International Convention on the Elimination of All Forms of Racial Discrimination (ICERD), the European Convention for the Protection of Human Rights and Fundamental Freedoms (ECHR), the American Convention on Human Rights (ACHR), and the African Charter on Human and Peoples' Rights (African Charter). Each provides substantial protection for the human rights of migrants, though none contains a categorical bar on distinctions against non-nationals and several include problematic provisions that create confusion concerning the scope of state obligation.

In general, differential treatment is permissible where the distinction is made pursuant to a legitimate aim, the distinction has an objective justification, and reasonable proportionality exists between the means employed and the aims sought to be realized.[17] The particular immigration status of a non-citizen may be relevant to the application of the proportionality principle, with greater rights adhering to settled migrants than to temporary visitors or to undocumented persons. The Convention on the Elimination of All Forms of Discrimination Against Women (CEDAW) and the Convention on the Rights of the Child (CRC) are especially relevant in regard to gender-based violence and family unification, special areas of vulnerability for migrants.[18]

The ICCPR, although not as widely ratified as other human rights treaties, is particularly important. The ICCPR protects many rights affected by migration control

---

1970 ICJ Reports 33-34; W. McKean, *Equality and Discrimination in International Law* (1983) p. 283 (speaking specifically of racial discrimination).

[15] UDHR Art. 21, defining political rights such as voting, holding public office, and public service, speaks of "everyone" having rights in "his country," which is taken as limiting these rights to citizens. The UDHR occupies a special place because of its influence on the formation of customary norms.

[16] "Everyone is entitled to all the rights and freedoms set forth in this Declaration, without distinction of any kind, such as race, colour, sex, language, religion, political or other opinion, national or social origin, property, birth or other status." National origin is generally understood to denote ethnic origin, rather than foreign nationality.

[17] Goodwin-Gill, *supra* note 2, at 78; Human Rights Committee, General Comment No. 18 (Non-discrimination) (1989), para. 13.

[18] CRC Art. 2(1) prohibits discrimination among groups of children, without specifically mentioning nationality or alienage, and Art. 2(2) prohibits discrimination against children based on their parents' "status."

measures, addresses discrimination in detail, and specifies non-derogable rights that are possessed by all human beings. Further, General Comment No. 15 of the Human Rights Committee provides guidance on the "position of aliens under the Covenant."[19] The following discussion of the ICCPR is also largely applicable to the three regional treaties, but noteworthy variations in the regional instruments are discussed below.

A State Party must ensure rights in the ICCPR to "all individuals within its territory and subject to its jurisdiction" (Article 2(1)), without mentioning reciprocity[20] and nationality. The general non-discrimination provisions in the same article and in Article 26 are open-ended (being illustrative and including "other status"), but do not specifically list nationality or alienage among the prohibited grounds of distinction. The non-discrimination provision in Article 4(1), relating to derogation, does not prohibit distinctions against non-nationals, but derogation is subject to a strict rule of proportionality.[21]

The rights in the ICCPR can be divided into five categories, as they relate to distinctions against migrants:

1. Some rights must be provided on an equal basis to nationals and migrants, either because the right is absolute or because selective denial would never be reasonable or proportionate: the right to life (Article 6); the prohibition on torture and cruel, inhuman, or degrading treatment or punishment (Article 7); the prohibition on slavery, servitude, and forced or compulsory labor (Article 8);[22] the humane treatment of prisoners (Article 10); imprisonment for contractual debt (Article 11); the right to leave the country (Article 12(2); equality before the law and fair trial rights (Article 14); prohibition on retroactive criminal penalties (Article 15); right to recognition as a person before the law (Article 16); freedom of thought, conscience, and religion (Article 18) freedom of opinion (Article 19(1)); the right to marry (Article 23); the right of children to measures of protection (Article 24); and the right of minorities to culture, religion, and language (Article 27).[23] Some of these rights are non-derogable under Article 4.[24] Harsh migration control mea-

---

[19] Human Rights Committee, General Comment No. 15 (The position of aliens under the Covenant) (1986).

[20] Friendship, commerce, and navigation treaties secure rights to certain foreign nationals on the basis of reciprocity, and still function as an important source, especially of economic rights for migrants. Treaties of economic union operate on a similar principle.

[21] According to Art. 4(1): "In time of public emergency which threatens the life of the nation and the existence of which is officially proclaimed, the States Parties to the present Covenant may take measures derogating from their obligations under the present Covenant to the extent strictly required by the exigencies of the situation, provided that such measures are not inconsistent with their other obligations under international law and do not involve discrimination solely on the ground of race, colour, sex, language, religion or social origin."

[22] The tie of nationality may subject citizens to national or military service and civil obligations that are excluded from the definition of forced labor in Art. 8(3)(c), while some migrants would be exempted.

[23] The Human Rights Committee in General Comment No. 15, para. 7, embraces aliens in Art. 27 on minority rights, but some scholars assert that these protections are limited to national minorities.

[24] Non-derogable articles are 6, 7, 8(1-2), 11, 15, 16 and 18.

sures may imperil the lives of migrants, and an important aspect of the right to life relates to disproportionate use of force in law enforcement. Required measures to prohibit advocacy of national and racial hatred (Article 20) must protect nationals and migrants alike.

2. Certain articles prohibit arbitrary state action that may permit narrow distinctions between nationals and migrants. For example, the prohibition on arbitrary arrest and detention does not exclude immigration detention only of migrants, but it limits detention and does not permit migrants to be treated differently in the criminal context. The right to judicial proceedings to challenge the lawfulness of detention applies in all contexts and is non-derogable.[25] The family is protected against "arbitrary or unlawful interference" (Article 17), and in certain (but not all) circumstances this may preclude deportation of family members.[26] A balance between state interests and family unity must be struck, similar to that which prevails in the application of Article 8 of the ECHR. The fact that a migrant is settled, rather than temporary or undocumented, will enter into this balance.

3. Distinctions against migrants may sometimes be justified under limitations clauses permitting restriction on grounds such as national security or public order, if legitimate state aims and proportional means exist. The rights affected include manifestation of religion (Article 18), freedom of expression (Article 19), and freedom of association (Article 22). Where migrants are subjected to expulsion in retaliation for their exercise of these human rights, the same rule of legitimate aims and proportional means should apply, although this issue is not clearly resolved.[27]

4. Certain political rights are explicitly limited to citizens, such as the right to take part in public affairs, to vote, and to have access to public service (Article 25). The right of the child to acquire a nationality (Article 24(3)) cannot reasonably be read to exclude the application of *jus sanguinis* principles that deny citizenship to children born to migrants in the State Party's territory.

5. Some provisions specifically protect migrants (Article 13 on expulsion), while others protect only nationals and lawfully present migrants (such as the right to internal freedom of movement in Article 12(1)). The debate as to whether the right to enter "his own country" (Article 12(4)) applies to long-resident migrants is unresolved.[28] Certain equal rights are of special value to migrants, such as the right to an interpreter in criminal proceedings (Article 14(3)(f)) and the right to recognition as a person (Article 16).

---

[25] Human Rights Committee, General Comment No. 29 (States of Emergency) (2001), para. 16.

[26] *Winata et al.* v. *Australia*, Comm. No. 930/2000, Decision of 26 July 2001, UN Doc. CCPR/C/72/D/930/2000 para. 7 (2001).

[27] Tiburcio, *supra* note 2, at 204, asserts that expulsion for expressive activity must be justified under the limitations clauses.

[28] Cholewinski, *supra* note 2, at 52. See the contribution of Vincent Chetail on this question in the present volume.

It is not possible here to note all the subtle variations in the civil and political provisions of the regional treaties. ECHR Article 16 is a rare instance of authorized discrimination against migrants; it enables State Parties to limit aliens' freedom of expression, association, and assembly by restricting the political activity of aliens. This political activity may apparently concern both the home and the host state. However, Article 16 has been given a narrow reading.[29] African notions of solidarity and friendly relations between states underlie provisions that permit restrictions on the political activity of migrants.[30] European regional trends appear to be in the direction of facilitating political participation by some migrants, for example through the Convention on the Participation of Foreigners in Public Life at the Local Level,[31] but ratification is too limited to permit any general conclusions regarding an emerging norm against traditional preferences for nationals in the enjoyment of political rights. To the extent that political rights for migrants are recognized, they concern settled migrants and political activity at the local level.[32]

Antiterrorism measures are sometimes targeted differentially at migrants. The application of non-discrimination norms to the expressive and associational activities of non-nationals is thus an important policy issue facing states. At the same time, the equality principle mandates that migrants be entitled to national treatment regarding physical security and fair trial. Rules on detention and expulsion, discussed below, also constrain antiterrorist measures. While derogation norms do not exclude all distinctions between nationals and migrants, they do prohibit racial and religious discrimination and impose strict rules of proportionality.

The economic, social, and cultural rights of migrants are addressed in more detail below, but it appears that non-discrimination principles operate more weakly for migrants regarding these rights than for many civil and political rights. As Ryszard Cholewinski notes, the "ICESCR affords less protection to aliens in comparison with the UDHR and the ICCPR."[33] The ICESCR includes an open-ended non-discrimination clause (Article 2(2), but permits limitations for the "general welfare" (Article 4). Economic rights may be limited for non-nationals by "developing countries," in an especially opaque provision (Article 2(3)). Migrants may, however, "have a right to the enjoyment of the minimum core content of rights guaranteed by the ICESCR."[34] Categorical exclusion of migrants from all economic, social, and cultural rights is not authorized. The proportionality principle would support some distinctions between different groups of non-citizens, for example with respect to the right to work.

Norms against racial and ethnic discrimination are especially relevant to migrants who compose minorities in their host state, but the ICERD introduces an "unfortunate"[35] ambiguity in Article 1(2), which disclaims application to "distinctions,

---

[29] Cholewinski, *supra* note 2, at 375-376 (discussing *Piermont* v. *France Judgment* of 27 April 1995, Ser. A, No. 314-A).

[30] African Charter Art. 23(2).

[31] 5 February 1992, *ETS* No. 144.

[32] Cholewinski, *supra* note 2, at 370-381.

[33] Id. at 56.

[34] Id. at 58.

[35] Id. at 62.

exclusions, restrictions or preferences ... between citizens and non-citizens." However, migrants who are victims of racial or ethnic discrimination may claim ICERD's protection despite their alienage, as indicated in the sparse jurisprudence of the Committee on the Elimination of Racial Discrimination.[36] Under Article 1(3), laws governing citizenship may not discriminate against persons of a particular nationality.

Violence against women implicates human rights norms of special relevance to women migrants, who suffer from a double vulnerability. Norms prohibiting gender-based discrimination and requiring action to combat violence against women apply to women migrants as well as to citizens. Migration control measures may inadvertently facilitate or aggravate violence against women (for example, by discouraging trafficking victims from contacting authorities).

In summary, migrants are entitled to equal protection with respect to many civil and political human rights, especially those relating to security of the person and fair process. All non-derogable rights demand equality, but others (such as the right to fair trial) do as well. Migration control measures must not encourage official and private anti-migrant violence. The strong link between racism, xenophobia, and human rights violations against migrants poses a significant challenge for states in devising migration policies that meet basic human rights standards. Migrants who are members of racial and ethnic minorities are entitled to protection from discrimination on those bases.

Alienage is a protected "other status" subject to non-discrimination norms, but reasonable and proportional distinctions may be drawn between nationals and migrants with respect to some rights, in particular political and expressive rights, some freedom of movement norms, and certain aspects of the right to family life. Non-discrimination norms appear to be a less powerful instrument regarding unequal treatment of migrants in the enjoyment of economic, social, and cultural (ESC) rights. However, states may be required to draw distinctions between groups of migrants who enjoy different levels of protection, and not all ESC rights permit categorical denial to migrants.

HUMAN RIGHTS OF MIGRANT WORKERS

The imminent entry into force of the 1990 International Convention of the Rights of All Migrant Workers and Members of Their Families (ICMW),[37] following a concerted effort to promote ratification, has given prominence to that sub-group of migrants who are migrant workers or members of their families.[38] The International Labor Organization (ILO) estimates that, of the roughly 150 million migrants in the

---

[36] *Yilmaz-Dogan* v. *the Netherlands*, Comm. No. 1/1984, UN Doc. A/43/18, Annex IV, 59-64. CERD General Recommendation No. XI (42) (Non-Citizens) (1993) provides little substantive guidance.

[37] At the time of writing, the necessary twenty ratifications had been completed; the treaty is expected to enter into force this year.

[38] The efforts are described by Patrick A. Taran in the IOM study, *supra* note 1, at 17-22.

world, between 36-42 million persons are migrant workers, and an additional 44-55 million are members of their families.[39] Key ILO conventions include the Convention Concerning Migration for Employment (No. 97) of 1949 and the Convention Concerning Migration in Abusive Conditions and the Promotion of Equality in Opportunity and Treatment of Migrant Workers (No. 143) of 1975, that precede UN codification in this field.[40]

Only a sketch of this important topic is possible here. Five issues merit emphasis. First, the migrant workers conventions are not widely ratified and a striking disparity in ratifications exists between sending states and receiving states. Second, these instruments are unique in treating nationality explicitly as a prohibited basis of distinction.[41] Equality is guaranteed especially in work-related matters such as remuneration and hours of work,[42] but equality is promoted in broader areas such as social security, access to employment, trade union freedoms, and cultural rights.[43] Third, migrant workers comprise several distinct groups with varying human rights issues, from multinational executives, to legally admitted skilled and unskilled workers in a range of occupations, to irregular migrants who occupy the lowest employment rungs. Fourth, the rights of irregular migrants are especially controversial, as are issues of family unity. Fifth, these conventions simultaneously promote measures to combat illegal migration.[44]

The breadth and complexity of the migrant workers conventions are sometimes cited as an explanation for their low rate of ratification. The ICMW pointedly encompasses *all* migrant workers – legal and illegal – and their family members. Resistance to legal obligations that might impede enforcement measures to combat illegal migration and preferences for nationals in economic matters also deter ratification. Briefly, the ICMW, in Part III, guarantees rights to all migrant workers and their families, restating with slight variation many fundamental rights (Articles 8-24, 29); providing national treatment in matters such as equal conditions of work (Article 25); trade union rights (Article 26); social security (Article 27); and basic education (Article 30); and dealing with matters of special concern to migrants, such as preservation of cultural identity (Article 31); and repatriation of savings (Article 32). Part IV provides more extensive guarantees, although not always national treatment, for migrants in a documented or regular situation, in matters ranging from liberty of movement (Articles 38-39) to access to employment (Articles 51-54). A Committee on the Protection of the Rights of All Migrant Workers and Members of

[39] R. Zegers de Beijl, Combatting Discrimination against Migrant Workers: International Standards, National Legislation and Voluntary Measures – The Need for a Multi-pronged Strategy, May 1997, available at http://www.ilo.org/public/english/protection/migrant/papers/disstrat/index.htm.

[40] The UN controversially decided to draft the ICMW despite the existence of the ILO conventions.

[41] ICMW Art. 7.

[42] ILO Convention No. 97 Art. 6(1).

[43] ILO Convention No. 143 Art. 10.

[44] ICMW Part VI. Convention No. 143 is split into two parts that can be separately ratified, one dealing with migration in abusive conditions and the other with equality of opportunity and treatment. Cholewinski, *supra* note 2, at 100. The UN Special Rapporteur on the human rights of migrants also is mandated to consider obstacles to the return of migrants who are undocumented or in an irregular situation. Commission on Human Rights resolution 1999/44.

Their Families will be established under Part VII of the ICMW, following its entry into force.

IMMIGRATION CONTROL MEASURES AND HUMAN RIGHTS

Distinctions between citizens and migrants are clearly permissible in the regulation of admission and expulsion. However, immigration control is constrained by human rights norms.

Substantive Human Rights Bars to Expulsion

Human rights treaties forbid the return (*refoulement*) of migrants to states where they would face certain violations of their rights. Article 3 of the Convention Against Torture and Other Cruel, Inhuman and Degrading Treatment of Punishment and Article 22 of the Convention on the Rights of the Child explicitly prohibit *refoulement* under specified conditions. The ban on returning migrants to torture may form an aspect of the customary law prohibition on torture, in light of general rules on state responsibility.[45] Some provisions of human rights treaties impose implicit *non-refoulement* obligations of an absolute character; most prominent among these are ICCPR Article 7 and ECHR Article 3 (concerning torture and cruel, inhuman, or degrading treatment or punishment).

Other provisions may implicitly limit the power of states to deport where the deprivation of rights outweighs the state's interest in migration control or public safety. The right to family life is especially relevant (ICCPR Articles 17 and 23; ECHR Article 8; ACHR Articles 17 and 19; African Charter Article 18, CRC Articles 3, 9, 10, and 16). Furthermore, the logic of the family life jurisprudence may extend to broader provision of subsidiary protection.[46]

Procedural Rights, Especially Relating to Expulsion and Consular Access

Human rights norms relating to expulsion of migrants are essentially procedural (for example, ICCPR Article 13), and provide that expulsion must be by a competent authority in accordance with law and that individuals should be permitted to give reasons why they should not be expelled. The European Court of Human Rights has demanded compliance with procedural fairness in the expulsion of irregular migrants under ECHR Protocol 4 Article 4; Protocol 7 Article 1 provides additional procedural protections for lawfully resident migrants.[47] The IACHR Special Rap-

---

[45] Art. 16 of the 2001 ILC draft Articles on State Responsibility (states that aid or assist other states to commit internationally wrongful acts).

[46] Commission of the European Communities, Proposal for a Council Directive laying down minimum standards for the qualification and status of third country nationals and stateless persons as refugees, or as persons who otherwise need international protection, COM (2001) 510 (2001/0207 CNS), 12 September 2001.

[47] *Conka* v. *Belgium*, App. No. 51564/99, Judgment of 5 February 2002, para. 63 (requiring "that the

porteurship has examined procedural rights related to expulsion.[48] While expulsion of enemy aliens was a traditional practice, modern norms may impose individualized procedural requirements.[49] The right to challenge an expulsion is vital to the right to seek asylum and to the human rights bars to *refoulement*, as well as to fundamental fairness.

Irregular migration is itself criminalized, increased international efforts are devoted to combating migrant smuggling, and many migrants are charged with ordinary criminal offenses. Migrants may be at a cultural disadvantage when involved in criminal proceedings. The right to consular notification and access guaranteed by the 1963 Vienna Convention on Consular Relations is a right of individuals that may also be asserted by means of diplomatic protection.[50] The Inter-American Court of Human Rights has characterized consular access as a human right.[51]

Detention

Migrants are differentially subject to immigration controls that often include a detention component.[52] The Human Rights Committee has indicated that, under the principle of proportionality, prolonged detention of migrants without a showing of necessity and periodic review may be arbitrary in violation of Article 9 of the ICCPR.[53] The Working Group on Arbitrary Detention of the UN Commission on Human Rights has adopted a set of ten principles relating to the detention of migrants, but these largely concern treatment of detainees rather than the basis for detention.[54] States have increasingly resorted to detention as a deterrent measure against irregular migration. The impact of these policies on asylum-seekers has been addressed by the UNHCR and scholars.[55]

Detention in connection with interdiction of seaborne migrants may implicate additional legal rules relating to rescue at sea and disembarkation. The UNHCR has cautioned that ships should not be used as floating detention centers.[56]

---

personal circumstances of each of those concerned had been genuinely and individually taken into account" under Protocol 4 Art. 4). The two Protocols have not been ratified by all Council of Europe states.

[48] See *supra* note 10, at 1440-1445.

[49] J. Henckaerts, *Mass Expulsion in Modern International Law and Practice* (1995).

[50] International Court of Justice, LaGrand Case (*Germany* v. *United States*), Judgment of 27 June 2001.

[51] Inter-Am. Ct. H.R., The Right to Information on Consular Assistance in the Framework of the Guarantee of the Due Process of Law, Advisory Opinion OC-16/99 (ser. A) No. 16 (1999).

[52] ECHR Art. 5(1)(f) specifically addresses arrest for immigration purposes.

[53] *A.* v. *Australia*, Comm. No. 560/1993, Views of 3 April 1997, UN Doc. CCPR/C/59/D/560/1993 (1997).

[54] Working Group on Arbitrary Detention, Deliberation No. 5: Situation Regarding Immigrants and Asylum-Seekers (providing, *inter alia*, a right to counsel, a right to be brought promptly before a judicial or other authority, prohibition on unlimited or excessively lengthy custody, and segregation from convicted prisoners).

[55] UNHCR, *Revised Guidelines: Applicable Criteria and Standards relating to the Detention of Asylum Seekers* (February 1999).

[56] UNHCR, *Rescue-at-Sea, Specific Aspects Relating to the Protection of Asylum-Seekers and Refugees*, Expert Roundtable, Lisbon, 25-26 March 2002, para. 7.

Indefinite detention without charge or trial is imposed selectively on non-citizens in some recent antiterrorism measures. Such policies can represent serious derogations from the prohibition on arbitrary detention, and are subject to searching review as to whether they are strictly required by the exigencies of an actual emergency threatening the life of the nation. The right to take judicial proceedings to challenge the lawfulness of detention is now widely regarded as non-derogable.[57]

Humanitarian law, including the Geneva Convention IV of 1949, regulates the internment of civilians who are nationals of enemy powers or who live in occupied territory, during armed conflict between states.

ECONOMIC, SOCIAL, AND CULTURAL RIGHTS

This complex topic embraces a range of discrete rights. Different categories of migrants enjoy different levels of protection in relation to particular rights; and a number of specialized regional and bilateral treaties provide reciprocal guarantees, sometimes of great complexity. Variations exist regionally and in state practice.[58] In general, categorical exclusions of migrants from economic, social, and cultural rights are impermissible and differential treatment must be justified. Article 2(3) of the ICESCR is unusual in authorizing categorical denial of "economic" rights to non-nationals in "developing countries," but the meaning of these terms is uncertain. Justification for adverse treatment may be relatively easy in some circumstances (for example, denying tourists access to the labor market), or it may involve a difficult balancing process (for example, determining whether minor children of asylum-seekers may be educated separately from the children of citizens and settled migrants).

Citizens of states belonging to an economic union may receive national treatment in matters such as employment, while other settled and temporary migrants are treated less favorably. The reciprocal benefits guaranteed in economic unions and bilateral arrangements extend only to specified beneficiaries, but patterns discernable in such agreements provide evidence of emerging general principles of law and customary norms.

Here it is possible only to identify some key rights governed by international standards, although few have an absolute or universal character:

* *Work*: Equality of employment conditions for those in the work force, including irregular migrants, is perhaps the least controversial norm, although many employers recruit irregular migrants precisely in order to provide substandard wages and working conditions. Labor union rights are also more securely protected than many employment-related rights. Social security rights are complex; reciprocal rules (for example, among EU states) may result in differential guarantees for different groups of migrants. Access to work is least securely protected, and re-

---

[57] Human Rights Committee, General Comment No. 29, para. 16.
[58] Cholewinksi and Tiburcio include partial surveys of state practice.

mains "one area where state sovereignty is prevalent and where countries are least inclined to realize equality between migrant workers and nationals."[59] Access to work is often linked closely to migration control, and some lawful migrants may be restricted to certain jobs or economic sectors while other migrants (asylum-seekers, for example, or family members of migrant workers), may face significant barriers. However, equality of treatment may exist within regional economic unions, and freedom of movement for employment is a major objective of such unions.

- *Education*: The right to primary education is perhaps the most compelling issue in this area, and universal entitlement appears protected by the ICESCR (Article 13); Convention on the Rights of the Child (Article 28); ECHR (Protocol 1 Article 2); the ICMW (Article 30); the OAS Charter (Article 47); and the American Declaration on the Rights and Duties of Man (Article XII). Reasonable and proportionate justification for denial of this right is difficult, because of the centrality of primary education to the child's ability to develop and to enjoy other rights.[60] Access to secondary, higher, and vocational education is addressed in these and other instruments as migrants may face discrimination. Equal access to financial assistance for education appears to be least securely protected.

- *Health and housing*: General economic, social, and cultural instruments protect these rights, and exclusion of migrants must be justified under their non-discrimination provisions. Irregular migrants comprise the most disadvantaged persons in respect of access to adequate housing, and may be the target of harsh enforcement measures (for example, forcible evictions) that implicate absolute rights, such as life and physical security. Denial of access to basic health care may also implicate these fundamental rights. Universal and regional migrant workers conventions address health and housing issues, and groups of migrants (nationals of certain favored states, lawful migrants, irregular migrants) may enjoy different levels of protection.

- *Cultural rights*: Migrants frequently differ in language, religion, dress, and other cultural practices from the societies in which they live. These variations may provoke intolerance in sectors of the host societies, and result in violations of basic civil and political rights discussed above. Freedoms of belief and thought are absolute, but manifestation may be subject to regulation. Non-discrimination principles require a reasonable and proportionate basis for state action that impinges on freedom of religion, expression, association, and participation in minority cultural practices. The rights of parents to pass on cultural practices may raise difficult issues (ranging from the debate over education in the mother tongue and culture versus education in the mainstream, to the need to protect children from

---

[59] Cholewinski, *supra* note 2, at 290.

[60] Tiburcio, *supra* note 2, at 161, concludes that "international law does not establish a definite rule," but this point is controversial.

harmful cultural practices such as female genital mutilation). Secular societies may attempt to suppress manifestation of religious beliefs (hijab or turbans, for example) that disproportionately affect migrants.

GAPS, OMISSIONS, AND AREAS FOR COOPERATION

The human rights treaty bodies have given relatively little attention to the human rights of migrants. Issuance of general comments could clarify many of the issues identified here. The human rights bars to expulsion are the subject of increasing adjudication at the international, regional, and national level, and greater clarity to this topic may result from the EU's harmonization of subsidiary protection. The human rights of migrant workers, especially the undocumented, remain contested and the pertinent ILO and UN treaties are still not widely ratified. The establishment of a Committee to implement the ICMW may provide a forum to help bridge this gap.

Selected Bibliography

ADEPOJU, A. – "Illegals and Expulsion in Africa: The Nigerian Experience," 18 *International Migration Review* (1984): 426.

AHMED, SYED REFAAT – *Forlorn Migrants: An International Legal Regime for Undocumented Migrant Workers* (2000).

ALLEWELDT, R. – "Protection Against Expulsion Under Article 3 of the European Convention on Human Rights," 4 *European Journal of International Law* (1993): 360.

AMERASINGHE, CHITTHARANJAN F. – *State Responsibility for Injuries to Aliens* (1967).

ANSAY, T. – "The New UN Convention in Light of the German and Turkish Experience," 25 *International Migration Review* (1991): 831.

AUKERMAN, M.J. – "Discrimination in Germany: A Call for Minority Rights," 13 *Netherlands Quarterly of Human Rights* (1995): 237.

BATTISTELLA, GRAZIANO – *Human Rights of Migrant Workers: Agenda for NGOs* (1993).

BÖHNING, W.R. – "The ILO and the New UN Convention on Migrant Workers: The Past and Future," 25 *International Migration Review* (1991): 698.

BORCHARD, EDWIN – *Diplomatic Protection of Citizens Abroad or the Law of International Claims* (1916).

BOSNIAK, LINDA – "Human Rights, State Sovereignty, and the Protection of Undocumented Migrants Under the International Migrant Workers Convention," 25 *International Migration Review* (1991): 737.

BOUDAHRAIN, A. – "The New International Convention: A Moroccan Perspective," 25 *International Migration Review* (1991): 866.

CATOR JULIE AND JAN NIESSEN (EDS.) – *The Use of International Conventions to Protect the Rights of Migrants and Ethnic Minorities* (1994).

CHOLEWINSKI, RYSZARD – *Borders and Discrimination in the European Union* (2002).

—. *Migrant Workers in International Human Rights Law: Their Protection in Countries of Employment* (1997).

—. "The Protection of the Right of Economic Migrants to Family Reunion in Europe," 43 *International and Comparative Law Quarterly* (1994): 568.

—. "The Racial Discrimination Convention and the Protection of Cultural and Linguistic Ethnic Minorities," 1991 *Revue de Droit International* 167.

COMMISSION ON HUMAN RIGHTS, Migrant Workers, "Report of the Special Rapporteur, Ms. Gabriela Rodríguez Pizarro," submitted pursuant to Commission on Human Rights Resolution 2000/48, UN

Doc. E/CN.4/2001/83 (2001).

—. "Report on mission to Ecuador," UN Doc. E/CN.4/2002/94/Add.1 (2002).

—. "Report on visit to Canada," UN Doc. E/CN.4/2001/83 Add. 1 (2000).

—. "Report of the Working Group of Intergovernmental Experts on the Human Rights of Migrants," UN Doc. E/CN.4/1999/80 (1999).

CROCK, MARY AND PENELOPE MATHEW – "Immigration and Human Rights in Australia," in D. Kinsey (ed.), *Human Rights In Australia: A Practical Guide* (1998).

DE LA VEGA, CONNIE – Review of Cholewinski, 21 *Human Rights Quarterly* (1999): 229.

DRZEMCZEWSKI, ANDREW – "The Position of Aliens in Relation to the European Convention on Human Rights: A General Survey," in *Human Rights of Aliens in Europe* (1985).

FITZPATRICK, JOAN M. (ED.) – *Human Rights Protection for Refugees, Asylum-Seekers, and Internally Displaced Persons: A Guide to International Procedures and Mechanisms* (2002).

FOURLANOS, GERASSIMOS – *Sovereignty and the Ingress of Aliens: With a Special Focus on Family Unity and Refugee Law* (1986).

FROWEIN, JOCHEN (ED.) – *Die Rechtsstellung von Ausländern nach staatlichem Recht und Völkerrecht (The Legal Position of Aliens in National and International Law)* (1987).

GARCÍA-AMADOR, F.V., LOUIS B. SOHN AND R.R. BAXTER – *Recent Codification of the Law of State Responsibility for Injuries to Aliens* (1974).

GHOSH, BIMAL (ED.) – *Managing Migration: Time for a New International Regime?* (2000).

GOODWIN-GILL, GUY – *International Law and the Movement of Persons between States* (1978).

GUILD, ELSPETH AND PAUL MINDERHOUD (EDS.) – *Security of Residence and Expulsion: Protection of Aliens in Europe* (2001).

HELTON, ARTHUR – "The New Convention from the Perspective of a Country of Employment: The U.S. Case," 25 *International Migration Review* (1991): 848.

HENCKAERTS, JEAN-MARIE – *Mass Expulsion in Modern International Law and Practice* (1995).

HUNE, SHEILA AND JAN NIESSEN – "Ratifying the UN Migrant Workers Convention: Current Difficulties and Prospects," 12 *Netherlands Quarterly of Human Rights* (1994): 393.

HUNE, SHEILA – "Migrant Women in the Context of the International Convention on the Protection of the Rights of All Migrant Workers and Members of Their Families," 25 *International Migration Review* (1991): 800.

INSTITUTE OF MEDICINE – *The Human Rights of Migrants* (2001).

KITAMURA, Y. – "Recent Developments in Japanese Immigration Policy and the United Nations Convention on Migrant Workers," 27 *University of British Columbia Law Review* (1993): 113.

KOJANEC, G. – "The UN Convention and European Instruments for the Protection of Migrants," 25 *International Migration Review* (1991): 818.

KYLE, DAVID AND REY KOSLOWSKI – *Global Human Smuggling: Comparative Perspectives* (2001).

LAYTON-HENRY, ZIG (ED.) – *The Political Rights of Migrant Workers in Western Europe* (1990).

LILLICH, RICHARD – *The Human Rights of Aliens in Contemporary International Law* (1984).

LOENEN, TITIA AND PETER R. RODRIGUES (EDS.) – *Non-Discrimination Law: Comparative Perspectives* (1999).

MACEWEN, MARTIN (ED.) – *Tackling Racism in Europe: An Examination of Anti-Discrimination Law in Practice* (1995).

MAX PLANCK INSTITUTE OF COMPARATIVE LAW – *The Legal Position of Aliens in National and International Law* (1987).

MCDOUGAL, MYRES, HAROLD LASSWELL AND LUNG-CHU CHEN – "Protection of Aliens from Discrimination and World Public Order: Responsibility of States Conjoined with Human Rights," 70 *American Journal of International Law* (1976): 432.

MCKEAN, W.A. – *Equality and Discrimination under International Law* (1983).

MIGRANT WORKERS, Report of the Special Rapporteur, Ms. Gabriela Rodríguez Pizarro, submitted pursuant to Commission on Human Rights Resolution 2001/52, UN Doc. E/CN.4/2002/94 (2002).

NAFZIGER, JAMES AND B.C. BARTEL – "The Migrant Workers Convention: Its Place in Human Rights Law," 25 *International Migration Review* (1991): 771.

NAFZIGER, JAMES – "The General Admission of Aliens under International Law," 77 *American Journal of International Law* (1983): 804.

NASCIMBENE, BRUNO (ED.) – *Expulsion and Detention of Aliens in the European Union Countries* (2001).

NIESSEN, JAN – "Immigrants and Migrant Workers," in A. Eide, C. Krause, and A Rosas (eds.). *Economic, Social and Cultural Rights: A Textbook* (1995).

NIESSEN, JAN AND PATRICK TARAN – "Using the New Migrant Workers' Rights Convention," 25 *International Migration Review* (1991): 859.

PELLONPÄÄ, MATTI – *Expulsion in International Law: A Study in International Aliens Law and Human Rights with Special Reference to Finland* (1984).

PLENDER, RICHARD – *International Migration Law* (2nd edn. 1988).

SECOND PROGRESS REPORT of the Special Rapporteurship on Migrant Workers and Their Families in the Hemisphere, Annual Report of the Inter-American Commission on Human Rights, OEA/Ser.L/V/II.111, Doc. 20 rev., Chapter VI (2001): 1417-1486.

SOHN, LOUIS B. AND THOMAS BUERGENTHAL (EDS.) – *The Movement of Persons Across Borders* (1992).

STAPLES, HELEN – *The Legal Status of Third Country Nationals Resident in the European Union* (1999).

SUB-COMMISSION on Prevention of Discrimination and Protection of Minorities, International Provisions Protecting the Human Rights of Non-Citizens, Study prepared by the Baroness Elles, UN Doc. E/CN.4/Sub.2/392/Rev.1 (1980), UN Sales No. E.80.XIV.2 (1980).

SUB-COMMISSION on the Protection and Promotion of Human Rights, The Rights on Non-citizens, Working paper submitted by Mr. David Weissbrodt in accordance with Sub-Commission decision 1998/103, UN Doc. E/CN.4/Sub.2/1999/7 (1999).

SWART, A.H.J. – "The Legal Status of Aliens: Clauses in Council of Europe Instruments Relating to the Rights of Aliens," 1980 *Netherlands Yearbook of International Law* 3.

SYMPOSIUM on International Migration in the Americas, Report of the Rapporteur (2000).

TIBURCIO, CARMEN – *The Human Rights of Aliens under International and Comparative Law* (2001).

WEINER, MYRON – *The Global Migration Crisis: Challenge to States and to Human Rights* (1995).

ZEGERS DE BEIJL, ROGER – "Combating Discrimination Against Migrant Workers: International Standards, National Legislation and Voluntary Measures – the Need for a Multi-pronged Strategy" (1997).

Chapter 11
FAMILY UNITY

Kate Jastram*

State sovereignty over borders is qualified by international legal rules protecting the family. Under certain circumstances, non-citizens can claim the right to family unity in their host states, depending on their immigration status and the nature of their relationship. This chapter surveys the state of international law with respect to family unity across international borders, and notes some of the special issues relevant to children who travel alone.[1]

A few words about terminology may be useful. The right to family unity is not expressed as such in international instruments. Family unity is the term generally used to describe the totality of the interlocking rights enumerated below, and covers, in the migration context, issues related to admission, stay, and expulsion. Family unity also indicates a more specific meaning relating to constraints on state discretion to separate an existing intact family through the expulsion of one of its members. Family reunification, or reunion, refers to the efforts of family members already separated by forced or voluntary migration to regroup in a country other than the one of their origin, and so implicates state discretion over admission. This chapter uses family unity in its broader meaning, unless the more specific one is clearly implied.

THE RIGHT TO FAMILY UNITY

A family's right to live together is protected by international law. There is universal consensus that, as the fundamental unit of society, the family is entitled to respect, protection, assistance, and support.[2] A right to family unity is inherent in recogniz-

* Acting Clinical Professor of Law, International Human Rights Law Clinic, University of California at Berkeley, Boalt Hall School of Law.

An earlier version of this paper benefited greatly from comments made by the participants at the International Legal Norms and Migration Project Conference, Geneva, 23-25 May 2002.

[1] Parts of this paper are drawn from K. Jastram and K. Newland, "Family Unity and Refugee Protection," *in* Refugee Protection in International Law: UNHCR's Global Consultations on International Protection (eds. Erika Feller, Volker Turk, and Frances Nicholson), Cambridge University Press, forthcoming June 2003.

[2] Universal Declaration on Human Rights, 1948, Art. 16(3); International Covenant on Civil and Political Rights, 1966, Art. 23(1); International Covenant on Economic, Social and Cultural Rights, 1966, Art. 10(1); American Convention on Human Rights, 1969, Art. 17(1); African Charter on Human and

ing the family as a group unit. The right to marry and found a family[3] also includes the right to maintain a family life together.[4]

The right to a shared family life draws additional support from the prohibition against arbitrary interference with the family.[5] In addition, states have agreed with unprecedented speed and unanimity[6] to an extensive codification of children's rights, including their right to live with their parents.[7] Both the father and the mother, irrespective of their marital status, have common responsibilities as parents and share the right and responsibility to participate equally in the upbringing and development of their children.[8]

The right to family unity is not limited to citizens living in their own state.[9] Cross-border family unity issues arise most frequently when a host state either seeks to deport one member of a family of non-citizens, or seeks to deny entry to an individual seeking to join family members already residing in the state. The corollary problem, that of a state of origin denying exit permission to an individual attempting reunification with family in another country, has become a less salient issue with the end of the Cold War.

As with the right to family unity, experts almost universally agree that there is a right under international law to family reunification.[10] The right has been character-

---

Peoples' Rights, 1981, Art. 18(1)(2); African Charter on the Rights and Welfare of the Child, 1990, Art. XVIII(1); Revised European Social Charter, 1996, Art. 16. See also Convention on the Rights of the Child, 1989, 5th preambular paragraph.

[3] Universal Declaration on Human Rights, 1948, Art. 16(1); European Convention for the Protection of Human Rights and Fundamental Freedoms, 1950, Art. 12; International Covenant on Civil and Political Rights, 1966, Art. 23(2); American Convention on Human Rights, 1969, Art. 17(2).

[4] Human Rights Committee, 39th session, 1990, *General Comment No. 19,* para. 5 (27 July 1990). See also E.F. Abram, "The Child's Right to Family Unity in International Immigration Law," 17(4) *Law and Policy* (1995) p. 407 and M.K. Eriksson, *The Right to Marry and Found a Family: A World-Wide Human Right* (1990) p. 135.

[5] Universal Declaration on Human Rights, 1948, Art. 12; European Convention for the Protection of Human Rights and Fundamental Freedoms, 1950, Art. 8; International Covenant on Civil and Political Rights, 1966, Art. 17; American Convention on Human Rights, 1969, Art. 11(2); Convention on the Rights of the Child, 1989, Art. 16.

[6] The Convention on the Rights of the Child, 1989, had 191 States Parties as of 15 June 2002.

[7] Convention on the Rights of the Child, 1989, Arts. 3, 9, and 10. See also the African Charter on the Rights and Welfare of the Child, 1990, Art. XIX(1); Vienna Declaration on Human Rights, 1993, para. 21.

[8] Convention on the Elimination of All Forms of Discrimination Against Women, 1979, Art. 5(b); Convention on the Rights of the Child, 1989, Art. 18(1). See also the Human Rights Committee, *General Comment No. 28 on Article 3*, UN Doc. CCPR/C/21/Rev.1/Add.10, para. 25 (29 March 2000).

[9] Human Rights Committee, 27th Session, 1986, *General Comment No. 15 on the Position of Aliens under the Covenant,* para. 7 (11 April 1986). See also UN Doc. E/CN.4/2001/83, para. 24 (9 January 2001), Report of the Special Rapporteur on the Human Rights of Migrants.

[10] See Report of the Special Rapporteur on the Human Rights of Migrants 2001, *supra* note 9, at para. 65. See also Summary Conclusions on Family Unity, UNHCR Global Consultations on International Protection Expert Roundtable, para. 1 (8-9 November 2001), found on www.unhcr.ch. In addition to Abram, *supra* note 4, see, for example, J. Apap and N. Sitarapoulos, "The Right to Family Unity and Reunification of Third Country Migrants in Host States: Aspects of International and European Law," in *Proceedings of the First European Congress for Specialist Lawyers in the Area of Immigration and Asylum in Europe (Odysseus Network), Brussels 1-2.12.2000* (forthcoming 2002); section 2:

ized as a self-evident corollary to the right to family unity[11] and the right to found a family[12] and has been linked to freedom of movement.[13] The few who see family reunification as not yet having attained the status of a right have not made a persuasive case addressing the significance of the Convention of the Rights of the Child.[14]

The right to family unity across borders intersects with the prerogative of states to make decisions on the entry or stay of non-citizens. The rights on which family unity is based are often qualified with provisions for the state to limit the right under certain circumstances. It should be noted, however, that the most important, and sometimes only, qualifier is the imperative to act in the best interests of the child. The nature of the family relationship shapes the right to family unity with minor dependent children and their parents having the strongest claim to remain together or to be reunited. Maintaining the unity of an intact family poses different issues than reconstituting a separated family. Finally, the immigration status of the various family members has an impact on how the right to family unity should be implemented.

THE RIGHT TO FAMILY UNITY: CATEGORIES OF CLAIMANTS

The right to family unity universally applies to all persons. The question, then, is not whether various categories of persons have the right to family unity, but rather which state(s) must act to ensure the right. The following discussion is organized by category of claimant for ease of analysis, not because of any hierarchy of entitlement.

Nationals: The right to marry is not limited to persons of the same nationality. However, for a citizen marrying a non-citizen, issues can arise when arbitrary re-

---

"An express right to family reunification is uniquely enshrined in Article 10.1 of the [CRC]." See also R. Perruchoud, "Family Reunification" XXVII(4) *International Migration* (1989) p. 519.

[11] See, for example, Human Rights Committee, *General Comment No. 15, supra* note 9, at para. 5. See also Executive Committee Conclusion No. 24 (XXXII) 1981, para. 1: "In application of the principle of family unity and for obvious humanitarian reasons, every effort should be made to ensure the reunification of separated refugee families."

[12] Human Rights Committee, 39th Session, 1990, *General Comment No. 19, supra* note 4, at para. 5. See also Conclusions on Family Reunification, XIIIth Round Table on Current Problems in International Humanitarian Law (1988), International Institute of Humanitarian Law, para. 2.

[13] See Abram, *supra* note 4, at 415.

[14] C.S. Anderfuhren-Wayne, for example, writing in 1996, notes the importance of reunification rights and the need for more specific international provisions regarding them, but cites only a 1988 report that pre-dates adoption of the CRC. C.S. Anderfuhren-Wayne, "Family Unity in Immigration and Refugee Matters: United States and European Approaches," 8(3) *International Journal of Refugee Law* (1996) p. 351 and accompanying n. 19. Van Krieken recently reiterated that the concept of reunification "is now slowly being codified," P.J. van Krieken, "Family Reunification," *in* P.J. van Krieken (ed.), *The Migration Acquis Handbook* (2001) p. 120 and P.J. Van Krieken, "Cairo and Family Reunification," 42 (2-3) *AWR Bulletin: Quarterly on Refugee Problems* (1995) p. 52, but the bulk of his analysis is based on a 1993 article. Van Krieken's 2001 article is, as he notes, based on and often identical to his 1995 piece, van Krieken, 2001, p. 128 and accompanying n. 23, which he in turn notes is based on his 1993 paper, van Krieken, 1995, p. 52 and accompanying n. 5.

strictions are imposed or significant delays are encountered, or when female citizens have lesser rights than male citizens, for example, in obtaining entry for their non-citizen spouses or in transmitting citizenship to their children.[15]

Migrants: Under the International Convention on the Protection of the Rights of All Migrant Workers and Members of their Families (not yet in force) states shall "take measures they deem appropriate" to facilitate reunification.[16] The degree of discretion retained by states with respect to migrant workers reflects an expectation that workers can return to their home countries if they wish to rejoin family members, although in practice this can be difficult. Family reunification is increasingly understood as a means of promoting the integration and securing the rights of migrants in their host societies.[17]

1951 Convention refugees: Refugees recognized under the 1951 Convention Relating to the Status of Refugees are usually in the most advantageous position of all non-citizens with respect to family unity. The particular vulnerability of refugees is recognized in the Final Act of the Conference of Plenipotentiaries that adopted the 1951 Convention, which recommends that states take necessary measures for the protection of the refugee family.[18] Family unity in the refugee context means granting refugee or a similar secure status to family members accompanying a recognized refugee. The country of asylum must likewise provide for family reunification, at least of close family members, since the refugee cannot by definition return to the country of origin to enjoy reunification there. The recent practice of Australia to deny family reunification possibilities to recognized refugees who arrive without documentation violates a number of provisions of international law, including Article 31 of the 1951 Convention.

Organization of African Unity (OAU)/Cartagena refugees: The OAU Convention governing the specific aspects of refugee problems in Africa does not make specific reference to family unity or reunification. The body of African human rights law, however, is a rich source for family rights. Like the OAU Convention, the Cartagena Declaration on Refugees guides countries in their response to mass influx, where refugee status is granted on a group basis. The Cartagena Declaration specifically acknowledges family reunification as a fundamental principle that should be the basis for humanitarian treatment in the country of asylum.

---

[15] See generally, Eriksson, *supra* note 4. Citizen children can often be reunited with non-citizen parents, but generally not until they reach the age of majority. Ireland's supreme court has ruled that a newborn citizen does not have the right to the company of its family in Ireland. *Lobe v. Minister of Justice, Equality and Law Reform* (2003), 1 ESC 1 (23 January 2003).

[16] International Convention on the Protection of the Rights of All Migrant Workers and Members of their Families, 1990, Art. 44(2).

[17] World Conference against Racism, Racial Discrimination, Xenophobia and Related Intolerance, Durban Declaration, para. 49 and Programme of Action, para. 28; Commission on Human Rights Resolutions 2002/59, para. 1 and 2001/56, para. 1.

[18] Final Act of the 1951 United Nations Conference of Plenipotentiaries on the Status of Refugees and Stateless Persons IV.B speaks of the unity of the family as an essential right of the refugee.

Mass influx: The right to family unity applies in situations of mass influx. Given the prevalence of family separation in mass influx, keeping or bringing family members together poses enormous practical problems.[19] Registration designed to identify separated families,[20] tracing, assistance with communication and transportation, and similar measures may help relatives within a mass of refugees to re-establish a family group.

In situations of mass influx, many of those seeking protection will fall within the 1951 Convention refugee definition. However, states sometimes respond with temporary protection when the number of people precludes individual status determination. The UNHCR's Executive Committee has specifically concluded that respect for family unity is a "minimum basic human standard" in such situations[21] and has called for family reunification for persons benefiting from temporary protection.[22] There is an emerging consensus for the need for prompt reunification during temporary protection.[23]

Beneficiaries of complementary forms of protection: Complementary protection refers to various types of status granted to people whose claims under the 1951 Refugee Convention have been rejected after an individual determination, but who have nevertheless been found to be in need of international protection.[24] Beneficiaries of complementary protection are entitled to respect for their fundamental human rights, including the right to family unity. The justification for refugee family reunification in a country of asylum derives from the refugee not being able to return home, and not from the Refugee Convention itself. Persons in an analogous situation of inabili-

---

[19] With respect to the Rwandan exodus, for example, see ICRC/UNHCR/UNICEF/IFRCRCS Joint Statement on the Evacuation of Unaccompanied Children from Rwanda, 27 June 1994; M. Merkelbach, "Reuniting Children Separated from their Families after the Rwandan Crisis of 1994: The Relative Value of a Centralized Database," 82 *ICRC* (2000) 351-366; C. Petty, "Family Tracing and Reunification – Safeguarding Rights and Implementing the Law," 4 *International Journal of Children's Rights* (1996) pp. 165-176.

[20] UNHCR, "Practical Aspects of Physical and Legal Protection with Regard to Registration," UN Doc. EC/GC/01/6*, 19 February 2001.

[21] Executive Committee Conclusion No. 22 ((XXXII) 1981 (II.B.2.(h)).

[22] Executive Committee Conclusion No. 15 (XXX) 1979 (e): "States should facilitate the admission to their territory of at least the spouse and minor or dependent children of any person to whom temporary refuge or durable asylum has been granted."

[23] The recent EU directive on temporary protection requires Member States to reunite from within the European Union close family members as well as unmarried partners if the State has similar treatment for them in its aliens law, and allows them to reunite other close dependent family members. Family members who are not in the European Union but wish to be reunited with a sponsoring relative will be able to do so on a showing that they are in need of protection. EU *Council Directive* 2001/55/EC of 20 July 200, on minimum standards for giving temporary protection in the event of mass influx of displaced persons and on measures promoting a balance of efforts between Member States in receiving such persons and bearing the consequences thereof, Art. 15. Temporary protected status (TPS) in the United States does not permit family reunification, but is not analogous to temporary protection as practiced in Europe. INA Section 244, 8 CFR Section 244.2.

[24] UNHCR, "Complementary Forms of Protection," UN Doc. EC/GC/01/18, 4 September 2001. UNHCR, "Complementary Forms of Protection: Their Nature and Relationship to the International Refugee Protection Regime," UN Doc. EC/50/SC/CRP.18, 9 June 2000.

ty to return home should benefit from the same application of the right in the country of asylum.

A number of countries,[25] but not all,[26] extend family reunification rights to beneficiaries of complementary protection. That some 1951 Convention refugees are erroneously granted only complementary protection is a concern in countries where there is a wide disparity in family reunification possibilities between the two categories.[27]

Asylum-seekers: Since a decision has yet to be made as to the legal status of asylum seekers, it may be difficult to determine where they should enjoy the right to family unity and reunification, or which state bears responsibility for giving effect to that right. If asylum determination systems were prompt and efficient, this lack of clarity would cause few problems. But asylum systems are notoriously neither prompt nor efficient, and the length of proceedings in many countries causes tremendous hardship, particularly when children are apart from parents.

The obvious answer is to expedite asylum determinations, but this worthy goal seems to recede in the distance. There is a general recognition, at least in principle, that separated children should benefit from expedited procedures, but such measures do not even begin to address the right of children left in a country of origin or in transit to family reunification; no state has adopted expedited procedures for asylum-seeking parents separated from their children. Resettlement is also difficult since resettlement countries often feel that the country where one family member has an application pending should accept the remaining family members.

Some limited steps have been taken to address the situation. Under the terms of the Dublin Convention, a member state is responsible for determining the status of an asylum-seeker with a close family member in that state who is a refugee recognized under the 1951 Convention.[28] Proposals presented by the European Commission for a revised Dublin Convention strengthen these provisions,[29] for example, by providing that the close family member need only have a pending asylum claim, as opposed to requiring that he or she be a recognized refugee. The European Commission adds further criteria including that, where an asylum-seeker is an unaccompa-

---

[25] The Council of Europe Committee of Ministers specifically recommends that family reunion provisions relating to refugees should apply. Council of Europe Committee of Ministers Rec. No. (2001) 18, 27 November 2001, on subsidiary protection, para. 6.

[26] The United States, for example, does not provide for family reunification with persons protected under the Convention against Torture. Pub. L. 105-277, 112 Stat. 2681-2822 (October 1998). This is problematic, not least because return is not necessarily envisaged as a durable solution for a person at risk of torture.

[27] Van Krieken, Family Reunification, *supra* note 14, at 61-62.

[28] Convention Determining the State Responsible for Examining Applications for Asylum Lodged in one of the Member States of the European Community, 1990, Art. 4.

[29] European Commission, "Proposal for a Council Regulation Establishing the Criteria and Mechanisms for Determining the Member State Responsible for Examining an Asylum Application Lodged in one of the Member States by a Third-Country National," COM (2001) 447 final, 26 July 2001, preambular paras. 6-7, Arts. 5-8.

nied minor, responsibility for considering the claim should lie with the state where there is a member of the family who is able to take in the minor. There is no stipulation as to the formal status of the other family member.

Similarly, the Parliamentary Assembly of the Council of Europe has recommended that members of the same family be allowed to reunite during status determination procedures.[30] The European Council on Refugees and Exiles has also recommended that members of a family who have been compelled to seek asylum in different countries be allowed to pursue their claims together in a single country.[31]

It is understandable that states are not eager to process family reunification applications for asylum seekers whose asylum applications they are having difficulty processing. Given the scarcity of state resources, however, it would be helpful to pursue possibilities for reuniting family members who are seeking asylum in various countries, particularly if determination of the claim has been pending, or is expected to take longer than six months. The grouping together of potentially related claims, witnesses, and evidence would be more cost effective than parallel procedures in different jurisdictions, and would promote more consistent decision-making.

CONSTRAINTS ON STATE DECISIONS TO EXPEL AND ADMIT

Expulsion

International human rights jurisprudence on family unity is most fully developed thus far in the context of expulsion, where an individual will assert the right to family unity as a defense against deportation.[32] Family unity in this regard may be seen as both a procedural right and a substantive one. As a matter of procedure, states are less free to expel a family member than a sole individual, and must consider the family interests involved. The Human Rights Committee, for example, has cited respect for family life as one factor that may provide non-citizens with the protection of the International Covenant on Civil and Political Rights (ICCPR) even in relation to entry or residence, notwithstanding the general state power over immigration.[33]

As a substantive matter, respect for the right to family unity requires balancing the state's interest in deporting the family member with the family's interest in remaining intact. In cases challenging deportation as a violation of ICCPR Article 17, which prohibits arbitrary or unlawful interference with privacy, family and home, the Human Rights Committee has examined whether the effects on the family of the separation would be disproportionate to the state's objectives in removing the individual.[34] The Human Rights Committee has considered on the one hand, length of

---

[30] Council of Europe Parliamentary Assembly, Rec. 1327 (1997), 24 April 1997, on the protection and reinforcement of the human rights of refugees and asylum-seekers in Europe, para. 8.vii.(p).

[31] ECRE, "Position on Refugee Family Unification," July 2000.

[32] ICCPR Art. 13 applies to all procedures aimed at the obligatory departure of an alien, whether described in national law as expulsion or otherwise. Human Rights Committee, *General Comment No.15, supra* note 9, at para. 9.

[33] Human Rights Committee, *General Comment No. 15, supra* note 9, at para. 5.

[34] See, for example, *Canepa* v. *Canada,* UN Doc. CCPR/C/59/D/558/1993 (20 June 1997), para. 11.4

stay in the host country, age, and the degree of the family's financial and emotional interdependence, and on the other hand, the state's interests in promoting public safety and in enforcing immigration laws. The Committee did not find an interference with family life to be arbitrary in two cases brought against Canada, each one concerning a single man in his thirties, with citizenship in a Western European country, who had lived in Canada since childhood, who had repeated criminal convictions, and who hoped to remain with parents and siblings.[35]

In contrast, the more recent case of *Winata v. Australia*,[36] held that the proposed removal of the stateless, formerly Indonesian, parents of a thirteen-year-old Australian citizen would violate a number of provisions of the ICCPR, including freedom from arbitrary or unlawful interference with the family, the entitlement of the family to protection by the state, and the right of the child to protection without discrimination. Although the Canadian cases cited in the preceding paragraph are clearly differentiated by the existence of a criminal record, it is worth noting that in both instances the men had been long-time legal permanent residents. In *Winata*, it is significant that the Human Rights Committee found in favor of the mother and father, even though they had been living illegally in Australia for many years, after initially entering on student and tourist visas, respectively. Australia's interest in enforcing its immigration law and its objections that the parents could not have had a reasonable expectation of maintaining their family life in Australia, given their own lack of status, were not sufficient to override the Human Rights Committee's focus on the length of the citizen child's time in Australia (from birth to age thirteen) and his complete integration into Australian society. In the Committee's words,

> "In view of this duration of time, it is incumbent on the State Party to demonstrate *additional factors* justifying the removal of both parents that go *beyond a simple enforcement of its immigration law* in order to avoid a characterization of arbitrariness."[37] (Emphasis added.)

This line of cases under the ICCPR suggests that, particularly when expulsion is threatened for immigration violations only, as opposed to criminal law convictions, and citizen children will be affected, states will find it difficult to rely solely on their interest in immigration enforcement to justify separating an intact family.

In assessing family unity cases involving children states must also take into account the best interests of the child. States seeking to separate families through deportation face significant constraints in the Convention on the Rights of the Child (CRC), which requires in Article 9 that states "*shall* ensure that a child *shall* not be separated from his or her parents against their will, except when ... such separation is *necessary for the best interests of the child.*" (Emphasis added)

There are procedural and substantive aspects to the best interests requirement. The Committee on the Rights of the Child's insistence on the procedural aspect is emphasized in its concluding observations on Norway. The Committee observed that

---

[35] *Canepa and Stewart v. Canada*, UN Doc. CCPR/C/58/D/538/1993 (16 December 1996).

[36] *Winata v. Australia*, UN. Doc. CCPR/C/72/D/930/2000 (16 August 2001).

[37] *Winata*, para. 7.

"when decisions to deport foreigners convicted of a criminal offense are taken, *profes-sional opinions* on the impact of such decisions upon the children of the deported persons are not *systematically* referred to and taken into consideration. ... [The Committee recommended that Norway] review the *process* through which deportation decisions are made to ensure that where deportation will mean the separation of a child from his or her parent, the best interests of the child are taken into consideration."[38] (Emphasis added.)

It has been held that the best interests principle has attained the status of customary international law.[39] In addition to near-universal adherence to the binding provisions of the CRC, state practice with respect to the right to family unity is regularly confirmed by the Commission on Human Rights.[40]

The substantive content of the best interests principle is not defined in the CRC. Nevertheless, certain elements emerge from other provisions of the Convention.[41] In the case of actions and decisions affecting an individual child, it is the best interests of that individual child that must be taken into account. It is in the child's best interests to enjoy the rights and freedoms set out in the CRC, such as contact with both parents (in most circumstances). Best interests must be determined on a case-by-case basis, taking into account the totality of the circumstances. The Committee on the Rights of the Child has, for example, urged states to take the principle into "full consideration" and to "consider the full implications" of it.[42] In this regard, it should be noted that CRC Article 12 mandates that the views of the child shall be heard "in any judicial and administrative proceedings affecting the child" and be given due weight in accordance with his or her age and maturity. It is certainly not always in the best interests of the child to remain with parents, as recognized in CRC Article 9. However, it should be noted that in sharp contrast to the ICCPR, which prohibits only "arbitrary and unlawful" interference with the family, the CRC does not recognize a public interest to be weighed against the involuntary separation of the family.[43] The only exception allowed is when separation is necessary for the best interests of the child.

---

[38] Concluding observations of the Committee on the Rights of the Child: Norway, UN Doc. CRC/C/15/Add. 126 (28 June 2000), paras. 30-31.

[39] See *Beharry* v. *Reno*, 183 F.Supp. 2d 584 (E.D. N.Y.), wherein a federal district court in the United States, which is not a State Party to the Convention on the Rights of the Child, ruled that the government must take into account customary international law principles regarding the best interests of the child in the case of an immigrant man slated for deportation for a criminal offense, who is also the father of a seven-year-old U.S. citizen daughter.

[40] Commission on Human Rights Resolutions 2001/75 on the Rights of the Child, UN Doc. E/CN.4/2001/75, para. 11(c), and 2000/85 on the Rights of the Child, UN Doc. E/CN.4/2000/85, para. 15(d). UNHCR's Executive Committee has also expressed its concern over the serious consequences of expulsion on family members of refugees, Executive Committee Conclusion No. 7 (XXVIII) 1997(b).

[41] See Human Rights Brief No. 1, The Best Interests of the Child, Australian Human Rights and Equal Opportunity Commission website, www.hreoc.gov.au/human_rights/briefs/brief_1.html (last update 2 December 2001) as of 17 July 2002.

[42] Concluding observations of the Committee on the Rights of the Child: Finland, UN Doc. CRC/C/15/Add.132 (16 October 2000), paras. 25-26.

[43] Abram, *supra* note 4, at 418. "Thus, a competent state authority may decide to deport a parent in accordance with municipal law for carefully weighed and relevant reasons, yet the separation of the

On the European level, Article 8 of the European Convention for the Protection of Human Rights and Fundamental Freedoms (ECHR) provides that everyone has the right to respect for his or her family life. This right shall not be interfered with unless in accordance with the law and necessary in the interest of national security, public safety, or the economic well-being of the country, or for the prevention of disorder or crime, for the protection of health or morals, or the protection of the rights and freedoms of others.

The ECHR provides protection from deportation under certain circumstances.[44] The European Court distinguishes between aliens seeking to avoid family separation through expulsion and aliens seeking entry for the purposes of family reunion. In expulsion cases, the Court has balanced the individual's rights against the community's interests in determining whether removal was necessary in a democratic society. This approach places a greater burden of justification on states, and the Court has tended to side with non-citizens wishing to prevent family separation.[45] In the recent case of *Boultif* v. *Switzerland,*[46] for example, the Court found in favor of a man whose residence permit in Switzerland had not been renewed due to a criminal conviction. Rejecting arguments that the man and his Swiss wife could enjoy family life in Algeria, the court found that the wife could not be expected to follow her husband there because she had never lived there, had no other ties with the country, and did not speak Arabic.

Admission

Family reunification requires a state to affirmatively allow entry to a person, as opposed to refraining from deporting someone, and thus is a right more encumbered by state discretion. Nevertheless, states are bound by international obligations toward the family both in this context and in the realm of family unity. These obligations are most pronounced in the Convention on the Rights of the Child, but support can be found in other international instruments, as well.

Under humanitarian law, states are obliged to facilitate family reunification "in every possible way."[47] Non-citizens, as noted above, are included in the ICCPR's

---

child from the parent may violate the state's obligations and the child's right to family unity under article 9."

[44] The European Court must first find that there is a "private and family life." The category of family that can claim protection is broader than that under the CRC, since a minor child-parent relationship is not necessarily required. *Marckx* v. *Belgium,* for example, recognized the ties between near relatives such as grandparents and grandchildren as being included in family life, 27 April 1979, Serie A No. 31. Same-sex relationships may also be protected, although under the rubric of private, rather than family, life. *X and Y* v. *UK,* European Commission on Human Rights Admissibility Decision of 3 May 1983, Appl. No. 9369/81.

[45] For example, *Berrehab* v. *the Netherlands,* Judgment of 21 June 1988, Appl. No. 10730/84; *Moustaquim* v. *Belgium,* Judgment of 25 January 1991, Appl. No. 12313/86. For analyses of ECHR jurisprudence see Apap and Sitarapoulos, *supra* note 10; H. Lambert, "The European Court of Human Rights and the Right of Refugees and Other Persons in Need of Protection to Family Reunion," 11 (3) *International Journal of Refugee Law* (1999) p. 431; Anderfuhren-Wayne, *supra* note 14, at 354.

[46] *Boultif* v. *Switzerland,* Judgment of 2 August 2001, Appl. No. 54273/00.

[47] Additional Protocol I, 1977, Art. 74. See also Protocol II, 1977, Art. 4 (3)(b).

family protection provisions and their right to family reunification may, under some circumstances, give rise to a state obligation outweighing its interest in control of borders.[48]

In examining the application of Article 5 of the Convention on the Elimination of All Forms of Racial Discrimination, which protects, among other rights, the right to marriage and choice of spouse, the Committee on the Elimination of Racial Discrimination has queried, for example, the United Arab Emirates as to what extent foreign workers are entitled to have their children join them.[49] The Committee on Economic, Social and Cultural Rights has expressed its concern with Canada's delay in reuniting recognized refugees with their families.[50] The UNHCR's Executive Committee has also addressed the issue of refugee family reunification on a number of occasions.[51]

The right to family reunification for minor children and their parents is codified in the CRC.[52] Several elements of this provision are worthy of note.[53] First, the explicit link to CRC Article 9 means that the obligation imposed to ensure the unity of families within the state also determines the state's action regarding families divided by its borders. Second, one of the CRC's achievements is the recognition that reunification may require a state to allow *entry* as well as departure. Third, children and parents have equal status in a mutual right; either may be entitled to join the other. Nor is it sufficient that the child be with only one parent in an otherwise previously intact family; the child has the right to be with both parents, and both parents have the right and responsibility to raise the child.

Finally, the obligation on states to deal with reunification requests in a positive and humane manner means, in most cases, an *affirmative* manner. The only limitation allowed is the one permissible under Article 9(1), if reunification would not be in the best interests of the child, or when the reunification will occur in another country. While Article 10 does not expressly mandate approval of every reunification application,[54] it clearly contemplates that there is at least a presumption in favor of approval.[55] States cannot maintain generally restrictive laws or practices regard-

---

[48] Human Rights Committee, *General Comment No. 19, supra* note 4 , at para. 5.

[49] Concluding observations of the Committee on the Elimination of Racial Discrimination: United Arab Emirates, UN Doc. CERD/C/279/Add.1, para. 550 (1995).

[50] Concluding Observations of the Committee on Economic, Social and Cultural Rights: Canada, UN Doc. E/C.12/1/Add.31, para. 37 (1998).

[51] Executive Committee Conclusions No. 1(XXVI) 1975(f); No. 9 (XXVIII) 1977; No. 24 (XXXII) 1981; No. 84 (XLVIII) 1997; No. 85 (XLIX) 1998 (u)-(x); No. 88 ((L) 1999. See also UNHCR *Handbook on Procedures and Criteria for Determining Refugee Status*, para. 186 (1992).

[52] Convention on the Rights of the Child, 1989, Art. 10(1) "In accordance with the obligations of States Parties under article 9, paragraph 1 [a child shall not be separated from his or her parents against their will], applications by a child or his or her parents to enter or leave a State Party for the purpose of family reunification shall be dealt with by States Parties in a positive, humane and expeditious manner."

[53] For a fuller discussion of the CRC, see Abram, *supra* note 4, at 421-425.

[54] The drafters did not want to appear to require prejudgment of such applications. S. Detrick, *The United Nations Convention on the Rights of the Child: A Guide to the "Travaux Preparatoires"* (1992) p. 206.

[55] Vienna Convention on the Law of Treaties, Art. 31(1). Although Anderfuhren-Wayne, *supra* note 14, at 351, asserted that states enjoy "extensive discretion" under Art. 10, she did not identify the basis

ing the entry of aliens for reunification purposes without violating the CRC.[56] Nor can states fail to provide and promote a procedure for reunification. The Committee on the Rights of the Child has urged Norway, notwithstanding that state's "very positive approach" to family reunification, to "establish a *standard procedure though which children* and other concerned persons ... *are informed* of the possibilities and procedures for family reunification and for these procedures to be implemented *systematically* in accordance with *set guidelines*."[57] (Emphasis added.)

Reservations made by a small number of states to the reunification provision provide additional confirmation that the CRC imposes a general duty to allow entry for family reunification purposes.[58] While it has been argued that state practice is not uniform,[59] outright failures to allow reunification are more properly seen as violations of the right, not as evidence that there is no right. Failures to allow reunification are certainly treated as such by the Committee on the Rights of the Child, which has used peremptory language in this regard, recommending for example that Australia introduce legislation and policy reform "to *guarantee* that children of asylum seekers and refugees *are* reunified with their parents in a speedy manner"[60] (emphasis added). Similarly, the committee expressed its concern with Austria's legislation on the right to family reunification, and recommended that Austria "take *all* necessary measures to ensure that *all* its domestic legislation is in *full conformity* with the principles and provisions of the Convention, and in particular with Articles 9, 10, 20, and 22"[61] (emphasis added).

As noted above, the European Court distinguishes between family separation through removal and family reunification through entry, taking a more restrictive view of the latter.[62] The Court's approach is to examine whether there is a possibility

---

for that discretion. To the contrary, the formulation of Art. 10 is considerably stronger than language commonly used to allow significant state discretion, such as "consider favorably," "take appropriate measures," or "in accordance with national law." See also, Van Krieken, "Family Reunification," *supra* note 14, at 123, who acknowledged that Art. 10 does not "leave much room for machination and manipulation."

[56] See, Abram, *supra* note 4, at 423-424. "A state cannot as a matter of law or policy determine that family reunification for a category of sundered families will take place somewhere else in the world, and that family unity will be respected only by ushering the local child or parent to the airport. There is no true observation of a right if that right cannot be realized except abroad. States do not normally have the power to ensure the realization of a right outside of their own jurisdiction. A policy to reject most requests of any category of persons to enter a country for purposes of family reunification, except under restrictive conditions or exceptional circumstances, violates the Convention."

[57] Concluding observations of the Committee on the Rights of the Child: Norway, UN Doc. CRC/C/15/Add.126, paras. 32-33 (28 June 2000).

[58] Abram, *supra* note 4, at 424; and G.S. Goodwin-Gill, "Protecting the Human Rights of Refugee Children: Some Legal and Institutional Possibilities," *in* J.D.H. van Loon and P. Vlaardingerbroek (eds.), *Children on the Move: How to Implement Their Right to Family Life* (1996) p. 103.

[59] Anderfuhren-Wayne, *supra* note 14, at 351-352.

[60] Concluding observations of the Committee on the Rights of the Child: Australia, UN Doc. CRC/C/15/Add.79, para. 30 (10 October 1997).

[61] Concluding observations of the Committee on the Rights of the Child: Austria, UN. Doc. CRC/C/15/Add.98, para. 9 (7 May 1999).

[62] Although, as Lambert, *supra* note 46, at 442, points out, it is regrettable that the Court has not said

of family life elsewhere, usually in the country of origin.[63] While the Court has tended to find that there is such a possibility, each case must turn on its own facts. In a recent case, the Court found in favor of Turkish parents legally residing in the Netherlands, with two children born there, seeking to bring their oldest, Turkish-born daughter to join them.[64] The Court emphasized in particular the difficulties that the Dutch-born and educated children would have in Turkey. This useful focus on the realities of the family's life and the situation in their country of origin lends additional weight to efforts to reunify families of refugees and other persons in need of international protection, since they are not able to return to their country. There are, in addition, family reunification principles pertaining specifically to those in need of international protection that have been codified in the CRC,[65] and in regional instruments in Africa, Europe, and Central America.[66]

DEFINITION OF THE FAMILY

There is not a single, internationally accepted definition of the family, and international law recognizes a variety of forms.[67] The existence of a family tie is a question of fact, to be determined on a case-by-case basis. Certainly the nuclear family is the most widely accepted for family unity and reunification purposes.[68] In the European context, the amended proposal for a Council directive on the right to family reunification would also include unmarried partners living in a durable relationship with the applicant, if the legislation of the member state concerned treats such a relation-

why it observes such a distinction. Any refusal to allow entry, especially to a child, suggests a strong expectation that the parent will have to return to country of origin.

[63] *Ahmut* v. *the Netherlands*, 28 November 1996, No. 73/1995/579/665, and *Gul* v. *Switzerland*, 19 February 1996, No. 53/1995/559/645.

[64] Affaire *Sen* c. *Pays-Bas* [judgment available in French only], Arrêt de 21 décembre 2001, requete n. 31465/96.

[65] Convention on the Rights of the Child, 1989, Art. 22(2).

[66] African Charter on the Rights and Welfare of the Child, 1990, Art. XXIII(2). European Union Council Directive 2001/55/EC, 20 July 2001, n. 24 above, Art. 15. Council of Europe Committee of Ministers Rec. No. (2001) 18, 27 November 2001, *supra* note 25, at. para. 6; Council of Europe Committee of Ministers Rec. No. R (2000) 9, 3 May 2000, on temporary protection, para. 4; and Council of Europe Committee of Ministers Rec. No. R (99) 23, 15 December 1999, on family reunion for refugees and other persons in need of international protection. Council of Europe Parliamentary Assembly, Rec. 1327 (1997), n. 31 above, para. 8.vii.(o)-(q). Cartagena Declaration on Refugees, 1984, Conclusion III (13).

[67] See, for example, Human Rights Committee, *General Comment No. 28, supra* note 8, at para. 27; Human Rights Committee, *General Comment No. 19, supra* note 4, para. 2; Human Rights Committee, 32nd session, 1988, *General Comment No. 16*, para. 5 (8 April 1988). See also Apap and Sitaropoulos, *supra* note 10, at section 1, and more generally, G. van Bueren, "The International Protection of Family Members Rights as the 21st Century Approaches," 17 (4) *Human Rights Quarterly* (1995) pp. 733-740.

[68] See, for example, Council of Europe Committee of Ministers Rec. No. R (99) 23, *supra* note 66, at para. 2. See also Lambert, *supra* note 45, at 430; van Krieken, Family Reunification, *supra* note 14, at 122; and A. Hurwitz, "The 1990 Dublin Convention: A Comprehensive Assessment," 11 (4) *International Journal of Refugee Law* (1999) p. 653.

ship as corresponding to that of married couples.[69] The International Convention on the Protection of the Rights of All Migrant Workers and Members of the Families (MWC) includes persons who have a relationship with the migrant worker that, according to applicable law, produces effects equivalent to marriage.[70]

International humanitarian law recognizes that a family consists of those who consider themselves and are considered by each other to be part of the family, and who wish to live together.[71] In the refugee context, states have shown a willingness to promote liberal criteria with a view toward comprehensive reunification of families.[72] There is also extensive support on the European level for a wider acceptance of other family members, including the elderly, infirm, or otherwise dependent.[73]

Given the range of variations on the notion of family, a flexible approach is needed.[74] One useful limiting factor recognized by many states in determining whether more distant family members should be reunited is dependency.[75]

SPECIAL ISSUES IN THE MIGRATION OF CHILDREN

Non-citizen children are covered by the provisions of the CRC[76] and by human rights law generally. Transit and host states must act in their best interests,[77] take into account their views,[78] and provide them the opportunity to be heard in any judicial or administrative proceeding that affects them.[79]

Children are found outside their country of nationality for a variety of reasons, and the usual analytical categories for adults do not easily fit their complex circumstances. Given children's special vulnerabilities, notions of forced versus voluntary migration used to differentiate refugees from migrants, and notions of coercion versus consent for distinguishing trafficking from smuggling, are not always particular-

---

[69] Commission of the European Communities Amended Proposal for a Council Directive on the Right to Family Reunification, Brussels 10.10.2000 COM (2000) 624 Final, 1999/0258 (CNS), Art. 5.1. (a).

[70] International Convention on the Protection of the Rights of All Migrant Workers and Members of the Families, 1990, Art. 44(2).

[71] Y. Sandoz, C. Swinarski, and B. Zimmermann (eds.), *Commentary on the Additional Protocols* (ICRC, 1987), para. 2997.

[72] UNHCR Executive Committee Conclusion No. 88 (L) 1999 (b)(ii), "Protection of the Refugee's Family."

[73] Council of Europe Parliamentary Assembly, Rec. 1327 (1997), *supra* note 30, para. 8.vii.(o); Commission Amended Proposal for a Council Directive on the Right to Family Reunification, *supra* note 69, at Art. 5.1. (d)-(e). For ECHR jurisprudence, see Lambert, *supra* note 45, at 435-436.

[74] UNHCR, "Background Note: Family Reunification in the Context of Resettlement and Integration," Annual Tripartite Consultations on Resettlement, 20-23 June 2001, para. 14.

[75] UNHCR's operational definition is that a dependent person relies for his or her existence substantially and directly on another person, in particular because of economic reasons, but also taking emotional dependency into consideration. UNHCR *Resettlement Handbook*, ch. 4.6.5.

[76] Convention on the Rights of the Child, 1989, Art. 2.

[77] Id. at Art. 3.

[78] Id. at Art. 12(1).

[79] Id. at Art. 12(2).

ly helpful.[80] States have a tendency to veer between welfare protection on the one hand, focusing on these aliens as children, and immigration control on the other, focusing on these children as aliens.[81] The detention of children is a particularly reprehensible aspect of the latter approach, rightly condemned as illegal and inhumane, but clung to by unimaginative or callous bureaucrats as an enforcement tool in too many countries.[82]

In the asylum context, accompanied children rarely have their claims heard, even if theirs are potentially stronger than those of their parents. States have difficulty assessing claims of separated children due to the lack of relevant country of origin information,[83] and, all too frequently, a failure to properly conceptualize the harm done to children as falling within the ambit of the 1951 Convention.[84] One researcher's tentative conclusion is that, as compared to adult asylum-seekers, fewer separated children are granted asylum, and even fewer are returned, a muddled policy response that reveals states' uncertainty in dealing with such children.[85] Even if recognized, the refugee child faces enormous obstacles in achieving family reunification. States' policy concerns not to reward families for sending anchor children are too often allowed to override the child's right to be with his or her family. Even adult refugees in states with well-functioning asylum systems often face lengthy delays in being reunited with their children.[86]

Migrant children are increasingly likely to be smuggled or trafficked, in part because of restrictions on entry imposed by wealthy destination countries.[87] They are, in many ways, invisible – out of sight of their parents, their governments, and the

---

[80] See J. Bhabha, "Lone Travelers: Rights, Criminalization, and the Transnational Migration of Unaccompanied Children," 7 *University of Chicago Law School Roundtable* (2000) p. 269.

[81] See J. Bhabha, "Minors or Aliens? Inconsistent State Intervention and Separated Child Asylum Seekers," 3 *European Journal of Migration and Law* (2001) p. 293.

[82] See UN Doc. E/CN.4/2001/83/Add.1 (21 December 2000), para. 86, Addendum to the Report of the Special Rapporteur on the Human Rights of Migrants, on her Visit to Canada. See also A. Hunter, "Between the Domestic and the International: The Role of the European Union in Providing Protection for Unaccompanied Refugee Children in the United Kingdom," 3 *European Journal of Migration and Law* (2001) p. 393, and G. Sadoway, "Canada's Treatment of Separated Refugee Children," 3 *European Journal of Migration and Law* (2001) pp. 366-369.

[83] See A. Hunter, *supra* note 82, at 395.

[84] For a laudable recent attempt to address some of these difficulties, see Directorate of Immigration Finland, *Guidelines for Interviewing (Separated) Minors*, November 2001. See also, UNHCR, *Guidelines on Policies and Procedures in Dealing with Unaccompanied Children Seeking Asylum*, 1 February 1997; Separated Children in Europe Programme, A Joint Initiative of UNHCR and International Save the Children Alliance, 'Statement of Good Practice," October 2000; Action for the Rights of Children CD-ROM Resource Pack, August 2001; and UN General Assembly, "Protection and Assistance to Unaccompanied and Separated Refugee Children," UN. Doc. A/56/333, 7 September 2001.

[85] Bhabha 2001, *supra* note 81, at 312-313.

[86] See, for example, G. Sadoway, *supra* note 82, at 349.

[87] 2001 Report of the Special Rapporteur on the Human Rights of Migrants, *supra* note 9, at para. 62. See also, for example, G. Thompson, "Guatemala Intercepts 49 Children Illegally Bound for U.S.," *The New York Times*, 8 April 2002, p. A2. "Guatemalan authorities intercepted some 49 children, from toddlers to teenagers, who were being illegally transported from El Salvador to the United States, in what authorities said today was part of a highly organized smuggling network. ... American officials said most of the children were being transported to the United States to be reunited with parents."

society in which they now live. Reliable information on the numbers and conditions of migrant children is difficult to obtain.[88] A minimal necessary first step for states seeking to address these issues is to maintain gender and age disaggregated statistics on all categories of non-citizen children, including most obviously (and easily), those in detention.

Families separated by migration "are becoming increasingly common, and will become a defining characteristic of societies in many countries in the twenty-first century."[89] Equally defining will be the efforts of families to reunite through migration, and the ways in which states will choose to respond.

Selected Bibliography

ABRAM, E.F. – "The Child's Right to Family Unity in International Immigration Law," 17(4) *Law & Policy* (1995).

ANDERFUHREN-WAYNE, C.S. – "Family Unity in Immigration and Refugee Matters: United States and European Approaches," 8(3*) International Journal of Refugee Law* (1996).

APAP, J. AND N. SITAROPOULOS – "The Right to Family Unity and Reunification of Third Country Migrants in Host States: Aspects of International and European Law," in *Proceedings of the first European Congress for Specialist Lawyers in the Area of Immigration and Asylum in Europe (Odysseus Network), Brussels 1-2.12.2000* (2002).

BHABHA, J. – "Minors or Aliens? Inconsistent State Intervention and Separated Child Asylum Seekers," 3 *European Journal of Migration and Law* (2001).

—. "Lone Travelers: Rights, Criminalization, and the Transnational Migration of Unaccompanied Children," 7 *University of Chicago Law School Roundtable* (2000).

J. BHABHA AND W. YOUNG – "Not Adults in Miniature: Unaccompanied Child Asylum Seekers and the New US Guidelines," 11 *International Journal of Refugee Law* (1999).

BOELES, P. – "Directive on Family Reunification: Are the Dilemmas Resolved?" 3 *European Journal of Migration and Law* (2001).

DETRICK, S. – *The United Nations Convention on the Rights of the Child: A Guide to the "Travaux Preparatoires"* (1992).

ERIKSSON, M.K. – *The Right to Marry and Found a Family: A World-Wide Human Right* (1990).

GOODWIN-GILL, GUY S. – "Protecting the Human Rights of Refugee Children: Some Legal and Institutional Possibilities," in J. Doe, H. van Loon and P. Vlaardingerbroek (eds.), *Children on the Move: How to Implement Their Right to Family Life* (1996).

HUNTER, A. – "Between the Domestic and the International: The Role of the European Union in Providing Protection for Unaccompanied Refugee Children in the United Kingdom," 3 *European Journal of Migration and Law* (2001).

JASTRAM, K. AND K. NEWLAND – "Family Unity and Refugee Protection," in Refugee Protection in International Law: UNHCR's Global Consultations on International Protections (eds. Erika Feller, Volker Turk, and Frances Nicholson) Cambridge University Press, forthcoming June 2003.

LAMBERT, H. – "The European Court of Human Rights and the Right of Refugees and Other Persons in Need of Protection to Family Reunion," 11 (3) *International Journal of Refugee Law* (1999).

MERKELBACH, M. – "Reuniting Children Separated from their Families after the Rwandan Crisis of 1994: The Relative Value of a Centralized Database," 82 *ICRC* (2000).

MOTOMURA, H. – "The Family and Immigration: A Roadmap for the Ruritanian Lawmaker," 43 (4) *American Journal of Comparative Law* (1995).

---

[88] Bhabha 2000, *supra* note 80, at 273-278.

[89] UN. Doc. E/CN.4/2000/82 (6 January 2000), para. 84, Report of the Special Rapporteur on the Human Rights of Migrants.

NYKANEN, E. – "Protecting Children? The European Convention on Human Rights and Child Asylum Seekers," 3 *European Journal of Migration and Law* (2001).

PETTY, C. – "Family Tracing And Reunification – Safeguarding Rights And Implementing The Law," 4 *International Journal of Children's Rights* (1996).

VAN KRIEKEN, P.J. – "Family Reunification," in P.J. van Krieken (ed.), *The Migration Acquis Handbook* (2001).

SADOWAY, G. – "Canada's Treatment of Separated Refugee Children," 3 *European Journal of Migration and Law* (2001).

UNHCR – "Background Note: Family Reunification in the Context of Resettlement and Integration," Annual Tripartite Consultations on Resettlement, 20-23 June 2001.

Chapter 12
CHILDREN, MIGRATION AND INTERNATIONAL NORMS

Jacqueline Bhabha*

HISTORICAL BACKGROUND

Among migration experts, recognition of the distinctive situation of children as international migrants often comes as something of an afterthought. International migration is typically assumed to be an activity of adults or families, crossing borders in search of employment, safety, or family reunification. Insofar as attention turns to the specific problems of vulnerable groups amongst this population, it tends to be directed to the needs of the disabled, the elderly, or, most commonly, women-and-children, conceived of as one entity, one word virtually. Yet it is only from a perspective that takes the adult male as norm, that women and children merge as a group, "the other."[1] In the context of family migration, where women and children travel as part of a male-headed household, their situation in relation to migration law and policy is comparable. As autonomous or unaccompanied migrants, however, be they dependent relatives following to join resident family members, refugees, or trafficked persons, their circumstances and needs differ significantly. Critically, whereas only a subset of women migrants has specific gender-based vulnerabilities, all child migrants, whether or not their migration is linked to child specific exploitation, by virtue of their minority require special protection, either by family, other private entities, or state authorities. Merging the two groups into one perpetuates the assumption of common dependency and inferiority.

International law has long recognized the distinctive needs of some groups of child migrants. In 1924, acting on the principle that "mankind owes to the child the best it has to give,"[2] the League of Nations adopted the Declaration of the Rights of

---

* Executive Director, University Committee on Human Rights Studies, Harvard University. I would like to thank Elena Klau for her superb research assistance.

[1] In terms of the scale of migration, women and children outnumber adult men. Of 150 million migrants worldwide, it is estimated by the International Labor Organization (ILO) that 36-42 million are migrant workers and 44-55 million are members of their families, see www.ilo.org/public/english/protection/migrant/papers/disstrat/index.html.

Female-headed migrant households are less likely to have adult male family members accompanying than male. According to UNHCR, women constitute 51% of the 6.1 million refugees for whom information by gender is available. UNHCR Population Data Unit, *Women, Children and Older Refugee: The Sex and Age Distribution of Refugee Populations with a Special Emphasis on UNHCR Policy Priorities*, 19 July 2001, para. 14. http://www.unhcr.ch.

[2] Preamble, Declaration of the Rights of the Child 1924 (Declaration).

the Child. This was the first international human rights declaration adopted by any inter-governmental entity, preceding the Universal Declaration on Human Rights by nearly a quarter of a century. Two of the five principles articulated by the 1924 Declaration define rights relevant to child migrants. Article 3, a precursor of attention to the special needs of refugee children, states: "The child must be *the first* to receive relief in times of distress."[3] Article 4, reflecting the long-standing concern about child exploitation and trafficking, stipulates that "The child – must be protected against every form of exploitation."

Both categories of child migrants, victims of exploitation and refugees, have been addressed by specific early international migration documents. The first in time were anti-trafficking treaties that focused on criminalizing the recruitment and transportation of young girls for prostitution. The 1910 International Convention for the Suppression of White Slave Traffic required State Parties to punish anyone who hired, abducted, or enticed for immoral purposes any woman under the age of twenty-one; the 1921 International Convention for the Suppression of the Traffic in Women and Children expanded the protective measures to children of either sex. The scope of protections was further enlarged by the 1956 UN Supplementary Convention on the Abolition of Slavery, the Slave Trade and Institutions and Practices Similar to Slavery, to encompass all forms of child exploitation, including labor exploitation, whether by parents or others.[4]

Child refugees have been the subject of international concern since the inception of an international refugee regime. The 1946 Constitution of the International Refugee Organization (precursor to the United Nations High Commissioner For Refugees), adopted to regularize the status of World War II refugees, included as one of four categories of persons defined as refugees, a group of orphans under sixteen.[5] International recognition of the particular vulnerability of refugee children thus predates recognition of the distinctive difficulties of refugee women by about forty years. This contrasts interestingly with the approach of early international humanitarian law. The 1949 Geneva Convention IV Relative to the Protection of Civilian Persons in Time of War expressly granted a general entitlement to special treatment in international armed conflicts to the wounded and sick, and to expectant mothers, but not to children.[6] It was not until the 1977 Geneva Protocol I that the broad

---

[3] Declaration, *supra* note, 2 at Art. 3. A noticeable feature of the Declaration is the absolute primacy afforded to the child's need for protection and relief ("the child must be *the first*"). This is modified in subsequent documents. Thus the 1959 Declaration of the Rights of the Child stipulates that children shall be "among the first" to receive protection and relief, a more realistic approach given the likely need for expert adult assistance, see G. Van Beuren, *The International Law on the Rights of the Child* (1995) pp. 32-38.

[4] Article 1(d) renders unlawful "Any institution or practice whereby a child or young person under the age of 18 years is delivered by either or both of his natural parents or by his guardian to another person, whether for reward or not, with a view to the exploitation of the child or young person or of his labor."

[5] Annex 1, Part 1, sect. A, Art. 4.

[6] Geneva Convention IV Relative to the Protection of Civilian Persons in Time of War 1949 (GC IV) Art. 16. The Convention does, however, provide for special treatment of children in a range of particular circumstances.

principle of children's entitlement to special treatment in such circumstances was codified.[7]

GENERAL PRINCIPLES

The effort to protect children, including child migrants, through legally binding conventions was crystallized by the 1989 Convention on the Rights of the Child (CRC), the most rapidly and widely ratified of all international human rights treaties,[8] which codified and expanded international, regional, and bilateral agreements on child-specific rights and protection. Children, including child migrants, are thus afforded more comprehensive protection in international law than any other broad social group. Following a continuing and increasingly accepted trend, the CRC defined a child as "every human being below the age of 18 years unless, under the law applicable to the child, majority is attained earlier."[9] Where relevant, norms that apply generally to everyone or to no one also apply to children, even when they are not specifically enumerated. Most significant for child migrants are norms relating to the various aspects of freedom of movement, non-discrimination, nationality, economic, social and cultural rights (in particular education and health), and detention. This chapter will outline these general principles, central topics of other chapters in this collection, as they relate to child migrants. In addition, states have developed norms and policies for a subset of migration circumstances that are especially relevant to child migrants. These include questions of family unity, refugee protection, smuggling and trafficking, and transnational adoption. These topics will also be given attention.

Freedom of Movement

States enjoy broad discretion in the admission and expulsion of aliens, including alien children, to and from their territory. As a result, no right to freedom of movement is enshrined in international law.[10] However, state discretion is circumscribed by human rights laws that have curbed this classic arena of sovereign state autonomy. Freedom of movement can be conceptualized as consisting of three necessary

---

[7] Geneva Protocol I 1977 (GPI) Art. 77(1).

[8] The Convention was adopted by consensus by the General Assembly on 20 November 20 1989; it entered into force in record time on 2 September 2 1990.

[9] CRC Art. 1. Like adulthood, childhood is a social construct that has traditionally lacked clarity and consistency in terms of its definitional boundaries. Conceived of more as an incomplete, "comparative negative," not yet adult, than a rights-imbued human status, the concept has been applied to a range of ages. Van Beuren, *supra* note 3, at 11. Other terms associated with childhood, but with varying meanings and connotations, are also commonly used: minor, juvenile, infant, adolescent. Confusion can arise when several terms are used in the same text without definition, as in the UNHCR, *Handbook on Procedures and Criteria for Determining Refugee Status* (1979) para. 219 [hereafter *UNHCR Handbook*]. See J. Bhabha, "Minors or Aliens? Inconsistent State Intervention and Separated Child Asylum-Seekers," 3 *European Journal of Migration and Law* (2001) pp. 283-314, 297.

[10] See the contribution of Vincent Chetail in the present volume.

components, the right to leave a country, the right to enter a country, and the right to remain in a country. Article 10(2) of the CRC states that children have a right to leave any country, including their own, "subject only to such restrictions as are prescribed by law and which are necessary to protect the national security, public order (*ordre public*), public health or morals or the rights and freedoms of others and are consistent with the other rights recognized in the present Convention."[11] Custody agreements[12] and prohibitions on child exploitation[13] are permissible restrictions; bureaucratic delays, unreasonably high fees for the issuance of travel documents, restrictions on family members traveling together, or punitive expulsion of children from their school to discourage travel abroad are not.[14] The right to leave a country is moot without the correlative right to enter another country. Whereas children have a general right to leave *any* country (subject to the qualifications above), they only have a general right to enter their *own* country[15] (including a country they have never resided in, but of which they are nationals by virtue of *jus sanguinis*);[16] foreign countries have a wide scope for setting admission criteria, subject to compliance with their international obligations.[17] These include obligations in respect of non-discrimination and prohibition on inhuman treatment,[18] *non-refoulement* obligations in respect of refugees[19] and, most significantly for children, the obligation to consider "the best interests of the child"[20] and to respect family unity.[21] In practice,

---

[11] Many other international and regional human rights instruments have a similar provision, see Universal Declaration on Human Rights (UDHR) Art. 13; International Covenant on Civil and Political Rights (ICCPR) Art. 12(2); International Convention on the Elimination of All Forms of Racial Discrimination (ICERD) Art. 5(d)(ii); International Convention on the Rights of All Migrant Workers and Members of their Families (ICMW), not in force as of 28 July 2002. Art. 8; European Convention for the Protection of Human Rights and Fundamental Freedoms (ECHR) Protocol 4 Art. 2; American Convention on Human Rights (ACHR) Art. 22(2); African Charter on Human and Peoples' Rights (African Charter) Art. 12(2).

[12] CRC Art. 11(2); Hague Convention on the Civil Aspects of International Child Abduction (Hague Abduction Convention) Art. 13; European Convention on Recognition and Enforcement of Decisions Concerning Custody of Children and on Restoration of Custody of Children.

[13] CRC Art. 19.

[14] Human Rights Committee (HRC) General Comment No. 27, para. 17.

[15] CRC Art. 10(2); see also UDHR Art. 13(2); ICCPR Art. 12(4); ICERD Art. 5 (d) (ii); ECHR Protocol 4 Art. 3(2); ACHR Art. 22(5); African Charter Art. 12(2). Scholars dispute whether the phrase "own country" accords rights to long-term lawful residents as well as nationals. See HRC General Comment No. 27, para. 20.

[16] H. Hannum, *The Right to Leave and Return in International Law and Practice* (1987) p. 56. Restrictions or unreasonable delays in the issuance of passports to children who are citizens by descent, or who seek to return to their country having traveled on false documents to secure illegal entry, constitute violations of states' obligations.

[17] ICCPR Art. 12(2); ICERD Art. 5; ECHR Protocol 4 Art. 29(2); ACHR Art. 22; African Charter Art. 12(2).

[18] HRC General Comment No. 15, para. 5.

[19] CRC Art. 22; Convention on the Status of Refugees (CSR) Art. 33(1); Organization of African Unity (OAU) Convention Art. II(4).

[20] CRC Art. 3.

[21] CRC Art. 9; ICCPR Art. 23(1); International Covenant on Economic, Social and Cultural Rights (ICESCR) Art. 10(3); HRC General Comment No. 15, para. 5, 7.

the separation of children from their families, discussed in more detail below, remains one of the most urgent human rights issues. Like the right to enter, the right to remain in a state other than one's own is restricted, though states have wide discretion in devising grounds for removal, deportation, or expulsion.[22] State practice towards child migrants has generally been more generous in relation to expulsion than it has in relation to admission. The case law of the European Court of Human Rights is illustrative of this difference.[23]

Non-discrimination

International law does not prohibit all distinctions between people, just those which are arbitrary, disproportionate, or unjustifiable.[24] Given the moral and legal imperative to treat all human beings, including children and non-citizens, as of equal worth,[25] the onus is on those who seek an exception to the equality principle to justify it. Article 2(1) of the CRC prohibits discrimination in relation to the rights set out in the Convention, both between adults and children, and between different groups of children on the basis "of the child's or his or her parent's or legal guardian's race, color, sex, language, religion, political or other opinion, national, ethnic or social origin, property, disability, birth or other status."[26] This broad principle requires states parties to the CRC to not only prevent discrimination, but also to take action to ensure the positive enjoyment by children of rights on a par with adults.[27] No equivalent general codification of the non-discrimination rights of migrants exists. Instead, one can distinguish three different sets of norms. In some situations (e.g., with respect to the prohibition on cruel, inhuman, or degrading treatment or punishment[28]), aliens are entitled to the same treatment as nationals; thus a country that considers female genital circumcision to be cruel, inhuman, or degrading treatment cannot exempt non-citizen children from protection.[29] In a second set

---

[22] ICCPR Art. 13; CSR Arts. 32, 33; Convention Against Torture (CAT) Art. 3; ECHR Art. 3,8,14; Declaration On The Human Rights of Individuals Who are not Nationals of the Country in which They Live, United Nations General Assembly (UNGA) Res. 40/144 of 13 December 1985, Art. 2(1). See the contribution of David Martin in the present volume.

[23] Contrast *Berrehab* v. *The Netherlands*, Judgment of 21 June 1988, Appl. No. 10730/84, and *Moustaquim* v. *Belgium*, Judgment of 25 January 1991, Appl. No. 12313/86 with *Ahmut* v. *The Netherlands* (73/1995/579/665) judgment of 28 November 1996. See J. Bhabha, "Enforcing the Human Rights of Citizens and Non-Citizens in the Era of Maastricht: Some Reflections on the Importance of States," 29 *Development and Change* (1998) pp. 697-724, 718.

[24] Judge Tanaka Dissenting Opinion in South West Africa Cases (Second Phase) ICJ Reports 1966, at 305, 306; Belgian Linguistic Case ECHR (1968) judgment of 23 July 1968, 34.

[25] UDHR Preamble and Art. 1; ICCPR Preamble; ICESCR Preamble.

[26] Similar language, though not limited to children, is contained in many other instruments, see UN Charter Art. 1(3), 55(c); UDHR Art. 2; ICCPR Art. 2; ICESCR Art. 2(2); ECHR Protocol 12. The prohibition on discrimination "irrespective of ... national, ethnic or social origin" is generally understood to refer to ethnic origin rather than nationality. Nationality would therefore come within the rubric of "other status" by virtue of the *eiusdem generis* rule.

[27] Van Beuren, *supra* note 3, at 40.

[28] ICCPR Art. 7; ECHR Art. 3; ACHR Art. 5(2); ACHR Art. 13 (1),(2); African Charter Art. 5.

[29] See also CRC Art. 24 that obliges states parties to take effective measures against traditional

of situations, though the same norms apply, distinctions between citizens and aliens are permissible;[30] thus restriction of the right to freedom of expression or association may be justified on grounds of national security or public order, subject however to the general requirement of legitimacy and proportionality.[31] Curtailment of cultural practices in relation to dress or religious worship would have to meet these stringent requirements. In a third set of situations, special rules give rise to a difference in treatment between citizens and aliens; for example the dependent children of a diplomatic agent have rights to diplomatic immunity[32] and non-citizen children in custody or detention have rights of consular notification and access.[33] In general the requirement in Article 3(1) of the CRC that the best interests of the child should be a primary consideration in all state actions concerning children limits the scope of permissible discrimination against alien children. Historically many invidious distinctions against children have been justified in terms of their need for protection. A striking contemporary example is the United States and Canadian governments' justification for the incarceration of particular groups of separated child asylum-seekers in terms of their need for protection from the predatory reach of traffickers.[34] Such distinctions should be prohibited since they are not in the best interests of the child. Alternative methods for securing safety, regularly used for children facing comparable risks of domestic abuse or kidnapping in contested custody situations, are available. These may include secure shelters run by non-governmental organizations and specialist state child welfare services.

Nationality

The right of every child to acquire a nationality is enshrined in international law.[35] Though states have considerable discretion in devising rules about the acquisition and loss of nationality, this discretion is limited by international law. Particular attention is paid to the avoidance of statelessness[36] – states are under an obligation to grant nationality to children born or abandoned in their territory who would otherwise be stateless[37] and to facilitate the naturalization of refugees.[38] The principle of

---

practices affecting the health of minors; there is scholarly debate about whether all forms of female circumcision are *ipso facto* harmful to health, see R. Shweder, "What About Female Genital Mutilation? And Why Understanding Culture Matters In The First Place," *in* R. Shweder, M. Minow and H. Rose Markus (eds.), *Engaging Cultural Differences: The Multicultural Challenge in Liberal Democracies* (2002) pp. 216-251.

[30] A particularly broad exemption from the application of the general non-discrimination norm to distinctions between citizens and non-citizens is contained in CERD Art. 1(2), though this cannot be used to justify race or ethnic discrimination, *Yilmaz-Dogan* v. *Netherlands*, Committee on the Elimination of Racial Discrimination Comm. 1/1984, UN Doc. A/43/18, Annex IV, 59.

[31] ICCPR Art. 19,22; ECHR Art. 10, 16; African Charter Art. 23(2).

[32] Vienna Convention on Diplomatic Relations Art. 37(1).

[33] Vienna Convention on Consular Relations, Art. 36.

[34] Bhabha, *supra* note 9, at 300.

[35] CRC Art. 7; UDHR Art. 15; ICCPR Art. 24(3)

[36] CRC Art. 7(2).

[37] European Convention on Nationality (ECN) Art. 6.

[38] CSR Art. 34.

non-discrimination prohibits differences in the treatment of nationals based on the method of acquisition (birth on the territory, descent, or registration).[39] In states that operate the principle of *jus soli*, children of illegal entrants and visitors are included.[40] Acknowledging the realities of a globalizing world, states – including those traditionally opposed – are increasingly tolerating dual or multiple nationalities, as when children automatically acquire several nationalities at birth.[41] There is also a growing consensus that states should facilitate the acquisition of nationality by second and third generation immigrants, including children, and by adopted children. Given that one of the critical attributes of nationality is the entitlement to remain in the territory indefinitely, irrespective of criminal convictions or antiterrorist measures, acquisition of the nationality of the state of residence is likely to be a critical safeguard for immigrant children.[42]

Economic, Social and Cultural Rights

International law recognizes a broad range of economic, social and cultural rights, including the rights to education and to health, which have to be progressively realized. Special emphasis is placed on states' obligations towards children. Thus, though "everyone has the right to education,"[43] it is only primary education that is compulsory and must be made available free to all.[44] "Treaty law is clear. *All* children who live in states which are party either to the International Covenant on Economic, Social and Cultural Rights (ICESCR) or the CRC are entitled to receive free primary education."[45] Even states that are not parties to these treaties, such as the United States, have consistently recognized the rights of non-citizen children, in-

---

[39] ECN Art. 5(2); however this apparently does not exclude discrimination in rules regulating the loss of nationality. A recent German nationality law requires second-generation immigrant children who acquired their parents' nationality by descent and German nationality by birth on the territory to choose one nationality when they turn eighteen, but no such requirement is applied to children of mixed marriages. See the contribution of Kay Hailbronner in the present volume.

[40] This may give rise to controversy, as is currently the case in Ireland in relation to the so-called "passport babies" – e.g., children born to rejected asylum-seekers from the Balkans. The Irish Supreme Court has ruled that newborn citizens do not have a right to enjoy the company of the family in Ireland if this conflicts with immigration control requirements. *Lobe v. Minister for Justice, Equality and Law Reform* (2003), 1 ESC 1 (23 January 2003).

[41] ECN Art. 14.

[42] The significant increase in applications by U.S. resident aliens for naturalization following the events of 11 September 2001, suggests popular recognition of this fact; naturalization applications between May 2001 and May 2002 saw a 65% jump compared with the previous 12 months, from nearly 315,000 to about 520,000, K. Franklin, "Citizenship Applications on Rise Since 9/11, INS Official Reports," *The Virginian Pilot*, 3 August 2002.

[43] UDHR Art. 26(1).

[44] CRC Art. 28(1); ICESCR Art. 13; CSR Art. 22; ECHR Protocol 1 Art. 2; ICMW Art. 30.

[45] Van Beuren, *supra* note 3, at 235. This is widely recognized. Many states accord education rights beyond primary school and in line with provisions for domestic children to migrant children, including children seeking asylum, see for example, Country Reports on Belgium, Denmark, Germany in IGC, *Report on Unaccompanied Minors: Overview of Policies and Practices in IGC Participating States* (Secretariat on the Inter-Governmental Consultations on Asylum, Refugee and Migration Policies in Europe, North America and Australia, July 1997), 88, 151, 196.

cluding those who are undocumented, to free primary education.[46] The CRC requires State Parties to ensure that the right to education is achieved "on the basis of equal opportunity."[47] Differential treatment of migrant children, for example by mother tongue teaching, must therefore be justified in terms of the "best interest" principle and applicable non-discrimination provisions.[48] A fear that domestic primary schools may be swamped by children of asylum-seekers, recently voiced by the UK Home Secretary,[49] as a justification for denying these children access to mainstream schools falls foul of these provisions. Also relevant to the rights of migrant children and their families are states' obligations to respect the rights of parents in regard to religious and moral education of their children;[50] however, states have no duty to provide instruction in line with such parental choices.

Similarly, while international law establishes a universal right to enjoyment of "the highest attainable standard" of health,[51] there is a particular focus on the health of mother and child[52] and on primary health care.[53] State policies of prolonged and harsh detention of children seeking asylum,[54] including the separation of such children from their parents,[55] and the incarceration of unaccompanied migrant children,[56] have deleterious health consequences that are inconsistent with international obligations.[57] Recent evidence on the progressively deteriorating health of some immigrant child populations also suggests the need for more vigilance to these obli-

---

[46] *Plyler* v. *Doe*, 457 U.S. 202 (1981).

[47] CRC Art. 28(1).

[48] For example a UNESCO Convention and Recommendation against Discrimination in Education (adopted by the General Conference of UNESCO on 14 December 1960) includes a provision granting equal access to education to children who are resident and foreign nationals, Art. 3(e); however, a prohibition on differences in treatment of pupils except on the basis of merit or need in respect of school fees, scholarships, or other forms of assistance is confined to differences *between nationals*, Art. 39(c).

[49] BBC, "Blunkett Talks Tough on Asylum," 24 April 2002,
http://news.bbc.co.uk/hi/english/uk_political/newsid_1947000/1947160.stm.

[50] UDHR Art. 26(3); ICESCR Art. 13; ICCPR Art. 18(4); ECHR Protocol 1 Art. 2. By contrast the CRC has no such provision, though it gives children themselves the right to participate in decisions to ensure that their education conforms to their own religious and moral convictions, see Van Beuren, *supra* note 3, at 243.

[51] CRC Art. 24; UDHR Art. 25; ICESCR Art. 12; ICERD Art. 5; ACHR Additional Protocol Art. 10; African Charter Art. 16; ICMW Art. 38 (right to emergency medical care).

[52] UDHR Art. 25(2); ICESCR Art. 12(2)(a).

[53] CRC Art. 24(2)(b).

[54] Australian practice at the Woomera Detention Centre, see P. Barkham, "No Waltzing in Woomera," *The Guardian*, 25 May 2002, at 24.

[55] U.S. Policy see Human Rights Watch (HRW), *Detained and Deprived of Rights: Children in the Custody of the U.S. Immigration and Naturalization Service*, December 1998; C. Nugent and R. Schulman, "Giving Voice to the Vulnerable: On Representing Detained Immigrant and Refugee Children," 78 *Interpreter Releases* (2001) p. 1569.

[56] Human Rights Watch (HRW), *Slipping Through the Cracks: Unaccompanied Children Detained by the U.S. Immigration and Naturalization Service* (1997).

[57] A judge reviewing the detention for over six months of twelve Chinese children by the Canadian authorities commented: "Almost all of [the children] have lost weight and become increasingly withdrawn and timid. They have been visited by a doctor only once and this doctor did not speak any of the languages spoken by the minors." Gao (Litigation Guardian of V Canada (Minister of Citizenship and Immigration) 2000 Carswell Ont. 2646, Docket 00-CV-192960, Judgment of 27 July 2000.

gations.[58] UNHCR Guidelines on Refugee Children[59] state that immediate family re-union is critical to the mental health of the refugee child.

Detention

Immigrant detention, which by definition impacts discriminatorily on non-citizens, does not, per se, violate the prohibition on arbitrary arrest and detention; however, such detention must conform with domestic law and be reasonable in length.[60] Children must "be accorded treatment appropriate to their age"[61] and detention is only to be used "as a measure of last resort and for the shortest possible period of time;"[62] moreover, international law requires that the best interests of the child be a primary consideration.[63] According to the UNHCR, separated[64] children seeking asylum should not be detained.[65] Moreover there are special rules that establish minimum international standards for the fair and humane treatment of *any* child in detention. These include a requirement that legal procedures be prompt, expeditious, and at no cost for detained children without adequate means,[66] that detention should only be in facilities guaranteeing a reasonable degree of personal privacy[67] and meaningful activities and programs promoting the development and health of the young person;[68] and that children in detention should be separated from non-family adults.[69] Several states, including the United States and Australia, routinely ignore these provisions in their treatment of migrant children.[70] According to the UN Special Rapporteur on

---

[58] M.M. Suarez-Orozco, "Everything You Ever Wanted to Know about Assimilation but Were Afraid to Ask," *in* Shweder, *supra* note 29, at 31.

[59] UNHCR, *Guidelines on Refugee Children* (1988).

[60] ICCPR Art. 9; ECHR Art. 5(1)(f); prolonged detention without evidence of necessity may violate the principle of proportionality see *A. v. Australia,* CCPR/C/59/D/560/1993 (1997) communication of HRC.

[61] ICCPR Art. 39.

[62] CRC Art. 37(b). See also UN Rules for the Protection of Juveniles Deprived of their Liberty I.2.

[63] CRC Art. 3.

[64] Children outside their country without their families have in the past generally been termed unaccompanied children. However, many such children are not in fact literally unaccompanied, at least not for their entire journey or stay; they may be escorted by family acquaintances, co-villagers, paid smugglers, or traffickers working within criminal networks. Accordingly, following a growing trend initiated by the Separated Children in Europe Program, the term separated is preferred throughout this text. See M. Ruxton, *Separated Children Seeking Asylum in Europe: A Programme for Action* (2000).

[65] UNHCR, *Note on Policies and Procedures in dealing with Unaccompanied Children Seeking Asylum* (1996) section 7.6.

[66] UNHCR Policies, sections 5, 8. UNHCR also recommends the appointment of a legal guardian for separated detained children.

[67] UN Rules IV D.

[68] UN Rules II.12.

[69] UN Rules II C 29.

[70] HRW, *supra* note 56, HRW, *supra* note 55. Despite widespread criticism the Australian federal government has refused to change its migrant child detention policy: according to Prime Minister John Howard, "It's not a policy we like having to implement but in the face of attempts by people to come to this country illegally there is really no alternative." http://canberra.yourguide.com.au/detail.asp?class, visited on 23 July 2002. Some other states have time and age limits on detention of child asylum-seek-

the human rights of migrants, such practices are not only inhumane but illegal;[71] they have attracted widespread condemnation.

FAMILY UNITY

International law protects the right to form a family[72] and to enjoy a shared family life,[73] it calls for the "widest possible protection and assistance" for the family,[74] and it prohibits arbitrary or unlawful interference with the family.[75] It considers the family to be "the natural environment for the growth and well-being of all its members *and particularly children.*"[76] Taken together these provisions constitute a strong international legal norm protecting the right to family unity. For children, the norm is particularly compelling. CRC Article 9(1) states: "States parties *shall ensure* that a child shall not be separated from his or her parents against their will, except when competent authorities subject to judicial review determine, in accordance with applicable law and procedures, that such separation *is necessary for the best interests of the child.*" This rule applies to *all* children within the jurisdiction of a State Party, including immigrant and refugee children residing within the state.[77] The child's right to family unity can be conceptualized as comprising two distinct elements: the right not to be separated from the family, and the right, once separated, to be reunited.

The Right Not to be Separated

The right of a child not to be separated from his or her family consists of two state obligations:[78] a negative obligation requiring states not to interfere with family unity; and a positive obligation to take all necessary measures to assure the realization of the child's right to family unity. The *only* exhaustive limitation on these obligations is where separation is necessary for the best interests of the child. Decisions in the immigration context are covered by the obligation,[79] unless specifically excepted by State Party reservations, understandings, or declarations.[80] Serious harm

---

ers (e.g., Belgium, see ICG Report *supra* note 45, at 88), yet others prohibit detention of such children (though disputes about age may result in significant numbers of children being detained). Amnesty International, *Most Vulnerable of All: The Treatment of Unaccompanied Children in the UK* (1999).

[71] UN Doc. E/CN.4/2001/83/Add.1(21 December 2000) para. 86.

[72] UDHR Art. 16.

[73] F.E. Abrahm, "The Child's Right to Family Unity in International Immigration Law," 17(4) *Law and Policy* (1995) p. 407.

[74] ICESCR Art. 10(1).

[75] CRC Art. 16; UDHR Art. 12; ICCPR Art. 17; ECHR Art. 8; ACHR Art. 11(2).

[76] CRC Preamble.

[77] Abrahm, *supra* note 73, at 416-417. The following paragraphs draw extensively from this article and from the paper on family unification by Kate Jastram prepared for this collection.

[78] CRC Art. 9.

[79] CRC Art. 9(4).

[80] Several states have attached such reservations. The UK reservation, for example, stipulates that

to the child in the parental home or the absence of viable alternatives would meet this standard for separation; deportation of a criminal alien parent that imposed the separation of child from parent would not unless this was necessary for the child's best interest.[81] Even if the family could avoid separation by following the deportee, the State Party has an obligation under the CRC, prior to expulsion of a family member, to consider whether such uprooting would in fact cause family separation because of the magnitude of practical adaptation difficulties; the child's views would have to be given due weight[82] and the child's best interests would have to be a primary consideration. Thus, under the CRC, the negation of family unity can only be justified by the private interest of a child. The European Convention for the Protection of Human Rights and Fundamental Freedoms (ECHR) jurisprudence, discussed below, provides useful guidance for construing adaptation and relocation difficulties. The CRC approach to enforced separation contrasts with the general principle in CRC Article 3 that makes "best interest" a primary, but not as in Article 9 *the paramount*, consideration governing all other state actions concerning children. The Australian High Court has ruled that ratification of the CRC provides parents and children with a legitimate expectation that the principle of family unity will be adhered to.[83] The CRC approach also contrasts with the approach of other international human rights conventions that allow interference with a child's family life in a broader range of circumstances justified by public interest.[84] Thus, the International Covenant on Civil and Political Rights (ICCPR) prohibits only arbitrary or unlawful interference with family life; the Human Rights Committee (HRC) has determined that this provision protects children's right to family unity despite state immigration control laws in a range of circumstances.[85] The ECHR permits interference with a child's right to respect for his or her private or family life only when such interference is in accordance with the law (i.e., is both lawful and legitimate) and "*necessary* in a democratic society in the interests of national security, public safety, or the economic well-being of the country, for the prevention of disorder or crime, for the protection of health or morals, or for the protection of the rights or freedoms of others." Both citizen[86] and alien[87] children living with their parents as

---

the CRC will not affect implementation of domestic immigration and nationality legislation, unless this amounts to violation of an additional right, e.g., the right to respect for family life under ECHR Art. 8. Germany's declaration protects its ability to exclude unauthorized aliens and to distinguish between nationals and aliens in matters of immigration control. Of course reservations are only effective insofar as they do not contradict norms of *jus cogens* and customary international law, see Van Beuren, *supra* note 9, at 55-57.

[81] See *Beharry* v. *Reno*, US Dist. Ct., EDNY, 8 January 2002, 2002 US Dist. LEXIS 757 (though the United States is not a party to the CRC, a federal district court judge ruled that customary international law principles relating to the best interests of the child should be taken into account in the deportation decision of a criminal alien with a seven-year-old citizen child).

[82] CRC Art. 9(2), Art. 12.

[83] *Minister for Immigration and Ethnic Affairs* v. *Ah Hin Teoh*, 183 *CLR* 273 (1995) (Austr.).

[84] ICCPR Art. 17(1); ECHR Art. 8(2).

[85] HRC General Comment No. 15 para. 7, General Comment No. 19 para. 5; Communication No. 930/2000, UN Doc. CCPR/C/72/D/930/2000, para. 8 (16 August 2001) holding that proposed removal of parents of thirteen-year-old Australian would violate the Convention.

[86] *Beldjoudi* v. *France*, Appl. No. 120083/86. In some states, the principle of family unity for citi-

well as children with ties to non-custodial divorced parents[88] have benefited from this widely used provision. Expulsion of a non-custodial parent that would prevent regular contact with the child, for example where the custodial parent remains with the child in the home country, has been held to be a violation of the ECHR Article 8 right to respect for family life, even when the closeness between the non-custodial parent and the child is not officially established.[89] Though the ECHR judicial institutions have tended to view family unity and the right to respect for family life as a privilege of parents earned by good behavior or responsible parental involvement rather than as a right of children, the jurisprudence provides a useful guide for considering how to assess the difficulty of child relocation. The age of the child, and the linguistic, emotional, educational, socioeconomic environment to which the child would be moving, are relevant factors to be considered when evaluating whether the harm of dislocation is proportionate to the benefit of controlling immigration (younger children are more easily relocated). A small disparity in environmental conditions between the deporting and the receiving state is less likely to give rise to a finding of a violation. Taken together, these international law protections of the right of children not to be separated from their family place a heavy burden on states to justify contrary measures.[90] They require states to afford deportable aliens the right to a hearing prior to expulsion where family unity will be disrupted.[91] The CRC transforms this heavy burden into a binding obligation.

The Right to Family Reunification

From a child's standpoint, family separation caused by the expulsion of a parent can be as devastating as family separation caused by the refusal to allow reunification: the resulting disruption of family unity is the same. This moral equivalence is recognized by the CRC that codifies a child's right to reunification following family separation.[92] The requirement that State Parties deal with an application for family reunification by a child or his or her parents in a "*positive*, humane and expeditious manner" is violated by the long waiting periods, aggressive adversarial questioning

---

zen children has been derived from domestic constitutional norms, see *Fajujonu* v. *Minister for Justice* (1989) 2. *Irish Reports* 151. (Irish case) However, The Irish Supreme Court has recently restricted the scope of this decision. *Lobe* v. *Minister for Justice, Equality and Law Reform, supra* note 40. Usually the right of the citizen child to family unity is limited by the principle of proportionality, which allows for deportation of the alien relative where a serious criminal offence has been committed. E.Z. Friedler, "From Extreme Hardship to Extreme Deference: United States Deportation of its Own Children," 22 *Hastings Constitutional Law Quarterly* (1995) p. 491. In France, undocumented parents of citizen children, while not granted legal status as relatives of citizens, are not deported; they are considered "non-expulsables" but also "non-regularisables," J. Simeant, *La Cause des Sans-Papiers* (1998) p. 137.

[87] *Moustaquim* v. *Belgium*, Appl. No. 12313/86.

[88] *Berrehab* v. *The Netherlands*, Appl. No. 10730/84.

[89] *Ciliz* v. *The Netherlands*, Appl. No. 29192/95.

[90] See *Fadele Family* v. *UK* Appl. No. 13078/870; see also report of Australian Human Rights Commission on Complaint of Mr. and Mrs. M. Yilmaz, cited *in* Van Beuren, *supra* note 9, at 81-82.

[91] ICCPR Art. 17; see *Beharry* v. *INS*, 2002 U.S. Dist. Lexis 757.

[92] CRC Art. 10(1).

of dependents seeking admission and narrow eligibility criteria that characterize many domestic immigration systems. Article 10(1) of the CRC further provides that attempts by a child to secure family reunification should not entail "adverse consequences" for members of the child's family; current U.S. practice by which detained children seeking asylum are used as bait to detain their undocumented parents violates this provision. Other international law instruments recognize family reunification rights in some circumstances;[93] yet whether they afford any such general right is not resolved.[94] In practice, as stated earlier, states have afforded greater protection to children where families have resisted exclusion than where they have attempted reunification,[95] even where young children living on their own in their country of origin would face institutionalization or severe hardship in the absence of reunification with a parent.[96] At the same time, most states have family reunification provisions in their domestic immigration laws, though with considerable variations.[97] Where family reunification cannot take place in the country of residence of a separated child, e.g., because of a risk of persecution, family unity should be protected by allowing admission of non-resident children.[98] The Convention on the Status of Refugees (CSR) does not enshrine any right to family reunion for refugees;[99] however the CRC, in addition to the general right to family unity under Articles 9 and 10, requires positive action by states to facilitate the family reunification of refugee and asylum-seeking children.[100] Though the CRC affords parents and children a mutual right to be joined by each other, in practice, states have generally not afforded separated children, including refugee and citizen children, the right, while minors, to secure their parents admission for reunification. This asymmetry between parents and children violates both the right to family unity and the nondiscrimination

---

[93] ICCPR HRC General Comment No. 19 para. 5; *Abdulaziz, Cabales, and Balkandali* v. *UK*, Appl. No. 00009214/80(1985); African Charter on the Rights and Welfare of the Child Art. XXIII(2).

[94] Contrast R. Plender, *International Migration Law* (1988) p. 366, arguing against such a right, with Report of the Special Rapporteur on the Human Rights of Migrants 2001 para. 65 arguing in favor.

[95] For the special case of child abduction see CRC Art. 11 and Hague Abduction Convention, which requires States Parties to return a child wrongfully removed or retained to the country of habitual residence for a best interest determination to be made there, rather than – as previously – in the country of abduction. See also European Convention on Recognition and Enforcement of Decisions Concerning Custody of Children and on Restoration of Custody of Children.

[96] *Ahmut* v. *The Netherlands,* Appl. No. 73/1995/579/665; see also *Gül* v. *Switzerland,* Appl. No. 53/1995/559/645.

[97] Abrahm, *supra* note 77, at 400-406.

[98] The Australian temporary protection visa, which does not permit the holder to effect reunification with his or her spouse or minor children, violates this obligation.

[99] Though CSR and its 1967 Protocol are silent on the right to family reunification, the UNHCR Handbook (para. 186) and several UNHCR ExCom conclusions have addressed the topic of refugee family reunification. See also UNHCR, Guidelines on the Care and Protection of Refugee Children (1994); UNHCR, Guidelines on Policies and Protections in Dealing with Unaccompanied Minors Seeking Asylum (1997). See also "Recommendation B in Final Act to CSR," cited in G.S. Goodwin-Gill, "Protecting the Human Rights of Refugee Children: Some Legal and Institutional Possibilities," *in* J. Doek, H. van Loon, and P. Vlaardingerbroek (eds.), *Children on the Move: How to Implement their Right to Family Life* (1996) 97.

[100] CRC Art. 22(2).

norm.[101] Where children cannot be expected to seek family reunification in the home country, as is manifestly the case for separated child refugees, the absence of a legal right to bring parents to join them (until the parents become elderly and dependent) consigns these children to permanent family separation. Similarly placed adults, by contrast, are uniformly allowed such family reunification rights with respect to their minor children. This asymmetry in the family reunification rights of children and adults is unjustifiable, and one of the clearest examples of neglect of a child-specific focus in current migration norms. International law also protects the rights to family unity of children of migrant workers,[102] and of civilians, including children, separated by war[103] and of residents of occupied territories.[104]

REFUGEE PROTECTION

As stated earlier, international law has recognized the special needs of refugee children. International norms apply to both refugee[105] and children's rights.[106] The CRC, unlike the CSR, includes within the scope of its refugee protection provisions, both children who have already been accorded refugee status by the host state and children who are seeking asylum.[107] According to one scholar this scope must now be considered expanded to encompass UNHCR's even more inclusive definition that embraces "children who are refugees, returnees, asylum-seekers and displaced persons of concern to UNHCR."[108] UNHCR has recognized the centrality of the CRC as "a normative frame of reference."[109] In addition to protections specific to refugees, several general protection obligations are particularly relevant, including the right to public education,[110] housing,[111] health care,[112] and social security,[113] and the obliga-

---

[101] W. Ayotte, *Information on Separated Children Arriving in Western Europe: Why They Travel and How They Arrive* (2000).

[102] ICMW Art. 44(2).

[103] GC IV Art. 26; GP I Art. 74.

[104] GC IV Art. 24; Regulations Annexed to the Hague Convention Respecting the Laws and Customs of War on Land 1907, Art. 46.

[105] "The term 'refugee' shall apply to any person who ... owing to a well-founded fear of being persecuted for reasons of race, religion, nationality, membership of a particular social group or political opinion, is outside the country of his nationality and is unable or, owing to such fear, unwilling to avail himself of the protection of that country; or who, not having a nationality and being outside the country of his former habitual residence is unable or, owing to such fear, is unwilling to return to it." CSR Art. 1(2) as amended by 1967 Protocol.

[106] CRC Art. 22.

[107] CRC Art. 22(1). This article has also been held to cover rejected child asylum-seekers, see Van Beuren, *supra* note 9, at 362.

[108] Abrahm, *supra* note 77, at 425-426, citing UNHCR Policy on Refugee Children, UNHCR Doc. EC/SCP/82.

[109] Goodwin-Gill, *supra* note 99, at 102.

[110] CRC Art. 28; CSR Art. 22; the right to elementary education is the same as for national children, to higher education the same as for settled aliens, CSR Art. 22(2).

[111] CSR Art. 21.

[112] CRC Art. 24.

[113] CRC Art. 26; CSR Art. 24.

tion to ensure the survival and development of the child,[114] that no child is subjected to torture or cruelty,[115] and that any child deprived of a family environment is given special protection.[116] Moreover, refugee children must be given "appropriate" protection and assistance to enable them to attain such rights[117] – this should include assistance in tracing family members, access to legal representation, interpreters, counseling, and appropriate fostering arrangements.

There is no lower age limit to the well-established international right to claim asylum or resist *refoulement* to a persecuting or torturing country.[118] This follows from the general non-discrimination principle outlined above. Any of the five grounds enumerated in the CSR refugee definition can apply to a child. Recent jurisprudential developments have expanded the meaning of persecution, the pivotal threshold concept in the refugee definition, and the ground of membership in a particular social group, the most expansive of the five grounds, to encompass various child-specific forms of persecution, including child abuse, child sale and trafficking, vulnerabilities arising out of being a street child, a member of a gang, or behaviors which, while not rising to the threshold of persecution for an adult, do so for a child (e.g., witnessing death of close relatives).[119]

Generally, when children seek refugee protection as part of a family group, no special legal problems arise despite their pervasive legal invisibility and the absence of any provisions in the CSR assimilating an adult refugee's child to his or her refugee status.[120] However, it is when children are separated from family that they encounter particular legal hurdles; no direct path to asylum or family reunification is assured. Neither the CSR nor the CRC offer an adequate system of international protection. This is one of the most serious shortcomings of the international normative framework as regards protection of child migrants. The CRC's system of vertical control through reporting obligations, complemented by the involvement of the UNHCR and the horizontal cooperative arrangements envisaged by the Hague Adoption and Abduction conventions go some way, but much stronger international cooperation and supervision are required to prevent vulnerable migrant children from falling through the numerous cracks that arise in domestic protection. Many states have adopted inconsistent policies towards such children, veering between concern for them as particularly vulnerable migrants, and hostility to them as peculiarly unpredictable illegal aliens.[121] Such policies frequently violate CRC obligations, particularly the best interests principle and the unrebuttable obligation to

---

[114] CRC Art. 6(2).

[115] CRC Art. 37.

[116] CRC Art. 20.

[117] CRC Art. 22(1).

[118] UDHR Art. 14; CSR Art. 32, 33; ICCPR Art. 13; CAT Art. 3; ECHR Art. 3; OAU Convention; Cartagena Declaration on the Problems of Refugees and the Displaced in Central America.

[119] Bhabha, *supra* note 9.

[120] According to the UNHCR Handbook, "dependants are normally granted refugee status according to the principle of family unity," para. 184; and their dependency operates in favor of children (para. 185). An exception are situations where the child's claim is stronger than the parents, but is neglected because of the adult-centric bias.

[121] Bhabha, *supra* note 9, at 299-324.

promote family unity. Adult (including parental) assessments of what constitutes a child's best interests may conflict with the child's right to have his or her expressed views taken into account.[122]

Substantive and procedural guidelines addressing issues facing separated child asylum-seekers have been developed at an international,[123] regional,[124] and national[125] level. Several problems have attracted particular attention but remain unresolved through non-implementation of guidelines. These include measures to address the absence of adequate legal representation or guardianship arrangements; unreliable or harmful age determination procedures; the protracted and often inconclusive nature of legal proceedings to secure permanent legal status; the abusive use of detention, including in some cases punitive measures; the vulnerabilities arising out of smuggling and trafficking arrangements, and the failure to promote family reunification in the receiving or home country. The lacuna in legal responsibility for decisions affecting refugee children is a serious gap in protection. Child refugees do not usually fall afoul of the exclusion provisions in CSR;[126] however, the special circumstances of child soldiers may give rise to exclusionary concerns that have to be balanced against the best interests principle.[127]

---

[122] CRC Art. 12. For example, while a welfare professional may consider a separated child asylum-seeker best off returned to his or her home, the child may oppose such action.

[123] The 1979 UNHCR Handbook devotes seven paragraphs to unaccompanied minors, paras. 213-219; since 1986 the situation of refugee children has been accorded special attention, see EXCOM General Conclusion No. 41(XXXVII) 1986 para.(m) Conclusion 91; EXCOM No. Conclusion 47 (XXXVIII) 1987; UNHCR, Refugee Children: Guidelines on Protection and Care (1994); UNHCR, "Guidelines on Policies and Procedures in Dealing with Unaccompanied Minors Seeking Asylum" (1997).

[124] EU Council Resolution on "Unaccompanied Minors who are Nationals of Third Countries," *Official Journal* C 221 (1997). See A. Hunter, "Between the Domestic and the International: The Role of the European Union in Providing Protection for Unaccompanied Refugee Children in the United Kingdom," 3 *European Journal of Migration and Law* (2001) 393. See also D. Pearl and C. Lyons, "The Treatment by the European Union of Unaccompanied Minors," *in* N. Lowe and G. Douglas (eds.), *Families across Frontiers* (1996) pp. 435-448.

[125] The first child-specific national guidelines for separated children seeking asylum were promulgated by Canada; these were limited to procedural and evidentiary issues, Immigration and Refugee Board, "Child Refugee Claimants: Procedural and Evidentiary Issues," Ottawa, September 1996. See UNHCR, *Separated Children Seeking Asylum in Canada* (2001); G. Sadoway, "Canada's Treatment of Separated Refugee Children," 3 *European Journal of Migration and Law* (2001) p. 366. In 1998 the United States issued "Guidelines for Children's Asylum Claims" which also included substantive legal standards expanding the concept of persecution to include child-specific situations, U.S. Department of Justice, Immigration and Naturalization Service, 10 December 1998. See J. Bhabha and W. Young, "Not Adults in Miniature Unaccompanied Child Asylum Seekers and the New U.S. Guidelines," 11(1) *International Journal of Refugee Law* (1999). Considerable U.S. public concern relating to the treatment of separated child migrants, particularly following the Elian Gonzalez case, has resulted in congressional moves to legislate a wide range of desirable policy changes, see Unaccompanied Alien Child Protection Act of 2001 [S.121; H.R.1904], which at the time of this writing is being incorporated into the far-ranging Homeland Security legislation before Congress, see Title XII of Lieberman substitute to H.R. 5005, S 2541.

[126] CSR Art. 1(F).

[127] W.H. Perlmutter, "An Application of Refugee Law to Child Soldiers," 6(2) *Georgetown Public Policy Review* (2001) pp. 137-153; M.S. Gallagher, "Soldier Boy Bad: Child Soldiers, Culture and Bars to Asylum," 13(3) *International Journal of Refugee Law* (2001) pp. 310-353.

SMUGGLING AND TRAFFICKING

International norms relating to abusive child migration practices have a long history.[128] Recent concern has focused on two aspects, criminalization of the practices themselves and protection of the victims.[129] Children (along with women) have been a distinct focus of attention because of their particular vulnerability to exploitation and their need for special protection.[130] In general, these measures have starkly failed to prevent proliferation or protect intended beneficiaries; the carefully integrated, transnational scope of the illegal networks contrasts with ineffective interstate attempts at collaboration. Implementation, rather than elaboration of further norms, thus remains the critical challenge.[131] Though smuggling and trafficking are both part of the expanding illegal global migration business, they are conceptually and legally distinct. From the viewpoint of states, they are closely linked as variants of this business, from the viewpoint of migrants, they may be diametrically opposed, one a life line, the other a life sentence. A measure of definitional clarity and consensus, following decades of doctrinal wrangling, has been achieved through the adoption by the General Assembly of two protocols to the UN Convention Against Transnational Organized Crime.[132] Reports of the UN Special Rapporteur on the Sale of Children, Child Prostitution and Child Pornography, have also focused international attention on exploitative child migration.[133]

The Smuggling Protocol defines and establishes as a criminal offense the smuggling of migrants;[134] endangering the lives or safety of migrants is an aggravating

---

[128] See text *supra* note 4.

[129] CRC Arts.11, 34, 35. See V. Muntabhorn, this volume.

[130] ICMW; European Social Charter Art. 7; OAU Banjul Charter Art. 7; Hague Convention on the Protections of Children and Cooperation in Respect of Inter-Country Adoptions (Hague Convention); ILO Convention No. 182 Concerning the Prohibition and Immediate Action for the Elimination of the Worst Forms of Child Labor; Optional Protocol to the CRC Sale of Children, Child Prostitution and Child Pornography. Trade organizations, such as the WTO, have conspicuously failed to address the question of abusive international trade in human services, including exploitative child labor. For a detailed account see J. Bhabha, "Lone Travelers: Rights, Criminalization, and the Transnational Migration of Unaccompanied Children," 7 *University of Chicago Law School Roundtable* (2000) pp. 269-294. See also Communication from the Commission to the Council and the European Parliament, *Combating Trafficking in Human Beings and Combating the Sexual Exploitation of Children and Child Pornography,* COM (2000) 854 (final).

[131] Some states, e.g., China, have implemented draconian punitive measures including executions against traffickers, AP, "Child Traffickers executed in China," 26 April 2000.

[132] Protocol against the Smuggling of Migrants by Land, Sea and Air, supplementing the United Nations Convention against Transnational Organized Crime, A/55/383, Annex III (Smuggling Protocol); Protocol to Prevent, Suppress and Punish Trafficking in Persons, especially Women and Children, supplementing the United Nations Convention against Transnational Organized Crime, A/55/383/Annex II. (Trafficking Protocol). As of July 2002 the smuggling protocol had 101 signatories and 11 parties; and the trafficking protocol had 104 signatories and 12 parties. Both protocols need 40 parties to come into force.

[133] E/CN.4/1991/51, E/CN.4/1992/55 and Add.1; E/CN.4/1993/67 and Add.1; E/CN.4/1994/84 and Add.1 (visit to Nepal); E/CN.4/1997/95/Add.1 (visit to the Czech Republic) and Add.2 (mission to the United States on issue of commercial sexual exploitation of children); E/CN.4/1997/71 see particularly para. 49-145.

[134] Smuggling is defined as "the procurement, in order to obtain, directly or indirectly, a financial

circumstance. The Protocol encourages State Parties to facilitate the speedy return to their country of origin of smuggled persons. No explicit mention is made of the rights of child refugees or other child victims of human rights violations, though smuggled persons, including children, are not to be prosecuted for their unauthorized mode of entry. Children are significantly implicated in smuggling operations as refugees seeking asylum[135] and as separated family members seeking reunification.[136] In these contexts relevant international refugee and family unity protections apply. In practice, many states violate these provision, by detaining such children or expelling them without allowing access to due process procedures mandated by international law.

Children are disproportionately implicated in trafficking because of their particular vulnerability to exploitation for sex (servicing pedophile proclivities or as a presumed hedge against HIV/AIDS), for abusive adoption,[137] or as slave laborers.[138] International law prohibits all forms of child exploitation.[139] The Trafficking Protocol defines and criminalizes trafficking in persons, *especially women and children*.[140] By contrast with earlier treaties,[141] it includes not just coercion but abuse of

---

or other material benefit, of the illegal entry of a person into a State Party of which the person is not a national or a permanent resident," Smuggling Protocol Art. 3.

[135] According to one expert, "a very large number – perhaps the majority" of asylum-seekers in Europe have been smuggled or trafficked because of the difficulties of regular access, J. Morrison, *The Trafficking and Smuggling of Refugees: The End Game in European Asylum Policy* (July 2000) p. 24.

[136] "Guatemalan authorities intercepted some 49 children, from toddlers to teenagers, who were being illegally transported from El Salvador to the United States, in ... a highly organized smuggling network. ... American officials said most of the children were being transported to the United States to be reunited with parents." G. Thompson, "Guatemala Intercepts 49 Children Illegally Bound for U.S." *New York Times*, 8 April 2002, A2.

[137] Numerous baby smuggling rings illegally selling to unwitting adopters have been uncovered, see, e.g., D.M. Halbfinder, "Three Charged with Running Mexican Baby-Smuggling Ring," *New York Times*, 28 May 1999, A1 (describing the sale of at least seventeen Mexican infants for a minimum of $20,000 each to unwitting New York adopters). See also Report of Special Rapporteur on sale of children, child prostitution and child pornography, E/CN.4/1994/84, 14 January 1994, para. 48-63. (Report by SR on Sale of Children.)

[138] A UNICEF report identified Mexico as the main source of infants and children trafficked into the United States to be given in illicit adoptions or handed to prostitution rings; it cites a CIA study indicating that 50,000 women and children were smuggled into the United States in 1999 for purposes of prostitution or illegal adoption, M. Leon, "Children Smuggled into U.S. for Adoption, Prostitution," http://www.thenewsmexico.com/noticia.asp, visited on 1 July 2002. There are also reports, many difficult to substantiate, of child trafficking for sale of their organs, Report by SR on sale of Children, 1994, para. 53; 100-113; Report by SR on sale of Children, A/50/456 20 September 1995, para. 49-50.

[139] CRC Art. 36; ICESCR Art. 10(3).

[140] Trafficking in persons is defined as "the recruitment, transfer, harboring or receipt of persons, by means of the threat or use of force or other forms of coercion, of abduction, of fraud, of deception, of the abuse of power or of a position of vulnerability or of the giving or receiving of payments or benefits to achieve the consent of a person having control over another person, for the purpose of exploitation. Exploitation shall include, at a minimum, the exploitation of the prostitution of others or other forms of sexual exploitation, forced labor or services, slavery or practices similar to slavery, servitude or the removal or organs." Trafficking Protocol Art. 3. The European Framework proposal by contrast places the suppression of fundamental rights at the core of their definition, see Communication from the Commission to the Council and the European Parliament, *Proposal for a Council Framework Decision on Combating Trafficking in Human Beings* Art. 1, COM (2000) 854 final.

authority as a component of trafficking, a more comprehensive range of illicit purposes of trafficking and broader enforcement and (non-mandatory) protective measures. One clear goal of the Protocol is to substitute protection for criminalization of trafficked persons. This includes an option for states parties to permit such persons to remain on the territory, including permanently. Several special victim protection provisions are particularly relevant to children, including legal assistance, counseling services, and the availability of shelter and medical help. The rights of child refugees and victims of human rights violations are specifically protected.[142] In addition a wide range of anti-trafficking regional,[143] bilateral,[144] and national measures[145] exist; many, but not all, include some human rights safeguards. However, state practice routinely violates international protective provisions. For example, a report released at the time of this writing by the UN Special Rapporteurs on Arbitrary Detention and on the Sale of Children, child prostitution and child pornography criticized the Guatemalan government for jailing foreign girls after rescuing them from traffickers.[146]

TRANSNATIONAL ADOPTION

Whereas early systems of adoption were primarily intended to satisfy parental needs, the modern child-centered approach derives its force from the universal principle that the child should grow up in a family environment.[147] The proliferation of transnational adoption reflects a supply and demand maldistribution geographically – a dramatic reduction in children available for adoption in developed states, and a staggering number of abandoned children in developing countries.[148] The potential for exploitation and the difficulties in assessing suitability of prospective adopters

---

[141] Though the problem of child trafficking has long been of international concern, earlier treaties failed to distinguish between and cover all forms of trafficking – slavery was the predominant concern. The CRC established an all embracing binding prohibition on child trafficking for the first time.

[142] UNHCR has called for international collaboration to prevent the exposure of refugee children to trafficking, EXCOM Conclusion (e) A/AC/96/702.

[143] European Social Charter Art. 7; Communication from the Commission to the Council and the European Parliament, *Combating Trafficking in Human Beings and Combating the Sexual Exploitation of Children and Child Pornography*, COM (2000) 854 (final); OAU Banjul Charter Art. 7; see P. Twomey, "Europe's Other Market: Trafficking in People," *European Journal of Migration and Law* (2000) pp. 6-36.

[144] Agreement to combat people smuggling between Australia and Thailand – Nationwide News Party Ltd, "People Smuggling Pact," *The Daily Telegraph* (Sydney) 7 July 2001.

[145] For example, the US Trafficking Victims Protection Act 2000, which envisages the possibility of permanent residence for trafficking victims but mandates collaboration with the prosecution of traffickers, even when fears of retaliation and personal safety are at issue.

[146] "UN Concerned for Treatment of Detained Trafficked Girls in Guatemala," owner-rapidresponse@casa-alianza.org, 15 July 2002.

[147] Preamble, CRC. However international human rights law does not enshrine any right to adoption.

[148] W. Duncan, "Regulating Intercountry Adoption – An International Perspective," *in* A. Bainham and D. Pearl (eds.), *Frontiers of Family Law* Part I (1993) pp. 40-51.

were clearly recognized by the Indian Supreme Court in a seminal, early judgment.[149] Since then international legal norms have been developed; they are not intended to *facilitate*, but rather to *regulate* transnational adoption to ensure respect for the best interests[150] of the child, cooperation among states to prevent abusive adoptions (disguised trafficking or sale), and international recognition of legal adoptions.[151] The same standards and safeguards applicable to national adoptions apply to transnational ones. States of origin and receiving states have tended to have different approaches to the acceptability of private adoptions.[152] The CRC favors government-controlled placement of transnational adoptees by "competent authorities or organs"[153] as opposed to independent private agencies. The Hague Convention on International Cooperation and Protection of Children in Respect of Inter-country Adoptions, however, does not rule out private adoptions; it establishes a system of State Central Authorities responsible for sponsoring adoptions directly or delegating this to accredited or competent and qualified bodies or persons.[154] States of origin have an obligation to ensure that local adoption options are explored before transnational adoption is permitted[155] and that consents to the adoption (including where appropriate by the child) have been obtained freely, on the basis of full information and without economic inducement;[156] receiving states must establish that the prospective adopters are qualified to adopt[157] and that the adoptee can enter and remain permanently. Special considerations apply to the adoption of separated child refugees,[158] including whether adoption is ever appropriate when surviving parents exist[159] and which country has the legal responsibility for deciding on adoption.[160]

---

[149] *Lakshmi Kant Pandey* v. *Union of India, 2 Indian Supreme Court Reports* (1984) 795, cited *in* Van Beuren, *supra* note 9, at 96.

[150] The UN Declaration on Social and Legal Principles Relating to the Protection and Welfare of Children with Special Reference to Foster Placement and Adoption, Nationally and Internationally governs the factors to be considered in determining best interest.

[151] CRC Art. 1; Hague Convention Art. 1. Inter-country adoption motivated solely by the poverty of the biological parents is contrary to international legal principles, Van Beuren, *supra* note 9, at 100.

[152] Duncan, *supra* note 148, at 45-46.

[153] CRC Art. 21(e).

[154] Hague Convention Art. 22(2).

[155] CRC Art. 21(c). This however does not justify rigid and protracted administrative practices, or the imposition of quotas on foreign adoptees, W. Duncan, "The Hague Convention on the Protection of Children and Co-operation in Respect of Inter-country Adoption 1993 – Some Issues of Special Relevance to Sending Countries," in E.D. Jaffe (ed.), *Intercountry Adoptions: Laws and Perspectives of "Sending Countries,"* (1995) pp. 217-228.

[156] Hague Convention Art. 4.

[157] Hague Convention Art. 5.

[158] Goodwin-Gill, *supra* note 99, at 104-108.

[159] According to UNHCR, adoption can be considered where reunion would either not be in the best interests of the child, or in not likely to be realized within a reasonable time, normally a minimum of two years, UNHCR, *Refugee Children: Guidelines on Protection and Care* (1994) pp. 130-131.

[160] The Special Commission on the Implementation of the Hague Convention recommended that the country in which the child was residing following displacement should take the place of the state of origin, see Hague Convention on Private International Law, Special Commission on the Implementation of the Convention on 29 May 1993, 17-21 October 1994, working Doc. No. 39 (21 October 1994) para.1.

Experts consider the current absence of jurisdictional competence on these questions to be a serious gap in international protection.[161]

Selected Bibliography

ABRAM, FRANK ELIAHU – "The Child's Right to Family Unity in International Immigration Law," 17(4) *Law and Policy* (1995).

AMNESTY INTERNATIONAL – *Most Vulnerable of All: The Treatment of Unaccompanied Children in the UK* (1999).

AYOTTE, WENDY – *Information on Separated Children Arriving in Western Europe: Why They Travel and How They Arrive* (2000).

BHABHA, JACQUELINE – "Minors or Aliens? Inconsistent State Intervention and Separated Child Asylum-Seekers," 3 *European Journal Migration and Law* (2001).

—. "Lone Travelers: Rights, Criminalization, and the Transnational Migration of Unaccompanied Children," 7 *University of Chicago Law School Roundtable* (2000).

—. "Enforcing the Human Rights of Citizens and Non-Citizens in the Era of Maastricht: Some Reflections on the Importance of States," 29 *Development and Change* (1998).

—. "Get Back to Where you Once Belonged: Identity, Citizenship and Exclusion in Europe," 20 *Human Rights Quarterly* (1998).

BHABHA, JACQUELINE AND WENDY YOUNG – "Not Adults in Miniature: Unaccompanied Child Asylum Seekers and the New U.S. Guidelines," 11(1) *International Journal of Refugee Law* (1999).

DUNCAN, W. – "The Hague Convention on the Protection of Children and Co-operation in Respect of Intercountry Adoption 1993 – Some Issues of Special Relevance to Sending Countries," in Eliezer D. Jaffe (ed.), *Intercountry Adoptions: Laws and Perspectives of "Sending Countries"* (1995).

GOODWIN-GILL, GUY S. – "Protecting the Human Rights of Refugee Children: Some Legal and Institutional Possibilities," in Jaap Doek, Hans van Loon and Paul Vlaardingerbroek (eds.), *Children on the Move: How to Implement their Right to Family Life* (1996).

—. "Unaccompanied Refugee Minors: The Role and Place of International Law in the Pursuit of Durable Solutions," 3 *International Journal of Children's Rights* (1995).

HANNUM, HURST – *The Right to Leave and Return in International Law and Practice* (1987).

HOLBORN, L. – "The United Nations and the Refugee Problem," 6 *The Year Book of World Affairs* (1952).

HUMAN RIGHTS WATCH – *Detained and Deprived of Rights: Children in the Custody of the U.S. Immigration and Naturalization Service* (1998).

—. *Slipping Through the Cracks: Unaccompanied Children Detained by the U.S. Immigration and Naturalization Service* (1997).

HUNTER, ALISON – "Between the Domestic and the International: The Role of the European Union in Providing Protection for Unaccompanied Refugee Children in the United Kingdom," 3 *European Journal of Migration and Law* (2001).

KUPER, JENNY – *International Law Concerning Child Civilians in Armed Conflict* (1997).

PEARL, DAVID AND CAROLE LYONS – "The Treatment by the European Union of Unaccompanied Minors," in Nigel Lowe and Gillian Douglas (eds.), *Families Across Frontiers* (1996).

PLENDER, RICHARD – *International Migration Law* (1988).

RESSLER, EVERETT M., NEIL BOOTHBY AND DANIEL J. STEINBOCK – *Unaccompanied Children: Care and Protection in Wars, Natural Disasters, and Refugee Movements* (1998).

RUXTON, MICHAEL – *Separated Children Seeking Asylum in Europe: A Programme for Action* (2000).

SADOWAY, GERALDINE – "Canada's Treatment of Separated Refugee Children," 3 *European Journal of Migration and Law* (2001).

VAN BEUREN, GERALDINE – *The International Law on the Rights of the Child* (1995).

---

[161] Goodwin-Gill, *supra* note 99, at 108.

LABOR, TRADE AND DEVELOPMENT

Chapter 13
LABOR MIGRATION

Virginia A. Leary*

INTRODUCTION

The extent of labor migration is overwhelming. It is estimated that 60 to 65 million people are economically active in a country other than their own.[1] They are often accompanied by their families and may or may not be legally in their country of work. Labor migration has become extremely complex. While migration to seek work has been going on for centuries, the extent of labor migration has grown exponentially. Economic differences between developed and developing countries, globalization and increased trade, and political problems have contributed to the increase in the movement of workers.

In the past, it was frequently unskilled workers who migrated; today many highly skilled workers, particularly computer and information experts, have joined the ranks of migrants. Migrant workers now range from young unskilled women leaving to work abroad as domestics to highly trained specialists sought after by developed countries. Trafficking of young women across national boundaries for sexual purposes is widespread. The International Labor Organization (ILO) has pointed out that "there are growing problems with irregular migration, illegal employment and exploitation. ... In some sectors, notably agriculture, construction, tourism and care of the aged, only foreign workers, particularly the undocumented, are willing to accept short-term, insecure jobs with little career opportunity."[2]

The ILO has listed the main types of labor migration:[3]

1. *Migration for training purposes* involves citizens from one country who spend a few months in a private or public enterprise in a more advanced country to acquire skills. There are relatively few of these types of migrants.

---

* Virginia A. Leary is the Alfred and Hanna Fromm Professor Emeritus of International and Comparative Law, University of California (Hastings) and Distinguished Service Professor Emeritus, State University of New York (Buffalo). She presently resides in Geneva, Switzerland, where she is the Director of a project on Social Aspects of Trade Liberalization at the Graduate Institute of International Studies.

[1] International Labor Office, GB.283/2/1, March 2002, para. 92.

[2] Id. at para. 94

[3] M.I. Abella, *Sending Workers Abroad* (2nd printing 2000), pp. 113-114.

T.A. Aleinikoff and V. Chetail (Eds.), Migration and International Legal Norms
© 2003, T.M.C. ASSER PRESS, *The Hague, The Netherlands, et al.*

2. *Professional, technical, and managerial workers, as well as businesspeople and people providing cross-border services* move across borders temporarily and without much regulation. Some move for personal advancement or business demands, while others are workers in project-tied work, particularly in the construction industry.

3. *Migration for ordinary employment purposes under contract auspices that are limited in time* "first took place on a large scale when individuals from the then backward Mediterranean countries moved north to countries such as Belgium, France, and Germany. Contract migrants can now be found in many other countries. For example, Arab States tend to admit most Arab workers and all workers from non-Arab countries, as contract workers with limited-duration permits. ... Seasonal migration for employment purposes ... is practiced in ... the vineyards of France and California, the construction sites of Switzerland and the hotels of the Caribbean."[4]

4. *Migration for ordinary employment purposes but under settlement auspices* (Australia, Canada, the United States, New Zealand, Singapore).

The large numbers of undocumented or illegal workers mainly in developed countries should be added to the above-listed ILO categories.

To a substantial extent, labor migration is carried out through private initiatives that are largely unregulated at the international level. National laws, however, often provide varying degrees of regulation. The first section of the chapter refers to private arrangements. Labor migration is also facilitated and organized by state-to-state agreements and by regional arrangements, such as the European Union, the Council of Europe, and NAFTA, referred to in the second section. The major international efforts to regulate labor migration by ILO conventions and by the UN International Convention on the Protection of Migrant Workers have had limited effect and are described in the third section. The fourth section refers to the human rights non-standard-setting approach to migration within UN human rights bodies; including the Working Group on Migration and the Special Rapporteur on the human rights of migrants.

PRIVATE ORGANIZATION OF LABOR MIGRATION

As noted by the ILO, "[m]uch of contemporary migration is organized by private intermediaries, not by states. ..."[5] State policies towards these private initiatives vary widely. Some states adopt a *laissez-faire* policy (Portugal and the United Kingdom) whereby the state imposes no standards and leaves details of the contract up to the worker and the foreign employer.

---

[4] Id. at 114.
[5] ILO, GB.283/2/1, March 2002, Summary.

More typical, however, is a *regulated system* where the sending state adopts laws and regulations governing private recruitment for employment abroad. The state may screen jobs offered abroad, regulate recruiters, and set minimum standards for labor contracts, but the allocation of labor is still left to the market (India). Some states have a *state-managed* system where the state itself sets up systems to recruit and place workers abroad, entering into agreements for the equal treatment of its nationals regarding labor and social security policies. The state thus adopts an active foreign employment policy (Korea, Pakistan, Philippines). Most states license enterprises engaged in labor recruitment.

An ILO publication[6] points out that private sector participation in labor recruitment has a number of advantages: such efforts are not constrained by budgetary processes; private sector resources can be mobilized and have greater flexibility than state enterprises; private initiative results in the development of new markets; and foreign employers may prefer to work with private firms. "The rapidity with which private resources can be mobilized to promote foreign employment was demonstrated during the boom in demand for expatriate labor in the Middle East during the late 1970s and early l980s ..." but "states "would be better placed to manage foreign employment if they had well-functioning public employment services that can also undertake recruitment and placement activities for foreign employers."[7]

BILATERAL AND REGIONAL ARRANGEMENTS

Bilateral Labor Agreements

Bilateral agreements between sending and receiving countries, which seek to ensure that migration takes place in an orderly and appropriate fashion, appear to be less common today than the private arrangements referred to above. In the l960s northern European countries suffering serious labor shortages entered into bilateral agreements with southern European and North African countries. In the 1970s European countries entered into bilateral agreements with developing countries like Bangladesh, Iraq, Jordan, and Gabon. Private agencies under state supervision were allowed to recruit.

Regional Arrangements

European Convention on Human Rights

Most of the norms on migrant labor in the European context relate only to nationals from European countries. However, the European Convention on Human Rights, adopted by the Council of Europe in 1950, applies to all persons within the ratifying states, including migrants, whether or not they are nationals of a European state. Its

---

[6] Abella, *supra* note 4.
[7] Abella, *supra* note 4, at 56-57.

provisions cover mainly civil and political rights and do not contain specific provisions on migrant labor.

The Council of Europe

The European Social Charter of the Council of Europe[8] contains provisions on economic and social rights, but it applies only to nationals of Council of Europe (COE) Member States who are parties to the Charter. Two provisions provide rights for migrant workers: Article 18, the right to engage in a gainful occupation in the territory of other contracting parties and Article 19, the right of migrant workers and their families to protection and assistance. The Charter's provisions are largely modeled on ILO conventions, although the Charter is formulated in terms of human rights and brings together in one instrument many provisions in various ILO conventions. By 2002, the Charter had received 24 ratifications. Three Protocols to the Convention have been adopted and a revised amended Charter was adopted in 1999 that provides for the possibility of individual complaints for violation of the Charter.

In 1977, a European Convention on the Legal Status of Migrant Workers[9] was adopted at the Council of Europe, but, as one author who has written extensively on migrant labor points out, it was adopted at an inopportune moment (during the major oil crisis of 1973-1974) and is weak in terms of the protection of migrant workers.[10] Only eight European countries have ratified the Convention.

The European Union

The European Union treaties contain extensive provisions concerning freedom of movement of workers among the Member States, as well as numerous provisions providing for full equality of migrant workers with nationals of the receiving state.[11] The Union system is clearly the most advanced system for protecting migrant labor, but it is limited to nationals from Member States. Workers from outside the Union are not similarly protected unless European states have either ratified relevant ILO conventions (since none has ratified the UN Convention on Migrant Workers), or if the sending state has entered into an Association and Cooperation Agreement with the Union. This is particularly unfortunate since most of the problems for migrant workers in Europe affect those coming from outside the Union.

NAFTA

The North American Free Trade Agreement (NAFTA), an agreement between Canada, Mexico, and the United States, does not purport to establish an economic, political, and monetary union like the EU. Its primary objectives are the facilitation of

---

[8] European Social Charter, 1961, Council of Europe, *ETS,* No. 35.

[9] European Convention on the Legal Status of Migrant Workers, 1977, Council of Europe, *ETS,* No. 93.

[10] R. Cholewinski. *Migrant Workers in International Human Rights Law* (1997) pp. 221-223.

[11] Id. at 224-404.

trade among the three countries, the expansion of a secure market for the goods and services of the agreeing states, and a predictable commercial framework for trade.

Chapter Sixteen of the Agreement contains extensive articles about the entry of businesspersons into the respective states. The first article reflects the preferential trading relationship between the parties, and emphasizes "the desirability of facilitating temporary entry on a reciprocal basis and of establishing transparent criteria and procedures for temporary entry, and the need to ensure border security and to protect the domestic labor force and permanent employment in their respective territories."

While NAFTA provides an orderly framework for the entry of businesspersons into the three states, the major labor migration among the three countries remains the clandestine entry of unskilled workers from Mexico into Canada and the United States.

INTERNATIONAL REGULATION

The international effort to develop norms on labor migration through legally binding conventions has had limited success. Changes in the form and extent of migrant labor have outrun the ability of the international community to cope with such changes through binding norms and treaties, and political opposition in receiving states constitutes a formidable obstacle to further international regulation. International treaties on migrant labor have been ratified primarily by sending states and not by receiving states, where abuses generally occur. Recognition of limited success through legally binding treaties has led to new non-standard-setting initiatives both at the ILO and the UN.

ILO and Labor Migration

The ILO, founded in 1919 and the only public international organization to survive World War II, has the longest history with migrant labor issues. With the drafting and adoption of the Migrant Workers' Convention in 1990, however, the UN has become as much a focus as the ILO for concern with migrant labor issues.

The protection of workers outside their native country has been a central concern of the ILO since its founding. The Organization's Constitution refers to the need for protection of "the interests of workers employed in countries other than their own." The problems of migrant workers were given special mention in the Philadelphia Declaration of 1944 concerning the aims and purposes of the Organization. Although the standards on migrant labor are not included among the "core labor standards" enunciated in the 1998 Declaration on Fundamental Principles and Rights at Work, the Declaration reaffirms the need to pay special attention to migrant labor.

Employer and employee organizations are full ILO members, a role not granted to non-governmental organizations in other UN bodies. However, employee representatives at the ILO have not been as actively involved in promoting measures regarding migrant labor as they have been for other issues of more concern to organized labor (i.e., freedom of association). An ILO publication on Migrant Workers commented, in an understated manner, on this lack of interest by both employees' and employers' organizations:

> "On the local level, both employers' and workers' organizations have clearly much to contribute to the protection of workers, and a host of local level initiatives can be identified. It can be argued, however, that the social partners have not been as active as they could have been in terms of promoting equality of opportunity and treatment of non-nationals in the workforce, though particular organizations can of course be singled out as having provided model initiatives in this area. It should be noted that, in the course of preparing this survey, very few of these organizations took the opportunity to communicate their comments to the Committee."[12]

The lack of the interest of ILO constituents – governments, labor, and employer organizations – inhibited ILO work on migrant labor despite formal commitments to regulating such labor since its founding.

ILO Migrant Labor Standards

The ILO has adopted two general conventions on migrant labor: Convention No. 97 in 1949 and Convention No. 143 in 1975, each accompanied by two recommendations more detailed than the Conventions. Convention No. 97 had received only 42 ratifications by 2002 and Convention No. 143 had received only 18 ratifications by the same date. At the time of the adoption of the 1949 ILO Convention, the primary focus was the organization and regulation of workers from developing countries. According to W.R. Bohning, "The objectives and the instruments were clearly biased in favor of the immigration countries."[13] Little attention was paid at the time to the effects of labor movements in developing countries. By the time of the adoption of the 1975 Convention, there was a clearer emphasis on the effects of labor migration for the sending countries.

Convention No. 97 consists of a core treaty with three annexes, some or all of which may be excluded by ratifying states. Annexes I and II deal with recruitment and conditions for migrants recruited by private groups and under government-sponsored arrangements; Annex III is concerned with the import of migrants' personal effects into countries of employment. The Convention itself consists of only ten substantive articles. Ratifying states are committed, *inter alia*, to maintain a free service to assist migrants by providing them with adequate information, preventing misleading propaganda relating to emigration, and assuring equality of treatment of migrant workers concerning remuneration, family allowances, membership in trade unions, and social security. Migration for Employment Recommendation No. 86 that accompanies the Convention includes in Annex, a "Model Agreement on Temporary and Permanent Migration for Employment, including Migration of Refugees and Displaced Persons," intended as a model for bilateral agreements. Convention No. 97 has been ratified by only 42 states.

---

[12] ILO, Migrant Workers, General Survey, International Labor Conference, 1999, para. 80.

[13] W.R. Böhning, quoted in Cholewinski, *supra* note 10, at 95.

Convention No. 143, drafted in 1975, has had even less success among ILO Member States, with only 18 ratifications. It consists of fourteen substantive provisions dealing with migration in abusive conditions and equality of opportunity and treatment for migrant workers. The Preamble to Convention No. 143 asserts that further standards in addition to Convention No. 97 were desirable in order to "promote equality of opportunity and treatment of migrant workers, [and] to ensure treatment at least equal to that of nationals." It is accompanied by Recommendation No. 151 providing additional detail on the provisions of the Convention relating to the equality of opportunity and treatment, the reunification of families, the promotion of health of migrant workers, social services, employment, and residence.

In one of the most comprehensive studies on the human rights of migrant workers, Ryszard Cholewinski observes that the ILO migrant worker conventions are "innovative, rich in detail and break new ground, particularly with respect to the question of free choice of employment and economic and social rights," but they have been essentially ignored by the international community, and especially by the receiving countries, [as] evidenced by the small number of ratifications.[14]

Limitations of ILO Standards on Migrant Labor

In 1999, the ILO Committee of Experts on the Application of Conventions and Recommendations made a study, referred to as a "General Survey," on the law and practice of states relating to the two major ILO migrant worker conventions and the relevant recommendations.[15] The study focused on the possible revision of the Conventions, to be discussed at a future meeting of the International Labor Conference.

The Survey pointed out that the contemporary relevance of the Conventions was limited by the following factors:

• gender stereotypes in place at the time the conventions were adopted are no longer valid since women migrating for employment have become a significant portion of migrant workers. The conventions provide no protection for women trafficked to work in the sex sector.

• the commercialization of recruitment with widespread abuses, largely occurring since the conventions were adopted, are insufficiently regulated by the conventions, and the increase in irregular migration creates difficulties regarding the definition of the fundamental rights of migrant workers.

• the effect of regional integration on the movement of workers across borders raises new issues of the effect on treatment of workers outside the region.

New ILO "Integrated Approach" to Migrant Labor Issues

In short, the ILO conventions are widely perceived as limited by their inability to deal with current labor migration issues, and the ILO itself has recognized the limi-

---

[14] Cholewinski, *supra* note 10, at 135.
[15] See *supra* note 13.

tations of standard-setting in dealing with the problem of migrant labor. The ILO has referred to the limited (and decreasing rate) of ratification of the migrant labor conventions and has proposed a general discussion of migrant labor at the 2004 International Labor Conference (ILC).

A report written in preparation for the 2004 meeting of the ILC suggests consideration of the following questions specifically relating to ILO convention and recommendation standards:

"Can the international standards be made more relevant in view of the emerging new forms of migration and the status of national law and practice for the protection of their rights? What approach should be taken to ensure wider ratification and application of ILO Conventions on migrant workers? Should the existing ILO standards be revised or promoted? How can complementarity be assured with the implementation and monitoring of the 1990 United Nations International Convention on the Protection of the Rights of all Migrant Workers and Members of Their Families?"[16]

The main part of the Report, however, focuses on the need for an *integrated approach* to labor migration, in which revision of ILO conventions would be but one aspect of a broader consideration of the subject. An integrated approach would cut across practically all spheres of the normative and technical activities of the ILO, including employment policy, right of workers to organize, social security, and social implications of globalization. The Report concludes:

"An integrated approach would thus comprise a programmatic response to the issues of migrant workers in a cooperative, complementary and comprehensive process among the various concerned ILO sectors and units. It would also allow for a more comprehensive review of the question of whether and how the instruments need to be revised."[17]

UN Migrant Workers' Convention: A Human Rights Approach

Human Rights Approach

In 1990, after ten years of negotiations, the UN General Assembly adopted the International Convention on the Rights of All Migrant Workers and Their Families.[18] Twenty states, all of them sending states, have ratified the Convention; and it is expected to come into force in 2003. The Convention represents a new approach to labor migration because it specifically adopted a human rights approach, was adopted by the UN General Assembly and not by the ILO, and is the only single multilateral instrument that contains a comprehensive set of standards for migrant workers. The Preamble states that the Convention utilizes the major United Nations human rights instruments, which are referred to by title.

---

[16] ILO, GB. 283/2/1, March 2002, Date, Place and Agenda of the 92nd Session of the International Labor Conference, para. 11.

[17] Id. at para. 108.

[18] International Convention on the Rights of All Migrant Workers and Their Families, 1990, U.N.G.A. Res. 45/158.

Lönnroth has suggested the following reasons for UN, as opposed to ILO, adoption of the Convention:[19]

- it was felt that the Convention would receive more attention if drafted by the General Assembly than by the ILO;

- it was desired to give more weight to human rights issues than was evident in the ILO conventions;

- there was apprehension from some countries about the participation of non-governmental organizations in the drafting of conventions at the ILO, particularly the role of employer organizations; and it was seen as preferable to have the drafting undertaken only by states without non-governmental participation.

While the ILO migrant labor conventions are based on a minimum standards approach to international regulation of migrant labor, the UN Convention adopts a human rights, non-discrimination, approach: individuals (migrant workers) must be treated in a non-discriminatory manner regardless of nationality. Unlike the ILO conventions, the UN Convention does not permit ratifying states to exclude certain categories of workers from its provisions.

Provisions

The UN Convention recognizes that undocumented migrants face more difficult conditions than legal migrants. The twenty-seven articles in parts II and III of the Convention list the rights of *all* migrant workers – mainly a repetition of the civil, political, economic, social, and cultural rights contained in the two major international covenants on human rights. Part IV, containing twenty articles, lists additional rights for *documented* or legal migrants, including the right to move freely within the state of employment, to have access to educational institutions, and a number of other rights providing for equality of treatment with nationals. A Committee on the Protection of the Rights of All Migrant Workers and Members of their Families will be set up to review the application of the Convention based on reports from ratifying states.

Campaign for Ratification

The human rights approach of the Convention received attention at the April 2002 meeting of the UN Human Rights Commission. A public meeting on the Convention was held with an impressive list of speakers, including Mary Robinson, the UN High Commissioner for Human Rights, representatives from the ILO and the Inter-

---

[19] J. Lönnroth, "The International Convention on the Rights of All Migrant Workers and Their Families in the Context of Nationality and International Regulation Policies," 25 *International Migration Review* (1991) 710, 728.

national Organization for Migration (IOM), as well as Gabriela Rodriguez, the Special Rapporteur on the Human Rights of Migrants. A Global Campaign for ratification of the Convention is under way, with a Steering Committee composed of the by Human Rights Watch, the International Commission of Jurists, ILO, IOM, Public Services International, and the World Council of Churches.

Having received the necessary ratifications, the Convention is likely to come into force by the end of 2003; however, it is not likely that it will be ratified in the near future by receiving states, whom it is most intended to regulate.

Undocumented Workers: US Supreme Court Case

Article 26 in Part III of the UN Convention relating to *all* workers – undocumented workers as well as legal migrants – is particularly interesting in view of the U.S. Supreme Court's decision in *Hoffman Plastic Compounds, Inc., Petitioner* v. *National Labor Relations Board*[20] which involved an undocumented worker (referred to in the decision as an "illegal alien") laid off by Hoffman because of his support for a union-organizing campaign. The Court decided that the alien was not entitled to back pay for the period he was laid off even though documented workers were entitled to back pay since the campaign had been a legitimate union organizing effort. The Court concluded that to award back pay to "illegal aliens would unduly trench upon explicit statutory prohibitions critical to federal immigration policy." While the *Hoffman* case does not say that undocumented aliens may not participate in union activities, it accepts that a company may penalize such workers for doing so. The UN Convention was not cited and was irrelevant to the decision of the Court since it has not been ratified by the United States.

Justice Stephen Breyer filed a strong dissent supported by Justices John Paul Stevens, David Souter, and Ruth Bader Ginsberg. The compelling dissent points out, *inter alia*, that the immigration laws provide for specific penalties for an employer knowingly employing an illegal alien and for an alien who submits false documents, but the immigration laws do not permit the employer to ignore labor laws with impunity; labor laws should not be used as a means of controlling immigration.

The United States has not ratified the UN Migrant Workers' Convention and is unlikely to do so; nevertheless, the decision of the Supreme Court merits attention in light of Article 26 of the Convention which provides that states parties should recognize the right of migrant workers to freely join trade unions, to take part in meetings and activities of trade unions, and to seek the aid and assistance of any trade union. The implication of this article is that all migrant workers, including undocumented, should not be penalized for trade union activities. The placing of the article in Part III relating to *all* workers demonstrates that it applies to undocumented as well as documented workers. These protections are similar to the right included in the Covenant on Civil and Political Rights (which has been ratified by the United States); for that Article 22 provides that *everyone* may form and join a trade union for the protection of his rights.

---

[20] 535 U.S. 137, 122 S.Ct. 1275 (2002).

UN NON-STANDARD SETTING ACTIVITIES – A HUMAN RIGHTS APPROACH

In 1997, the UN Human Rights Commission established the Working Group on Migrants with a mandate that does not relate solely to migrant workers, but is broad enough to cover issues relating to them. Its mandate is to gather all relevant information on the obstacles existing to the effective and full protection of the human rights of migrants and to elaborate recommendations to strengthen the promotion, protection, and implementation of the human rights of migrants.

De la Vega has focused on the Working Group's efforts relating to migrant labor and has pointed out limitations to its effectiveness: insufficient resources, lack of political will, and limited meeting periods of the Group. She argues that

> "… it is incumbent upon the Working Group to take concrete steps that will help to promote and protect the rights of migrant workers. Simply gathering more information will be insufficient. One step that could lead the Working Group on Migrants to make a difference in the lives of some migrant worker is to follow the precedent of the Working Groups on Enforced and Involuntary Disappearances and on Arbitrary Detention and establish a procedure that allows consideration of actual violations."[21]

In 2000, the Human Rights Commission appointed Gabriela Rodriguez Pizarro as the Special Rapporteur on the Human Rights of Migrants. While her mandate covers human rights issues relating to migration in general, the three reports that she issued to date (October 2002) contain numerous references to issues concerning migrant labor. Her 2001 report referred to a number of urgent appeals made by the Special Rapporteur to States concerning the situation of migrant workers: (1) an appeal to Argentina relating to alleged physical attacks against Bolivian workers in the town of Escobar; (2) a communication to the Spanish Government about the living and working situation of immigrant workers in an Andalusian town (including a large number of undocumented workers) relating to excessive hours of work and use of pesticides without security measures to lessen their effect on health; and (3) an appeal to the Dominican Republic concerning the long-standing situation of the difficult living and working conditions of Haitian migrant workers in the sugar cane fields. The Rapporteur received replies from governments concerning each of her observations.[22]

The Rapporteur visited Canada and Ecuador to discuss with the respective governments the issues concerning migration, including labor issues. A planned visit in September and October 2001 to the Mexican-U.S. border was postponed following the September 11 attacks in the Unites States.

In the absence of the entry into force of the UN Convention, these UN human rights initiatives have provided a focus for continuing concern about migrant workers. The Working Group and the reports of the Special Rapporteur will continue to

---

[21] C. De la Vega, "Book Review, Migrant Workers in International Human Rights Law, by Cholewinski," 21 *Human Rights Quarterly* (1999) pp. 229, 250.

[22] E/CN.4/2001/83, 9 January 2001.

be important even when the Convention comes into force as the number of ratifications will remain limited and will probably not include ratifications by receiving
states. Both the Working Group and the Special Rapporteur have relied on standards
elaborated in the Universal Declaration on Human Rights, and in other widely ratified human rights instruments and, to a lesser extent, on the less widely ratified ILO
conventions on migrant labor, as the basis for their actions.

CONCLUSION

The effort to regulate the movement of workers and to provide protection for this
vulnerable category has many gaps. Bilateral agreements between sending and receiving countries providing for orderly migration are less widespread than in the
past. An integrated system such as the European Union has extensive provisions
concerning workers from within the Union, but lacks provisions concerning workers
from outside the Union. ILO migrant worker conventions have not been widely ratified. The major UN convention on migrant labor has not yet come into force and is
not likely to attract ratifications from receiving states. Human rights conventions,
such as the European Convention on Human Rights and the International Covenants,
have not been widely applied to migrant workers.

International migration facilitates economic development and it provides millions
of workers the opportunity to better their economic situation by working abroad,
particularly skilled workers whose services are desired in developed countries. Nevertheless, the limited extent and lack of regulation for the majority of migrant workers who are not highly skilled is a serious problem, as has been pointed out by
numerous commentators and by UN and ILO studies. The international response remains inadequate.

Prejudice against foreigners, prevalent in almost every country, as well as economic advantages from the use of undocumented workers, have militated against
improving the conditions of migrant workers. Migrant workers are a largely vulnerable population with little opportunity to make their voices heard, either in sending
or receiving countries. The ILO conventions are being seen, even by the ILO, as not
reflective of contemporary problems of migrant workers, and the ILO questions the
standard-setting approach. The ratification of the UN Convention is viewed as a
positive step but will have little effect unless ratified by receiving states, an unlikely
prospect.

What is to be done in view of this pessimistic observation? The ILO and the UN
human rights bodies must continue to give prominence, particularly to the problem
of migration of unskilled workers but, ultimately, solutions must come from an en-
lightened and informed public opinion in receiving countries. The focus on migrant
workers by the human rights community is perhaps the most positive aspect of the
current situation. Whether or not developed states ratify the UN Convention, it is a
positive effort undertaken by a wide number of influential intergovernmental and
non-governmental organizations to focus attention on the plight of migrant workers.
The consideration of the revision of the ILO migrant workers conventions in 2004
and the adoption of an integrated approach to migrant labor should be given a high

profile by the ILO and by other interested governmental and non-governmental organizations. Despite these initiatives and efforts, one cannot be optimistic about the more serious problems involved in the movement of labor, in view of the economic and political obstacles to improving their status.

Selected Bibliography

BATTISTELLA, GRAZIANO (ED.) – *Human Rights of Migrant Workers: Agenda for NGOs* (1993).

BÖHNING, ROGER – "The ILO Convention and the New UN Convention on Migrant Workers: The Past and Future," 25 *International Migration Review* 698 (1991).

CHOLEWINSKI, RYSZARD – *Migrant Workers in International Human Rights Law* (1997).

DE LA VEGA, C. – "Review of Cholewinski, Migrant Workers in Human Rights Law," 21 *Human Rights Quarterly* 229 (1999).

GOODWIN-GILL, GUY – *International Law and the Movement of Persons between States* (1978).

LÖNNROTH, JUHANI – "The International Convention on the Rights of All Migrant Workers and Members of Their Families in the Context of Nationality and International Migration Policies," 25 *International Migration Review* 710 (1991).

PLENDER, RICHARD – *Basic Documents on International Migration Law* (2nd revised edition, 1997).

STALKER, PETER – *The Work of Strangers, A Survey of International Labour Migration* (1994).

—. *Workers without Frontiers, The Impact of Globalization on International Migration* (2000).

Chapter 14
TRADE LAW NORMS ON INTERNATIONAL MIGRATION

Steve Charnovitz*

In contrast to the Treaty Establishing the European Community, the World Trade Organization (WTO) does not aspire to the abolition, as between Member States, of obstacles to the free movement of goods, persons, services, or capital.[1] The WTO asserts a much less ambitious goal in its preamble, namely, "reciprocal and mutually advantageous arrangements directed to the substantial reduction of tariffs and other barriers to trade and to the elimination of discriminatory treatment in international trade relations."[2] In accordance with the WTO rules, each member government retains a great deal of latitude to determine how substantially its trade barriers should be reduced and how much market freedom to permit. Nevertheless, joint action to undo obstacles to the movement of goods, persons, services, and capital defines the current competence of the WTO.

The movement of people is a relatively new concern for the trading system. In the pre-WTO era of 1947-1994 under the General Agreement on Tariffs and Trade (GATT), almost no attention was paid to workers and professionals. In 1948, the United Nations Conference on Trade and Employment had included "skills" within the mandate of the prospective International Trade Organization,[3] but the ensuing treaty never went into force, and the topic of skills remained outside of the trading system until it was brought back during the Uruguay Round negotiations (of 1986-1994).

Attention to the movement of people fits comfortably into the equity and efficiency rationales for the trading system.[4] Just as barriers to the transborder move-

---

* Steve Charnovitz practices law at Wilmer, Cutler & Pickering in Washington, D.C.

[1] See Treaty Establishing the European Community, Art. 3.1(c).

[2] Marrakesh Agreement Establishing the World Trade Organization, preamble. This Agreement and all other WTO agreements discussed herein can be found in WTO, *The Legal Texts. The Results of the Uruguay Round of Multilateral Trade Negotiations* (1999).

[3] Art. 11.2(a) of the Charter of the International Trade Organization (ITO) had authorized the ITO, in collaboration with other inter-governmental organizations, to make recommendations for international agreements to assure just and equitable treatment for the enterprises, skills, capital, arts, and technology brought by one Member country to another. Charter for an International Trade Organization, available at http://www.worldtradelaw.net/misc/havana.pdf. An early report (1947) of an ITO drafting committee stated that the transit of persons was not within the scope of the Charter, while noting that it may be the concern of another international agency. WTO, *Guide to GATT Law and Practice* (1995) p. 214.

[4] D. Rodrik, Comments at the Conference on "Immigration Policy and the Welfare State," Trieste (23 June 2001), pp. 1, 2.

T.A. Aleinikoff and V. Chetail (Eds.), Migration and International Legal Norms
© 2003, T.M.C. ASSER PRESS, The Hague, The Netherlands, et al.

ment of goods will reduce economic efficiency, so too will barriers to the movement of labor. There are numerous border barriers and domestic non-tariff barriers that prevent the operation of an efficient and free market for individuals and man-made products. The equity rationale for the WTO is further justification for reducing barriers to the movement of people. For example, the "special and differential treatment" norm in many WTO agreements suggests that rich countries should be especially open to goods imported from poor countries in the interest of raising the income of those countries. This same equity norm could also justify greater openness by industrial countries to workers from the developing countries. Indeed, the WTO General Agreement on Trade in Services (GATS) calls on governments to make commitments for "the liberalization of market access in sectors and modes of supply of export interest" to developing countries.[5]

The new WTO trade negotiations launched in November 2001 in Doha, Qatar, promote further expansion of the current low level of governmental commitments on the movement of natural persons. Some progress is expected in the next few years as this issue is a priority for large U.S. and European corporations, and for many governments in poor countries.[6] At this time, it seems unlikely that any of the underlying WTO law on services will be changed. Rather, the negotiations will focus on the commitments that governments make to reduce their own barriers.

This chapter discusses how trade law addresses international migration. The first section review the WTO rules on the movement of natural persons and notes some issues lacking clarity. The second section looks at the actual liberalization agreed to at the WTO. The final section discusses proposals to improve the WTO's interface with migration issues.

WTO RULES ON THE MOVEMENT OF NATURAL PERSONS – THE NORM AND ITS GAPS

Formally speaking, the WTO does not confer on individuals a right to live and work in foreign countries. As many treaties do, the WTO protects the individual indirectly by imposing obligations on governments regarding how they treat persons. With a few exceptions, the WTO's obligations pertain only to aliens, not to nationals of that government. No individuals can directly enforce such obligations at the WTO.

Nevertheless, in a roundabout way, the WTO does make it easier for individuals to work in foreign countries. The relevant norms are contained in the GATS. These norms arise out of treaty law. Customary international law plays little role in the WTO. The GATS obligations (like all WTO obligations) are in effect only between WTO member countries (currently 144).

---

[5] General Agreement on Trade in Services (GATS), Art. IV:1(c).

[6] S. Ostry, "The Uruguay Round North–South Grand Bargain: Implications for Future Negotiations," *in* D.L.M. Kennedy and J.D. Southwick (eds.), *The Political Economy of International Trade Law* (2002) pp. 285-297.

GATS Article I recognizes four modes of trade in services.[7] The first mode deals with a service supplier in one country providing services to another country (e.g., editing services). The second mode deals with a service consumer from one country going to another country to receive the service (e.g., education or medical treatment). The third mode deals with a service supplier who has a commercial presence in the receiving country (e.g., a bank). The fourth mode deals with a natural person, who is a service supplier and has a presence in another country (e.g., a banker).

Mode 4 is the central concern of this article.[8] Under GATS, a natural person (a human) is distinguished from a juridical person (a corporation). The GATS makes it easier for aliens to work by calling on governments to reduce barriers and improve market access to natural persons supplying Mode 4 services. Although the term "work" is not used, it is the focus of Mode 4 because it seeks to enable the individual to trade services for money. One might cavil that GATS looks at a natural person only as a supplier of services, rather than as an individual, yet the practical effect of either view is the same.

The relevance of GATS to individual workers is somewhat clarified in the GATS Annex on Movement of Natural Persons Supplying Services Under the Agreement ("Annex on Movement"). The term "movement of natural persons" is used in the Annex, but not in the GATS itself. The Annex on Movement states that the GATS "shall not apply to measures affecting natural persons seeking access to the employment market of a [WTO] Member, nor shall it apply to measures regarding citizenship, residence or employment on a permanent basis."[9]

While this appears to be an enormous exclusion, the exact parameters are not sharply defined. The sentence above leaves the implication that GATS covers measures regarding employment on a *non-permanent* basis, and therefore presumably covers individuals seeking such temporary employment. Yet whether or not GATS applies to employment at all remains unclear.

At issue is how to interpret the provision in the Annex on Movement which suggests that GATS does not apply to persons seeking access to the employment market. When individuals are self-employed, they may be treated as being outside of the employment market. When individuals relocate to work for a company at its branch in a host country, they can be perceived as working outside the employment market of the host country because they do not place themselves on the market. A key unsettled question in WTO services law is whether the GATS Agreement applies to individuals who work for companies of the host country. For example, nurses and computer technicians may want to enter a country and work for its local employers. As yet, there is very little WTO case law to interpret GATS and no case law to inter-

---

[7] GATS Art. I:2. The GATS excludes services supplied in the exercise of governmental authority. Id. at Art. I:3(b). This exclusion will differ from country to country.

[8] Mode 2 is also important to individuals who may seek to cross borders in order to consume services in other countries. Many governments make it difficult to change visa status when an individual enters on an education visa.

[9] GATS Annex on Movement of Natural Persons Supplying Services under the Agreement ("Annex on Movement"), para. 2. The term permanent is not defined in the GATS.

pret Mode 4. It is interesting to note that several regional trade agreements contain provisions modeled on the GATS Annex on Movement.[10]

The exclusion of permanent migration from the GATS had been advocated from the beginning, even by free traders. For example, Jagdish Bhagwati wrote in 1986 that permanent migration flows "raise a different, and more difficult, set of issues which, if brought into the discussion, would compromise the possibility of making significant progress on the issue."[11] Bhagwati also observed that the issue of permanent migration "is generally judged by moral-philosophical principles very different from the utilitarian calculus that underlies the economic case for free trade and free investment flows."[12]

The GATS Annex on Movement states that GATS shall not prevent governments from applying measures to regulate the entry of natural persons into their territory, or to regulate their "temporary stay," including those measures necessary to protect the integrity of borders. This provision makes clear that Mode 4 access for individuals will be tempered by national immigration regulations on the right to enter. There is a further proviso that a government border measure not be applied in such a manner as to nullify or impair the benefits accorded in a specific trade commitment. Therefore, governments do not have absolute discretion in immigration policy. A footnote to this proviso makes clear that governments may require visas for nationals from some countries and not from others. Of course, each government remains in control of what specific commitments it bargains away, so these GATS jurisdictional provisions are merely guides for negotiations.

GATS Mode 4 applies notionally to any individual providing services, from a business executive to a laborer. Some governments sought a narrower coverage during the Uruguay round, but the developing countries insisted that GATS should at least provide the possibility of covering construction, tourist, and domestic workers.[13]

Mode 4 obligations are symmetric to the obligations in the other three modes. The GATS contains several core rules that include the most-favored-nation requirement (subject to exemptions), transparency of regulations, and a responsibility to enter into successive rounds of negotiations with a view to achieving higher liberalization.[14] In addition, each government is required to set out in a schedule[15] the ex-

---

[10] See J. Nielson, "Current Regimes for Temporary Movement of Service Providers," Paper Presented at the Joint WTO-World Bank Symposium on Movement of Persons (Mode 4) Under GATS, April 2002, paras. 32-38, available at http://www.wto.org/english/tratop_e/serv_e/symp_mov_natur_perso_april02_e.htm.

[11] J.N. Bhagwati, "Economic Perspectives on Trade in Professional Services," 1986 *University of Chicago Legal Forum* (1986) pp. 45, 49. See also id. at 50 (emphasizing that the temporary nature of factor relocation be made explicit).

[12] Id. at 52.

[13] C. Arup, *The New World Trade Organization Agreements. Globalizing Law Through Services and Intellectual Property* (2000) p. 125.

[14] GATS Arts. II, III, XIX:1, XIX:4.

[15] The schedule is the detailed list of services commitments made by each WTO Member country. Schedules have to be negotiated with other countries. Id. Arts. XVI:1, XX. A government may not amend its schedule, even to liberalize it, without concurrence of other WTO Members through a review process or through a negotiation. Id. Art. XXI.

tent of its own specific commitments and is prohibited from maintaining market access restrictions that are not listed on its schedule.[16] In sectors where specific commitments are undertaken, a government shall accord national treatment – meaning that the foreign supplier is to be treated no less favorably than the domestic supplier – unless the government reserves an exception.[17] Similarly, in sectors where specific commitments are undertaken, governments shall ensure that measures of general application are administered in a "reasonable, objective and impartial manner."[18] Furthermore, governments shall not apply licensing requirements and technical standards that (a) are not based on objective and transparent criteria, (b) are more burdensome than necessary to ensure the quality of the service, or (c) as a licensing standard would restrict the supply of a service.[19] When government authorization is required for the supply of the service, the competent authorities shall "within a reasonable period of time" inform the applicant of the decision.[20] Another key rule provides that governments shall institute judicial, arbitral, or administrative tribunals that can be invoked by an affected service supplier for a prompt review of administrative decisions.[21] These last two rules are examples of how the WTO indirectly accords procedural rights to individuals (although not enforceable by the individual in the WTO).[22]

The GATS rule on the qualifications of professionals has particular relevance for Mode 4. The GATS does not require a recognition of equivalent qualifications by foreign professionals. Instead, it encourages governments to recognize the education and experience obtained in foreign countries and the licenses and certifications granted.[23] In that regard, the GATS directs the destination country government to give a foreign government an adequate opportunity to seek the recognition of its education, experience, licenses, and certifications.[24]

The GATS is a complex agreement that contains many exclusions. One article allows governments to carry out international agreements to avoid double taxation even though it would lead to different treatment of nationals from different countries.[25] Another notable exclusion, Article V *bis* (Labor Markets Integration Agreements), states that the GATS shall not prevent WTO members from being a party to an agreement establishing full integration of labor markets, provided that the agreement exempts citizens of parties to the agreement from requirements regarding residency and work permits. A footnote explains that typically such agreements provide foreign citizens the right of free entry to the employment market, and include provisions concerning conditions of pay, conditions of employment, and social benefits.[26]

---

[16] Id. Arts. XVI, XX. An example of such a restriction is a quota on foreign employees. Id. Art. XVI:2(d).

[17] Id. Art. XVII.

[18] Id. Art. VI:1.

[19] Id. Art. VI:5.

[20] Id. Art. VI:3.

[21] Id. Art. VI:2.

[22] Steve Charnovitz, "The WTO and the Rights of the Individual," 36 *Intereconomics* (2001) p. 98.

[23] GATS, Art. VII:1.

[24] Id. Art. VII:2.

[25] Id. Art. XIV(e).

[26] Id. GATS Art. V *bis* n. 2.

The existence of Article V *bis* beclouds the applicability of GATS to the employment market. If GATS does not apply to the employment market in the first place, why is this article needed if it has relevance only to such a market? Furthermore, is the WTO staking out some competence on labor policy by insisting that recognized agreements have exemptions regarding residency and work permits? Time will tell.

The GATS exception for security is also ambiguous. The exception would permit a government to violate a GATS rule or a national schedule for various reasons, such as a war or international emergency.[27] Yet the exception is unclear as to whether a domestic emergency would qualify.

Pursuant to GATS, the governments negotiated an "Understanding on Commitments in Financial Services" that contains an outline of commitments, including one on the "temporary entry of personnel."[28] This provision states that when a foreign financial service supplier establishes a commercial presence in the receiving country, that government shall permit temporary entry of senior management personnel possessing proprietary information. In addition, subject to the availability of qualified specialists in the receiving country, the government shall permit the entry of temporary personnel who are computer specialists, telecommunications specialists, actuaries, or legal specialists. The specific commitments made in the financial services sector are touted as a model for other sectors in future negotiations.

In summary, the GATS is both a shallow and a potentially deep international agreement. It is shallow because a protectionist government can comply fully with GATS while refraining from opening its market to foreign individuals who are service suppliers.[29] It is deep in that a government can make binding commitments that will implicate its ability to regulate the domestic market, at least *vis-à-vis* foreign service suppliers.[30] It should also be noted that Mode 4 does not include any obligations for the country of origin to allow an individual to exit. For example, Bangladesh, India, Indonesia, and Pakistan often prohibit women from taking jobs abroad as domestic workers. Such restrictions are not covered by GATS. Thus, to the extent that GATS does prescribe a legal norm for migration, it is tentative and narrow.

To better describe the Mode 4 norm and its gaps, one might consider two comparative perspectives. First, how do Mode 4 obligations compare to other WTO obligations? Second, how do Mode 4 obligations fit into the broader international regime on the movement of people?

Consider the WTO obligations on the movement of goods, services, capital, technology, and people:

- Government regulations and taxes affecting the entry of foreign *goods* are supervised by extensive rules in several WTO agreements including the GATT, the Agreement on the Application of Sanitary and Phytosanitary Measures (SPS),

---

[27] Id. Art. XIV *bis*.

[28] WTO, Understanding on Commitments in Financial Services, para. B(9), available at http://www.wto.org/english/tratop_e/serv_e/21-fin_e.htm.

[29] P. Sauvé, "Trade, Education and the GATS: What's In, What's Out, What's All the Fuss About?" Paper Prepared for OECD/US Forum on Trade in Educational Services (23–24 May 2002), p. 11.

[30] See, e.g., text accompanying note 19.

and the Agreement on Technical Barriers to Trade (TBT). These obligations apply generally to all measures affecting goods, without any need for filing schedules.[31] For example, under GATT jurisprudence, taxes and regulations cannot be applied in a way to limit equal competitive opportunities for imported products. Under the SPS Agreement, sanitary measures shall be based on scientific principles.[32] Under the TBT Agreement, technical regulations shall not be more trade-restrictive than necessary to fulfill a legitimate objective.[33]

- The GATS leaves much discretion with governments as to the breadth of their commitments on *services*. In general, however, the first and third modes can extend beyond temporary relationships. For instance, under Mode 3, a service supplier can seek to have a permanent presence and provide services to anyone in host country. Of the four modes, Mode 4 provides the least discretion.

- With respect to restrictions on *capital* movements, the WTO contains some disciplines and exceptions, and establishes links to the International Monetary Fund.[34] In general, however, governments retain considerable discretion to impose restrictions.

- For *technology*, the Agreement on Trade-Related Aspects of Intellectual Property Rights (TRIPS) requires that governments recognize and safeguard the intellectual property of aliens. The TRIPS Agreement also calls for cooperation to prevent international trade in goods infringing intellectual property rights.[35] Beyond TRIPS, the WTO does not supervise government restrictions on technology transfer. For example, it is probably not a WTO violation for a government to prohibit imports of fetal stem cells for research, even when there is no scientific basis for doing so.

Viewed in this multifactor context, WTO supervision over national regulation of the movement of people is weaker than supervision of goods, other services, and technology. It is perhaps on par with the lenient supervision of national restrictions on capital movements. For example, with respect to people, the WTO permits market access barriers without regard to whether there would be less trade-restrictive ways to achieve a legitimate societal objective. As compared to other services, the obligations on Mode 4 are shallower because they apply only to transient movements. Furthermore, as will be discussed below, the national GATS schedules for Mode 4 typically impose pre-employment requirements and other contractual conditions on individuals that severely hamper economic freedom.

---

[31] The one exception is GATT Art. II which references each government's own tariff schedules.

[32] Agreement on the Application of Sanitary and Phytosanitary Measures (SPS), Art. 2.2.

[33] Agreement on Technical Barriers to Trade (TBT), Art. 2.2.

[34] See GATT Arts. XII, XV, XVIII:B; Agreement on Trade-Related Investment Measures, Annex, para. 2(b); GATS Arts. XI:2, XII, XVI:1 n. 8. GATS schedules can also include commitments on monetary remittances.

[35] TRIPS Art. 69.

Another way of assessing GATS Mode 4 is to see where it fits into the international regime on the movement, both permanent and temporary, of people across borders. The WTO putatively has no role in permanent movement. The main categories for temporary transborder movement are refugees, tourism, family visits, educational and cultural exchanges, transit, and work. The WTO is interested in only the last category, work, and, more specifically, only services work. Even then, the WTO does not seek to spur negotiations over many of the reasons a government might have for denying foreigners an opportunity to resettle, such as xenophobia. Negotiations are possible, however, in response to the motivation of economic protection. Thus, across the whole spectrum of issues regarding the movement of people that could be the subject of international law, WTO law covers only a very narrow band.

Of course, much of the spectrum is bereft of any international law, so the GATS Mode 4 band is significant. Furthermore, because Mode 4 has growing economic salience, the WTO rules are likely to grow deeper as governments make more commitments in successive trade rounds. Looking ahead, the WTO may become a fertile source of migration law norms.

SURVEY OF NATIONAL MODE 4 COMMITMENTS

The second part of this chapter looks briefly at what governments have agreed to do in multilateral GATS Mode 4 negotiations. As noted above, the GATS is a bottom-up regime, and so the amount of market accessibility depends on each government's own schedule of commitments. Unfortunately, as a study by the Organization for Economic Cooperation and Development has noted, "Even by the modest standards of Uruguay Round liberalization on trade in services, little was achieved on Mode 4."[36] In some instances, however, actual regulatory regimes may be more liberal than a government has obligated itself to follow.

The existing Mode 4 commitments by over one hundred countries are heavily tilted toward high-skilled persons.[37] About 42 percent of the horizontal commitments (i.e., applying to all sectors) relate to intra-company transferees; 28 percent relate to executives, managers, and specialists; 13 percent are visitors for sales negotiations, and 10 percent are other business visitors. The remaining 7 percent are independent contractors and others. The typical practice in national schedules is to allow executives to stay for two to five years, while business visitors are limited to ninety days. A five-year stay would seem tantamount to migration, or at least temporary migration. As Allison M. Young has observed, "the tension between [national]

---

[36] Organization for Economic Cooperation and Development, Working Party of the Trade Committee, "Service Providers on the Move: A Closer Look at Labour Mobility and the GATS," TD/TC/WTP(2001)26/FINAL, p. 5 (20 February 2002) [hereinafter OECD Study].

[37] The data in this and the next paragraph are drawn from WTO Council for Trade in Services, Presence of Natural Persons (Mode 4), Background Note by the Secretariat, S/C/W/75 (8 December 1998), Table 9. Some updated figures are updated in Antonia Carzaniga, "GATS, Mode 4 and the Pattern of Commitments," at 4 (11 April 2002), available at http://www.wto.org/english/tratop_e/serv_e/symp_mov_natur_perso_april02_e.htm.

trade officials and immigration and labor market development officials … is played
out in the schedules."[38]

About 17 percent of the commitments apply to low-skilled personnel, and these
are often limited by an economic needs test that excludes the alien unless there has
been a showing that qualified domestic workers are unavailable. Even when such a
need exists, the paperwork involved can be daunting. It is interesting to note that the
North American Free Trade Agreement (NAFTA) eliminates labor market certifications for the temporary entry of a few categories of workers, including traders and
investors, intra-company transferees, business visitors, and qualified professionals
defined through education or experience.[39] Applicable visa requirements, however,
continue to apply.

The GATS schedules show numerous restrictions on foreign workers. The most
common restriction is "pre-employment," meaning that a person must already be
employed by the company he will be working for in the host country. Furthermore,
Mode 4 entry and the corresponding work permit are normally confined to one sector or to one employer, and workers cannot freely move to another position or relocate geographically.[40] Some governments require that foreign workers be paid the
prevailing wage.[41] Some governments have reserved the right to suspend commitments in the event of a labor-management dispute.[42] Some forbid temporary migrants from purchasing real estate. Some mandate that specialists train local staff.
Together, these limitations undermine the significance of Mode 4 commitments.

PROPOSALS FOR IMPROVING THE WTO NORM AND ITS IMPLEMENTATION

The third part of this chapter looks at ways that the WTO might liberalize national
barriers to the movement of natural persons. This can occur if governments make
greater commitments in the ongoing WTO round. Some inspiration may be drawn
from the labor mobility provisions in regional trade agreements, which in many instances go beyond the GATS. For example, the European Free Trade Association
provides for the free movement of workers and the self-employed without requiring
visas, although there is a limit of ninety days per year for service providers.[43] The
Caribbean Community (CARICOM) provides for free movement and elimination of
work permits for university graduates and selected occupations, such as media,
sports, music and art, entertainment, and tourism.[44]

---

[38] A.M. Young, "Where Next for Labor Mobility Under GATS?" *in* P. Sauvé and R.M. Stern (eds.),
GATS 2000. New Directions in Services Trade Liberalization (2000) pp. 184, 187.

[39] North American Free Trade Agreement (NAFTA), 17 December 1992, Art. 1603. Temporary entry is defined as entry without the intent to establish permanent residence. The United States retains a
quota on Mexican professionals until 2004.

[40] R. Chanda, "Movement of Natural Persons and the GATS," *in* B. Hoekman, A. Mattoo and P. English (eds.), *Development, Trade, and the WTO. A Handbook* (2002) pp. 304, 305, 307.

[41] OECD Study, *supra* note 36, at 16.

[42] WTO Background Note, *supra* note 37, at para. 45.

[43] Nielson, *supra* note 10, at para. 20.

[44] Id. at para. 23.

This section will not delve into WTO negotiation strategies, but rather will discuss some key areas for new international cooperation. One idea being considered is the "GATS visa" tailored for service professionals temporarily working outside of their own country.[45] This would be a national visa category that a cooperating government would issue according to prescribed criteria. Because only a narrow range of individuals would qualify, the screening procedures could be separated from normal visa decisions. With streamlined administrative procedures, the visa could be provided within a few weeks. Ideally, such a GATS visa would be granted to qualified individuals without regard to the applicant's nationality. Such a non-discrimination feature seems unlikely, however, although the GATS visa itself may emerge from current negotiations. It is interesting to note that the Asia Pacific Economic Cooperation Forum has agreed to an APEC Business Travel Card to facilitate entry into thirteen participating economies without having to apply for a visa.

The GATS negotiations also address the economic needs test. A minimal action would be to increase transparency of how these tests are implemented.[46] A more important action would be to harmonize the tests so that government decisions are easily reviewable. Ideally, such tests would be banned as inconsistent with the spirit of the WTO. After all, governments cannot refuse to import foreign goods on the grounds that the goods are not needed because domestic substitutes are available. Similarly, the TRIPS Agreement does not permit a government to refuse to award a patent or copyright to a foreign national simply because the local economy does not need it.

Greater recognition of foreign licenses is another possible outcome of the Doha trade round. The GATS currently calls for cooperation between WTO members and relevant international and non-governmental organizations toward the adoption of common international standards for recognition and for the practice of services trades and professions.[47] Aside from this provision, little progress has occurred.

WTO negotiators may also consider ways to improve the mobility of Mode 4 service suppliers in receiving countries. At present, visas and work permits are used to control where individuals can conduct business. Entry and residency are often preconditioned on working for a particular company. Such restrictions on freedom of movement make no sense in a dynamic world economy, and are a good example of how the WTO treats people less favorably than products. Under the GATT rules, the exporter of a product does not have to name in advance the final consumer in the country of import.

Prevailing wage requirements are another barrier to trade in services. They are, in effect, a "social clause" for the receiving country motivated by the idea of taking wages out of competition.[48] If an alien service supplier seeks equal pay, vis-à-vis local workers, then she ought be able to insist on that pay level. Conversely, if the

---

[45] OECD Study, *supra* note 36, at 48 (Box 6).

[46] M. Hatcher, "Mode 4 Trade – The Protagonists' View," Paper Presented at the Joint WTO-World Bank Symposium on Movement of Persons (Mode 4) Under GATS, April 2002, available at http://www.wto.org/english/tratop_e/serv_e/symp_mov_natur_perso_april02_e.htm.

[47] GATS Art. VII:5.

[48] For a discussion of social clauses, see V. Muntarbhorn, "Child Rights and Social Clauses: Child Labor Elimination as a Social Clause?," 6 *Int'l J. Children's Rights* (1998) pp. 255, 270-271.

alien is willing to lower her expectation for compensation, then she ought to be able to do that too. Nevertheless, WTO member governments continue to reserve the right to prevent an alien provider from working for less than the prevailing host country wage. The WTO norm for goods is importation without quantitative restriction, with an equal opportunity to compete on price against domestically-produced goods in the receiving country.[49] Conversely, the WTO norm for people is to limit competition.

Another challenging issue is solving the unfairness to foreign workers when they have to pay social insurance taxes to the host country even though they will not receive any benefits. In many instances, this amounts to double taxation because the foreign worker is already paying social taxes in his home country.[50] As noted above, the GATS permits governments to undertake international accords to prevent double taxation,[51] yet no trade norm has emerged on social insurance. This would be a good topic for cooperation between the International Labor Organization (ILO) and the WTO, but the WTO has resisted undertaking any cooperation with the ILO. The ILO first addressed the problem of the transferability and totalization of social insurance as early as 1935 with the Convention concerning the Establishment of an International Scheme for the Maintenance of Rights under Invalidity, Old-Age and Widows' and Orphans' Insurance (No. 48). More recently, the ILO has legislated a framework Convention Concerning the Establishment of an International System for the Maintenance of Rights in Social Security (No. 157).

Promoting Cooperation

The issues in GATS Mode 4 are difficult as they lie at the intersection of trade, labor, and public security policies. If greater progress is to be made, governments will need to provide assistance to each other in identifying best practices. The GATS calls for technical assistance to developing countries,[52] but not in the reverse direction and not among industrial countries. The GATS also provides for consultation and cooperation with other international organizations having a mandate regarding services, but only a few organizations (such as the International Telecommunications Union) are invited to meetings of the WTO Council for Trade in Services. That parochialism should end: When the Council considers issues regarding natural persons, it ought to invite the ILO and the International Organization for Migration (IOM) to attend and to assist in capacity building efforts.

The mobility of natural persons is important to economic development, and therefore, the IOM, the ILO, and the Office of the U.N. High Commissioner for Refugees should also be invited to meetings of the WTO Committee on Trade and Development. The UN Environment Program (UNEP) and the World Intellectual Property Organization (WIPO) already have observer status there, and organizations con-

---

[49] Of course, the application of antidumping and countervailing duties will encroach upon this norm.

[50] R. Chanda, "Movement of Natural Persons and Trade in Services: Liberalising Temporary Movement of Labor under the GATS," Indian Council for Research on International Economic Relations, Working Paper No. 51, pp. 21, 42-43.

[51] GATS Art. XIV(e).

[52] GATS Art. XXV:2 (Technical Cooperation). See also Art. IV (Increasing Participation of Developing Countries).

cerned with migration and labor are as relevant as UNEP and WIPO. Repeatedly, the WTO could increase its cooperation with non-governmental organizations (NGOs) and the private sector, many of whom are deeply interested in how Mode 4 movements can enable development. At present, NGOs, including business NGOs, are not permitted to be observers in the GATS entities. In April 2002, the WTO and World Bank joined together in hosting a symposium on Movement of Persons Under GATS. This was a positive step in bringing the WTO together with other international organizations and in highlighting the link between Mode 4 and the development agenda.

The WTO competence over the temporary movement of individuals provides an opportunity for the WTO to adopt a more "people-centered"[53] approach to trade and development. Rather than perceiving the GATS commitments as only obligations between the WTO member governments, the WTO could write its rules so that governments acknowledge obligations to service suppliers in their juridical and natural embodiment. One step in that direction that has already been taken is the noteworthy language in the GATS Annex on Movement that states that "Natural persons covered by a specific commitment shall be allowed to supply the service in accordance with the terms of that commitment."[54] If the GATS were more widely perceived as international law that could help workers, then the GATS might enjoy greater support from the public. At present, the movement of natural persons is discussed in the WTO mainly as a services modality, rather than in the broader context of allowing workers to gain new skills and career opportunities.

The WTO might also look for ways to better link the trade regime to the human rights and humanitarian regimes. Trafficking in women and children falls under the rubric of transborder services, and yet the WTO is not even considering cooperative practices to combat such trafficking. Under Article 69 of the TRIPS Agreement, governments agree to cooperate with a view of eliminating international trade in goods infringing on intellectual property rights. Perhaps the WTO should make a parallel commitment in the GATS Agreement to eliminate international trade in sexual services as infringing on basic human rights.

Finally, the broad competence of GATS over services has led to the question of how the WTO could include worker agency services in schedules. As David Richardson explains, labor unions provide such services and can create countervailing market power to anti-competitive market power of firms.[55] Richardson proposes that the WTO take steps toward a market-supportive worker agency agreement at the WTO. At the recent WTO/World Bank Symposium, a representative of Public Services International called attention to the need for "GATS workers" to enjoy the fundamental worker rights declared by the ILO.[56] Such ideas will merit attention in promoting the Doha Development Agenda.

---

[53] See United Nations, Monterrey Consensus, A/CONF/198/3, para. 8 (30 January 2002).

[54] Annex on Movement, *supra* note 9, para. 3.

[55] J.D. Richardson, "Narrow New Issues as a Natural Way Forward for the WTO," Institute for International Economics (2001).

[56] M. Waghorne, Paper Presented at the Joint WTO-World Bank Symposium on Movement of Persons (Mode 4) Under GATS, April 2002, available at http://www.wto.org/english/tratop_e/serv_e/symp_mov_natur_perso_april02_e.htm.

CONCLUSION

In conclusion, the WTO's legal norm on the movement of people is in a nascent stage. Economic openness does not define the norm. The WTO does not demand even a minimal degree of openness, nor does trade law reflect obligations *erga omnes*. Rather, WTO law is a skein of obligations between governments as to how they regulate (or refrain from regulating) market access. Over time, however, the WTO will catalyze greater economic openness, including opportunities for individuals to sojourn and work outside of their home country. As that transpires, the international trade and migration law regimes will need to work more closely with each other.

Selected Bibliography

HOEKMAN, BERNARD, AADITYA MATTOO, AND PHILIP ENGLISH (EDS.) – Development, Trade, and the WTO. A Handbook (2002): 304, 305, 307.

KENNEDY, DANIEL L.M., AND JAMES D. SOUTHWICK (EDS.) – The Political Economy of International Trade Law (2002).

NIELSON, JULIA – "Current Regimes for Temporary Movement of Service Providers," Paper Presented at the Joint WTO-World Bank Symposium on Movement of Persons (Mode 4) Under GATS (April 2002).

OECD – Working Party of the Trade Committee. "Service Providers on the Move: A Closer Look at Labour Mobility and the GATS," TD/TC/WTP(2001)26/FINAL (20 February 2002).

SAUVÉ, PEIRRE AND ROBERT M. STERN (EDS.) – GATS 2000. New Directions in Services trade Liberalization (2000).

WTO – The Legal Texts. The Results of the Uruguay Round of Multilateral Trade Negotiations (1999).

WTO – Council for Trade in Services, "Presence of Natural Persons (Mode 4), Background Note by the Secretariat," S/C/W/75 (8 December 1998).

Chapter 15
DEVELOPMENT AND MIGRATION

B.S. Chimni*

INTRODUCTION

The relationship between development, migration, and international law is a complex one. It not only involves questions pertaining to the existence and implications of a right to development, but also to its linkages with the international law of migration, and to the translation of these linkages into the language of obligation and rights. This chapter merely touches on the international law of migration before examining the right to development in international law and identifying the legal obligations that flow from it in the domain of international migration.

INTERNATIONAL LAW OF MIGRATION

It follows from the general international law principle of sovereignty that a state has the right to determine who can enter and reside on its territory. In the words of one authority, "the reception of aliens is a matter of discretion, and every state is, by reason of its territorial supremacy, competent to exclude aliens from the whole or any part, of its territory."[1] However, this right is subject to a state observing its international legal obligations. Thus, for example, Article 2(1) of the 1965 Declaration on the Human Rights of Individuals Who are not Nationals of the Country in which They Live states:

> "Nothing in this Declaration shall be interpreted ... as restricting the right of any State to promulgate laws and regulations concerning the entry of aliens and the terms and conditions of their stay or to establish differences between nationals and aliens. However, such laws and regulations *shall not be incompatible with the international legal obligations of that State, including those in the field of human rights*" (emphasis added).

In 1999, the Human Rights Committee (HRC) confirmed this understanding in its General Comment No. 27 on "Freedom of Movement." It noted that:

---

* Professor of International Law in the School of International Studies, Jawaharlal Nehru University, New Delhi, India.

[1] Sir Robert Jennings and Sir Arthur Watts Harlow (eds.), *Oppenheim's International Law* (1992) p. 897.

T.A. Aleinikoff and V. Chetail (Eds.), Migration and International Legal Norms
© 2003, T.M.C. ASSER PRESS, The Hague, The Netherlands, et al.

"The question whether an alien is "lawfully" within the territory of a State is a matter governed by domestic law, which may subject the entry of an alien to the territory of a State to restrictions, *provided they are in compliance with the State's international obligations*," (paragraph 4, emphasis added.)

As the HRC had pointed out in its General Comment No. 15, "in certain circumstances an alien may enjoy the protection of the Covenant [i.e., International Covenant on Civil and Political Rights, 1966 (ICCPR)] even in relation to entry or residence, for example, when considerations of non-discrimination, prohibition of inhuman treatment and respect for family life arise."[2]

International refugee law also places certain constraints on state action. Article 33(1) of the 1951 Convention on the Status of Refugees provides, for instance, that no person can be returned, for any reason whatsoever, to the frontiers of territories where her life or freedom is in danger. The Convention principle of *non-refoulement* is a part of customary international law and therefore to be observed by states that are not party to the 1951 Convention.[3] The principle is also contained in human rights instruments such as Article 3 of the 1984 Convention against Torture.

RIGHT TO DEVELOPMENT IN INTERNATIONAL LAW

Hard Law

The contours and content of a right to development in international law are drawn by the UN Charter and international human rights covenants. Article 55 of the UN Charter requires the organization, *inter alia,* to promote "higher standards of living, full employment, and conditions of economic and social progress and development. ..." Significantly, under Article 56, "all Members pledge themselves to take joint and separate action in cooperation with the Organization for the achievement of the purposes set forth in Article 55."

The 1966 International Covenant of Economic, Social and Cultural Rights (ICESCR) incorporates more specific provisions in relation to a right to development, placing great emphasis on international cooperation and assistance for its realization. First, Article 2(1) calls upon all State Parties to "take steps, individually *and through international assistance and cooperation, especially economic and technical*, to the maximum of its available resources, with a view to achieving progressively the full realization of the rights recognized in the present Covenant by all appropriate means ..." (emphasis added). Second, Article 11(1) requires that State Parties "recognize the right of everyone to an adequate standard of living for himself and his family, including adequate food, clothing and housing, and to the continuous improvement of living conditions." Thereafter, it calls upon them to "take appropriate steps to ensure the realization of this right, recognizing to this effect *the essential importance of international cooperation*," albeit "based on free consent" (emphasis

---

[2] Human Rights Committee, *General Comment No. 15* (1986) para. 5.
[3] G.S. Goodwin-Gill, *The Refugee in International Law* (1996) p. 167.

added). Third, Article 11(2) provides, *inter alia*, that State Parties "recognizing the fundamental right of everyone to be free from hunger, shall take, individually *and through international cooperation*, the measures, including specific programs, which are needed. ..." (emphasis added). Fourth, Article 22 authorizes the UN Economic and Social Council (ECOSOC) to draw the attention of other UN bodies to "the advisability of international measures likely to contribute to the effective progressive implementation" of the ICESCR. Finally, Article 23 commits State Parties to "international action for the achievement of the rights" recognized in the ICESCR.

These provisions of the ICESCR create *an international obligation on developed State Parties to cooperate and grant assistance to developing countries to help realize the right to development*. Even writers skeptical of the existence of such a legal obligation concede that the relevant provisions cannot be emptied of content. Thus, for instance, analyzing the preparatory work, Alston and Quinn conclude that "... on the basis of the preparatory work it is difficult, if not impossible, to sustain the argument that the commitment to international cooperation contained in the Covenant can accurately be characterized as a legally binding obligation upon any particular state to provide any particular form of assistance." But as they go on to add, "It would, however, be unjustified to go further and suggest that the relevant commitment is meaningless. In the context of a given right it may, according to the circumstances, be possible to identify obligations to cooperate internationally that would appear to be mandatory on the basis of the undertaking contained in Article 2(1) of the Covenant."[4] The obligation to cooperate in realizing the right to development may be conceptualized as containing a negative and a positive duty. In the least, there would appear to be a negative duty on State Parties not to impede the development of underdeveloped states.[5]

But in its General Comment No. 3, the Committee on Economic, Social and Cultural Rights (CESCR) has gone further and stated that international cooperation for development, and thus the realization of economic, social, and cultural rights, *is an obligation* placed upon all states. The opinion of the CESCR bears citing at length:

"A final element of Article 2(1), to which attention must be drawn, is that the undertaking given by all States parties is 'to take steps, individually and through international assistance and cooperation, especially economic and technical. ...' The Committee notes that the phrase 'to the maximum of its available resources' was intended by the drafters of the Covenant to refer to both the resources existing within a State and those available from the international community through international cooperation and assistance. Moreover, the essential role of such cooperation in facilitating the full realization of the relevant rights is further underlined by the specific provisions contained in Articles 11, 15, 22 and

---

[4] P. Alston and G. Quinn, "The Nature and Scope of States Parties' Obligations under ICESCR," *in* H.J. Steiner and P. Alston (eds.), *International Human Rights in Context: Law, Politics, Morals* (2000) p. 1328.

[5] In the words of Craven, "... States could be said to have an initial duty to restrain themselves from any action that might impede the realization of economic, social, and cultural rights in other countries." M.C.R. Craven, *The International Covenant on Economic, Social, and Cultural Rights* (1995) p. 147. See also Umozurike as cited in D.J. Harris, *Cases and Materials on International Law* (1998) p. 907.

23. With respect to Article 22 the Committee has already drawn attention, in General Comment No. 2 (1990), to some of the opportunities and responsibilities that exist in relation to international cooperation. Article 23 also specifically identifies 'the furnishing of technical assistance' as well as other activities, as being among the means of 'international action for the achievement of the rights recognized.'

The Committee wishes to emphasize that in accordance with Articles 55 and 56 of the Charter of the United Nations, with well-established principles of international law, and with the provisions of the Covenant itself, international cooperation for development and thus for the realization of economic, social and cultural rights is an obligation of all States. It is particularly incumbent upon those States which are in a position to assist others in this regard."[6]

Soft Law

The view of the ICESCR gains strength and validity when one takes into account the soft law international instruments that embody, in one form or another, the right to development and underline the need to realize economic, social, and cultural rights. Thus, for instance, Article 22 of the Universal Declaration on Human Rights (UDHR) states, *inter alia*, that "Everyone, as a member of society, has the right to social security and is entitled to realization, through national effort and international cooperation ... the economic, social and cultural rights indispensable for his dignity and the free development of his personality." Article 28 further provides that "everyone is entitled to a social and international order in which the rights and freedoms set forth in this Declaration can be fully realized." The obligations specified in the UDHR are today part of customary international law. On the fiftieth anniversary of the UDHR, the UN General Assembly (UNGA) solemnly declared its commitment to it "as a common standard of achievement for all peoples and all nations and as a source of inspiration for the further promotion and protection of all human rights and fundamental freedoms – political, economic, social, civil and cultural – including the right to development."[7]

Without a doubt, the most relevant and significant text on the matter is the Declaration on the Right to Development (DRD) adopted by the UNGA in 1986 by a vote of 146 to 1 (United States) with 8 abstentions (Denmark, Federal Republic of Germany, Finland, Iceland, Israel, Japan, Sweden, and the United Kingdom).

From a migration perspective, it is important to stress that the DRD conceives of the right to development as both an *individual* and a *collective* right. Article 1(1) of the DRD states that "The right to development is *an inalienable human right* by virtue of which every human person and all peoples are entitled to participate in, contribute to, and enjoy economic, social, cultural and political development, in which all human rights and fundamental freedoms can be fully realized." (Emphasis added.) Article 2(1) further emphasizes that it is the "human person" who is the central subject of development. The issue whether the right to development is a human right

---

[6] CESCR General Comment No. 3 HRI/GEN/1/Rev.1 (1990) pp. 48, 52. Emphasis added.
[7] GA/Res/53/168, 11 February 1999, fiftieth anniversary of the Universal Declaration on Human Rights.

was effectively settled by the 1993 Vienna Declaration and Program of Action (VDPA) which reaffirmed that "the right to development, as established in the Declaration on the Right to Development, as a universal and inalienable right and an integral part of fundamental human rights."

The right to development is "a necessary precondition for the satisfaction of the social and economic rights of individuals."[8] In the opinion of Mohammed Bedjaoui:

"The right to development is a fundamental right, the precondition of liberty, progress, justice and creativity. It is the alpha and omega of human rights, the first and the last human right, the beginning and the end, the means and the goal of human rights, in short it is the *core right* from which all the others stem. ..." (Emphasis in original).[9]

But how is the right to development to be realized? Article 3 of DRD states, *inter alia*:

"1. States have the primary responsibility for the creation of national *and international conditions* favorable to the realization of the right to development.
3. States have the *duty to cooperate* with each other in ensuring development and *eliminating obstacles to development*. States should realize their rights and fulfill their duties in such a manner as to *promote a new international economic order* ... as well as to encourage the observance and realization of human rights" (Emphasis added).

Article 4 goes further and states:

"1. States have the duty to take steps, individually and collectively, to formulate international development policies with a view to facilitating the full realization of the right to development.
2. Sustained action is required to promote more rapid development of developing countries. As a complement to the efforts of developing countries, effective *international cooperation is essential* in providing these countries with appropriate means and facilities to foster their comprehensive development" (Emphasis added).

Finally Article 10 states:

"Steps should be taken to ensure the full exercise and progressive enhancement of the right to development, including the formulation, adoption and implementation of policy, legislative and other measures at the national and *international* levels" (Emphasis added).

In sum, the responsibility for the realization of the right to development rests on all States, i.e., the international community. As the independent expert on the right to development has noted, "every State having recognized the right to development is obliged to ensure that its policies and actions do not impede enjoyment of that right

---

[8] G. Abi-Saab, "The Legal Formulation of a Right to Development," *in* H. Steiner and P. Alston, *supra* note 4, at 1321.

[9] M. Bedjaoui, "The Right to Development," *in* H. Steiner and P. Alston, *supra* note 4, at 1321, emphasis in original.

in other countries and to take positive action to help the citizens of other States to realize that right."[10]

Customary International Law

Is the right to development a part of customary international law? Two elements must be present for a principle or norm to become a part of customary international law: a material element showing a uniformity and consistency of practice, and a psychological element (or *opinio juris*) that a particular practice is required by prevailing international law.[11] That is to say, there has to be a sense of obeying a legal obligation as opposed to a mere courtesy or acting on moral grounds.

There are divergent views on whether the right to development is a part of customary international law. According to Crawford, "the right to development is, outside specific contexts and specific instruments ... less well integrated into the body of international practice than the notion of permanent sovereignty."[12] Likewise, according to Harris, the fact that the Declaration on the Right to Development (1986) failed to attract the support of all developed states and embodies "a puzzling compromise text" leading to "resulting uncertainty as to both the meaning of the Declaration and whether it was intended to state law" argue against "regarding the Declaration as evidence that the right to development is a part of present customary international law."[13]

On the other hand, Bedjaoui contends "the right to development is, by its nature, so incontrovertible that it *should* be regarded as belonging to *jus cogens*."[14] While state practice does not go so far as to suggest the emergence of a peremptory norm of international law there, appears to be sufficient state practice to conclude the existence of a customary international law norm of right to development. This state practice is evidenced in a number of international declarations and resolutions adopted before and after the DRD. These include specific resolutions adopted by the UNGA;[15] the United Nations Human Rights Commission (UNHRC);[16] the Declaration on Permanent Sovereignty over Natural Resources (1962); the Declaration on Social Progress and Development (1969); the Declaration and Program of Action on a New International Economic Order (1974); the Charter of Economic Rights and Duties of States (1974); ILA's Seoul Declaration on the Progressive Development of Principles of Public International Law Relating to a New International Economic Order (1986); the Limburg Principles (1987); the Rio Declaration on Environment and Development (1992); the Vienna Declaration and Program of Action (1993); the Cairo Declaration of the International Conference on Population and Development

---

[10] ECOSOC, E/CN.4/1999/WE.a8/2, para. 59.

[11] I. Brownlie, *Principles of Public International Law* (1990) p. 5.

[12] Harris, *supra* note 5, at 724.

[13] Id.

[14] Bedjaoui, *supra* note 9, at 1323. Emphasis in original.

[15] The latest of which is GA/RES 56/150, 8 February 2002, The Right to Development.

[16] UNCR 2002. E/CN.4/RES/2002/69. Commission on Human Rights Resolution 2002/69: Right to Development.

(1994); the North Atlantic Free Trade Agreement (NAFTA) (1994); the Copenhagen Declaration of the World Summit for Social Development (1995); the Beijing Platform for Action of the Fourth World Conference on Women (1995); the Lome Convention IV (1995); the Declaration of the South Summit (2000); the United Nations Millenium Declaration (2000); the Brussels Declaration on Least Developed Countries (2001); and the Monterrey Consensus on Financing for Development (2002).

Three other points may be made in support of the contention that the right to development is a norm of customary international law. First, only the United States voted against the DRD. The other seven developed countries did not vote against the DRD but merely abstained. These states may be seen as "bound on the ground of acquiescence and tacit consent, since an abstention is not a negative vote."[17] This view is strengthened by the fact that the developed states have repeatedly accepted, as evidenced by the numerous declarations and resolutions, soft law principles in relation to promoting development in third world countries. Indeed, as Roland Rich points out, "States behave as if they are under an obligation to provide development assistance."[18] Furthermore, in a number of other international legal texts the developed countries (including the United States) have accepted granting special and differential treatment to developing countries, underlining the need for international cooperation in realizing right to development and undertaking international obligations in this regard.[19] Finally, international financial institutions like the World Bank have always provided concessional aid to the developing countries in a bid to realize the right to development.[20]

Second, the cited international declarations and resolutions have to be read in light of the obligations contained in the ICESCR to cooperate with and give assistance to developing countries. It is worth pointing out here that in General Comment No. 3 the ICESCR affirms such an obligation by noting "the importance of the Declaration on the Right to Development adopted by the General Assembly ... and the need for States parties to take full account of all of the principles recognized therein." It emphasized that "in the absence of an active program of international assistance and cooperation on the part of all those States that are in a position to undertake one, the full realization of economic, social and cultural rights will remain an unfulfilled aspiration in many countries."[21]

Third, attention may be drawn to the customary international law character of the UDHR that embodies the right to development.

In brief, there is substantial evidence to confirm that the right to development is part of customary international law. Its emergence as a norm of customary international law, it may be noted, does not require its acceptance by all states.[22] As the In-

---

[17] T.O. Elias, "Modern Sources of International Law," *in* W. Friedmann, L. Henkin, and O. Lissitzyn (eds.), *Transnational Law in a Changing World* (1972) p. 54.

[18] R. Rich, "The Right to Development: A Right of Peoples?," *in* J. Crawford (ed.), *The Right of Peoples* (1988) p. 46. See also the discussion of state practice on pp. 47-50.

[19] Thus, for example, the Final Act of the Uruguay Round of Trade Negotiations provides in the many texts that constitute it special and differential treatment to developing countries.

[20] See Rich, *supra* note 18, at 49.

[21] HRI/GEN/1/Rev.1, pp. 48, 52. Emphasis added.

[22] P. Malanczuk and M. Barton *Akehurst's Modern Introduction to International Law* (1997) p. 42.

ternational Court of Justice (ICJ) noted in the *Nicaragua* case, "the Court does not consider that, for a rule to be established as customary, the corresponding practice must be in absolute rigorous conformity with the rule."[23] The United States can, however, perhaps claim the status of a persistent objector.[24] Such a status allows a state "to contract out of a custom in formation."[25] However, in doing so it would be completely out of step with the wishes of the rest of the international community.

LINK BETWEEN DEVELOPMENT AND MIGRATION IN INTERNATIONAL LAW

While the right to development prescribes certain legal obligations for the international community, the question is how it impacts the domain of migration. The link between development and migration has been expressed in several international soft law instruments. For example, the Cairo Declaration on Population and Development (1994) (CDPD) notes that "in its diverse types, international migration is … affected by the development process. …" (paragraph 10.1). It therefore invited governments of countries affected by international migration to "aid developing countries and countries with economies in transition in addressing the impact of international migration" (paragraph 10.6). The CDPD also called upon states "to address the root causes of migration, especially those related to poverty" (paragraph 10.2). Likewise, the Bangkok Declaration on Irregular Migration (1999) (BDIM) states:

> "As the causes of irregular migration are closely related to the issue of development, efforts should be made by the countries concerned to address all relevant factors, with a view to achieving sustained economic growth and sustainable development … (paragraph 5).
> Donor countries, international organizations and NGOs are encouraged to continue assistance to developing countries, particularly the least-developed countries, in the region aimed at poverty reduction and social development as one means of reducing irregular migration …. (paragraph 7)."

However, the links between development and migration are yet to be fully mapped in the international law literature. This is unfortunate for there is undoubtedly a body of hard and soft law that places certain obligations on states with respect to their migration law and practices. Before identifying these obligations, the implications of specifying soft law obligations must be discussed. It is sometimes said that

---

[23] *Nicaragua* v. *US* (Merits), *ICJ Reports* (1986) p. 98.

[24] Thus, for example, the United States entered the following interpretative statement to the Rio Declaration on Environment and Development (1992): "The United States does not, by joining the consensus on the Rio Declaration, change its long-standing opposition to the so-called right to development. Development is not a right. On the contrary, development is a goal we all hold, which depends for its realization in large part on the promotion and protection of the human rights set out in the Universal Declaration on Human Rights." *Akehurst, supra* note 22, at 239.

[25] Brownlie, *supra* note 11, at 10.

"rules are either part of the law or legally not binding; they cannot be binding and not binding at the same time."[26] However, such a view tends to underestimate the power of the idea of legitimacy in international law and relations. The legitimacy of a rule, as the German thinker Jurgen Habermas points out, "cannot be reduced to the idea of a *balance of power* ... [for] impartiality in judging cannot be *replaced* by autonomy in will formation."[27] The rejection of the idea of "soft law" obligations, in other words, ignores "the elite bias found in legal positivism."[28] It also overlooks the fact that these obligations are embodied in international law texts after a great deal of deliberation, and their being couched in soft law language is no reflection on the persuasiveness of their content. To put it differently, the absence of consent of dominant states renders the norm "soft law," but it does not vitiate its claim on compliance based on the legitimacy of the rule in question. Soft law merely means that the rule in question cannot be enforced against duty holders. Subsequent state practice can quickly transform soft law obligations into enforceable norms of customary international law. Having said this, the different obligations on states with respect to their migration law and practices are identified below in the context of north-south relations.

Obligation to Cooperate and Conduct Dialogue in Good Faith

States have a duty to cooperate to find solutions to global migration (voluntary and forced) problems arising out of underdevelopment. This duty also flows from the general principle of international law requiring states to resolve problems through cooperation. As the authoritative Friendly Relations Declaration (1970) succinctly puts it, there is "the duty of States to cooperate with one another in accordance with the Charter."[29] The principle of cooperation above all means a rejection of unilateralism and a duty to enter into a dialogue with other states in the international community. However, at present, developed states have undertaken a number of measures that keep out voluntary and forced migrants without any serious consultation with the developing countries that bear their principal impact.[30] Any consultations must be informed by the principle of good faith. As the Friendly Relations Declaration notes, all states must "fulfill in good faith the obligations assumed by them in accordance with the Charter." This has also been emphasized in the jurisprudence of the International Court of Justice[31] and arbitration tribunals.[32]

---

[26] Rudolf Bernhardt as cited in B.H. Weston, R.A. Falk, and H. Charlesworth, *International Law and World Order: A Problem Oriented Coursework* (1997) p. 168. See also *Akehurst, supra* note 22, at 54.

[27] J. Habermas, *Moral Consciousness and Communicative Action* (1990) p. 72 (emphasis is in original).

[28] W.F. Felice, *Taking Suffering Seriously: The Importance of Collective Human Rights* (1996) p. 89.

[29] According to Louis Sohn, unanimously approved general assembly resolutions, such as the 1970 Declaration on Principles of International Law Concerning Friendly Relations and Cooperation Among States, may be seen as "leading to the creation new international law applicable to all States" and as representing "a new method of creating customary international law." Weston, Falk, and Charlesworth, *supra* note 26, at 164.

[30] B.S. Chimni, "Reforming the International Refugee Regime: A Dialogic Model," 14 *Journal of Refugee Studies* (2001) p. 154.

[31] See for example *North Sea Continental Shelf* case, Judgment, *ICJ Reports* (1969) 47. The Court observed:

Obligation to Address Root Causes of Migration

There is a soft law obligation to address the root causes of migration flows. The already cited CDPD and BDIM note that underdevelopment is a principal root cause to be addressed. The UNGA has also adopted resolutions pointing to the need for action in this direction. Thus, for example, the UNGA Resolution 41/70, 3 December 1986, endorsed the recommendations made in the report of the Group of Governmental Experts on International Cooperation to Avert New Flows of Refugees. The report stresses that Member States should cooperate "for the prevention of new massive flows of refugees" and calls upon states to give "greater support to those projects that directly or indirectly could help avert new massive flows resulting from the impact of social and economic factors."[33] Likewise, in 1996 the UNGA urged Member States and the United Nations system "to strengthen international cooperation in the area of international migration and development in order to address the root causes of migration, especially those related to poverty."[34] The connection has also been expressed in specific international legal texts such as C143 Migrant Workers (Supplementary Provisions) Convention (1975):

> "… in order to overcome underdevelopment and structural and chronic unemployment, the governments of many countries increasingly stress the desirability of encouraging the transfer of capital and technology rather than the transfer of workers in accordance with the needs and requests of these countries in the reciprocal interest of the countries of origin and the countries of employment. …"[35]

Obligation to Eschew Policies Causing Violation of Economic, Social, and Cultural Rights

In so far as there is an obligation on states to not impede the realization of the right to development, there is a duty on developed states and the institutions they control to not prescribe economic policies to developing countries that lead to the violation of human rights, a principal cause of migration. The structural adjustment programs (SAP) presently prescribed by international financial institutions by way of condi-

---

"[T]he parties are under an obligation to enter into negotiations with a view to arriving at an agreement, and not merely to go through a formal process of negotiation … [T]hey are under an obligation so to conduct themselves that the negotiations are meaningful, which will not be the case when either of them insists upon its own position without contemplating any modification of it. …"

[32] See for example Government of *Kuwait* v. *American Independent Oil Co.*, *ILR* 1982 pp. 519, 578. The tribunal observed: "the general principles that ought to be observed in carrying out an obligation to negotiate – that is to say, good faith as properly to be understood; sustained upkeep of the negotiations over a period appropriate to the circumstances; awareness of the interests of the other party; and a persevering quest for an acceptable compromise."

[33] Goodwin-Gill, *supra* note 3, at 514.

[34] GA/RES/50/123, 23 February 1996, International Migration and Development.

[35] In sum, as Cholewinski put it from the perspective of developed countries, "a comprehensive program of development is the sole answer to reducing the flow of labour migrants and preventing future and potentially damaging mass exoduses." R. Cholewinski, *Migrant Workers in International Law: Their Protection in Countries of Employment* (1997) p. 36.

tionalities is one such set of policies. Thus, for example, the UNHRC in a resolution entitled "Effects of the full enjoyment of human rights of the economic adjustment policies arising from foreign debt and, in particular, on the implementation of the Declaration on the Right to Development" has emphasized that

"the structural adjustment policies have serious implications for the ability of the developing countries to abide by the Declaration on the Right to Development and to formulate national development policies that aim to improve the economic, social and cultural rights of their citizens."[36]

In this regard, the CESCR in its General Comment No. 2 observes:

"A matter which has been of particular concern to the Committee in the examination of the reports of State Parties is the adverse impact of the debt burden and of the relevant adjustment measures on the enjoyment of economic, social and cultural rights in many countries ... Promoting 'the human dimension of development' requires that the goal of protecting the rights of the poor and vulnerable should become a basic objective of economic adjustment."

It follows that underdevelopment and the violation of social, economic, and cultural rights are root causes of voluntary and forced migration. Both the policies prescribed by developed countries (or the institutions controlled by them) that are responsible for it and the restrictive voluntary and forced migration regimes that they maintain are difficult to justify in international law.

Obligation to Create Opportunities for Legal Migration

Articles 55 and 56 of the UN Charter obligate states to strive to create *global* full employment opportunities. A number of soft law instruments strengthen this conclusion.[37] For instance, ILO Recommendation No. 86 Concerning Migration for Employment (Revised 1949) states in Article 4(1):

"It should be the general policy of members to develop and utilize all possibilities of employment and for this purpose to facilitate the international distribution of manpower and in particular the movement of manpower from countries which have a surplus of manpower to those countries that have a deficiency."

Likewise, the Barcelona Declaration adopted at the Euro-Mediterranean Conference in November 1995 acknowledges:

"... the importance of the role played by migration in their relationships...[and] agree[s] to strengthen [...] cooperation to reduce migratory pressures, among other things through vocational training programs and programs of assistance for job creation."

---

[36] UN Doc. E/CN.4/RES/1999/22, 23 April 1999.
[37] Some examples of such texts have already been cited in the context of obligations to address the root causes of migration.

The CDPD more specifically recommends that:

> "Governments of countries of destination are invited to consider the use of certain forms of temporary migration, such as short-term and project-related migration, as a means of improving the skills of nationals of countries of origin, especially developing countries and countries with economies in transition."

The soft law obligation to create greater opportunities for legal migration *is not an alternative* to the obligation to transfer resources to the developing countries. To put it differently, worker remittances to the home country should not be equated with the rendering of direct assistance to it.

Furthermore, there exist hard law obligations to promote migration of *trade related labor*. These flow from specific treaty regimes such as the General Agreement on Trade in Services (GATS) and North American Free Trade Agreement (NAFTA).[38]

Obligation to Respect the Principle of Burden Sharing

There are obligations flowing from the principle of international burden sharing which is, in the view of this author, a principle of customary international refugee law.[39] The characterization of burden sharing as a principle of customary international law can be sustained by weighing the following chain of evidence:

i. provisions of universal and regional conventions and declarations on refugees (1951 Convention, 1969 Organization of African Unity (OAU) Convention, 1984 Cartagena Declaration etc);

ii. conclusions adopted by the Executive Committee of the UNHCR;

iii. numerous resolutions of the UNGA and the ECOSOC calling for burden sharing in the context of different refugee flows;

iv. the texts of different plans and programs of action adopted by the international community, in particular the Declaration and Program of Action of the First and Second International Conference on Assistance to Refugees in Africa (ICARA I and II), the Comprehensive Plan of Action on Indo-Chinese Refugees (1989) (CPA), and the Declaration and Concerted Plan of Action in favor of Central American Refugees, Returnees and Displaced Persons (1989) (CIREFCA);

v. state practice relating to evacuation, resettlement, and local integration of refugees and financial assistance to host states and institutions such as the UNHCR; and

---

[38] For a detailed discussion see S. Charnovitz, "Trade Law Norms on International Migration," in this volume.

[39] B.S. Chimni, *International Refugee Law: A Reader* (2000) p. 146.

vi. the customary international law norm of assisting developing countries.[40]

A range of obligations flows from the principle of burden sharing. These include, *inter alia,* phased dismantling of the non-entrée regime; responding positively to third-country resettlement requests; increasing the funding for the UNHCR; providing greater material and financial assistance to first asylum host countries; eschewing burden escaping practices such as deducting from ODA money expended on the first year of taking care of asylum-seekers/refugees;[41] and not offering aid which is used to violate the spirit of the principles of burden sharing and *non-refoulement*.[42]

Obligations Towards Aiding Return and Post-conflict Peace Building

Finally, a soft law obligation to assist in the return of refugees to post-conflict countries and in post-conflict peace building has emerged in the context of the reintegration of refugees in the country of origin. A UN Security Council (UNSC) Presidential Statement in February 2001 noted "the quest for peace requires a comprehensive, concerted and determined approach that addresses the root causes of conflicts, including their economic and social dimensions."[43] From this perspective flow specific soft law obligations with respect to the return of refugees. For instance, landmines represent a major obstacle to the return of refugees and displaced persons and to reconstruction activities. This has been the experience of returns to all post conflict societies, including Cambodia, Afghanistan, Mozambique, and Angola. The UNGA has in this regard called for greater contributions from donor countries.[44]

Likewise, there is a need for assistance in relation to the effective disarmament, demobilization, and reintegration (DDR) of former combatants in post-conflict societies. Without some degree of predictability of funding for DDR operations, the entire peace process and, along with it, the refugee return process can be jeopardized.[45]

---

[40] Id., at 146-152

[41] *Global Humanitarian Assistance (GHA)* (2000) p. 105.

[42] For instance, as a part of the effort to construct a non-entrée regime the EU has "unilaterally incorporate[d]" the States of Central and Eastern Europe (CEECs) into the emerging regional asylum regime. It has engaged "in a new form of development aid" which aims at "the transformation and development of the state monopoly of force" in CEECs, in particular the police and secret services." S. Lavenux, *Safe Third Countries: Extending the EU Asylum and Immigration Policies to Central and Eastern Europe* (1999) p. 83. For example, Germany concluded readmission agreements with Poland in 1993 and the Czech Republic in 1994. To implement them, it gave Poland DM 120m and the Czech Republic DM 60m (Id. at 15). This aid sought to "diminish the financial burden resulting from the amendments of the German asylum law and the readmission agreement[s]" to deal with increased flows of asylum-seekers and refugees (Schieffer cited in Id.). Out of the DM 120 m given to Poland only a mere 13 percent was earmarked for asylum infrastructure. Contrast this to the fact that Official Development Assistance (ODA) has fallen in the past decade (GHA, *supra* note 41, at 88).

[43] UN Security Council SC/7014, 4278th Meeting (AM) 20 February 2001, Presidential Statement. The text is available at http://www.un.org/News/Press/docs/2001/sc7014.doc.htm.

[44] GA 1999, *supra* note 7.

[45] UNSG, Report of the Secretary-General on the Work of the Organization GAOR: fifty-fifth session Supp. No. 1 (A/55/1) (2000), para. 72. See also S. Ogata, "Briefing to the Security Council" New York, 10 November 2000. Text available at www:\\http.unhcr.ch.

The UNSC has therefore recognized that adequate and timely funding for DDR is critical to the successful implementation of a peace process.[46] The UNSG has on this assumption proposed to "include comprehensive disarmament, demobilization and reintegration programs ... for future peace operations so that the General Assembly can review proposals for funding demobilization and reintegration programs, in the start-up phase, through the mission budgets."[47] But much more funding from the developed countries would be required to sustain the peace and refugee return process.

---

[46] United Nations S/2000/108, 20 October 2000, Report of the Secretary-General on the Implementation of the Report of the Panel on United Nations Peace Operations Contents, ¶ 26.

[47] Id.

EMERGING TOPICS

Chapter 16
HUMAN RIGHTS AND THE INTEGRATION OF MIGRANTS

Walter Kälin*

INTEGRATION OF MIGRANTS

The Notion of Integration

The integration of migrants is not a legal concept, although some states have either explicitly addressed this issue in their legislation or are planning to do so.[1] Integration is a notion that it is used in different contexts with very different meanings.

According to the New Oxford Dictionary of English, the term "integrate" has two meanings: to (1) "combine (one thing) with another so that they become a whole ...; and (2) to bring into equal participation in or membership of society or in an institution or body...; [to] come into equal participation in or membership of society or in an institution or body." [2] In the migration context, integration is used in both senses, each with a particular emphasis on how the relationship between immigrants and the receiving society is or should be shaped. The idea of bringing immigrant groups into a society refers to the cultural dimension of integration, i.e., the homogenization of beliefs and values, lifestyles, and modes of social behavior. The emphasis on participation or membership in institutions and bodies refers to full and equal access to the status systems of a society (labor, education, housing).

Assimilation and social integration are often combined when discussing integration.[3] But taking into account the very complex relationship between the cultural and

---

* Professor of Constitutional and International Law, Faculty of Law, University of Bern. I would like to thank Mirjam Baldegger for her valuable assistance in the preparation of this article. Part of this article is based on W. Kälin, *Grundrechte im Kulturkonflikt* (2000).

[1] See, e.g., paras. 43-45 of the new German Aliens Law (Aufenthaltsgesetz) and Arts. 51-57 of the Draft Aliens Law of Switzerland submitted to the Swiss Parliament by the Swiss Federal Council in March 2002.

[2] *The New Oxford Dictionary of English* (1998) p. 949.

[3] See, e.g., the definition of refugee integration given by Peer Baneke, the Secretary General of the European Council on Refugees and Exiles (ECRE): ... a long-term process of change which places demands on both receiving societies and the refugees and/or communities. From a refugee perspective, it requires a preparedness to adapt to the lifestyle of the host society without having to lose one's own cultural identity. From the point of view of the host society, integration requires a willingness to adapt public institutions to changes in the population profile, accept refugees as part of the national community, and take action to facilitate access to resources and decision-making processes" (quoted in Report of the Third European Conference on the Integration of Refugees, Brussels, 25-27 November 1999, p. 7, available at: www.refugeenet.org/documents/ volg.php3?ID=185).

T.A. Aleinikoff and V. Chetail (Eds.), Migration and International Legal Norms
© 2003, T.M.C. ASSER PRESS, The Hague, The Netherlands, et al.

the structural aspects of integration, the two elements should be distinguished. The social sciences do not use uniform terminology to describe how immigrants and the majority communities grow closer to one another. Still, the differentiation of this process has become standard,[4] even if terminology is not.

Cultural assimilation describes the process of growing participation in the culture and values of the host society. It leads to the cultural absorption of migrants into the host society, making cultural differences disappear to a large extent. This requires migrants to give up their cultural identity and take on, in the sense of acculturation, the values and behaviors of the host society. The opposite of cultural assimilation is cultural diversity or, as it is often called, multiculturalism.

Narrowly defined, integration denotes the incorporation of migrants into, and their participation in the structures of the host society at all levels. This so-called *structural* or *social integration* takes place in various areas. One can speak of economic integration as access to economic opportunities, in particular labor, of all kinds and on all levels; of integration into the educational system as access to non-segregated primary schools and to higher education; and of social integration as access to the status system of the host society. The opposite of structural and social integration is exclusion or marginalization. Social integration is absent if migrants are "marginalized in three interrelated ways: economically, through unemployment or low-status work that is insecure; socially, through poor education and vulnerability to crime, drugs, and household disintegration; and politically, by their powerlessness to influence decision-making."[5]

This terminology makes clear that integration is not a static concept but a process. This process is both a reality of and a challenge for every society and, as such, is not limited to the phenomenon of migration. Culturally diverse societies or societies that are strongly stratified along class lines are constantly faced with issues of integration not very different from the problems of societies that have to deal with culturally different or socially marginalized immigrants. On the other hand, there is no necessary link between migration and problems of integration. Such problems are largely absent where migrants have close cultural or family ties to the receiving country or where migrants are well educated, economically well-off, and socially accepted as group of persons enriching the cultural life of a country.

Cultural Assimilation and Social Integration – A Complex Relationship

The relation between social integration and cultural assimilation is complex. First, it is unclear to what extent social integration is possible without cultural assimilation and to what extent cultural assimilation facilitates social integration. While, for ex-

---

[4] The following definitions follow H.-J. Hoffmann-Nowotny, *Chancen und Risiken multikultureller Einwanderungsgesellschaften, Forschungspolitische Früherkennung* No. 119 (1992), p. 12. UNRISD, Social Integration: Approaches and Issues, Briefing Paper No. 1, World Summit for Social Development, March 1994, pp. 5-6, distinguishes between social integration as inclusionary goal and the creation of common identities.

[5] N. Van Hear, *Migration, Displacement and Social Integration*, UNRIS. Occasional Paper No. 9, World Summit for Social Development, Geneva 1994, n. 21.

ample, successful social integration is hardly possible without knowledge of the language used in everyday life, a high degree of assimilation does not always guarantee successful integration as exclusion and racism may occur between groups with similar backgrounds.[6] But there are cases of immigrant groups who became very successful in their host societies although they retained many of their cultural traditions.[7]

Second, states receiving considerable numbers of immigrants have adopted very different approaches to the relationship between integration and assimilation. These policies can often be traced back to one of the following models:[8]

- *Assimilation to the dominant culture* based on common civic values (the traditional "French" model). The ideal is that immigrants become full citizens indistinguishable from the majority population.

- *Creation of a common culture* in the sense of a "melting pot" (the traditional "American" model). Immigrants have to accept, but also to contribute to, a common culture based on civic virtues (e.g., the "American way of life"). Cultural diversity is relegated to the private sphere where it may flourish.

- *Multiculturalism,* i.e., the protection or even encouragement of cultural diversity not only in the private but also in the public sphere (the "Canadian" model). Immigrants must not give up their culture but all are obliged to embrace the ideal of tolerance *vis-à-vis* other ways of life.

- *Separation* in that immigrants do not have to assimilate to the dominant culture because they are not expected to remain for long, but, at the same time, they are denied social integration to a large extent (the traditional "German" and "Swiss" guest-worker model). Full social integration is only granted once the immigrants have fully assimilated to the dominant cultural patterns of the country.

While no country is strictly following these models today, they nevertheless shape national policies in a manner that clearly differentiates countries from each other.

The Relevance of Human Rights for the Integration of Migrants

As integration is not a legal concept, international law does not contain norms specifically addressing the issue. In particular, there is no general "right to integration" of migrants and no corresponding duty of states to integrate. Similarly, human rights law neither contains a general prohibition of an assimilation policy nor obligates states to take measures to facilitate the assimilation of migrants. Thus, international

---

[6] Consider, for example, racism against white Christians from the Balkans in Western Europe or instances of "new" racism between persons of the same color in South Africa.

[7] Some examples are East Asian immigrant communities in the United States, Indians in East Africa, and Lebanese traders in Western Africa.

[8] See Van Hear, *supra* note 5, at 18-20.

law, in most cases, does not require states to adopt a particular course of action in integrating and assimilating migrant populations. Nevertheless, it does limit state policies and gives them certain directions. In particular, human rights law contributes to the integration of migrants in the following ways:

- If the opposite of integration is social exclusion,[9] then the *prohibition of discrimination* is probably the most important safeguard in the area of integration as it prohibits the exclusion of migrants and the denial of their access to labor, education, health services, etc., on the basis of their race, color, language, religion, national or social origin, or other status (below, The Basic Principles of Non-discrimination).

- Non-discrimination, while prohibiting exclusion, is not sufficient to guarantee inclusion of migrants where other obstacles not based on discriminatory treatment make access difficult for migrants. Here, *economic, social, and cultural rights* may facilitate or even assure the integration of migrants (below, Human Rights and the Social Integration of Migrants).

- *Civil and political rights* are relevant to the issue of assimilation. Freedoms such as religion, language and marriage, and the protection of privacy and family life allow everyone, including migrants, to choose their own cultural identity and, thus, allow migrants to keep their cultural traditions. To a large extent, these guarantees prohibit forced assimilation. On the other hand, there are limits to tolerating certain cultural practices: Where they violate the rights of others, authorities must intervene to protect the victims (below, Human Rights and the Cultural Integration of Migrants).

This chapter discusses these three dimensions with regard to those among today's migrants who have a regular permit to stay and to work in the host country and who are likely to reside there permanently or at least for a prolonged period of time. It does not address the complex legal position of long-term illegal migrants whose presence is unknown to or tolerated by the authorities.

THE BASIC PRINCIPLE OF NON-DISCRIMINATION

The Relevance of Non-Discrimination for the Integration of Migrants

Equality of treatment and non-discrimination by the state are of paramount importance for the integration of migrants. Immigrants' access to employment, housing, and education is significantly limited or made impossible if the state, through its laws or administrative practices, disadvantages them in these areas. Examples of such laws or practices are regulations requiring that certain jobs be held by nationals

---

[9] See *supra* the section on the notion of integration.

or a legal requirement that makes access to the housing market more difficult for extended families. Therefore, in many areas, compliance with the prohibition of discrimination by the legislator and authorities facilitates integration. Non-discrimination forbids placing limitations on a person's access to institutions or to public benefits on the grounds of race, religion, ethnic origin, and similar reasons. Non-discrimination thus prevents governments from utilizing cultural arguments to justify disadvantages for some groups. Authorities must, in this regard, not only be "color-blind" but also "culture-blind." Most often, this approach will facilitate the integration of immigrants as they will be treated the same way as the citizens of the country.

Thus, the equal treatment of migrants without regard to national, ethnic, or religious origins facilitates their integration in most cases. However, equal treatment leads to segregation if rules of general application cause disadvantages for certain migrant groups because their situation is very different from that of the majority population. Where a rule's apparently neutral criteria result in *indirect discrimination*, having disproportionately negative impacts on specific groups of migrants, the state must acknowledge the disadvantages the criteria have on these groups and re-establish de facto equality by not allowing their members to be subject to such rules. The dispensation from dress codes at the workplace, which allows members of certain immigrant communities to accept a job without having to sacrifice the demands of their religion, or the availability of special burial grounds for certain religions serve to improve these persons' integration into society. These cases clearly show how tolerance toward migrants who want to keep their cultural traditions and belong to cultural minorities can ease their integration into the structures of the majority society. The refusal to take into account these persons' religious preferences would force them to either assimilate, and thereby lose an important part of their identity, or, if they hold on to their beliefs nevertheless, to retreat to the outer edges of society and become even more marginalized.

The Notion of Discriminatory Treatment of Migrants

Non-Discrimination

The prohibition of discrimination is a basic principle of international law that protects not only the citizens of a country but also all foreigners, including migrants. Thus, Article 2(1) of the International Covenant on Civil and Political Rights (ICCPR)[10] states that "[e]ach State Party to the present Covenant undertakes to respect and to ensure *to all individuals within its territory and subject to its jurisdiction* the rights recognized in the present Covenant, without distinction of any kind, such as race, colour, sex, language, religion, political or other opinion, national or social origin, property, birth or other status," (emphasis added) and Article 26 ICCPR guarantees *to all persons* equality before the law and equal protection by the law without any discrimination.

---

[10] International Covenant on Civil and Political Rights (ICCPR), 16 December 1966, 999 *UNTS* 171.

Non-discrimination clauses are part of the 1948 Universal Declaration on Human Rights (Article 2) and of many of the human rights treaties, including Article 2(2) of the International Covenant on Economic, Social and Cultural Rights (ICESCR);[11] Article 2(1) of the Convention on the Rights of the Child (CRC);[12] Article 14 of the European Convention on Human Rights (ECHR);[13] Article 1(1) of the American Convention on Human Rights;[14] and Article 2 of the African Charter on Human and Peoples Rights.[15]

Two questions arise regarding the integration of migrants: is it permissible to make certain distinctions between migrants and citizens, and is it permissible to make distinctions among migrants from different countries of origin?

Distinctions Between Citizens and Migrants

International law does not prohibit all distinctions between citizens and migrants. Article 1(2) of the International Convention on the Elimination of All Forms of Racial Discrimination stresses that its prohibition of racial discriminations does "not apply to distinctions, exclusions, restrictions or preferences made by a State Party to this Convention between citizens and non-citizens," meaning that differential treatment of citizens and non-citizens as such does not amount to racism. The International Convention on the Protection of the Rights of All Migrant Workers and Members of Their Families (MWC)[16] prohibits the discrimination of migrant workers based on their "sex, race, colour, language, religion or conviction, political or other opinion, national, ethnic or social origin, nationality, age, economic position, property, marital status, birth or other status," but does not contain a general prohibition on all distinctions between migrants and citizens of the country concerned. On the regional level, Article 16 of the ECHR entitles State Parties to impose "restrictions on the political activity of aliens."

However, human rights law does outlaw distinctions that amount to discrimination. In this regard, Article 26 of the ICCPR "guaranteeing to all persons equal and effective protection against discrimination on any ground such as race, colour, sex, language, religion, political or other opinion, national or social origin, property, birth or other status" and prohibiting such discrimination is of particular importance for migrants because of the autonomous nature of this provision, i.e., its applicability in areas not covered by any other guarantee of the Covenant.[17] The Human

---

[11] International Covenant on Economic, Social and Cultural Rights (ICESCR), 16 December 1966, 993 *UNTS* 3.

[12] Convention on the Rights of the Child (CRC), 20 November 1989, UNGA Res. 44/25.

[13] European Convention for the Protection of Human Rights and Fundamental Freedoms (ECHR) of 4 November 1950, *ETS* 5.

[14] American Convention on Human Rights of 22 November 1969, Organization of American States (OAS), *Treaty Series* No. 35.

[15] African Charter on Human and Peoples Rights of 26 June 1981, 21 *ILM*, 1982, 58.

[16] International Convention on the Protection of the Rights of All Migrant Workers and Members of Their Families of 18 December 1990 (hereinafter "MWC"), UNGA Res. 45/158 (not yet in force).

[17] M. Nowak, *U.N. Covenant on Civil and Political Rights – CCPR Commentary* (1993), pp. 465-466.

Rights Committee has stressed that distinctions made between citizens and non-citizens are not based on race or national origin but on "other status."[18] Such distinctions amount to prohibited discrimination if they cannot be justified on reasonable and objective grounds.[19]

Prohibitions of discrimination are also important for migrants in the context of limitations on rights guaranteed by human rights conventions. Article 2(1) of the ICCPR obliges States parties "to respect and to ensure to all individuals within its territory and subject to its jurisdiction the rights recognized in the present Covenant, without distinction of any kind, such as race, colour, sex, language, religion, political or other opinion, national or social origin, property, birth or other status." The Human Rights Committee has stressed that "the general rule is that each one of the rights of the Covenant must be guaranteed without discrimination between citizens and aliens. Aliens receive the benefit of the general requirement of non-discrimination in respect of the rights guaranteed in the Covenant, as provided for in Article 2 thereof. This guarantee applies to aliens and citizens alike."[20] The same must be true regarding the prohibition of discrimination in the exercise of economic, social, and cultural rights (Article 2 of the ICESCR).

While it is true that the ICCPR allows the permission for entry to be "subject to conditions relating, for example, to movement, residence and employment."[21] Articles 2(1) of the ICCPR and 2(2) of the ICESCR ensure that once admitted, migrants enjoy the same treatment as the citizens unless more restrictive limitations are justified by reasonable and objective grounds. Regarding the right of movement, "[d]ifferences in treatment in this regard between aliens and nationals, or between different categories of aliens" must "be justified under Article 12, paragraph 3" of the ICCPR;[22] they must be "necessary to protect national security, public order (*ordre public*), public health or morals or the rights and freedoms of others."

On the regional level, Article 14 of the ECHR outlaws discriminatory limitations of the rights guaranteed by the Convention in very much the same way as Article 2 of the ICCPR. Article 14 does not prohibit, in the area of migration law, all distinctions made between citizens and non-citizens but requires that such distinctions be based *on objective and reasonable grounds*. In Europe, the status of aliens was regarded as an objective and reasonable justification for many distinctions made between migrants and citizens of the country concerned.[23] More recently, the European

---

[18] See also Human Rights Committee, Communication No 196/1985, *Ibrahima Gueye et al.* v. *France*, views adopted 3 April 1989, para. 9.4. See also Communication No. 965/2000, *Mümtaz Karakurt* v. *Austria*, views adopted on 4 April 2002, Individual Opinion by Sir Nigel Rodley and Martin Scheinin.

[19] *Gueye, supra* note 18, at para. 9.5.

[20] Human Rights Committee, The Position of Aliens under the Covenant: General Comment No. 15, adopted on 11 April 1986, para. 2, reprinted in Compilation of General Comments and General Recommendations Adopted by Human Rights Treaty Bodies, 26 April 2001, UN Doc. HRI/GEN/1/Rev.5.

[21] Id. at para. 6.

[22] Id. at para. 8.

[23] See, e.g., European Commission on Human Rights, 17 December 1976, Application 7729/76, *Agee* v. *UK*, DR 7, 164 (176): "[The applicant's] status as an alien would in itself provide objective and reasonable justification for his being subject to different treatment in the field of immigration law to persons holding United Kingdom citizenship."

Court of Human Rights held, however, that the lack of citizenship alone could not justify all distinctions between citizens and migrants; it stressed that according to Article 14 of the ECHR, such distinctions must be based on *"very weighty reasons"* if they affect the exercise of rights and freedoms guaranteed by the Convention.[24]

Full equality between migrants and citizens is granted only on the basis of specific treaty provisions binding those states that have ratified it. The most prominent example is Article 43 of the MWC[25] which, however, has not yet been ratified by any state receiving a substantial number of immigrants.

Distinctions Among Migrants

Distinctions among migrants coming from different countries of origin are more problematic than those between citizens and non-citizens as they are based on the national or ethnic origin of the persons concerned, i.e., on elements listed as particularly suspect classifications in all human rights conventions. The distinctions are admissible only if justified by especially important reasons. Such reasons may be found in the very close relations between the two countries in question. Thus, the European Commission of Human Rights concluded that preferential treatment of migrants from former colonies did not constitute discrimination.[26] Likewise, the European Court of Human Rights regarded the treatment accorded by EU Member States to citizens of other Member States as permissible although it was not available to persons originating from countries outside the EU.[27] Refusal to grant the same treatment to migrants from other countries can be justified by the lack of reciprocity, i.e., by the fact that free movement and equal treatment of migrants from one's own country have not been accepted by the migrants' countries of origin. In this sense, the Human Rights Committee accepts "that an international agreement that confers

---

[24] European Court of Human Rights, Judgment of 31 August 1996, *Gayguz* v. *Austria*, para. 42. Despite this formulation, the Court upheld a decision denying social security benefits to a migrant worker equal to those provided to Austrian citizens, thus indicating that it is not yet ready to fully consider unlawful distinctions in those areas of the law where migrants traditionally are treated differently. See U. Davy, "Überregionales und regionales Völkerrecht," *in* Ulrike Davy (ed.), *Die Integration von Einwanderern* (2001) p. 66.

[25] Art. 43: "1. Migrant workers shall enjoy equality of treatment with nationals of the State of employment in relation to: (a) Access to educational institutions and services subject to the admission requirements and other regulations of the institutions and services concerned; (b) Access to vocational guidance and placement services; (c) Access to vocational training and retraining facilities and institutions; (d) Access to housing, including social housing schemes, and protection against exploitation in respect of rents; (e) Access to social and health services, provided that the requirements for participation in the respective schemes are met; (f) Access to cooperatives and self-managed enterprises, which shall not imply a change of their migration status and shall be subject to the rules and regulations of the bodies concerned; (g) Access to and participation in cultural life."

[26] See European Court of Human Rights, *Abdulaziz, Cabales and Balkandli* v. *UK*, Series A, No. 94, p. 54, para. 113.

[27] European Court of Human Rights, *Moustaquim* v. *Belgium*, Series A, No 193, para. 49. Such preferential treatment is also part of the 1999 Treaty between the European Communities and its Members States, and Switzerland on the Free Movement of Persons. See Art. 9 of Annex I to the Treaty providing for equal treatment with citizens in many areas.

preferential treatment to nationals of a State Party to that agreement might constitute an objective and reasonable ground for differentiation" if such treatment is based on reciprocity.[28] However, even in such cases, differential treatment is not automatically admissible. In the *Karakurt* case, the Human Rights Committee correctly stressed, in the case of distinctions between migrants from the EU and other countries, that "no general rule can be drawn therefrom to the effect that such an agreement in itself constitutes a sufficient ground with regard to the requirements of Article 26 of the Covenant. Rather, it is necessary to judge every case on its own facts."[29] In the case at issue, the Committee held that there were no reasonable grounds to justify the exclusion of non-EU nationals from being eligible to be elected to the work-council that firms of a certain size must set up in order to allow representation of the interests of the employees *vis-à-vis* the employer.[30]

HUMAN RIGHTS AND THE SOCIAL INTEGRATION OF MIGRANTS

Types of Obligations

There is no general right to integration and no corresponding duty of states in international law which leaves governments room to opt for a particular approach to the integration of migrants. However, human rights law can contribute in different ways to the social and economic integration of migrants. Economic, social, and cultural rights are particularly relevant in this regard, as they address issues such as education, labor, housing, or health that, together with the protection of family life, are of utmost importance for the integration of migrants. As many of these areas are discussed in other contributions to this volume,[31] the following discussion is limited to basic principles and examples taken from the areas of education and housing.

In order to identify basic legal principles that may inform any integration policy, it is helpful to recall the basic obligations imposed by such rights on states. The Committee on Economic, Social and Cultural Rights has stressed that like all human rights, these human rights impose "three types or levels of obligations on States parties: the obligations to *respect*, to *protect* and to fulfil...the obligation to *fulfil* incorporates both an obligation to *facilitate* and an obligation to *provide*."[32] In addition, states must refrain from discriminatory treatment on all levels.[33] The duty to respect obliges states "not to take any measures that result in preventing" access to available work, housing, education, and other goods and services covered by economic, so-

---

[28] *Karakurt, supra* note 18, at para. 8.4, summarizing its views in Communication No. 658/1995, *van Oord* v. *The Netherlands,* views adopted 23 July 1997, para. 8.4.

[29] *Karakurt, supra* note 18, at para. 8.4.

[30] Id.

[31] See the contributions of Virginia Leary, Peter Van Krieken, and Kate Jastram in the present publication.

[32] Committee on Economic, Social and Cultural Rights, The right to Adequate food, General Comment No. 12, 1999, reprinted in Compilation of General Comments and General Recommendations Adopted by Human Rights Treaty Bodies, 26 April 2001, UN Doc. HRI/GEN/1/Rev.5.

[33] Art. 2(2) ICESCR. See also *supra* the section on the basic principle of non-discrimination.

cial, and cultural rights; the "obligation to protect requires measures by the State to ensure that enterprises or individuals do not deprive individuals of" such access, and the "obligation to *fulfil (facilitate)* means the State must proactively engage in activities intended to strengthen people's access to and utilization of resources and means to ensure their livelihood ... . Finally, whenever an individual or group is unable, for reasons beyond their control, to enjoy" a relevant right "by the means at their disposal, States have the obligation to *fulfil (provide)* that right directly."[34]

Main Principles

Based on these different levels of human rights obligations, it is possible to identify the following principles that should inform the integration policies of states:

(1) *States must not interfere with efforts of migrants to integrate.* The duty to respect obliges states to refrain from prohibiting migrants access to services, institutions, and goods relevant for economic, social, and cultural rights that are available to them. The right to access can be limited only if, in accordance with Article 4 of the ICESCR, such limitations are provided for by law and are necessary for the promotion of "the general welfare in a democratic society." In the area of education, migrants cannot be excluded from access to government-run secondary schools or, within the limits of capacity, to public universities,[35] and they cannot be prohibited from sending their children to private schools.[36] Regarding the right to housing, migrants cannot be prohibited from renting housing from the private market and are protected against governmental measures of forced evictions.[37]

(2) *States must protect efforts of migrants to integrate against interference by third parties.* This is particularly relevant for migrants who may become victims of biases of or discrimination by employers, owners of apartments, and the like. Examples include Article 43(1)(d) of the MWC guaranteeing migrant workers "protection against exploitation in respect of rents," and Article 70 of the MWC obliging States Parties to "take measures not less favourable than those applied to nationals to ensure that ... living conditions of migrant workers and members of their families in a regular situation are in keeping with the standards of fitness, safety, health and principles of human dignity." Article 13 of the European Migrant Workers Convention[38] contains similar guarantees. According to its

---

[34] Committee on Economic, Social and Cultural Rights, General Comment No. 12, *supra* note 32, para. 15. Similarly, The Right to Education, General Comment No. 13 (Compilation, *supra* note 32), para. 47.

[35] Art. 13(2)(b) and (c) ICESCR.

[36] Art. 13(3) ICESCR.

[37] On the prohibition of forced evictions and permissible exceptions, see Committee on Economic, Social and Cultural Rights, The Right to Adequate Housing: Forced Evictions, General Comment No. 7, 1997, reprinted in: Compilation of General Comments and General Recommendations Adopted by Human Rights Treaty Bodies, 26 April 2001, UN Doc. HRI/GEN/1/Rev.5.

third paragraph "[e]ach Contracting Party undertakes to protect migrant workers against exploitation in respect of rents, in accordance with its laws and regulations on the matter." The fourth paragraph obliges each Party to "ensure, by the means available to the competent national authorities, that the housing of the migrant worker shall be suitable." Arguably, these provisions do not go beyond the obligations already inherent in the right to adequate housing as provided for by Article 11 of the ICESCR.

(3) *States must actively promote the integration of migrants by providing necessary services and goods.* Unlike the obligations to respect and to protect, the obligation to fulfill is, in principle, programmatic. Article 2 of the ICESCR requires States "to take steps ... to the maximum of its available resources, with a view to achieving progressively the full realization of the rights recognized in the present Covenant by all appropriate means, including particularly the adoption of legislative measures." This can be interpreted as an obligation to actively facilitate and promote, by appropriate legislative and other means, the integration of migrants if they face obstacles in this regard because they cannot fully enjoy their economic, social, and cultural rights. This idea has been specifically spelled out in the migrant workers conventions. Article 43 and 45 of the MWC grant migrant workers and their family members "equality of treatment with nationals of the State of employment" in relation to access to educational institutions and services and to vocational training. On the regional level, Article 14 of the European Migrant Workers Convention contains the same guarantee. Its second paragraph states that in order to "promote access to general and vocational schools and to vocational training centres, the receiving State shall facilitate the teaching of its language or, if there are several, one of its languages to migrant workers and members of their families." The fourth paragraph stresses that the "workers' previous attainments, as well as diplomas and vocational qualifications acquired in the State of origin, shall be recognised by each Contracting Party in accordance with arrangements laid down in bilateral and multilateral agreements." The promotion of education for migrant children has also been included in statements adopted at international conferences. Paragraph 10.12 of the Report of the 1994 Cairo International Conference on Population and Development[39] urges states to make, in the context of "the integration of documented migrants having the right to long-term residence," special efforts "to enhance the integration of the children of long-term migrants by providing them with educational and training opportunities equal to those of nationals."

(4) *Integration policies must respect the prohibition of discrimination.* States must refrain from discriminatory measures on all levels of obligations. As outlined above,[40] all distinctions between citizens and migrants, or among migrants

---

[38] European Convention on the Legal Status of Migrant Workers of 24 November 1977, *ETS* 093.

[39] Report of the International Conference on Population and Development (Cairo, 5-13 September 1994), 18 October 1994, UN Doc. A/CONF.171/13.

which affect their ability to integrate, must be based on objective and reasonable grounds.

Problems

Migrants who are lawfully in the host country are entitled to many of the human rights guarantees relevant for their social integration. Despite the fact that international law allows the identification of clear duties of states regarding the integration of migrants, the present stage of the development of international law is affected by several weaknesses.

The normative character of relevant economic, social, and cultural rights is clear in theory. In practice, however, these rights lack sufficient clarity regarding the specific obligations of states. These rights are, however, less important for migrants than one would expect. In particular, human rights law does not sufficiently address the question of binding obligations of states to take positive measures for facilitating and promoting the social integration of migrants. Furthermore, while it is accepted that economic, social, and cultural rights cannot be limited in discriminatory ways, it is largely unclear which distinctions between migrants and the citizens are admissible and which are not. The continuing existence of permissible distinctions, in itself, is an obstacle to the social integration of migrants.

Specific treaties on the rights of migrants try to remedy these weaknesses but they have not yet been accepted by a sufficient number of countries receiving relevant numbers of migrants.[41]

HUMAN RIGHTS AND THE CULTURAL ASSIMILATION OF MIGRANTS

Basic Tensions

From a human rights perspective, the issue of cultural assimilation of migrants is complex because of a deep tension between two basic principles. On the one hand, human rights such as the freedoms of religion, association, expression of opinion, and marriage or the right to privacy and to the protection of one's own family life guarantee cultural autonomy. The same is true for certain economic, social, and cultural rights, such as the right to education.[42] Human rights protect the cultural identity of everyone, including migrants, thus giving legal force to the idea that the respect for human beings requires a recognition of their identity, as, otherwise, individuals are degraded.[43] Therefore, to allow for cultural diversity is a significant element of each freedom that must be respected and protected.

---

[40] *Supra*, section on the basic principle of non-discrimination.

[41] The Migrant Workers Convention has not been ratified by any country with a substantial number of migrants, and as few as eight states have ratified the European Convention on the Legal Status of Migrant Workers.

[42] See Art. 13(3) ICESCR obliging states parties to the ICESCR to respect "the liberty of parents ... to ensure the religious and moral education of their children in conformity with their own convictions."

On the other hand, a certain basis of commonly accepted values is necessary in every state and every society for a minimal degree of cohesion. States based on the ideals of the rule of law can survive as such only if everyone similarly accepts plurality, the need for tolerance *vis-à-vis* persons who express dissent, and the principle that individuals may not resort to violence in situations of interpersonal conflicts. Therefore, basic values and principles such as equality, non-discrimination, refraining from violent solutions to conflict, and tolerance of other opinions must be defended in such states against culturally-based claims for other values.

Another tension exists between freedom and equality. Freedom requires allowing for the maximum degree of cultural diversity, whereas the principles of equality and non-discrimination demand that, in principle, laws do not differentiate between persons with different cultural backgrounds and authorities remain "culture-blind."

International law leaves enough room for states to define their own way for handling these tensions, but sets certain limits to what states can do.

Main Principles

States May Foster Cultural Assimilation

Apart from some exceptional cases,[44] the laws of a given country can be enforced *vis-à-vis* migrants in the same way as its citizens, and it is legitimate to take measures aimed at ensuring respect for such laws by migrants. This minimal degree of assimilation to the legal order of the host country is necessary everywhere, regardless of whether a country pursues a policy of assimilation or fosters cultural diversity.[45] States also have a right – and sometimes even a duty[46] – to make sure that the basic values of democratic societies, such as a minimal degree of respect of and tolerance for others or the abandonment of the use of violence in interpersonal relationships, are accepted by everyone in the society including migrants.[47] In addition, human rights law does not protect the demands of migrants to be shielded from contacts with those aspects of mainstream culture that they reject. In other words, while human rights law protects migrants in maintaining their cultural traditions, they do

---

[43] See C. Taylor, "The Politics of Recognition," *in Multiculturalism and The Politics of Recognition* (1992) p. 25, stressing that "our identity is partly shaped by recognition or its absence, often by the *mis*recognition of others, and so a person or group of people can suffer real damage, real distortion, if the people or society around them mirror back to them a confining or demeaning or contemptible picture of themselves. Non-recognition or *mis*recognition can inflict harm, can be a form of oppression, imprisoning someone in a false, distorted, and reduced mode of being."

[44] *Supra*, section on the notion of discriminatory treatment of migrants and section on main principle of human rights and the cultural assimilation of migrants.

[45] See *supra*, section on the integration of migrants, cultural assimilation, and social integration.

[46] Such an obligation often derives from the fact that many human rights guarantees require states not only to respect the rights of individuals but also to actively protect persons against infringements of their rights by third parties.

[47] See also *infra*, section on the rights and cultural assimilation of migrants, states opting for cultural diversity must respect certain limits of tolerance.

not guarantee that these traditions will remain unaffected by developments in the host society.

States aiming to be culturally homogeneous may opt for an active policy of assimilation that goes beyond these minimal requirements. From a human rights perspective, such a policy does not raise problems where it is based on mere encouragement (e.g., voluntary educational programs) or on incentives (e.g., rewards for language skills). Although human rights law contains certain prohibitions on forced assimilation,[48] states are entitled to enforce assimilation where a specific function can only be properly performed if the person ceases to insist on cultural practices incompatible with a particular task, provided such limitations are prescribed by the law, pursue a legitimate public interest, and are necessary in the circumstances. Thus, states are allowed to demand from migrants that they possess a degree of language ability necessary to function properly in a given society. Another example can be found in countries insisting on the religious neutrality of schools where teachers can be required not to wear clothing with strong religious connotations, such as an Islamic headscarf or the frock of a Catholic monk.[49]

It is important to realize that allowing a certain degree of cultural diversity may facilitate the integration of migrants where adherence to a cultural tradition is compatible with the relevant institutions or where structural requirements can be adapted to the cultural practices in question without significantly diminishing the functioning of the institution. In these cases, respect for diversity makes access easier for migrants insisting on keeping their cultural practices and, therefore, reduces their marginalization. Certain migrants want to become integrated but are hindered from doing so when, for instance, their religious beliefs or practices are not accepted. Yet because the wearing of a headscarf does not negatively affect the performance of a student, assimilation should not be entered in this context. In contrast, a prohibition on wearing such clothing might make parents decide not to send their daughter to school and thus handicap her integration. Similarly, excused school absences for religious holidays or complete exemption from classes, such as swimming, that conflict with the religious duties of female students permit migrant religious minorities to send their children to public schools. This not only furthers the structural integration of such groups, but also helps to expose such children to the values of the majority in the host state. This socialization process that occurs in schools serves, in the long-term, to let the group partially accept the basic values of the majority population in the host country. Assimilation is more likely to occur in such a manner than if these persons were forced to retreat into the cultural ghetto of ethnic or religious-based private schools.

---

[48] *Infra*, section on the rights and cultural assimilation of migrants, state promoting assimilation must respect the prohibition of forced assimilation.

[49] See, e.g., Swiss Federal Tribunal ATF 123 I 296, *X c. Conseil d'État du canton de Genève*, judgment of 12 November 1997, prohibiting a teacher in a public school in Geneva from wearing the Islamic head-scarf (hijab). The Tribunal argued that it would violate the neutral character of public schools if teachers would be allowed to wear "strong religious symbols."

States Promoting Assimilation Must Respect the Prohibition of Forced Assimilation

Assimilation policies must, by virtue of international law, respect the prohibition of forced assimilation. As the Human Rights Committee has stressed, aliens

> "have the right to freedom of thought, conscience and religion, and the right to hold opinions and to express them. Aliens receive the benefit of the right of peaceful assembly and of freedom of association. They may marry when at marriageable age. ... In those cases where aliens constitute a minority within the meaning of Article 27, they shall not be denied the right, in community with other members of their group, to enjoy their own culture, to profess and practise their own religion and to use their own language."[50]

While these guarantees do not prohibit measures aimed at encouraging or facilitating cultural assimilation, they grant migrants the right to oppose measures of assimilation imposed on them against their will if the cultural practices in question are protected by relevant human rights guarantees. Human rights such as the freedom of religion, the right to protection of family life, or the right to privacy protect them against forced assimilation, unless specific restrictions of the exercise of these rights are justified in accordance with the relevant limitation clauses of human rights treaties.

Of particular interest is Article 27 of the ICCPR protecting persons who belong to an ethnic, religious, or linguistic minority against any denial of their "right, in community with the other members of their group, to enjoy their own culture, to profess and practise their own religion, or to use their own language." This guarantee prohibits, in particular, "all forms of integration and assimilation pressure."[51] The Human Rights Committee has stressed that groups of migrant workers may fall under the notion of minority,[52] although it did so without clarifying the conditions necessary for such a classification. Arguably, migrant groups constitute a minority protected by Article 27 of the ICCPR if they live in a country for prolonged periods of time, i.e., when several generations have kept their ethnic, religious, or linguistic identity.

Human rights provisions specifically prohibiting measures that pressure migrants to assimilate also exist outside the context of minority protection. At the level of soft law, states have agreed that aliens have the "right to retain their own language, culture and tradition."[53] According to Article 29(1)(c) of the CRC, the education of the child should be directed to the development of respect "for the national values of the country in which the child is living" but at same time to "his or her own cultural identity, language and values, ... [and] the country from which he or she may originate." According to Article 12 of the MWC, "[m]igrant workers and members of their families shall not be subject to coercion that would impair their freedom to

---

[50] Human Rights Committee, General Comment No. 15 (1986), para. 7.

[51] Nowak, *supra* note 17, p. 502.

[52] See note 50, and General Comment No. 23 (1994), para. 5.2.

[53] Declaration on the Human Rights of Individuals Who are not Nationals of the Country in which They Live, G.A. Res. 40/144, annex, 40 U.N. GAOR Supp. (No. 53) at 252, U.N. Doc. A/40/53 (1985), Art. 5(1)(f).

have or to adopt a religion or belief of their choice" (paragraph 2), and States Parties have to respect "the liberty of parents, at least one of whom is a migrant worker, ... to ensure the religious and moral education of their children in conformity with their own convictions." In these provisions the MWC does not go beyond what is already guaranteed by the ICCPR and other relevant human rights conventions. Thus, e.g., Article 18(2) of the ICCPR protects everyone against "coercion which would impair his freedom to have ... a religion or believe of his own choice," and Article 13(3) of the ICESCR protects the right of parents to decide the religious and moral education of their children.

States Opting for Cultural Diversity Must Respect Certain Limits of Tolerance

Migrants do not enjoy full freedom to retain their own culture as there are limitation clauses to the international human rights conventions. Limitations necessary to safeguard public goods can be imposed where the exercise of certain freedoms endangers the public safety, order, health, or morals. Duties to protect the fundamental rights and freedoms of others may oblige states to intervene if certain cultural practices endanger other individuals.

This is especially true if the victims of certain cultural practices do not belong to that particular group. However, even if violations happen inside a group of migrants, they must not be tolerated, in particular where a certain behavior is prohibited by international law (e.g., forced marriages[54] and female genital mutilation[55]), where the protection of the needs of the child against serious dangers of physical or psychological abuse justify a state's intervention,[56] or where adults are involuntarily endangered by serious physical or psychological harm (for example when they are not allowed to leave a particular group).[57]

In such cases, group autonomy in their internal matters is limited because victims of internal oppression have a right to the same protection from private suppression and abuse as everybody else in that country. The denial of state intervention in these cases would mean that, for instance, children or women would be denied protection only because they belong to a minority group among the migrants which, in itself, would constitute a form of discrimination.

Selected Bibliography

DAVY, U. (ED.) – Die Integration von Einwanderern (2001).
HECKMANN F. AND W. BOSSWICK W. (EDS.) – Migration Policies: A Comparative Perspective (1995).
HOFFMANN-NOWOTNY H.-J. – Chancen und Risiken multikultureller Einwanderungsgesellschaften (1892).

---

[54] Art. 23(2) CCRP.

[55] Art. 24 CRC obliging States to take effective measures against traditional practices affecting the health of minors.

[56] Art. 3 CRC obliging States to primarily consider "the best interests of the child" when taking any measures affecting the child.

[57] This is a consequence of the duty of states under human rights treaties to not only respect but also to protect the life and physical integrity of individuals.

KÄLIN, WALTER – *Grundrechte im Kulturkonflikt* (2000).

KYMLICKA ,W. – *Multicultural Citizenship. A Liberal Theory of Minority Rights* (1995).

POULTER, S. – *Ethnicity, Law and Human Rights, The English Experience* (1998).

SCHNAPPER, D. – *La France de l'intégration* (1991).

SCHUCK P. AND R. MÜNZ – *Paths To Inclusion: The Integration Of Migrants In The United States And Germany* (1998).

TAYLOR, CH. – *Multiculturalism and "The Politics of Recognition"* (1992).

VAN HEAR, N. – *Migration, Displacement and Social Integration* (1994).

Chapter 17
HEALTH AND MIGRATION: THE HUMAN RIGHTS AND LEGAL CONTEXT

Peter van Krieken*

This chapter explores prevailing international legal norms pertaining to migration in the context of public health, and various entitlement paradigms governing access to health care both for migrants and nationals. States face significant challenges in regard to admission decisions, integration, and return of various categories of migrants. Specifically, state authorities grapple with policy questions concerning denial of entry to migrants due to public health concerns, requirements of health insurance, or some financial coverage prior to entry; extension or curtailment of state health insurance coverage following admission; and the role of health as a factor in expulsion decisions (particularly migrants originating from countries where their access to health services is not assured).

The chapter's first section outlines how far various international conventions have come in defining health as a universally applicable human right. Even without considering the unique situation of migrants, this section shows the difficulty faced by most states and regional bodies in accommodating this positive entitlement within political, economic, and social realities. Jurisprudential trends on the right to health are also analyzed. The second section examines international, regional, and national norms governing migration and health. The analysis is keyed to various stages in the migration process – pre-departure and admission, post-arrival and settlement, and return and expulsion.

HUMAN RIGHTS AND HEALTH: JURISPRUDENTIAL BASIS AND APPLICABILITY

General Principles

Human rights may be conceived in negative and affirmative terms, limiting state action in some cases and requiring the state to play an active role in others. Social and economic rights generally fall into the second category.

* Dr. van Krieken, lectures at Webster University, Leyden, St. Louis and serves with the Netherlands Ministry of Justice.

The author is grateful to Dr. Aleinikoff and Dr. Grondin for their pertinent and constructive suggestions.

T.A. Aleinikoff and V. Chetail (Eds.), Migration and International Legal Norms
© 2003, T.M.C. ASSER PRESS, *The Hague, The Netherlands, et al.*

The right to health contains elements of both: a state should not intervene in someone's health, meaning that the state should respect the integrity of the body, should neither torture nor impose diseases. At the same time, we associate a "right to health" with an obligation on the part of the community to provide adequate health services. Provisions in a number of international legal instruments describe this second, affirmative, meaning of a right to health:

- "everyone has the right to a standard of living adequate for the health and well being [, ...] including medical care" (Universal Declaration on Human Rights [UDHR], Article 25);
- "everyone has the right to benefit from any measures enabling him to enjoy the highest possible standard of health attainable" (European Social Charter, part I, 11);
- "the State Parties recognize the right of everyone to the enjoyment of the highest attainable standard of physical and mental health" (International Covenant on Economic, Social, and Cultural Rights [ICESCR], Article 12.1);
- "everyone shall have the right to health, understood to mean the enjoyment of the highest level of physical, mental and social well-being" (Additional Protocol [1988] to the American Charter on Human Rights, Article 10.1)

Many of the human rights instruments go one step further, describing more particular aspects of a right to health. These include:

- motherhood and childhood are entitled to special care and assistance (UDHR 1948, Article 25.2);
- anyone without adequate resources has the right to social and medical assistance (European Social Charter, part I, 13; and Article 13);
- the steps to be taken by the states parties shall include the creation of conditions which would assure to all medical service and medical attention in the event of sickness (ICESCR, Article 12.2.d);
- states shall take the necessary measures to protect the health of their people and to ensure that they receive medical attention when they are sick (African Charter on Human Rights, Article 16.2).

Perhaps the best (and fairly realistic) commitment that has been ratified is the 1988 Additional Protocol to the American Convention on Human Rights in the Area of Economic, Social and Cultural Rights (Article 10.2):

"In order to ensure the exercise of the right to health, the States Parties agree to recognize health as a public good and, particularly, to adopt the following measures to ensure that right:
(a) Primary health care, that is, essential health care made available to all individuals and families in the community;
(b) Extension of the benefits of health services to all individuals subject to the State's jurisdiction;
(c) Universal immunization against the principal infectious diseases;
(d) Prevention and treatment of endemic, occupational and other diseases;

   (e) Education of the population on the prevention and treatment of health problems, and

   (f)   Satisfaction of the health needs of the highest risk groups and of those whose poverty makes them the most vulnerable."

Finally, notice should be taken of the role of international cooperation. Under Article 2(1) of the ICESCR, states parties commit to undertaking steps – "individually and through international assistance and cooperation, especially economic and technical" – to achieve progressively the rights recognized in the Covenant, including the right to health.

Limitations in Applicability

The terms "adequate," "highest possible standard," and "highest level," which appear in the international legal materials quoted above, are problematic. As noted in the 2000 World Health Organization (WHO) report, "if services have to be provided to all, then not all services can be provided."[1] It is generally recognized that much more is possible technically than financially. Almost by definition, the standards and levels differ from country to country. As is true for virtually all the economic and social rights, it is not possible to assume or impose absolute norms (unlike civil and political rights – torture is forbidden in each and every country, in each and every form). Although the ICESCR guarantees "the highest attainable standard of physical and mental health," under Article 2(1) of the Covenant states commit themselves to undertake steps "to the maximum of [their] available resources" toward "achieving progressively the full realization" of rights recognized in the Covenant.[2]

    Furthermore, services vary within states, depending on whether they are provided for free or covered by insurance and whether persons have insurance. Each country and each system will have to decide which services are free, which ones fall under the prevailing insurance system, and which services persons must pay for. In the United States, for example, some 30 million persons lack any insurance, and have access only to that care provided by programs that serve the poor. In some countries in the North, persons over sixty years old have no access to kidney dialysis; and effective anti-cholesterol drugs are available for free in some countries but not in others.[3] It is obvious that health and the right to health are relative concepts.

    In 2000, the Committee on Economic, Social, and Cultural Rights issued a General Comment on the ICESCR that supplies important guidance on the concept of a right to the highest attainable standard of health.[4] The Comment provides a feasible

---

[1] The World Health Report 2000 (Health Systems: Improving Performance) p. xiv.

[2] Art. 2(1).

[3] Consider also the so-called DALE ("disability adjusted life expectation") phenomenon, which attempts to calculate whether it is worth the investment to start treatment. Some countries (and hence insurance companies) have a maximum of say $ 35,000 early, meaning that a treatment of $ 100,000 should ensure a life expectancy of at least three years.

[4] Committee on Economic, Social and Cultural Rights, Twenty-second session, Geneva, 25 April-12 May 2000; Agenda item 3: The right to the highest attainable standard of health: 11 August 2000. E/C.12/2000/4, CESCR General Comment No. 14.

approach, and one likely to represent a consensus view.[5] It states that "progressive realization means that States parties have a specific and continuing obligation to move as expeditiously and effectively as possible towards full realization" of the Convention's guarantee of the right to the enjoyment of the highest attainable standard of physical and mental health.[6] It is recognized that the precise nature of the facilities, goods, and services will vary according to numerous factors, including the country's developmental level; and that services will frequently remain out of reach for certain groups of society because payment for health services is to be considered a normal feature. Yet, the General Comment stresses that "States have a special obligation to provide those who do not have sufficient means with the necessary health insurance and health-care facilities."[7]

Emerging Jurisprudence on the Right to Health

The commitment set forth in the 1988 Protocol to the American Convention on Human Rights is of both a humanitarian and utilitarian character. The Protocol is, to a great extent, achievable because it limits itself to primary health care, immunization, endemic diseases, highest risk group, and the like, and focuses on access without indicating that those services should be free. Of greatest interest for the present study is the provision's guarantee of rights to "all individuals" subject to a State's jurisdiction – language that would cover immigrants, migrant workers, refugees and their families, and citizens. (This language should be contrasted with Article 2.3 of the ICESCR, which provides that "Developing countries with due regard to human rights and their national economy, may determine to what extent they would guarantee the economic rights in the present Covenant to non-nationals.")

Jurisprudence on the scope and applicability of the right to health is only now emerging. Nonetheless, a few interesting illustrations can be given. It is, for instance, possible to submit complaints to the Inter-American Commission on Human Rights (IACHR) on the basis of the right to health as provided in the American Declaration. Thus, in the case of the Yanomani Indians, the IACHR declared that the right to health in Article XI of the American Declaration had been violated.[8] The

---

[5] The Committee stated in paras. 5 and 6 of this General Comment:

The Committee is aware that, for millions of people throughout the world, the full enjoyment of the right to health still remains a distant goal. Moreover, in many cases, especially for those living in poverty, this goal is becoming increasingly remote. The Committee recognizes the formidable structural and other obstacles that result from international and other factors beyond the control of States, and impeding the full realization of Art. 12 in many States Parties.

With a view to assisting States Parties' implementation of the Covenant and the fulfilment of their reporting obligations, this General Comment focuses on the normative content of Art. 12 (Part I), States Parties' obligations (Part II), violations (Part III), and implementation at the national level (Part IV), while Part V deals with the obligations of actors other than States Parties. The General Comment is based on the Committee's experience in examining States Parties' reports over many years.

[6] Id. at para. 31.

[7] Id. at para. 19. See also para. 43(a), noting as "core obligation" a state's duty to "ensure the right of access to health facilities, goods and services on a non-discriminatory basis, especially for vulnerable and marginalized groups."

[8] *Annual Report of the Inter-American Commission on Human Rights*, 1984-1985, Resolution No.

government of Brazil was held to have failed to protect the Yanomani against the exploitation of the rainforest and the detrimental health effects that could be caused. Similarly, with the adoption of a complaint procedure under the European Social Charter (ESC) of the Council of Europe, the right to protection of health in the ESC will become susceptible to (quasi-) judicial review. This procedure will, however, only allow specific organizations, not individuals, to submit complaints.

Cases raising claims to a right to health may also arise at the national level. In some countries either a constitutional or international right to health has been given effect in domestic courts. Whereas some of these cases involve a right to certain healthcare facilities, others concern a right to environmental health. In a 1992 Colombian case about the terminal illness of an AIDS patient, the Colombian Supreme Court ruled that the state was required, under a provision in Colombian constitution guaranteeing a right to health (Article 13), to provide special protection when the lack of economic resources "prevents a person from decreasing the suffering, discrimination, and social risk involved in being afflicted by a terminal, transmissible, and incurable illness." To this end, the Court decided that the hospital was required to provide the AIDS patient with the necessary services. With regard to environmental health, the well-known 1993 Philippine *Minors Oposa* case[9] is significant. In that case the Philippine Supreme Court ruled that the state should stop providing logging licences to protect the health of present and future generations. The decision was based on Article II of the Declaration of Principles and State Policies of the 1987 Philippine constitution, which sets forth the rights to health and ecology.

The right to health may also be implicated in cases based on protections of other civil and political rights. Again, such protections may concern access to a certain healthcare facility or protection against environmental health threats. A case indirectly involving a right to access to healthcare services has been brought before the Human Rights Committee (HRC). This body has adopted the practice of considering Article 26 of the International Covenant on Civil and Political Rights (ICCPR) (non-discrimination) as an autonomous provision that may include the prohibition of discriminatory actions with relation to social rights. In *Hendrika S. Vos* v. *the Netherlands* (1989), the HRC considered whether the denial of a disability benefit constituted a violation of the article. Although the HRC held that there was no violation of Article 26, the fact that the HRC tested the denial of the sickness benefit against Article 26 shows its willingness to treat claims to social rights under the non-discrimination clause.

The Indian Supreme Court ruled that on the basis of the right to life contained in the Indian constitution, the claimant had a right to the available emergency medical treatment. It explained that:

"providing adequate medical facilities for the people is an essential part of the obligations undertaken by the Government in a welfare State.... Article 21 imposes an obligation on the State to safeguard the right to life of every person. Preservation of human life is thus

---

12/85, Case No. 7615; see also the publication P. Van Krieken (ed.), *Health, Migration and Return* (2001) p. 28.

[9] Included in 33 *ILM* 173 (1994).

of paramount importance. ... Failure on the part of a Government hospital to provide timely medical treatment to a person in need of such treatment results in a violation of his right to life guaranteed under Article 21."[10]

HEALTH REGULATIONS, MIGRATION, AND MIGRANTS

If state discretion is limited to some degree by human rights principles of non-discrimination, states nevertheless possess another source of authority – that is, the general power to regulate immigration – that has a direct impact on immigrants' health and access to health care. Thus, states have traditionally imposed a range of health-related conditions on entry, including requirements that migrants be healthy, have health insurance, or have other financial means to take care of their medical needs. This section examines existing regulations, their rationale, and the complexity of their application. Examples of adjudicated cases are used to explore how these laws are enforced at the various stages of the migration process, while the human rights dimension of the above section is invoked as relevant in each case.

Most of the epidemiological studies on the health status of migrants in host countries are from traditional countries of immigration, which often have a more selective and controlled movement of people coming into their countries. American, Canadian, and Australian studies have reported on migrants' health risks towards infectious diseases, mental health, and women's and child health. There is, in comparison, only a paucity of such studies looking at the health status of migrants in European countries. These countries, which were historically ones with net emigration, only quite recently started to realize that Europe had become a continent of immigration.[11] Consequently, comparatively speaking, population movements towards Europe tend to be less orderly, with large numbers of refugee claimants and asylum-seekers, and irregular and undocumented immigrants, and, to a lesser extent, labor migrants. Furthermore, the right of free movement of European Union citizens within the European Union countries increases population mobility. The changing world brought by globalization will compound the difficulty of managing health of a mobile population, particularly in managing the public health. Nowadays, the movement of people between their countries of origin and their new countries (the returnees or returned migrants), leisure travel of new migrants, and international travelers bring new challenges where traditional measures of exclusion, confinement, and quarantine become obsolete.

---

[10] Communication No. 218/1986, Views of 29 March 1989, UN DC A/44/40, annex X sect G, pp. 232-240; see also Van Krieken, *supra* note 8, at 29.

[11] See, e.g., R.T. Appleyard, "Migration and Development: A Global Agenda for the Future," *International Migration Quarterly Review*, vol. XXX 1992, Special Issue: Migration and Health in the 1990s; and R. Lohrmann, *International Migration: Trends and prospects*, International Social Security Association Ed., Migration: A Worldwide Challenge for Social Security (1994).

Pre-departure and Admission

The resurgence of classical infectious diseases, such as tuberculosis, and the emergence of new, previously unknown diseases such as HIV/AIDS have regenerated interest in migration and border health control. In countries with traditional and controlled immigration flows, health and medical regulations constitute the most ancient border entry requirements and predate immigration laws. Traditional countries of immigration, such as Australia, Canada, New Zealand, and the United States, usually conduct pre-departure medical screening. (Countries of more recent immigration, such as the European countries, generally conduct post-arrival screening, which is usually triggered by a requirement to obtain a work permit or simply by the immigration status of being refugees.) Screening generally includes testing to detect active tuberculosis and identifying migrants who have been infected. Most of these states also require mandatory testing for HIV. The criteria to determine who will be screened prior to arrival are usually based on prevalence rate of a specific infectious disease in country of origin, the category of application, the migrant's occupation in receiving country, and the migrant's expected length of stay in the host country.

The rationale for the pre-departure immigration health assessment is often regulatory in context and application and may not represent state-of-the-art public health practice.[12] Nations that have health components in their immigration process often base them on two basic principles:

1. *Protection of public health*: The intent of these practices is to prevent the introduction of infectious or communicable disease carried by migrants. Most attention in the traditional migration receiving countries is focused on tuberculosis, vaccine-preventable diseases, parasitic disease, and sexually transmitted diseases. These practices are applied to immigrants and refugees and, in some nations, some long-staying visitors such as students.[13]

---

[12] Some countries do not have legal provisions nor do they wish to have any that will assess certain categories of migrants for infectious tuberculosis, such as long-term visitors. Instead, such countries would focus on apparent higher-risk category such as the refugees. However, when comparing the migrants screened for infectious pulmonary tuberculosis, IOM's Migration Health Services Division detected as much, if not slightly more, tuberculosis, among the non-refugee population than among the refugees. The difference was that approximately 8% more cases of active tuberculosis were detected among migrants, despite the fact that the refugee population screened was 10% larger than the migrant's population. Comparatively, in a host country, Stephen Weis and his group, in a recent study published in 2001, found non-immigrant visitors to be an important source of tuberculosis morbidity, reporting more multi-resistant tuberculosis among the non-immigrant visitors than among the refugees and permanent resident immigrants. S.E Weis, et al., "Tuberculosis in the Foreign-born Population of Tarrant County, Texas by Immigration Status," 164 *American Journal of Respiratory* and *Critical Care Medicine* (2001) pp. 953-957. These two observations therefore challenge the wisdom of any national regulation wishing to manage migration public health of screening migrants for infectious diseases based on immigration status or category. Consequently, the public health practice of targeting surveillance programs around the world to either exclusively refugees or permanent residents should be re-visited.

[13] For instance, in the recent Netherlands Aliens Act, in force since 1 April 2001, it has been stated:

1. An application for the issue of a residence permit for a fixed period as referred to in section 13 may be rejected if (...)

2. *Reduction of burden on publicly funded services*: The intent of regulations in this area is to reduce the costs or demands for health care or social services that migrants may require after their arrival. Attention is therefore focused on chronic, high treatment cost diseases and is most often observed in nations that have state-supported national insurance health plans. These practices are applied to immigrants but often waived for refugees.

At the multilateral level, the International Health Regulations, adopted in 1969 and amended in 1973 and 1981, provide the framework for international cooperation. The stated purpose is "to ensure maximum security against international spread of diseases with minimum interference with world traffic and trade." The main objectives are to provide for the consistent application of routine, preventive measures (e.g., at ports and airports), the use by all of internationally approved documents (e.g., vaccination certificates), and the formal notification to the World Health Organization (WHO), and implementation of predetermined measures, in the event of the occurrence of cholera, plague, or yellow fever. The Regulations are currently being revised in order to better adapt them to the present volume of international traffic and trade and to take account of trends in the epidemiology of infectious diseases, including shifting the focus from the three diseases mentioned above to other health emergencies of international concern.[14]

Post-arrival and Settlement

We can differentiate among a number of post-entry scenarios, depending on a migrant's status (lawful-unlawful or temporary-settled) and whether a migrant has health insurance. It is also relevant whether the state is seeking to expel a migrant or to deny access to health services.

As noted above, international law non-discrimination norms apply to immigrants, but do not necessarily condemn all differences in treatment between citizens and non-citizens. Differential treatment occurs in several ways. Many states condition eligibility for health benefits or insurance based on an immigrant's status (excluding, for example, temporary workers or undocumented migrants). Some states recognize eligibility only after a certain number of years of residence. Recent changes in policy in Denmark, for example, deny migrant workers access to social welfare during the first seven years of their (legal) stay. They are, of course, free to take health insurance, but access to health care is then the result of a contractual relationship rather than the obligation of the receiving society toward newcomers. In reality a condition for legal stay is a work permit that should include health insurance (either directly or through the employer with an insurance company in the country of

---

(d) the alien constitutes a threat to public policy or national security;

(e) the alien is not prepared to submit to a medical examination performed in the interests of public health in order to check for the presence of a disease designated by or pursuant to the Infectious Diseases Act or to undergo medical treatment for such a sickness; (...)

(g) this is necessary in the public interest, other than on the grounds referred to at (a) to (f).

[14] WHO, *International Travel and Health*, Annex 2.

temporary residence, or by the individual with an insurance company in the country of origin).[15]

For lawfully residing immigrants, it is doubtful that illness alone can be grounds for withdrawing a residence permit, unless it would concern matters of national security or a "danger to the community."[16] Furthermore, settled lawful immigrants are generally understood to have greater claims to state-provided benefits than temporary migrants. The pending EU/EC directive concerning the status of third-country nationals who are long-term residents demonstrates the trend here.[17] The draft directive provides enhanced protection against expulsion for long-term residents, stating that such decisions may be taken by member states only where a long-term resident's conduct "constitutes an actual and sufficiently serious threat to public order or domestic security that it affects a fundamental interest in society." (Article 13.1) The directive also affirms the principle that long-term residents must have the same social protection entitlements as nationals – including family allowances, retirement pensions, sickness insurance, and unemployment benefits (Article 12.d).[18]

Migrant workers would not fall under the proposed EU directive on long-term residents, but rather under a proposed directive focusing on employment and self-employment. Although the directive states that workers from non-EU states are entitled to equal treatment with EU citizens regarding "social security including healthcare," the directive would also permit revocation of a residence permit if a period of unemployment exceeded a certain period of time.[19] This carries the implicit suggestion that such workers should not become a financial burden for the host state, and that continued residence *cum* treatment is not assured.

As to migrants residing illegally in a state, it is up to the insurance company whether access to health services can be granted. The illegal stay, of course, may be grounds for expulsion. Whether or not that would amount to inhuman treatment under ECHR's Article 3 will be examined below.

Denials of emergency assistance – even to undocumented migrants – is difficult to justify. Significantly, the 1990 UN Convention on the Protection of the Rights of All Migrant Workers and Members of their Families (Article 28) provides:

---

[15] It should be noted (a) that Denmark, through a Protocol to the 1997 Treaty of Amsterdam, has decided not to become a member of a common (EC) migration regime; and (b) that it would be of interest to see how the European Court or the Committee under the ICESCR would evaluate this rule if it came before them.

[16] Compare the exception to the *non-refoulement* principle as per Art. 33.2 of the 1951 Refugee Convention.

[17] These proposals have been well received and might be adopted as binding before the 1st of May 2004. By that time the transition period for Justice and Home Affairs (TEU-TEC) comes to an end. See for details P. Van Krieken (ed.), *The Migration Acquis Handbook* (2000) and IOM's 2002 publication Van Krieken and Ungureanu (eds.), *The Migration Acquis* (2002) Update.

[18] Council Directive concerning the status of third-country nationals who are long-term residents, COM (2001) 127 (final), 13 March 2001.

[19] Council Directive on the conditions of entry and residence of third-country nationals for the purpose of paid employment and self-employed economic activities, COM (2001) 386 final, 11 July 2001, Art. 11(1)(f)(iv), Art. 10 (three months per year in the first years of stay; six months per year after two years of stay).

"Migrant workers and members of their families shall have the right to receive any medical care that is urgently required for the preservation of their life or the avoidance of irreparable harm to their health on the basis of equality of treatment with nationals of the State concerned. Such emergency medical care shall not be refused them by reason of any irregularity with regard to stay or employment."

Although this Convention will soon enter into force, no country of the North has ratified it – a fact related to general attitudes relating to irregular migrants. Yet, most EU countries will not deny health services in the case of an emergency to that group. Although it could be argued that this is a voluntary and not a legal obligation, the trend may eventually create a custom. It is questionable whether the non-discrimination principle would come to the fore, as long as labor migration is considered a contractual relationship with a spelled-out condition and the person concerned has his or her own society in which to enjoy the services as agreed upon and possible in that society. The latter alternative is not available to the refugee, who, of course, should enjoy virtually the same treatment as nationals under Article 24 of the 1951 Refugee Convention.[20]

Immigrant access to medical services and benefits in the country of settlement has been tested in several court cases. *Gaygusuz* v. *Austria*[21] concerned the refusal by Austrian authorities to grant emergency assistance to an unemployed man of Turkish nationality, who had exhausted his entitlement to unemployment benefits, on the ground that he did not have Austrian nationality. The European Court of Human Rights found this decision to be in breach of Article 14 of the ECHR (non-discrimination) in conjunction with Article 1 of the First Protocol (peaceful enjoyment of possessions). The Court's finding was based in particular on the fact that the applicant had made contributions to the unemployment insurance fund. It is likely that similar conclusions would apply to claims to entitlement to medical care if based on contributions. The full scope of the problem becomes visible when looking at the situation of individuals who have not made any contribution to any public system of health care and where facilities would need to be provided on the basis of a principle of charity rather than that of mutual assistance. Yet, it should be stressed that the degree of severity of suffering required to engage the responsibility of the public authorities under Article 3 of the Convention (forbidding inhuman or degrading punishment or treatment) is particularly high.[22]

It has also been suggested that Article 8 of the ECHR – which provides for the right to respect of private life and is concerned with imposing on states both a nega-

---

[20] This article reads: "The Contracting States shall accord to refugees lawfully staying in their territory the same treatment as is accorded to their nationals in respect of the following matters ... (b) social security."

[21] 39/1995/545/631.

[22] As pointed out above, the degree of severity of the suffering required to engage the responsibility of the public authorities under Art. 3 of the Convention is particularly high. It is for this reason also that an application introduced in the eighties before the Commission by a destitute woman who could not afford to pay her electricity bills, whose electricity supply had been cut off by the Belgian authorities, and who argued her case on the basis of Art. 3 of the Convention as the lack of heating seriously affected the well-being of her children and herself was unsuccessful (14641/89).

tive and a positive obligation of non-interference – could constitute a basis on which aliens who are denied a minimum of care required by their health conditions could successfully argue their case, to the extent that physical integrity is an inherent part of this guarantee. However, the structure of Article 8 is quite different from that of Article 3. Where Article 3 contains an absolute prohibition, Article 8 permits interferences (in disregard of positive or negative undertakings), provided such interference pursues a legitimate aim and that the contested measure is proportionate to the aim pursued. In the application of this balancing a case of interference with an individual's right to respect for physical integrity, the following elements affect the weight given to the various interests: the gravity of the disease, the availability of medical care in the receiving country, the basis for the underlying deportation order (such as illegal entry, or the existence of a criminal record), and the existence of family life. The few cases brought before the Convention bodies do not cover the full range of health care; they concerned situations of medical treatment of illnesses and not, for example, access to birth assistance or to care for the elderly or physically or mentally handicapped, areas in which considerations pertaining to physical integrity are equally relevant.

Return and Expulsion

An important question arises under human rights law whether returning persons to countries where they may not have access to adequate health services constitutes inhuman or degrading treatment. These issues have been examined under the European Court of Human Rights in a variety of cases.[23] More often than not, return has been allowed.

In the 1990 case *Cruz-Varas*,[24] a Chilean was sent back home while his case was still pending in Strasbourg. The Court ruled that deportation did not amount to a breach of Article 3, despite the fact that the claimant suffered from PTSS and that his mental health deteriorated upon deportation.

In *Tanko* v. *Finland*,[25] the Commission indicated that a lack of care may amount to a situation in which Article 3 may be violated. The case concerned a Ghanaian whose application for political asylum had been rejected, and who thereupon submitted that he would face serious problems due to an eye disease. The Commission was of the opinion that appropriate drugs could be taken home to the country of origin and that the "real risk" criterion – an essential element of Article 3 jurisdiction – had not been met.

In *D.* v. *UK*,[26] the Court stated that "aliens who have served their prison sentences and are subject to expulsion cannot in principle claim any entitlement to remain on the territory of a contracting state in order to continue to benefit from medical, social or other forms of assistance provided by that state during their stay in prison."

---

[23] Until November 1998 (the entry into force of Protocol 11) a Commission would take the decision whether a case would be admissible.

[24] 46/1990/237/307.

[25] 23634/94.

[26] 146/1996/767/964.

The Court nevertheless ruled that Article 3 applies to inhuman treatment brought about by unintentional acts and that the expulsion of a foreigner dying from AIDS to a country that lacks the appropriate means of treatment would constitute a violation of this provision. The Court underlined that in arriving at its conclusion it had taken into account "the very exceptional circumstances" and the "compelling humanitarian considerations at stake."

The UK, in its reaction, stated that

> "the court did insist that the case had very special circumstances, i.e., the almost total absence of medical and social care in St. Kitts for this particular individual, the critical stage of his fatal illness, i.e., very near to death and the care from which he would be wrenched. It was therefore concluded that the numbers of cases to which the expanded Article 3 could apply is very small."[27]

In March 1998, the European Commission concluded that repatriation of an ex-Zairean who had both the AIDS virus and Kaposi Syndrome to the newly renamed Democratic Republic of Congo would constitute a violation of Article 3. In its report the Commission stated that repatriation of a person to a country where he would probably not be able to benefit from the necessary medical treatment and where he would have to confront an illness such as AIDS at an advanced stage, all alone, without family support, would constitute an ordeal preventing him from preserving his human dignity while his illness pursued its inevitably painful and fatal course. The French decided to settle this case out of court, and agreed to grant the ex-Zairean a residence permit.

Two months later, the Commission made public a decision on the admissibility of an application lodged by a Ugandan national who was HIV positive and faced with repatriation from Finland where he had been sentenced to over eleven years in prison.[28] In this case repatriation was not believed to be a violation of Article 3. This, in spite of submissions (i.e., medical opinions) that interruption of the medication would result in an acceleration of the illness; adequate medical treatment in Uganda could not be assured (*cure*); and there was a lack of friends and relatives in Uganda (*care*). The applicant claimed that if he were returned, he would be treated as an outcast and would lack the means to receive proper care, whether medical or psychological. The Commission, however, held that the illness had "not yet reached such an advanced state that ... deportation would amount to treatment proscribed by Article 3." In reaching this conclusion, it took the situation and conditions in Uganda into due account. The Commission distinguished the case of the ex-Zairean on the grounds that there the infection had already reached an advanced stage neces-

---

[27] The UK stressed that in their opinion Art. 3 of the ECHR could be held to be limited to intentional acts of the authorities or from non-state bodies. The UK indicated that "The Court ruling in this case means that Art. 3 can also apply where the source of the offending treatment arises from factors outside the control of the authorities there and even when, in itself, the treatment does not infringe Convention standards." Quite remarkably, experts indicate that St. Kitts is one of the few Caribbean countries that has a medical school/faculty (Cuba and Jamaica being the other ones). Raoul Wallenberg Institute, Report No. 31: *Health Gaps and Migratory Movements* (2000) p. 64.

[28] Karara, 40900/98.

sitating repeated hospital stays and that the care facilities in the receiving country were precarious.

The benchmarks would thus appear to be the state of the illness and the conditions in the country of origin. Importantly, it was implicitly held that although the illness might, upon the return, become more manifest and that although interruption of the medication would result in the acceleration of the illness, return would not, ipso facto, amount to a breach of Article 3. This includes the assumption that the level of treatment in Uganda is well below the level of treatment in Finland – meaning that the emphasis lies with the *possibility* of treatment in general, not the *level* of treatment. Likewise, in the 1999 case of *SCC* v. *Sweden*[29] relevant considerations were the recent and early diagnosis and treatment, the availability of treatment in the receiving country, and the fact that relatives of the applicant lived there. This underscores that the Court makes an overall assessment, taking into account all the circumstances surrounding the case.

Departure to Seek Medical Assistance

Finally, it might be argued that a "right to health" imposes a duty on states not to prevent residents from trying to obtain essential health care, goods, and services beyond state borders if they are not available at home. This issue was discussed at a September 2000 expert meeting,[30] focusing on paragraph 39 of the CESCR's General Comment, in which the Committee deals with the notion that "States parties have to respect the enjoyment of the right to health in other countries." There was general consensus among the experts, based on the submissions by Professor Cees Flinterman, that the paragraph concerned may amount to a right to seek these services abroad – i.e., the right to leave one's country – but does not include the right to have one's country of origin pay for services not available at home, nor that access to health services in another country should be automatic or free. Of course, the migrant may be able to purchase services outside his or her country of origin, and persons frequently undertake international travel for precisely this reason.

CONCLUSIONS

The right to health as a concept has as yet not firmly matured into a consistently applicable, enforceable concept, much less a transportable one.

Developments indicate that minimum services (primary health care) need to be provided to persons within a state, irrespective of immigrant status. This is based more on pragmatic economic and public health rationales for such access to primary

---

[29] 46553/99.

[30] The expert meeting – with participation of experts from IOM, WHO, the ECHR, the judiciary, academia, and the executive – mainly focused on the return issue. Medical experts, economists, and, of great interest, experts in ethics (both migration and medical) contributed. The end-result was a publication that favors a multidisciplinary approach: Van Krieken, *supra* note 8. The above paragraph on the General Comment (GC) is based on pp. 47-48 of Van Krieken; the GC itself can be found there on pp. 48-67.

health care than on the rights-based framework of various human right conventions. Furthermore, states are generally entitled to limit entry to their territory; health-related reasons for denying admission and residence are common state practice; and access to local social welfare may be limited in the contractual relationship between a community and newcomers. There is no basis for a claim that a difference in health services in the country of origin and the country of settlement alone can give rise to a legitimate expectation of a right to enter and reside in a state not one's own. Developing norms may suggest that long-settled immigrants are entitled to health-care benefits and services on terms provided generally to citizens, and expulsion of persons with a long-term residence permit solely because they are ill is not permitted. Finally, cases in which non-citizens contest expulsion based on a claim of illness and lack of facilities in the country of origin are likely to succeed only under special circumstances.

The health-migration interface deserves to be elaborated upon, at the legislative and policy frameworks level, as well as in immigration and health care standards of practice. As that effort continues, two frameworks for analysis will need to be utilized. The first is the moral imperative reflected in human rights law. The second is the new knowledge that modern public health science has brought to bear on previous theories that have governed immigration control in the past.

INTERNATIONAL COOPERATIVE EFFORTS

Chapter 18

ILLUSTRATION OF MULTILATERAL, REGIONAL AND BILATERAL COOPERATIVE ARRANGEMENTS IN THE MANAGEMENT OF MIGRATION

International Organization for Migration

INTRODUCTION

In recent years, migration has featured highly on the agendas of a number of international, regional, and subregional bodies. Governments of states of origin, transit, and destination increasingly employ cooperative arrangements and agreements in addressing such concerns as reducing the causes of irregular migration, regulating entry and stay, safeguarding basic human rights of migrants, and promoting democracy while giving impetus to economic development. These cooperative arrangements address a broad array of migration concerns and take the shape of bilateral and multilateral arrangements, including those of a regional nature.

Other chapters discuss interstate cooperation in the management of migration found in international conventions and instruments. This chapter highlights other types of arrangements, primarily of a more informal and non-binding nature, intended, *inter alia*, to regularize migratory movements and facilitate cross-border flows. They take the form of memoranda of understanding, statutes, plans of action, and declarations.

The sheer number and variety of these arrangements, and the difficulty of access to some (particularly bilateral agreements), makes it infeasible to provide a comprehensive catalogue of all the existing arrangements. Consequently, this paper provides an overview of the major types of cooperative arrangements utilized by states today in managing migration and includes illustrations of each.

GENERAL CHARACTERISTICS OF MULTILATERAL, REGIONAL, AND BILATERAL MANAGEMENT ARRANGEMENTS

Multilateral Arrangements

Multilateral arrangements are a classic tool used by states in shaping their conduct towards one another through reaching understandings with regard to a particular

T.A. Aleinikoff and V. Chetail (Eds.), Migration and International Legal Norms
© 2003, T.M.C. ASSER PRESS, The Hague, The Netherlands, et al.

subject matter. In the field of migration, this approach offers to states of origin, transit, and destination the opportunity for dialogue and the possibility for multilateral coordination leading to common policies and practice.

As an example, one of the first multilateral arrangements concerning the movement of persons was concluded by the Nordic States in 1954, establishing the Common Nordic Labor Market.[1] Through this arrangement, nationals are granted permission to work in any one of the Member States without a work permit – thereby allowing for the free movement of labor. Progress achieved by this arrangement led to the Benelux Economic Union that ensures the free movement of persons, goods, capital, and services between the Member States (discussed below under the section concerned with trade).

The majority of multilateral arrangements currently adopted by states to address migration take the form of non-binding Declarations or Plans of Action endorsed by consensus at the conclusion of an international conference.

Regional Arrangements

In the absence of a global migration regime during the 1990s, multilateral arrangements with a regional focus in the form of Regional Consultative Processes (RCPs) have emerged as viable mechanisms of cooperation intended to enhance the management of migration, particularly that of irregular migration. RCPs offer distinct frameworks for addressing issues of common concern to participating states of individual geographical regions. Presently, RCPs exist in the Americas, Europe, East and South Asia, and Africa. They are especially important in light of their focus on information sharing and by reflecting regional understandings and facilitating consistency in adopting strategies leading to regional solutions. To date, most Plans of Action or other conclusions adopted by consensus emanating from RCPs are informal and non-binding – these features constitute key factors attracting states' participation in these processes.

Bilateral Arrangements

Early arrangements regulating international migration date back to the late eighteenth and nineteenth century. These bilateral treaties in consular agreements or treaties of Friendship, Commerce and Navigation (FCN) were concerned primarily with trade between nations, based on the principle of most favored nation treatment. They also provided a right to enter ports of the territories of each party wherever foreign commerce was permitted in order to attend to commercial affairs and a limited right of establishment or residence by the citizens of State Parties.[2] These early

---

[1] They include Denmark, Finland, Norway, and Sweden. See S. Collinson, *Europe and International Migration* Royal Institute of International Affairs (1993).

[2] See for instance, the Treaty of Commerce and Navigation between Argentina and the United States of 27 July 1853; between Austria-Hungary and the United States of 27 August 1829, Treaty of Friendship, Limits, and Navigation Between Spain and the United States of 27 October 1795; Peace, Friendship, Limits, and Settlement between the United States and Mexico, 2 February 1848; Jay's Treaty of

bilateral agreements regulating movement of natural persons linked with economic activities are the precursors to those currently being developed multilaterally pursuant to the General Agreement on Trade in Services (GATS) with respect to the temporary movement of service providers.

For many years, cooperation between governments in the management of migration has taken place through bilateral arrangements. These arrangements effectively manage migration flows due to their adaptation to the particular interests of the parties concerned and to their possibilities for concrete results. In the area of labor migration, for instance, bilateral agreements emerged in the 1960s and 1970s as the most frequent tool employed by western European states facing serious labor shortages and labor-supplying states willing to supply temporary migrant workers. A review of the use of bilateral arrangements shows there has been a steady increase in the number concluded from 1950 through 1990 and an unprecedented burst since 1991.

ILLUSTRATION OF VARIOUS TYPES OF ARRANGEMENTS

Multilateral Arrangements

Numerous international conferences were convened in the 1990s to address migration, either exclusively or as part of consideration of other subjects. Global conferences such as the 2001 Durban World Conference Against Racism, Racial Discrimination Xenophobia and Related Intolerance, and the 2002 Johannesburg World Summit on Social Development, regularly and increasingly include in the Declarations or Plans of Action, adopted by consensus at the conclusion of the conference, sections or paragraphs devoted to migration issues. These non-binding declarations of the views of or calls to action for the international community reflect the increasing importance of migration on the international policy agenda.

Chapter X of the Cairo Programme of Action

None of the recent multilateral statements on migration is as comprehensive or focused as that adopted at the International Conference on Population and Development held in Cairo, 5-13 September 1994 (UN ICPD).[3] Chapter X of the Programme of Action[4] is devoted to migration, refugees, asylum-seekers, and displaced persons.

Amity, Commerce and Navigation between Britain and the United States of 19 November 1794. *http:/ /www.yale.edu/lawweb/avalon/amerdipl.htm*.

[3] The Conference was attended by representatives of 183 states and numerous intergovernmental organizations, and NGOs. The participants heard over 230 speakers, including 155 UN Member States and observers, 24 UN agencies, programmes, and funds, 15 intergovernmental organizations, and 37 non-governmental organizations. See, http://www.iisd.ca/linkages/cairo.html.

[4] The Programme of Action of the UN ICPD, a non-binding declaration adopted by consensus by the 183 participating states, builds on the international consensus developed at the World Population Conference at Bucharest in 1974 and the International Conference on Population at Mexico City in 1984 on the need to consider the broad issues of and interrelationships between population, sustained economic growth, and sustainable development.

It offers a comprehensive overview of the challenges linked to the movement of persons. The objectives under Chapter X include cooperation: to address the root causes of undocumented migration; to reduce substantially the number of undocumented migrants, while ensuring that those in need of international protection receive it; to prevent the exploitation of undocumented migrants and to ensure that their basic human rights are protected; to prevent all international trafficking in migrants, especially for the purposes of prostitution; and to ensure protection against racism, ethnocentrism, and xenophobia.[5]

In Chapter X, participating states noted that international migration policies need to take into account economic constraints of the receiving country, the impact of migration on the host society, and its effects on states of origin. Chapter X presents the advantage of a balanced approach to the needs and obligations of states of origin, transit, and destination, as well as to the rights and obligations of migrants. For instance, documented migrants are described as "those who satisfy all the legal requirements to enter, stay and, if applicable, hold employment in the country of destination." In light of their status, the UN ICPD recognizes that the integration of documented migrants into the host society is generally desirable, and consequently, it is important to extend to them the same social, economic, and legal rights as those enjoyed by citizens, in accordance with national legislation. Moreover, the UN ICPD supports the view that family reunification of documented migrants is an important factor in international migration. Also important is the protection of documented migrants and their families from racism, ethnocentrism, and xenophobia, and respect of the physical integrity, dignity, religious beliefs, and cultural values. Additionally, the UN ICPD specified the benefits of documented migration to the host country, and remittances of documented migrants to their states of origin as a very important source of foreign currency contributing to improving the well-being of relatives in the states of origin.[6]

The UN ICPD describes undocumented or irregular migrants as "persons who do not fulfill the requirements established by the country of destination to enter, stay or exercise an economic activity." The UN ICPD expressed the position that "[i]t is the right of every nation State to decide who can enter and stay in its territory and under what conditions. Such right, however, should be exercised taking care to avoid racist or xenophobic actions and policies."[7]

Despite regular reference to the Conference's achievements, the implementation of the various recommendations remains limited. This effort to establish a firm international cooperative platform to tackle migration management challenges remains the most significant contribution at the global level to understanding the complexities of migration and to addressing migration comprehensively but has not resulted in the convening of an international conference on migration.[8]

---

[5] Id. at Point 10.16.

[6] Id. at Point 10.9.

[7] Id. at Point 10.15.

[8] Five years after the UN ICPD, a review was conducted in New York in June 1999, referred to as UN ICPD + 5. The outcome document entitled "Proposals for Key Actions for the Further Implementation of the Programme of Action of the International Conference on Population and Development"

Regional Arrangements – Regional Consultative Processes on Migration

Multilateral arrangements in the migration field with a regional focus – referred to generally as Regional Consultative Processes (RCPs) – follow in large measure the suggested objectives and actions set forth under Chapter X of the Cairo Programme of Action. RCPs emphasize a cooperative, non-binding approach to migration management based on dialogue and shared interests.[9] Usually launched through an international conference focused on a particular migration issue or phenomenon of concern to participating states, RCPs have become, in most instances, on-going fora for the exchange of information and exploration of common approaches to the management of migration. In most cases, RCPs are not constituted under United Nations auspices or as part of a treaty body and any understandings reached are not legally binding.

Europe

The CIS Conference Process was launched in 1996 following endorsement by UN General Assembly Resolution 50/151 of 1995 calling on the UN High Commissioner for Refugees (UNHCR) to convene a regional conference to address the problems of refugees, displaced persons, other forms of involuntary displacement, and returnees in the states of the Commonwealth of Independent States and relevant neighboring states. Spearheaded by Russia, the UNHCR, the International Organization for Migration (IOM), the Organization for Security and Cooperation in Europe (OSCE) and its Office for Democratic Institutions and Human Rights (ODIHR), the CIS Conference Process adopted a Programme of Action in May 1996.[10]

The Programme of Action includes measures aimed at establishing national migration systems and developing appropriate policies and operational activities; preventive measures to address the causes of possible displacement; measures strengthening international cooperation and cooperation with the relevant international organizations and non-governmental organizations; and the implementation and follow-up of activities in order to ensure the sustainability of the Conference process. One of the distinctive features of the CIS Conference Process is its emphasis on NGO participation and the development of local NGO capacity.[11]

---

was considered to be an important achievement. An entire section (section C) of the document is devoted to international migration. For more information and the relevant documents, see http://www.unfpa.org/icpd/index.htm.

[9] See generally, A. Klekowski von Koppenfels, *The Role of Regional Consultative Processes in Managing International Migration*, IOM Migration Research Series No. 3, May 2001 (hereinafter "Klekowski").

[10] CIS CONF/1996/6/Suppl. 11 June 1996, UNHCR, Geneva 1996, points 4 and 5 of Declaration. The participating states are: Armenia, Azerbaijan, Belarus, Georgia, Kazakstan, Kyrgyzstan, Moldova, the Russian Federation, Tajikistan, Turkmenistan, Ukraine, and Uzbekistan. See also "The CIS Conference on Refugees and Migrants," UNHCR Refugees Magazine, 1 May 1996, available at www.unhcr.ch.

[11] Id. at 21-22.

The Budapest Group was launched in 1991 with an immediate aim of preventing illegal migration from eastern and central Europe toward western Europe and establishing sustainable systems for orderly migration in the wider European region.[12] Although the initial meeting focused on border control and preventing East-West irregular migration, the Budapest Process has gradually expanded its focus to the management of irregular migration, including the smuggling of migrants. The 1997 Prague Ministerial Conference of the Budapest Group adopted non-binding recommendations covering the following areas: harmonization of legislation to combat trafficking in aliens; pre-entry and entry control, in particular the approximation of visa regimes; return to country of origin and readmission agreements; information exchange on illegal migration; technical and financial assistance to Central and Eastern European states; and linkage between trafficking in aliens and other forms of organized crime. In the autumn of 2001, a working group emerged on asylum and irregular migration.[13]

Americas

Launched in 1996 in Puebla, Mexico, the first Regional Conference on Migration (RCM) endeavored to sketch integrated migration management approaches to issues of relevance to the region.[14] The second RCM, in Panama in 1997, established the Regional Consultative Group, commonly referred to as the Puebla Process, and adopted a Plan of Action to advance toward a better administration of migratory phenomenon.[15] The Puebla Plan of Action calls for cooperation in exchanging information on migration policies, addressing the links between migration and development, combating migrant trafficking, cooperating on the return of extra-regional migrants, respecting human rights, and promoting technical cooperation.[16] The fourth RCM in El Salvador in 1999 focused on migration issues related to hurricane Mitch, while the fifth RCM held in March 2000 in the United States (Washington), reaffirmed the participating states cooperative undertaking.

---

[12] Participants are: Albania, Australia, Austria, Belarus, Belgium, Bosnia and Herzegovina, Bulgaria, Canada, Croatia, Cyprus, Czech Republic, Denmark, Estonia, Finland, France, Georgia, Germany, Greece, Hungary, Iceland, Ireland, Italy, Latvia, Liechtenstein, Lithuania, FYR Macedonia, Malta, Moldova, the Netherlands, Norway, Poland, Portugal, Romania, Russian Federation, Slovakia, Slovenia, Spain, Sweden, Switzerland, Turkey, Ukraine, United Kingdom, the United States, and the European Commission. The International Centre for Migration Policy Development (ICMPD) in Vienna is in charge of the Secretariat of the Budapest process. For more information, see www.icmpd.org.

[13] Klekowski, *supra* note 9, at 10.

[14] Representatives of the following states attended this first conference: Belize, Canada, Costa Rica, El Salvador, Guatemala, Honduras, Mexico, Nicaragua, Panama, and the United States. Representatives of the IOM, the Economic Commission for Latin America and the Caribbean (ECLAC), the Inter-American Development Bank (IDB), and UNHCR also participated. See the "Joint Communiqué, Regional Conference on Migration," at www.rcmvs.org.

[15] The Member States are: Belize, Canada, Costa Rica, Dominican Republic, El Salvador, Guatemala, Honduras, Mexico, Nicaragua, Panama, and the United States.

[16] The third RCM, in Canada in February 1998, focused on the return of extra-regional migrants and the reintegration of regional migrants.

The Puebla Process was initially intended to serve as a forum for dialogue and exchange of information on the movement of extra-regional migrants transiting through the region to the United States and Canada. It has since expanded its scope of engagement by including technical cooperation activities. Indeed, the positive experience of the Puebla Process in mobilizing resources and stimulating concrete action in response to the displacements caused by Hurricane Mitch has served not only to strengthen the Puebla Process itself, but also to inspire other RCPs to look at possible concrete action based on the relationships and understandings forged through these informal fora.

Using as theme "Towards Regional Solidarity in Security and Migration," the seventh RCM took place in Antigua, Guatemala, in May 2002. The participants acknowledged the important role played by migration policies in the area of regional security, as well as the need to adopt essential actions for the security of the region within a framework of full respect for the human rights of migrants, particularly in terms of distinguishing positive and beneficial migration flows. To this end, they approved a Declaration Against Terrorism and recommended that Member States of the RCM sign, ratify, and implement the United Nations Convention against Transnational Organized Crime, as well as the two supplementary Protocols: Protocol to Prevent, Suppress and Punish Trafficking in Persons, Particularly Women and Children; and the Protocol Against Smuggling of Migrants by Land, Sea and Air.[17]

The South American Migration Dialogue, also known as the Lima Process, started in Lima, Peru, in July 1999, brings together annually representatives from South American states to exchange views on the migration situation in their states and to open up channels for dialogue and cooperation. In an effort to consolidate and apply in South America progress achieved at the regional level, participants adopted the Lima Declaration. This document sets forth the resolve of the group to monitor migration trends in the region to analyze and cooperate in order to find solutions consistent with the interests of the countries involved.

A Final Declaration and Plan of Action was endorsed by the participants at the Third South American Conference on Migration held in August 2002 in Ecuador. Under this Declaration, the participants reaffirmed, *inter alia*, their commitment and the will of their governments to promote safe migration and to strengthen the mechanisms to combat illegal trafficking of persons. They also expressed their resolve to establish a New International Migratory Order, structured according to certain fundamental concepts including: shared responsibility between states of origin and destination over migration; the fight against illegal trafficking of persons; and linking the phenomenon of international migration more closely to the processes of overall development. The Plan of Action provides for various activities geared at strengthening the ability of the participating states to manage migration problems.[18]

---

[17] http://www.rcmvs.org/RCM_in_brief.doc.

[18] Representatives of the following states attended the meeting: Argentina, Bolivia, Brazil, Colombia, Chile, Ecuador, Guyana, Paraguay, Peru, Uruguay, and Venezuela.

Asia-Pacific

Two RCPs are operating in East and Southeast Asia. The Manila Process was launched by the IOM through a 1996 conference addressing problems linked to migrant trafficking and irregular migration in the region. The Inter-Governmental Asia-Pacific Consultations on Refugees, Displaced Persons and Migrants (APC), was also established in 1996, and is cosponsored by the IOM and the UNHCR. The Manila Process brings together states of the region[19] to address migrant trafficking and irregular migration. At the initial conference, participants expressed an interest not only in the prevention and control of trafficking, but also in root causes of migration, particularly linked to issues of development. The APC provides governments of Asia and Oceania[20] with a forum for consultations on a broad range of issues concerning population movements in the region, including those of refugees and displaced persons. The two processes were strengthened by the ministerial-level International Symposium on Migration entitled "Towards Regional Cooperation on Irregular/Undocumented Migration," which brought together representatives of Asian states in Bangkok on 23 April 1999, to consider international migration within the context of regional cooperation on irregular migration. The Bangkok Declaration on Irregular Migration was adopted at this meeting and provides, *inter alia*, that migration, particularly irregular migration, should be addressed in a comprehensive and balanced manner, considering its causes, manifestations, and effects, both positive and negative, in the states of origin, transit, and destination; orderly management of migration, particularly irregular migration and trafficking, will require the concerted efforts of states concerned; regular migration and irregular migration should not be considered in isolation from each other; and in order to achieve the benefits of regular migration and reduce the costs of irregular migration, the capacity of states to manage movement of people should be enhanced through information sharing and technical and financial assistance.[21]

The Bali Ministerial Conference on People Smuggling, Trafficking in Persons and Related Transnational Crime, held in Bali in February 2002, offered an unprecedented opportunity for officials from the extended region of Asia (including Turkey) to exchange information and to examine new strategies that could be implemented to combat smuggling and trafficking.[22] Additionally, other topics were discussed including the root causes of irregular movement and how to build on existing efforts to curb such movement of people; and the Afghan refugee crisis and immigration administration issues. The participants agreed that two ad-hoc experts' groups (one on international and regional cooperation with New Zealand serving as

---

[19] Representatives of the following states attended the meeting: Australia, Bangladesh, Brunei Darussalam, Cambodia, China, Indonesia, Japan, Republic of Korea, Lao PDR, Malaysia, Myanmar, New Zealand, Papua New Guinea, the Philippines, Singapore, Sri Lanka, Thailand, and Vietnam, as well as the Hong Kong Special Administrative Region participated in the meeting.

[20] Id.

[21] http://www.thaiembdc.org/info/bdim.html.

[22] Cohosted by Indonesia and Australia, a total of thirty-four ministers attended the conference from thirty-eight states in the Asia Pacific, the Middle East, and other regions, as well as the United Nations Transnational Administration in East Timor (UNTAET), IOM, and UNHCR.

coordinator; the other on policy issues, legal frameworks, and law enforcement issues, with the Kingdom of Thailand serving as coordinator) would be established for follow-up purposes.

Africa

In West Africa, the Regional Consultative Process known as the Dakar Process was launched in collaboration with IOM, the Economic Community of West African States (ECOWAS), and the West African Economic and Monetary Union (UEMOA), through the West African Ministerial Meeting on the Participation of Migrants in the Development of their Country of Origin held in October 2000.[23] The Dakar Declaration that emerged from this meeting reflects the region's concern with migration and the promotion and maintenance of peace and stability in the region. The Dakar Declaration focuses on the protection of migrants and the effective channeling of remittances toward activities that can enhance economic development.[24] Follow-up proposals were adopted by ECOWAS governments at the meeting.

The first step towards the implementation of the Dakar Declaration and follow-up proposals were achieved through a seminar organized jointly by IOM and the International Migration Policy Programme (IMP) on 8–21 December 2001. The seminar focused on government capacity building in migration policy development and management based on regional cooperation.[25]

At an October 2002 meeting sponsored jointly by the IOM and ECOWAS, in Dakar, Senegal, the implementation of the Dakar Declaration and follow-up process was established as the Migration Dialogue for West Africa (MIDWA).[26] The general goal of this RCP is to enhance regional harmonization in migration management toward economic development. MIDWA's objectives are to: combat trafficking in persons; address issues linked to labor migration; monitor the activities of the Permanent Observatory for West African International Migration (in data gathering); and promote peace and stability in West Africa.

Migration and Dialogue for Southern Africa (MIDSA) was created in 2000 from a technical cooperation workshop for senior government officials from the thirteen

---

[23] Representatives of the following states attended the meeting: Burkina Faso, Cape Verde, Cote d'Ivoire, The Gambia, Guinea, Guinea-Bissau, Liberia, Mali, Niger, Nigeria, Senegal, Sierra-Leone, and Togo. Representatives of the following additional states attended the meeting as observers: Belgium, France, Italy, the Netherlands, Portugal, United Kingdom, Spain, Switzerland, and the United States.

[24] Klekowski, *supra* note 9, at 15. See also http://www.iom.int/africandiaspora/pdf/Dkr%20Declaration_eng_131000.pdf

[25] Representatives of sixty states attended the seminar including the fifteen Member States of ECOWAS: Benin, Burkina Faso, Cape Verde, Ivory Coast, Gambia, Ghana, Guinea, Guinea-Bissau, Liberia, Mali, Niger, Nigeria, Senegal, Sierra-Leone, and Togo and Mauritania, together with fifty international experts, representatives of international institutions and Government observers from Belgium, France, Italy, the Netherlands, Portugal, South Africa, Switzerland, and the Unites States.

[26] Representatives of the following states participated at this meeting: Benin, Burkina Faso, Cape Verde, Côte d'Ivoire, Gambia, Ghana, Guinea, Guinea-Bissau, Liberia, Mali, Mauritania, Niger, Nigeria, Senegal, Sierra Leone, and Togo. International organizations directly involved are: ECOWAS jointly with IOM and ILO, UNHCR, WFP, OCHA, UNICEF, UNAIDS, IMP, OAU, and UEMOA.

Southern African governments of the Southern African Development Community (SADC) on migration management.[27] Hosted by the IOM, the United Nations Institute for Training and Research (UNITAR), and the International Migration Policy Programme (IMP), participants recognized the need "to develop, in conjunction with the Southern African Development Community (SADC), a forum for further exchange of information, experience and perspective among Governments on migration policy and practice, to facilitate cooperation." Themes of common interest explored through MIDSA by means of technical cooperation training and information sharing include border control and labor migration.

Inter-regional

The development in October 2002 of the Western Mediterranean Conference on Migration (5 + 5 Dialogue), involving five European states of transit and destination on the northern shore of the Mediterranean and five North African states of origin on the southern shore,[28] offers an example of efforts to improve understanding of migration dynamics across regions. The 5+5 Dialogue shared information and best practices, and explored common principles for cooperation in managing cross-regional flows while tackling issues relating to migration and development (the role of diaspora, labor migration, integration). The Tunis Declaration[29] calls for information exchange and analysis of migration trends toward the following objectives: reinforcing cooperation to prevent and combat illegal migration including trafficking in human beings; supporting comprehensive development efforts so as to prevent illegal migration; reinforcing the integration process in host states, and protecting human rights and fundamental freedoms of migrants while emphasizing migrants' duties and obligations.[30]

The Inter-Governmental Consultations on Asylum, Refugee and Migration Policies in Europe, North America and Australia (IGC) (1985)[31] emerged from a meeting organized by the IOM and the UNHCR to consider issues relevant to "The Arrivals of Asylum-Seekers and Refugees in Europe." The IGC has expanded its areas of interest since that time, but remains an informal, non-decision-making forum focused on information exchange and discussion of policy directions among the participating governments. The IGC's areas of interest include: entry, border control, labor migration, refugees, asylum, country of origin information, data, return, irregular migration, smuggling and trafficking, and technology.[32] While neither decision-making nor operational in focus, this forum is regarded as the most established

---

[27] Southern African Migration Project – MIDSA (http://www.queensu.ca/samp/MIDSA.htm)

[28] Representatives of the following states attended the meeting: Algeria, France, Italy, Libya, Malta, Morocco, Mauritania, Spain, Tunisia, and Portugal.

[29] The Tunis Declaration is available at www.iom.int.

[30] Ibid.

[31] The participating states are: Australia, Austria, Belgium, Canada, Denmark, Finland, Germany, Ireland, Italy, the Netherlands, Norway, Spain, Sweden, Switzerland, the United Kingdom, and the United States. The European Commission, IOM and UNHCR participated as observers.

[32] Klekowski, *supra* note 9, at 9-10.

consultative mechanism on migration and has certainly influenced both understanding of migration issues and the policy direction of the participating states.

The Asian-African Legal Consultative Organization (AALCO) was established in New Delhi, India, (originally as the Asian-African Legal Consultative Committee) as an outcome of the Conference of Afro-Asian Nations, in Indonesia on April 1955.[33] The AALCO is an advisory body to its member governments in the field of international law and serves as a forum for Asian-African cooperation in legal matters. The protection of migrant workers has appeared as an agenda item at every annual session of the AALCO since 1991. Regular annual discussions on the subject have culminated in the submission by the Secretariat in June 2001 of a Draft Model Agreement. This Draft establishes a legal framework for cooperation between AALCO Member States in matters relating to migrant workers between states of origin and states of destination-employment and more effectively prevents and combats transnational crime, including trafficking and smuggling, while furthering the protection of the human rights of migrant workers. Membership adoption of the agreement would establish a mechanism for cooperation in the management of migration. It is anticipated that the Draft Model Agreement will be the subject of debates at the next annual session of the AALCO scheduled for March 2003.

The third Asia-Europe Ministerial Conference on Cooperation for the Management of Migratory Flows between Europe and Asia (ASEM) was held in Lanzarote, Spain, in April 2002.[34] Views were exchanged on recent trends in migratory movements between Asia and Europe; and the need to reach mutual understanding with the view to address migration in a comprehensive and balanced manner, considering its causes, manifestations, and effects. Several conclusions reached at other regional processes on migration were reiterated at the conclusion of the conference.[35] They include the need to further strengthen economic cooperation; narrow the gap between the developed and developing ASEM members, and thus eradicate the root of illegal immigration; cooperate in fighting against illegal immigration among ASEM members; establish a regular cooperative system for exchanging information; and seize the criminals organizing illegal immigration.[36] The Ministers noted progress achieved in the management of migration through regional efforts and agreed to present the results of this conference at the Fourth Asia-Europe Summit (ASEM 4) in Copenhagen, Denmark, in September 2003.

---

[33] Member States in Africa are: Botswana, Egypt, Gambia, Ghana, Libya, Mauritius, Nigeria, Senegal, Sierra Leone, Somalia, Sudan, Tanzania, and Uganda. In Asia they are: Bahrain, Bangladesh, China, India, Indonesia, Iran, Iraq, Japan, Jordan, Korea (DPR), Korea (R.), Kuwait, Malaysia, Mongolia, Myanmar, Nepal, Oman, Pakistan, Palestine, Philippines, Qatar, Saudi Arabia, Singapore, Sri Lanka, Syria, Thailand, United Arab Emirates, and Yemen. In the European Union they are Cyprus and Turkey. Permanent observers are two: Australia and New Zealand. See http://www.aalco.org.

[34] They include the fifteen EU Member States and 10 Asian states: Brunei, China, Indonesia, Japan, South Korea, Malaysia, the Philippines, Singapore, Thailand and Vietnam (http://europa.eu.int/comm/external_relations/asem/intro/).

[35] The Declaration of the ASEM Conference on Cooperation for the Management of Migratory Flows between Europe and Asia is available at http://europa.eu.int/comm/external_relations/asem/min_other_meeting/mig.htm.

[36] Id.

THEMATIC ARRANGEMENTS

The following section presents a number of migration management themes that are the subject of interstate cooperative arrangements.

Refugees

A few examples exist of regional initiatives forging concrete durable solutions to problems linked to refugees and population displacement. The achievements of these initiatives serve as models to further inter-agency and inter-governmental collaboration, to promote protection and serve the needs of migrants and the uprooted, and to facilitate durable solutions. Two of these models will be discussed below – the Comprehensive Plan of Action for Indo-Chinese Refugees (CPA) and the International Conference on Central American Refugees (CIREFCA) – as they constitute innovative cooperative solutions to international humanitarian crises.

The Comprehensive Plan of Action for Indo-Chinese Refugees

The CPA was adopted following an International Conference on Indo-Chinese Refugees convened by the Association of Southeast Asian (ASEAN) nations. The Conference was held in close cooperation with the UNHCR and other states concerned with the problems posed by the continuing exodus by sea into the South-East Asian region of large numbers of refugees and asylum-seekers from Vietnam and the Lao People's Democratic Republic. The objective was to adopt a comprehensive and solutions-oriented approach to this humanitarian crisis, and to study the push-off policies of some governments.[37]

A series of multilateral consultations brought together representatives of states most directly concerned by the continuing outflow of Indo-Chinese refugees. A Declaration and a Comprehensive Plan of Action were adopted as the basis of a comprehensive approach and durable solution to the continuing problem of Indo-Chinese asylum-seekers and refugees. The Comprehensive Plan of Action covered various aspects of the Indo-Chinese refugee problem, including the question of clandestine departures, regular departure programs, reception of new arrivals, refugee status, and the promotion and implementation of durable solutions, notably resettlement and repatriation. A coordinating committee established detailed modalities for its implementation.

The CPA stands as a striking example of the use of a conference to forge an international consensus on solutions to a pressing international humanitarian problem. The CPA established the international, regional, and bilateral frameworks that reoriented migratory trends in the region. While not legally binding, the CPA secured the commitment of regional governments to permit persons arriving by boat to disem-

---

[37] See, Office of the United Nations High Commissioner for Refugees: International Conference on Indo-Chinese Refugees. Report of the Secretary-General [Annex: Declaration and Comprehensive Plan of Action (CPA)]. For many documents relevant to the CPA see http://www.unhcr.ch/.

bark on coastal land, and to have access to housing and care pending resolution of their refugee claims. The CPA required resettlement states to accept for resettlement those determined to be refugees, and required the states of origin to accept the return without retribution of those found not to be in need of international protection. A confluence of humanitarian and political imperatives created the will of the international community to solve this particular pattern of outflows.

The International Conference on Central American Refugees (CIREFCA)

The International Conference on Central American Refugees, known by its Spanish acronym CIREFCA, was convened in May 1989 by the governments of Central America and Mexico in collaboration with the UNHCR and the United Nations Development Programme (UNDP) to examine needs and specific proposals for practical solutions to refugee problems. The seven participating governments of the region committed to the goal of linking emergency assistance to ongoing development plans through coordination between the UNHCR and the UNDP.[38]

CIREFCA addressed problems related to the regional crisis caused by the movement of approximately two million people, including refugees, displaced persons, and returnees in the aftermath of the conflicts in El Salvador, Guatemala, and Nicaragua throughout the 1980s. The Conference was convened to initiate a process leading to durable solutions to these population displacements. Launched as a Conference, CIREFCA became an initiative connected with the ongoing peace process in the region and lasted two additional years (until 1994) permitting more time to achieve its goals beyond the three years originally envisaged.

CIREFCA represents the culmination of a series of earlier efforts to extend protection to refugees. Taking into consideration the 1984 Cartagena Declaration, which reflects the expanded definition of a refugee of the 1974 Organization of African Unity's refugee convention, CIREFCA reinforced the broad protection needs of refugees within the particular regional context of that time. As an arrangement offering a forum for dialogue in a war-torn region, CIREFCA achieved many of its goals effectively and constitutes an example for its political contribution in furthering peace and reconciliation, and in promoting protection of and long-term solutions for refugees, displaced persons, and returnees.

Border Management

Border management involves facilitating authorized flows of business people, tourists, migrants, and refugees and the detection and prevention of illegal entry of aliens into a given country. Increasingly, states, especially those that share borders, cooperate in identifying irregular and unauthorized entries. Measures to manage

---

[38] The seven participating regional governments were: Belize, Costa Rica, El Salvador, Guatemala, Honduras, Mexico, and Nicaragua. The conference attracted attention at the highest political levels in Central America, and in international donor states, the concerned agencies of the UN system and nongovernmental organizations – both international and local academics and refugees themselves (http://www.refugees.org/world/articles/centralamerica_wrs93.htm).

borders include the imposition by states of visa requirements, carrier sanctions against transportation companies bringing irregular aliens to the territory, and interdiction at sea.[39] At the European Union (EU) level, the 1985 Schengen Agreement[40] and the 1990 Convention Implementing the Schengen Agreement[41] developed practical implementing measures to abolish internal borders and to achieve the free movement of persons. The aim of the free circulation area[42] essentially translates into not being required to present a valid travel document when moving within Schengen territory.

The 1985 Schengen Agreement offers a framework, setting out short-term and long-term measures that would have to be undertaken, while defining the major issues, goals, and means of enhancing cooperation in the areas listed under the Agreement: free movement of persons, protection of public order and public safety, combating drug trading and illegal entry. The 1990 Schengen Implementing Convention sets the objective of free circulation within the Schengen Member States while at the same time counterbalancing measures such as external border controls, a common visa policy, police and judicial cooperation, and information exchange.

The Schengen Agreements abolished the control of identity cards and passports for crossing the internal frontiers between the Member States of the Schengen

---

[39] See generally, Art. 2.1 of the Declaration on the Human Rights of Individuals Who Are Not Nationals of the Country in Which They Live, GA Res. 40/144 13 (1985) reaffirming states' prerogative to allow or deny entry. See also G.S. Goodwin-Gill, "Migration: International Law and Human Rights," in Bimal Ghosh (ed.), *Managing Migration; Time for a New International Regime?* (2000) pp. 172-173.

[40] France and Germany had agreed to start an inter-governmental initiative to abolish border controls between both states by setting up the Schengen Agreement on 14 June 1985. Belgium, the Netherlands and Luxembourg, which had gained some experience in this field since the founding of the Benelux Economic Union in 1960, soon joined this initiative. The Agreement was supplemented by the Schengen Implementing Convention of 19 June 1990. The Schengen Member States are: Austria, Belgium, Denmark, France, Finland, Germany, Greece, Iceland, Italy, Luxembourg, the Netherlands, Norway, Portugal, Spain, and Sweden. For texts of the Schengen Agreement and the Convention Implementing the Schengen Agreement, see, http://www.auswaertiges-amt.de/www/en/willkommen/einreisebestimmungen/schengen_html.

[41] Participation in the Schengen Agreements is reserved only for Member States of the European Union. The Convention implementing the Schengen Agreement signed at Schengen on 19 June 1990 is subject to approval or ratification in accordance with the constitutional provisions of the State Parties. The Convention entered into force for Belgium, Germany, France, Luxembourg, and the Netherlands on 1 September 1993, for Portugal and Spain on 1 March 1994, for Italy on 1 July 1997, for Greece and Austria on 1 December 1997. Only two Member States of the EU, the UK and Ireland, remain outside the scope of the Schengen Agreements. Iceland and Norway, not being EU Member States and therefore not able to fully accede to the Schengen Convention signed "Cooperation Agreements" with the Schengen Executive Committee, enabling them to be an "associate member," without the right to decision. Iceland and Norway undertook, under this Agreement, all the obligations stemming from the Schengen Agreements and they also have the responsibility to guarantee at their frontier "the level of Schengen security." See http://www.fecl.org/circular/4302.htm.

[42] Art. 14.2 of the Treaty Establishing the European Community (EU Treaty) states that: "The internal market shall comprise an area without internal frontiers in which the free movement of goods, persons, services, and capital is ensured in accordance with the provisions of this Treaty." See, EU *Official Journal* C 340, 10 November 1997, pp. 173-308, also, http://www.eel.nl/treaties/cons2en.htm.

Agreement.[43] The Schengen Agreements also aim at reinforcing the security of citizens by improving police, judicial, and administrative cooperation between the Member States and establishing a common information system.[44]

In the Americas, the U.S.-Mexico Binational Commission was established in 1981 as a forum for regular cabinet-level exchanges between the two states on a wide range of issues, including border cooperation. On this subject, the two states have entered into an arrangement referred to as Border Liaison Mechanism (BLM). Launched in 1993, the BLM has matured into an effective tool to manage cases related to alien smuggling and violation of the border on both sides. The two states consider the BLM as a unique mechanism that enhances the ability of the United States and Mexico to resolve border issues in a cooperative and pragmatic manner.[45]

In January 2002, the U.S. government issued "Fact Sheet: Border, Security, Smart Borders for the twenty-first century that specifies the new approach to border management. The two principles are that air, land, and sea borders of the United States must provide a strong defense for the American people against all external threats, most importantly international terrorists; and that America's border must be highly efficient, posing little or no obstacle to all legitimate trade and travel.

Under the Smart Border scheme, the United States and Mexico entered into the U.S.-Mexico Border Partnership Action Plan which consists of a twenty-two point Agreement containing provisions to tackle various types of border concerns. For instance, point 6 deals with cross-border cooperation and revitalizing existing bilateral coordination mechanisms at the local, state, and federal levels, with a specific focus on operations at border crossing points. Under point 11, the parties reaffirmed their commitment to curb the smuggling of people, expand the Alien Smuggling and Trafficking Task Force, and establish a law enforcement liaison framework to enhance cooperation between United States and Mexican federal agencies along the U.S.-Mexico border.[46]

In December 2001, the United States and Canadian governments concluded an agreement to build a smart border for the twenty-first century. Border agencies from both countries have made significant progress in implementing key elements of the agreement. The agreement is based on the Canada-U.S. Smart Border Declaration wherein the two countries declared their commitments, *inter alia*, to work together to address threats to the public and their economic security; and develop a zone of confidence against terrorist activity, while creating a unique opportunity to build a

---

[43] See, in particular, Art. 2 of the Schengen Implementing Convention: "Internal borders may be crossed at any point without any checks on persons being carried out." The presentation of papers is abolished at internal borders for all nationals of the Schengen area as well as for nationals of third states. However, some security controls are still maintained. For insuring the security of the citizens, an identity control can take place close to the frontier at airports, ports, and railway stations that are open to external traffic.

[44] The Schengen Information System (SIS) deals with information concerning the entry of third country nationals, issuing visas, and police cooperation. See http://ue.eu.int.

[45] http://www.state.gov.

[46] http://www.state.gov/p/wha/rls/fs/8909.htm.

smart border for the twenty-first century that securely facilitates the free flow of people and commerce.[47]

The Central American Organization on Migration (OCAM) (for which IOM acts as an advisory and technical body) was established in 1990 by the Directors of Migration of Costa Rica, El Salvador, Guatemala, Honduras, Nicaragua, and Panama. OCAM's focus is to facilitate joint initiatives in the field of migration through the harmonization and standardization of policies and legislation on migration control that simultaneously facilitate border transit. The Information System on Migration in Central America (SICA), together with the virtual Secretariat, contribute to reinforce institutional coordination efforts on policies and procedures for sound migration management in the region.[48]

In Africa, the 1975 Economic Community of West African States (ECOWAS) adopted the Treaty of Lagos, which guarantees freedom of movement and residence, as well as equality of treatment in relation to cultural, religious, economic, professional, and social activities for nationals of all ratifying states. The 1979 Protocol to this Treaty entitles all citizens of ECOWAS to travel visa-free for a period of ninety days and to reside on the territory of any Member State.[49]

Through the Treaty Establishing the African Economic Community that entered into force on 12 May 1994, the Member States agreed to adopt necessary measures to achieve progressively the free movement of persons, and to ensure the enjoyment of the right to residence within the community.[50]

The Treaty of the Southern African Development Community (SADC) that entered into force on 5 October 1993 aims at developing policies toward the progressive elimination of obstacles to the free movement of persons, capital, and labor within the region. As a result, a Draft Protocol on the Free Movement of Persons in the Southern African Development Community (SADC) was announced in June 1995, and was replaced in 1997 by the Draft Protocol on the Facilitation of Movement of Persons in the Southern African Development Community. The 1997 Draft Protocol aims at: facilitating the movement of citizens of Member States within the region by gradually eliminating obstacles which impede such movement; expanding the network of bilateral agreements towards a multilateral regional agreement; cooperating in preventing the illegal movement of citizens of Member States and the illegal movement of nationals of third states within and into the region; cooperating in improving control over external borders of the SADC community; and promoting common policies on immigration matters. The Protocol has yet to be adopted due to diverging interests between states of origin and destination within the region.[51]

---

[47] http://www.dfait-maeci.gc.ca/anti-terrorism/declaration-en.asp.

[48] See generally International Organization for Migration, *The State of Migration Management in Central America* (2002).

[49] http://www.ecowas.int.

[50] http://www.dfa.gov.za/for-relations/multilateral/eccas.htm. See Chapter VI Art. 43.

[51] http://www.sadc.int/.

Arrangements for Return and Readmission of Persons without Authorization to Stay

There are numerous bilateral arrangements (and only a few multilateral arrangements) that provide for the orderly return of migrants to their states of origin. It is recognized under general international law principles that states have the right to remove aliens without authorization to stay, consistent with their international law obligations.[52] By the same token, states have an obligation to readmit their own nationals. This responsibility is reflected in various arrangements entered into by governments to provide for the readmission of their own nationals and is recognized by the UN General Assembly, including the need to facilitate the return of nationals who are not refugees.[53] Moreover, the right of an individual to return is enshrined under international law.[54]

Generally, states encounter few difficulties in returning irregular migrants, including rejected asylum-seekers, provided that their identity and citizenship are established and the country of origin agrees to readmit. However, problems arise when the country of origin refuses to accept returnees, imposes administrative and procedural requirements aimed at preventing returns, and irregular migrants cannot be adequately identified. Moreover, it is more difficult to return a migrant when the person has been present in the host country for a substantial period of time and has established roots.

Arrangements Relating to Voluntary Returns

The return of migrants and asylum-seekers is usually arranged through bilateral or multilateral arrangements between the states concerned, with a supportive role of humanitarian organizations. Return arrangements contain elements to deal humanely and effectively with persons such as rejected asylum-seekers, in accordance with relevant international standards and in a spirit of international cooperation.

---

[52] For example, Art. 33 of the 1951 Refugee Convention provides particularly that "[n]o Contracting State shall expel or return ("refouler") a refugee in any manner whatsoever to the frontiers of territories where his life or freedom would be threatened on account of his race, religion, nationality, membership of a particular social group or political opinion" The Convention against Torture and Other Cruel, Inhuman or Degrading Treatment or Punishment also contains in its Art. 3 a *non-refoulement* provision, which forbids expulsion, return, or extradition "where there are substantial grounds for believing that [the person] would be in danger of being subjected to torture." See Human Rights, A Compilation of International Instruments, United Nations, 1993, for Refugee Convention see vol. I (Second Part), p. 634; for Convention Against Torture, see vol. I (First Part), p. 293.

[53] See General Assembly Resolutions: 45/150 of 14 December 1990, para. 9, 46/106 of 16 December 1991, para. 10; 47/105 of 16 December 1992, para. 10.

[54] The right to return is contained in several human rights instruments, such as Art. 13(2) of the Universal Declaration on Human Rights; Art. 12(4) of the International Covenant on Civil and Political Rights; Art. 5(d)(ii) of the International Convention on the Elimination of All Forms of Racial Discrimination; and in regional human rights conventions as well as in the national legislation of various states. Id., note 54, Human Rights, A Compilation of International Instruments, vol. I (First Part).

Return of Extra-regional Migrants

At the regional level, efforts are being deployed by states of origin, transit, and destination, through RCPs, to implement practical cooperation programs aimed at the orderly return of extra-regional migrants stranded in states of the region. To this end, a Draft Multilateral Cooperation Program for the Assisted Return of Extra-Regional Migrants Stranded in Member States is currently under the consideration of the participating states of the Puebla Process.[55]

The Draft Cooperation Program provides for return operations to be consistent with the national laws of the States Parties and their obligations, under international humanitarian law, human rights law, and international refugee law. A distinctive feature of this proposed Cooperation Agreement is that it includes the IOM as an implementing party to make the relevant arrangements and to ensure that voluntary returns are conducted in dignity.

Under the Smart Border Declaration, the United States and Canada are working toward ensuring comprehensive and permanent coordination of information sharing in matters relating to border crossing. The two countries are developing means to address legal and operational challenges to joint removals, and coordinating initiatives to encourage uncooperative states to accept the return of their nationals (point 27).[56]

The Regional Cooperation Model functioning between Australia and Indonesia (which apparently is not yet in the public stream)[57] increases the capacity of the two countries to deal with irregular migrants and people-smuggling. This arrangement is intended to deter potential irregular migrants and smugglers, while strengthening the international protection framework by providing early access to a refugee status determination process.

Return of Qualified Nationals

While the emigration of labor has reduced unemployment and increased remittances to many developing states, alarms are again being sounded over the potential damage that the emigration of the highly skilled can cause to their development aspirations. A significant number of immigrants with professional qualifications are increasingly recruited for employment in more developed states where skilled labor is needed to sustain the rapid growth of the new knowledge industries.

---

[55] The VI Regional Conference on Migration (RCM) took place in San Jose, Costa Rica in March 2001, with the participation of the Member States of Belize, Canada, Costa Rica, the Dominican Republic, El Salvador, Guatemala, Honduras, Mexico, Nicaragua, Panama, and the United States of America. The participants adopted a "Framework for the Implementation of the General Program of Cooperation of the RCM for the Return of Extra-regional Migrants" as a point of reference for the negotiation of accords between IOM and Member States of the RCM, in accordance with the legal framework of each country. http://usinfo.state.gov/regional/ar/6thrcm.htm.

[56] See http://www.canadianembassy.org/border/declaration-e.asp.

[57] See transcript of press conference between Immigration Minister Philip Ruddock and Defense Minister Peter Reith at http://www.minister.immi.gov.au/media/transcripts/transcripts01/indonesia_050901.htm.

The Return of Qualified Nationals (RQN) Programme administered by the IOM and the Transfer of Knowledge Through Expatriate Nationals (TOKTEN), sponsored by the UNDP, constitute two arrangements intended to have an impact on development in states of origin. The implementation of return of talent programs represents an effort to address the problems linked to "brain drain" in states of origin while contributing to development.[58]

Readmission Arrangements

Readmission arrangements negotiated directly between the concerned states include agreements providing for procedures for the return of irregular aliens to their states of residence. Persons to be readmitted by a contracting party on the request of another contracting party are a country's own nationals and, under certain conditions, third country nationals or stateless persons who have passed through the border of the requested country or been granted permission to stay there. Readmission agreements may be concluded to solve current return problems, to formalize a return situation, or to prevent the occurrence of return problems in the long run. These results are distinguished from the arrangements discussed above as they involve involuntary return or deportation.

Bilateral and multilateral readmission agreements to readmit nationals have existed for centuries. In the nineteenth century for instance, various treaties were concluded between Switzerland, Germany, and Italy on the obligation to readmit their own nationals.[59] Since that time, several states have entered into bilateral and multilateral readmission agreements. The IGC reported that as of August 1999, 220 of the 230 existing readmission agreements were concluded since 1990 and 170 of them concern Central and East European states.[60]

The multilateral readmission agreement concluded between the Schengen states and Poland providing for the readmission of irregular migrants stands as an example of other such types of agreements. The 1985 Schengen Agreement provides for a common approach to visa policies and asylum procedures and imposes the obligation to readmit on the state that issued the visa or right of residence to the irregular alien.[61]

Readmission agreements provide procedures under which readmissions are to be conducted. They cover such issues as: readmission of own nationals; readmission in

---

[58] E/ECA/IDRC/IOM/2000/L. UN Economic and Social Council, Economic Commission for Africa, Report on Regional Conference on Brain Drain And Capacity Building in Africa, 22-24 February 2000, Addis Ababa. See http://www.iom.int/search/query.idq?CiRestriction=tokten.

[59] See K. Hailbronner, "Readmission Agreements and the Obligation on States under Public International Law to readmit their Own and Foreign Nationals," *in* 57 *ZaöRV* (1997) p. 6.

[60] P.J. Van Krieken (ed.), *The Migration Acquis Handbook* (2001) pp. 425-426.

[61] The Convention Determining the State Responsible for Examining the Applications for Asylum Lodged in Member States of the European Communities (Dublin Convention), signed in Dublin on 15 June 1990, is not a readmission agreement proper, but in practice, it serves as one in that it determines the EU Member State responsible for examining an application for asylum that is lodged within the territory of the Member State.

the case of third-country nationals; means of proving[62] or presuming[63] nationality; time limits for requests for readmission and the reply to the request; transit arrangements when necessary; exchange of personal data regarding person to be readmitted and data protection; and cost of transport.[64]

Generally, readmission agreements are implemented at points of entry, so long as nationality can be proved or substantiated. However, the procedure is complicated by instances involving individuals with multiple nationality, permanent residence in a third country, or criminals, as state obligations to readmit can be restricted for such categories of persons. For example, the readmission agreement between Switzerland and Bulgaria of 18 July 1994 limits the obligation to readmit if the person can enter a third State.[65]

A uniform picture of bilateral and multilateral readmission agreements cannot be established. However, bilateral agreements with states of origin often include development-related incentives for the latter and basic formulations pertaining to processing modalities facilitating forced and/or voluntary returns.

Labor Migration

Labor migration involves work performed by documented or undocumented and regular or irregular migrants. It includes semiskilled and unskilled workers, free-moving migrants, and frontier workers moving to secure employment or to undertake self-employment. Traditionally, labor migration is arranged through formal agreements negotiated between the relevant government(s) or between governments and either employers or industrial associations. Agreements typically provide for both permanent and temporary entries while enabling employers to recruit a specified number of workers from overseas in response to identified or emerging labor market (or skill) shortages in a given country's labor market. Although labor migration has increased considerably, the bulk of it is organized by private entities – including those without authorization and sometimes with the assistance of criminal organizations – adding to the difficulties inherent in regulating labor migration.[66]

During the 1960s, bilateral cooperation arrangements were entered into between European states facing labor shortages (such as the Federal Republic of Germany, France, Switzerland, Belgium, and the Netherlands) and labor-supplying states (such as Spain, Greece, Portugal, Turkey, Algeria, Morocco, and Tunisia). These arrangements provided for non-discrimination with respect to conditions of employment, remuneration, and social security. In the 1970s, many Middle Eastern states became migrant workers recruiting pools. In addition to bilateral arrangements, framework

---

[62] Such as: identity cards, a minor's travel documents in lieu of passport, provisional identity papers, service record books, and military passes. Hailbronner, *supra* note 59, at 253.

[63] Such as: official service pass, a company pass, driving license, extract from register office records, photocopies of the above documents, the language of the person concerned. Id.

[64] See, i.e., Recommendation of 30 November 1994 concerning a specimen bilateral readmission agreement between a Member State of the European Union and a third country, Id. pp. 247-248, citing *Official Journal* C 274, 19 September 1996, p. 20-24 .

[65] Hailbronner, *supra* note 59, at 9.

[66] International Labor Conference, GB.283/2/1, Geneva, March 2002, p. 27.

agreements consisting of Statements of Cooperation emerged in certain parts of the world as a preferable tool in recruiting workers by private agents with general state supervision. Agreements illustrative of these arrangements are between Bangladesh and Libya; Pakistan and Jordan; the Philippines and Gabon; the Islamic Republic of Iran, Iraq and Jordan; Vietnam and Jordan. Labor migration arrangements between states of the former Soviet Union also emerged during the 1970s and 1980s.[67]

In addition to recruitment agreements concluded between Governments, conditions of employment include migration management terms regarding, *inter alia*, the acceptance of returnees by the state of origin and the granting of access to labor employment opportunities to the state of origin. An example is the agreement entered into by Spain with Ecuador on 25 January 2001. The Agreement provides that Spain would increase trade and development opportunities for Ecuador and the latter would facilitate the voluntary return of its nationals in an irregular situation in Spain.[68]

Labor migration at the EU level under the Treaty of Amsterdam is connected with the principle of free movement of persons within the EU.[69] The Treaty distinguishes between different categories of EU citizens, i.e., workers, self-employed persons, providers, or receivers of services. It regulates their rights to reside and work within a Member State, the social advantages they are granted, and their social security rights.[70]

The Community Charter of the Fundamental Social Rights of Workers (1989) is the basic document determining the treatment of workers within the region. While Title I of the Community Charter details rights such as freedom of movement, employment and remuneration, improvement of living and working conditions, and social protection, Title II of the Community Charter makes it clear that the Member States are generally responsible for guaranteeing fundamental social rights in accordance with national practices. Although not legally binding in itself, this document establishes guiding principles for the treatment of Community nationals and non-nationals in the employment field.[71]

In the Americas, the North American Free Trade Agreement (NAFTA) provides for the issuance of special visas and deals with migration issues through the North American Agreement on Labor Cooperation.[72]

---

[67] M. Abella, *Sending Workers Abroad* (1997) p. 64.

[68] Citation omitted – Document is not in the public domain.

[69] Treaty of Amsterdam, Title III: Free Movement of Persons, Services and Capital and Title XI, Social Policy, Education, Vocational Training and Youth.

[70] The most important regulations include: (i) Regulation No. 1612/68/EEC, dealing principally with equality of treatment with respect to access to employment, working conditions, social and tax advantages, trade union rights, vocational training and education, and guidelines for family reunification (amended by Regulation No. 312/76 of 9 February 1976 and No. 2434/92 of 27 July 1992); and (ii) Regulation No. 1408/71/EEC relating to the application of social security regimes to employed persons and the self-employed and to members of their families who move within the Community (amended by Regulation No. 1606/98/EC, 29 June 1998). The regulations are found in R. Plender (ed.), *Basic Documents on International Migration Law* (2nd revised edn., 1997).

[71] http://www.europarl.eu.int/workingpapers/soci/104/part2_en.htm.

[72] http://www.nafta-sec-alena.org/english/index.htm.

In Latin America, the Southern Common Market Pact (MERCOSUR) of 1995 formalized the current informal flow of workers across the internal borders of the region. The signatories to the Cartagena Agreement or Andean Pact, approved in 1977, the creation of the Andean Migration for Employment Instrument (decision 116) and, in 1996, the creation of the "Andean Migration Card" which aims to facilitate migration flows in the sub-region (decision 397).[73]

The Andean Instrument on Labor Migration, attached to the Simon Rodriguez Agreement on Socio-Labor Integration and signed by the Member States of the Cartagena Agreement of 1973, establishes the procedures for the recruitment and protection of workers.[74] Widely applied in the region during the 1970s as a guideline to developing labor migration policies, the decline in the application of the Andean Instrument in the 1980s was followed by efforts in the 1990s to revive its relevance with respect to free movement of persons in the Andean region. In this regard, agreement was reached in 1999 at the Second Conference of Ministers of Labor of the Andean Group to reactivate the Simon Rodriguez Agreement on Socio-Labor Integration.[75]

In the Arab Region, the primary document concerned with migration is the Agreement of the Council of Arab Economic Unity (1965). Established in 1957 by a resolution of the Arab Economic Council of the Arab League, the Council's focus is regional and is devoted to achieving economic integration through the framework of economic and social development. The Agreement provides for freedom of movement, employment, and residence and abolishes certain restrictions upon movement within the region.[76] In 1968, the Arab Labor Organization developed the Arab Labor Agreement, intended to facilitate labor movement in the region, and giving priority within the region to Arab workers.[77]

In the 1970s measures strengthening the provisions of the Arab Labor Agreement were undertaken with the goal of retaining jobs for Arab workers and deporting non-Arab workers from the region. This focus on reducing the participation of external migrants from the Arab labor market is apparent throughout the 1980s, with the

---

[73] http://www.idrc.ca/lacro/investigacion/mercosur.html.

[74] The Andean Community is an economic and social integration organization with international legal status. It comprises the following states: Bolivia, Colombia, Ecuador, Peru, and Venezuela, and the bodies and institutions of the Andean Integration System (SAI). Its early beginnings date back to 1969, when a group of South American states signed the Cartagena Agreement, also known as the Andean Pact. See http://www.imf.org/external/np/sec/decdo/acuerdo.htm.

[75] See Final Declaration of the Meeting of Ministers of Labor of the Andean Community – Declaration of Cartagena de Indias adopted by the Ministers of Labor of the Member Countries of the Simón Rodríguez Convention on Social and Labor Integration, meeting in Cartagena de Indias in May 1999 for the purpose of making an assessment of the present state of Andean Community integration in the social and labor areas and of proposing mechanisms for its reactivation. The Andean Labor Ministers approved an action plan for creating jobs and guaranteeing labor rights. See http://www.comunidadandina.org/ingles/document/Act_n9.htm.

[76] Membership is composed of Egypt, Iraq, Jordan, Kuwait, Libya, Mauritania, the Palestine Liberation Organization, Somalia, The Sudan, Syria, United Arab Emirates, and Yemen. See http://www.arab.de/arabinfo/arabeco.htm.

[77] http://www.arab.de/arabinfo/arabeco.htm. See also ILO Regional migration instruments at http://lanic.utexas.edu/.

adoption of the Strategy for Joint Arab Economic Action and the Charter of National Economic Action. Under the Strategy "Arab manpower must be resorted to increasingly to reduce dependence on foreign labor." Additionally, under the Charter of National Economic Action legal barriers between nationals and migrants from other Arab states are to be eliminated, providing for freedom of movement and equality of treatment. The Arab Declaration of Principles on the Movement of Manpower (1984) underlined the need to give preference to Arab nationals and calls for the strengthening of regional bodies and intra-regional cooperation.[78]

In Asia, an important proportion of the migrant workforce is absorbed within the region. While in the 1970s Asian states were admitting less than 6 percent of the region's labor migrants (for the most part, male unskilled labor), during the second half of the 1990s, over 40 percent of this group (for the most part female domestic workers) was moving through states in the region (this consideration excludes movements of labor within China and India).[79]

Labor migration in Asia is generally arranged by the private sector. Exceptions include agreements between Malaysia and Bangladesh for the supply of plantation labor. Much effort is deployed in states of destination within the region to maintain flexibility in the recruitment of migrant workers despite attempts by states of origin to impose more control over migration processes.

The movement of highly skilled labor migrants into the states of the region is clearly related to the flows of foreign direct investments. Other related factors lie in state policies to provide specifically for the liberal admission of managers and technical personnel needed to facilitate the establishment of subsidiaries or branches of transnational corporations in states such as Singapore, China, and Vietnam. While Asia constitutes the dominant region of origin of Information Technology (IT) workers to North America and Australia, access to the agreements pertaining to such recruitment is restricted as most occurs privately.

The states of Asia and the Pacific have not as of yet established regional agreements or institutions dealing specifically with labor migration. In Africa, at the sub-regional level, there are a number of instruments addressing the problems specifically related to intra-regional labor migration. In this regard, the Central African Customs and Economic Union[80] adopted an agreement in 1973, which recognizes the principle of non-discrimination on the grounds of nationality in employment, remuneration, and other working conditions, providing that the labor migrants are already in possession of a job offer.[81]

Labor Migration of Talented and Highly Skilled Professionals

Migration of highly skilled professionals and non-return of "advanced and talented students" due to better wages, career development opportunities, and working condi-

---

[78] Id. ILO Regional migration instruments.

[79] Id.

[80] Established in December 1964, this body was created to promote the establishment of a Central African Common Market. Its membership includes Cameroon, Central African Republic, Chad, Republic of the Congo, Equatorial Guinea, and Gabon.

[81] http://www.dfa.gov.za/for-relations/multilateral/eccas.htm.

tions are common in relation to states of origin and destination. With trade barriers falling and technology recognizing neither borders nor nationality, individual initiative and talent are increasingly recognized as a valuable global resource. Demands in the field of information technology and access to student talents has triggered competition among the traditional countries of immigration (TCIs) which include the United States, Canada, Australia, and New Zealand.

It has been reported that these four TCIs account for between 1.2 and 1.3 million legal permanent immigrant entries per year. In this context, the TCIs have established and maintain large and complex arrangements for admitting foreign workers for certain types of employment, both permanently and temporarily. TCIs also rely on immigration to enhance their economic competitiveness.

TCIs have set into place special arrangements to facilitate immigration by removing administrative barriers to hiring right out of school foreign students who demonstrate talent. They provide for the admission, both permanently and temporarily, of foreign workers with strong human capital qualifications. In this respect two groups of foreigners have been particularly targeted: information and communications technology professionals and foreign students. Admission formulae include the availability of the Working Holiday Makers visa, which allows some tourists to obtain short-term employment legally; regional reciprocal arrangements such as the Trans-Tasman Travel Arrangement, which gives reciprocal entry, work, and establishment rights to citizens of both Australia and New Zealand; and the visa-free entry and rights to employment between the United States and Canada in about seventy professional occupations under NAFTA.

Another example of a labor migration arrangement for the highly skilled is the "German Green Card" program for IT specialists. Germany's shortage of IT staff forced the government to launch the program in 2000 in an effort to sustain economic growth. Through this arrangement, the process of bringing in non-European Economic Area (EEA) nationals to work as IT professionals in Germany is radically streamlined enabling foreign IT specialists to acquire work and residency permits with a minimum of red tape. The German Green Card Program is intended to last through 2003, and a maximum number of 20,000 citizens of nations outside the European Union will be allowed to enter Germany and hold jobs in its information technology sector.[82]

Potential Remittances Arrangements

Migrant remittances are linked to labor migration and the effect of migration on development. Remittances constitute the most significant and visible economic and social impact of the migration phenomenon for migrant-sending states.

Efforts to improve transaction efficiency and reduce transfer costs, which are now estimated at 15 percent of the amount remitted, include proposals submitted by Multilateral Investment Fund Managers. The managers seek to demonstrate ways to reduce the cost of remittances through competition among financial institutions and

---

[82] http://www.germany-info.org/relaunch/welcome/work/greencard.html.

to provide attractive investment opportunities in the home states that can help build sustainable projects to enhance local communities over the long term, thereby reducing dependency and contributing to development.[83] This promising venture is one example among a few. To date, arrangements to market the transfer of remittances toward economic development remain to be established, despite the apparent leverage remittance money could have in boosting economic development.[84]

An example of a government-sponsored arrangement is established under the scheme negotiated by the Mexican Government with banks and wire transfer agencies in the United States. According to this arrangement, in effect as of December 2001, approximately fifteen banking institutions and their branches allow documented and undocumented migrants from Mexico to open bank accounts upon presentation of identification cards provided by Mexican consulates. This arrangement enables migrants' relatives in the country of origin to withdraw funds for a cost of about US$ 3 per transaction – far less than the usual money transfer fee.[85]

Remittances and savings of migrants have also been a subject in regional processes and international conferences. For example, at the West African Regional Ministerial Conference on the Participation of Migrants in the Development of their Country of Origin in Dakar, Senegal, in October 2000, the participating states committed themselves "to strengthening relations between migrants and their States of origin, by creating favorable conditions for migrants' remittances and savings."[86]

Moreover, at the UN ICPD, it was concluded that "orderly international migration can have positive impacts on both the communities of origin and the communities of destination, providing the former with remittances and the latter with needed human resources. International migration also has the potential of facilitating the transfer of skills and contributing to cultural enrichment."[87]

Migration and Trade-in-Services

Trade-in-services has no direct links to immigration policy, yet factors relating to the issuance of visas for the cross-border movement of persons in order to provide services and deliver products brings trade within the ambit of migration concerns. Multilateral economic agreements, such as those relating to trade-in-services, that are rooted in the principle of reciprocity and partnership impose upon states the need

---

[83] http://www2.iadb.org/exr/idbamerica/English/OCT01E/oct01e3-b.html. See generally "Migration And Sustainable Development The Remittances Link," by S. Stanton Russell Remarks for UN Economic Social Council (ECOSOC) Substantive Session, 2 July 2002, referring to P. Serrano, "ECLAC's Experiences with the Productive Use of Remittances by Central American Emigrants," paper presented at conference on "Approaches to Increasing the Productive Value of Remittances," see also, Manuel Orozco, "Globalization and Migration: the Impact of Family Remittances in Latin America," paper presented at same conference sponsored by the Inter-American Foundation and the World Bank, held 19 March 2001, report September 2001, pp. 10 and 31.

[84] Id.

[85] Id. p. 8 citing G. Thompson, "Big Mexican Breadwinner: the Migrant Worker," *The New York Times*, 25 March 2002, p. A3.

[86] Id., note 25.

[87] See UN ICPD Programme of Action, September 1994 – http://www.iisd.ca/linkages/cairo.html.

to codify reciprocal access for each other's nationals in the fields of business, trade, investment, and cultural exchanges. Trade is intimately linked to the movement of people in providing services and promoting the sale of goods and services in foreign markets.

At the multilateral level, the World Trade Organization (WTO) Agreements do not cover labor mobility *per se*. The movement of natural persons as service suppliers is covered by the GATS under Mode 4 and is specified as "the supply of a service ... by a service supplier of one Member, through presence of natural persons of a Member in the territory of another Member." Labor mobility under the GATS is limited to the temporary movement and cover of independent service suppliers and the self-employed. It applies to foreign employees of foreign companies established on the territory of a Member State (see GATS Annex on Movement of Natural persons Supplying Services under the Agreement). The GATS does not provide for full labor or service supplier mobility and does not impinge on Governments' right to regulate entry and stay of individuals. However, Member States may carve out regulatory arrangements relating to work and labor (usually short of permanent migration) and access to the labor market that do not nullify or impair commitments undertaken under the GATS.

Because labor mobility arrangements vary depending on a range of factors, including the geographical proximity of the parties, Regional Trade Agreements (RTAs) are used by Member States to regulate the movement of (higher skilled) workers.

Labor Mobility within Europe

Labor mobility constitutes a fundamental aspect of the single European market. Article 14 of the EU Treaty specifies that "[t]he internal market shall comprise an area without internal frontiers in which the free movement of goods, persons, services and capital is ensured."

The Agreement on the European Economic Area (EEA)[88] expands the scope of the EC Treaty on free movement of persons to allow EEA nationals to enter any EU and European Free Trade Association (EFTA) state for the purpose of employment as self-employed, service providers, or recipients.[89] Further expansions are provided for under the Agreement Amending the Convention Establishing the EFTA. This Agreement, signed on 21 June 2000, enlarges the EFTA area and provides for free movement of persons, including the self-employed and persons with no gainful employment, who would otherwise have sufficient financial means (within certain specific limitations).[90]

---

[88] EEA agreements are concluded with the following States: Austria, Belgium, Denmark, Finland, France, Germany, Greece, Iceland, Ireland, Italy, Liechtenstein, Luxembourg, the Netherlands, Norway, Portugal, United Kingdom, Spain, and Sweden. See http://europa.eu.int/comm/competition/international/3a01en.html.

[89] EFTA is an international organization comprising four states: The Republic of Iceland, The Principality of Liechtenstein, The Kingdom of Norway and The Swiss Confederation. EFTA has headquarters in Geneva and offices in Brussels and Luxembourg. See http://secretariat.efta.int/.

[90] http://www.efta.int/docs/surv/Publications/AnnualReport/1997/persons.htm.

Labor Mobility and Other Regional and Bilateral Arrangements[91]

While at the EU level the degree of liberalization of trade allows for general mobility of people and confers immigration rights, the majority of RTAs are more limited and facilitate mobility within the confines of applicable domestic immigration and migration legislation. States parties retain their sovereign rights to grant and refuse residence permits and visas; provisions of trade agreements cannot be used to challenge immigration decisions. Hence, Member States are free to apply measures regulating the entry of natural persons onto their territories and to ensure the orderly movement of persons across their borders, so long as such regulations do not impair or nullify benefits accrued to a Member State under the terms of WTO commitments (paragraph 4 of Annex).

NAFTA predates and provides guidance to the GATS. NAFTA does not create a common market for the movement of labor. Both NAFTA and the Canada-Chile Free Trade Agreement provide for the temporary entry of businesspersons and highly skilled workers within the territories of the Member States. More specifically, the two agreements identify four categories of travelers eligible for temporary entry: traders and investors, intra-company transferees, business visitors, and professionals. Although general immigration regulations such as visas continue to apply, other regulations such as labor certification or labor market assessments, to ensure that a person is not displacing the labor market, are no longer applicable.[92]

In South America, the Southern Common Market Agreement (MERCOSUR) constitutes a replica of the GATS. Provisions relating to access to labor markets and right of entry and stay of foreigners are regulated by the individual Member States.[93]

The Caribbean Community (CARICOM) under Protocol II: Establishment, Services and Capital (1998) provides for the free movement of university graduates, other professionals and skilled persons, and members of selected occupations, as well as freedom of travel and exercise of a profession for CARICOM nationals.[94]

The ASEAN Free Trade Area (AFTA) provides for general coverage of trade in services but does not contain specific provisions regulating labor mobility.[95] The

---

[91] The discussion below on the various labor mobility arrangements in regional trade agreements are informed in part by a paper submitted by Julia Nielson, Trade Directorate of OECD, at Joint WTO-World Bank Symposium on Movement of Natural Persons (Mode 4) under the GATS, WTO, Geneva, 11-12 April 2002. See Current Regimes for Temporary Movement of Service Providers, Labour Mobility in Regional Trade Agreements.

[92] NAFTA membership includes the following states: Canada, Mexico, and the United States. See generally http://www.sice.oas.org/summary/nafta/nafta16.asp.

[93] MERCOSUR membership includes the following states: Argentina, Brazil, Paraguay and Uruguay. See http://search.yahoo.com/bin/search?p=MERCOSUR.

[94] CARICOM membership includes the following states: Antigua and Barbuda, the Bahamas, Barbados, Belize, Dominica, Grenada, Guyana, Haiti, Jamaica, St Kitts and Nevis, St Lucia, St Vincent and the Grenadines, the Republic of Suriname, and Trinidad and Tobago. See http://www.caricom.org/expframes2.htm.

[95] ASEAN Free Trade Area membership includes the following states: Brunei, Darussalam, Indonesia, Laos, Malaysia, Myanmar, Philippines, Russia, Singapore, Chinese Taipei, Thailand, the United States, and Vietnam. See http://www.south-asia.com/saarc/sapta.htm.

Asia-Pacific Economic Cooperation Forum (APEC)[96] in its Bogor Declaration, places emphasis on human resources development, and provides for no market access arrangements on labor mobility but facilitates entry. APEC has established a scheme streamlining temporary entry, stay, and departure processing of business people. The South Asian Association for Regional Cooperation (SAARC) established under the South Asian Preferential Trading Arrangement contains no provision on trade in services. However, it facilitates business travel via a simplification of visa procedures and visa exemption to ease trade and tourism within the region.

The Australia New Zealand Closer Economic Relations Trade Agreement (ANZCERTA) Services Protocol provides for full market access (Article 4) and national treatment (Article 5) for all service suppliers between the two states.[97] It is important to note that the ANZCERTA does not provide for full labor mobility. Nationals of the two states are free to live and work indefinitely in either country under the Trans-Tasman Travel Arrangement (limitations apply for instance to persons with criminal records). The arrangement is not part of the ANZCERTA and consists of a series of immigration procedures applied by each country.[98]

The New Zealand-Singapore Closer Economic Partnership provides for the movement of natural persons and contains the same provisions as GATS. The parties are to review their schedules of commitments every two years until they achieve free trade in services by 2010 (Article 20.4).[99]

In Africa, under the Treaty for a Common Market for Eastern and Southern Africa (COMESA) provision is made for a community within which goods, services, capital, and labor will be free to move across national borders of the Member States. The treaty is envisaged to come into force in 2025. In the meantime, the implementation of a protocol on the gradual relaxation and eventual elimination of visa requirements and a protocol on the free movements of persons, labor, services, and the right to establish residence are setting up the context for the treaty.[100] The Southern African Development Community (SADC) is intended to promote the free movement of goods and services within the region but does not contain provisions for free movement of labor or service suppliers.[101]

---

[96] APEC membership includes the following states: Australia, Brunei, Darussalam, Canada, Chile, China, Hong Kong, China, Indonesia, Japan, Korea, Malaysia, Mexico, New Zealand, Papua New Guinea, Peru, the Philippines, Russia, Singapore, Chinese Taipei, Thailand, the United States, and Vietnam. See 1994 Bogor Declaration at http://www.apecsec.org.sg/.

[97] ANZERTA came into force in 1983. See generally, http://www.mft.govt.nz/for.html.

[98] http://www.nzimmigrationguide.co.nz/NZ_Immigration_Monitor_06.htm.

[99] New-Zealand-Singapore Closer Economic Partnership Agreement provides under Art. 72 for the Movement of Natural Persons who are service suppliers. See http://www.executive.govt.nz/minister/sutton/singapore/.

[100] COMESA membership includes the following states: Angola, Burundi, Comoros, Democratic Republic of Congo, Djibouti, Egypt, Eritrea, Ethiopia, Kenya, Madagascar, Malawi, Mauritius, Namibia, Rwanda, Seychelles, Sudan, Swaziland, Zambia, and Zimbabwe. Chapter 28 of the COMESA Treaty concerns the Free Movement of Persons, Labour, Services, Right of establishment and Residence. Art. 164 provides in part that the Member States "agree to adopt, individually, at bilateral or regional levels the necessary measures in order to achieve progressively the free movement of persons, labour and services and to ensure the enjoyment of the right of establishment and residence by their citizens within the Common Market." See http://www.comesa.int/backgrnd/backtr28.htm.

[101] SADC membership includes the following states: Angola, Botswana, Democratic Republic of

The U.S.-Jordan Free-Trade Agreement provides for labor mobility and is covered under the section on trade and services. The Agreement goes beyond the GATS and includes specific provisions regarding visa commitments. Similarly, the EU-Mexico Free Trade Agreement addresses labor mobility through trade-in-services. This Agreement is limited to service suppliers under the GATS, excludes access to labor markets, and provides for each party to maintain the right to regulate entry and stay in accordance with their immigration legislation.[102]

CONCLUSION

The various multilateral, regional, and bilateral arrangements discussed above reveal that migration is a field ripe with examples of cooperation. They show the willingness of states to engage in cooperative efforts with a view to achieve the promises of orderly migration.

In tackling migration management issues, states from various regions use different arrangements, depending on the particular migratory issue to be addressed. More generally, they shape their approaches in view of their perspectives as states of origin, transit, or destination, but also in view of shared understandings and a commitment to cooperation.

Recent arrangements on migration focus on cooperative efforts to combat irregular migration, eradicate smuggling and trafficking, and mitigate brain drain while maximizing the benefits of remittances with the view to contributing to sustainable development of states of origin and eventually reducing the incentive to migrate. Safeguarding the fundamental human rights of migrants, preventing their exploitation, and securing protection from persecution of those in need also constitute priorities of states in their management migration arrangements.

While these arrangements address the pressing issues of the day, they also point to a need for a framework built on certain fundamental premises, including the need for interstate cooperation based on common understandings and shared appreciation of good practices in migration management. Most arrangements contribute to improving migration management, particularly when they incorporate burden and responsibility sharing among states. However, arrangements based on internationally recognized good practices would serve to establish the groundwork for a global approach to migration management.

Confidence building through informal cooperative arrangements discussed above facilitates international cooperative coordination benefiting states of origin, transit, and destination and lays the foundation for such a global approach.

Congo, Lesotho, Malawi, Mauritius, Mozambique, Seychelles, South Africa, Swaziland, Tanzania, Zambia, and Zimbabwe. See Declaration and Treaty of SADC and Agreement Amending the Treaty of SADC at http://www.sadc.int/english/protocols/agreement_amending_the_treaty_of_the_sadc.html.

[102] http://www.sice.oas.org/Trade/us-jrd/usjrd.asp.

ANNEX

Annex
BASIC INSTRUMENTS ON INTERNATIONAL MIGRATION LAW

I. UNIVERSAL INSTRUMENTS

1) United Nations Instruments

United Nations Charter, adopted 26 June 1945, TS No. 993, entered into force 24 October 1945.

Universal Declaration on Human Rights, adopted 10 December 1948, G.A. Res. 217A (III).

Convention on the Suppression of Trafficking and the Exploitation of the Prostitution of Others, adopted 21 March 1950, 96 UNTS 271, entered into force 25 July 1951.

Geneva Convention Relative to the Protection of Civilian Persons in Time of War, adopted 12 August 1949, 75 UNTS 287, entered into force 21 October 1950.
   Protocol Additional II to the Geneva Conventions of 12 August 1949, and relating to the Protection of Victims of Non-International Armed Conflicts, adopted 12 December 1977, 1125 UNTS 609, entered into force 7 December 1978.

Convention relating to the Status of Refugees, adopted 28 July 1951, 189 UNTS 137, entered into force 22 April 1954.
   Protocol relating to the Status of Refugees, adopted 31 January 1967, 606 UNTS 267, entered into force 4 October 1967.

Convention relating to the Status of Stateless Persons, adopted 28 September 1954, 360 UNTS 117, entered into force 6 June 1960.

Standard Minimum Rules for the Treatment of Prisoners, adopted 30 August 1955, by the First United Nations Congress on the Prevention of Crime and the Treatment of Offenders, UN Doc. A/CONF.6/1, Annex I, A (1956), adopted 31 July 1957 by the Economic and Social Council, E.S.C. Res. 663C (1957), amended E.S.C. Res. 2076 (1977).

Convention on the Nationality of Married Women, adopted 20 February 1957, 309 UNTS 65, entered into force 11 August 1958.

Agreement relating to Refugee Seamen, adopted 23 November 1957, 506 UNTS 125, entered into force 27 December 1961.
   Protocol relating to Refugee Seamen, adopted 12 June 1973, 965 UNTS 445, entered into force 30 March 1975.

Convention on the Reduction of Statelessness, adopted 30 August 1961, 989 UNTS 175, entered into force 13 December 1975.

Vienna Convention on Diplomatic Relations, adopted 18 April 1961, 500 UNTS 95, entered into force 24 April 1964.

Vienna Convention on Consular Relations, adopted 24 April 1963, 596 UNTS 261, entered into force 19 March 1967.

UN Declaration on Territorial Asylum, adopted 14 December 1967, UNGA Res. 2312 (XXII).

International Covenant on Civil and Political Rights, adopted 16 December 1966, 999 UNTS 171, entered into force 23 March 1976.
First Optional Protocol to the International Covenant on Civil and Political Rights, adopted 16 December 1966, 999 UNTS 171, entered into force 23 March 1976.

International Covenant on Economic, Social and Cultural Rights, adopted 16 December 1966, 999 UNTS 3, entered into force 3 January 1976.

International Convention on the Elimination of All Forms of Racial Discrimination, adopted 21 December 1965, 660 UNTS 195, entered into force 4 January 1969.

Convention on the Elimination of All Forms of Discrimination Against Women, adopted 18 December 1979, 1249 UNTS 13, entered into force 3 September 1981.

Declaration on the Elimination of All Forms of Intolerance and Discrimination Based on Religion or Belief, adopted 25 November 1981, G.A. Res. 36/55.

Convention Against Torture and Other Cruel, Inhuman and Degrading Treatment or Punishment, adopted 10 December 1984, 1465 UNTS 85, entered into force 26 June 1987.

Declaration on the Human Rights of Individuals who are not Nationals of the Country in Which They Live, adopted 13 December 1985, G.A. Res. 40/144.

G.A. Resolution 41/70 endorsed the recommendations made in the report of the Group of Governmental Experts on International Cooperation to Avert New Flows of Refugees, adopted 3 December 1986.

UN Declaration on Social and Legal Principles Relating to the Protection and Welfare of Children with Special Reference to Foster Placement and Adoption, adopted 3 December 1986, G.A. Res. 41/85.

Declaration on the Right to Development, adopted 4 December 1986, G.A. Res. 41/128.

Body of Principles for the Protection of All Persons under Any Form of Detention or Imprisonment, adopted 9 December 1988, G.A. Res. 43/173.

Convention on the Rights of the Child, adopted 20 November 1989, 1577 UNTS 44, entered into force 20 September 1990.
Optional Protocol to the Convention on the Rights of the Child on the Sale of Children, Child Prostitution and Child Pornography, adopted 25 May 2000, G.A. Res. 54/263 (annex II).

International Convention on the Protection of the Rights of All Migrant Workers and Their Families, adopted 18 December 1990, G.A. Res. 45/158 (annex), 30 ILM 1521 (1991).

Declaration on the Rights of Persons Belonging to National or Ethnic, Religious or Linguistic Minorities, adopted 18 December 1992, G.A. Res. 47/135.

Declaration on the Elimination of Violence Against Women, adopted 20 December 1993, G.A. Res. 48/104.

Cairo Declaration of the International Conference on Population and Development, adopted 13 September 1994, UN Doc. A/CONF.171/13 and Add. 1.

Copenhagen Declaration of the World Summit on Social Development, adopted 12 March 1995, UN Doc. A/CONF.166/9

G.A. Resolution on International Migration and Development, adopted 23 February 1996, G.A. Res. 50/123.

G.A. Resolution on Assistance to refugees, returnees and displaced persons in Africa, adopted 12 February 1999, G.A. Res. 53/126.

G.A. Resolution on the Effects of the Full Enjoyment of Human Rights of the Economic Adjustment Policies arising from Foreign Debt and, in particular, on the Implementation of the Declaration on the Right to Development, adopted 23 April 1999, UN Doc. E/CN.4/RES/1999/22.

United Nations Convention against Transnational Organized Crime, adopted 15 November 2000, G.A. Res. 55/25.
   Protocol to Prevent, Suppress and Punish Trafficking in Persons, Especially Women and Children, supplementing the United Nations Convention against Transnational Organized Crime, adopted 15 November 2000, G.A. Res. 55/25.
   Protocol against the Smuggling of Migrants by Land, Sea and Air, supplementing the United Nations Convention against Transnational Organized Crime, adopted 15 November 2000, G.A. Res. 55/25.

G.A. Resolution on the Right to Development, adopted 8 February 2002, G.A. Res. 56/150.

2)   International Labor Organization Instruments

Convention No. 48 concerning the Establishment of an International Scheme for the Maintenance of Rights under Invalidity, Old-Age and Widows' and Orphans' Insurance, 22 June 1935, available in ILO, International Labor Conventions and Recommendations, vol. 1 (ILO, 1996).

Convention No. 97 of 1949 concerning Migration for Employment (Revised), adopted 1 July 1949, 120 UNTS 71, entered into force 22 January 1952.

Convention No. 118 concerning Equality of Treatment of Nationals and Non-Nationals in Social Security, adopted 28 June 1962, 494 UNTS 271, entered into force 25 April 1964.

Convention No. 143 concerning Migrations in Abusive Conditions and the Promotion of Equality of Opportunity and Treatment of Migrant Workers, adopted 24 June 1975, 1120 UNTS 324, entered into force 9 December 1978.

Convention No. 157 concerning the Establishment of an International System for the Maintenance of Rights in Social Security, 21 June 1982, ILO Official Bulletin (1982) Series A, No. 2, p. 61.

Convention No. 182 concerning the Prohibition and Immediate Action for the Elimination of the Worst Forms of Child Labour, adopted 1 June 1999, 38 ILM 1207, entered into force 19 November 2000.

3)   Other Multilateral Instruments

International Convention for the Suppression of White Slave Traffic, adopted 4 May 1910, 101 UNTS 98, entered into force 4 May 1949.

International Convention for the Suppression of the Traffic in Women and Children 1921, 13 UNTS 53, adopted 30 September 1921, entered into force 15 June 1922.

International Convention for the Suppression of the Traffic in Women in Full Age, adopted 11 October 1933, 150 LNTS 431, entered into force 24 August 1934.

General Agreement on Trade in Services, adopted 15 April 1994, 33 ILM 1168, entered into force 1 January 1995.

II. REGIONAL INSTRUMENTS

1) European Instruments

a) *Council of Europe*

European Convention for the Protection of Human Rights and Fundamental Freedoms, 4 November 1950, ETS 5, entered into force 3 September 1953.
> Protocol No. 4, 16 September 1963, ETS 46, entered into force 2 May 1968.
> Protocol No. 7, 22 November 1984, ETS 117, entered into force 1 November 1988.
> Protocol No. 12, 4 November 2000, ETS 177.

European Convention on Social and Medical Assistance, adopted 11 December 1953, ETS 14, entered into force 1 July 1954.
> Protocol to the European Convention on Social and Medical Assistance, adopted 11 December 1953, ETS 14a, entered into force 1 July 1954.

European Convention on Establishment, adopted 13 December 1955, ETS 19, entered into force 23 February 1965.

European Convention on Extradition, adopted 13 December 1957, ETS 24, entered into force 18 April 1960.

European Agreement on Regulations governing the Movement of Persons between Member States of the Council of Europe, adopted 13 December 1957, ETS 25, entered into force 1 January 1958.

European Agreement on the Abolition of Visas for Refugees, adopted 20 April 1959, ETS 31, entered into force 4 September 1960.

Convention on Reduction of Cases of Multiple Nationality, adopted 6 May 1963, ETS 43, entered into force 28 March 1968.
> First Protocol Amending the Convention on Reduction of Cases of Multiple Nationality, adopted 24 November 1977, ETS 95, entered into force 8 September 1978.
> Second Protocol Amending the Convention on the Reduction of Cases of Multiple Nationality and Military Obligations in Cases of Multiple Nationality, adopted 2 February 1993, ETS 149, entered into force 24 March 1995.

European Social Charter, adopted 18 October 1961, ETS 35, entered into force 26 February 1965.
> Revised European Social Charter, adopted 3 May 1996, ETS 163, entered into force 1 July 1999.

European Convention on the Legal Status of Migrant Workers, adopted 24 November 1977, ETS 93, entered into force 1 May 1983.

European Agreement on Transfer of Responsibility for Refugees, adopted 16 October 1980, ETS 107, entered into force 1 December 1980.

European Convention on Recognition and Enforcement of Decisions Concerning Custody of Children and Restoration of Custody of Children, opened for signature on 20 May 1980, ETS 105, entered into force 1 September 1983.

European Convention for the Prevention of Torture and Inhuman or Degrading Treatment, adopted 26 November 1987, ETS 126, entered into force 1 February 1989.

European Convention on the Participation of Foreigners in Public Life at the Local Level, opened for signature 5 February 1992, ETS 144, entered into force 1 May 1997.

Framework Convention for the Protection of National Minorities, opened for signature 1 February 1995, ETS 157, entered into force 1 February 1998.

European Convention on Nationality, adopted 6 November 1997, ETS 166, entered into force 1 March 2000.

b)   European Union

Convention determining the State responsible for examining applications for asylum lodged in one of the Member States of the European Communities (Dublin Convention), adopted 14 June 1990, 20 ILM 425 (1991), entered into force 1 September 1997.

Convention applying the Schengen Agreement of 14 June 1985 between the Governments of the States of the Benelux Economic Union, the Federal Republic of Germany and the French Republic on the Gradual Abolition of Checks at the Common Frontiers, adopted 14 June 1990, 30 ILM 83, entered into force 1 September 1993 and implemented from 26 March 1995.

Conclusion on countries in which there is generally no serious risk of persecution, adopted 30 November and 1 December 1992, SN 2836/93 (WGI 1505).

Resolution on manifestly unfounded applications for asylum, adopted 30 November and 1 December 1992, SN 2836/93 (WGI 1505).

Resolution on a harmonized approach to questions concerning host third countries, adopted 30 November and 1 December 1992, SN 2836/93 (WGI 1505).

Resolution on the harmonization of national policies on family reunification, adopted 1 June 1993, SN 2828/1/93 (WGI 1497).

Council resolution of 20 June 1994 on limitations on admission of third-country nationals to the Member States for employment, OJ 1996 C 274/3.

Council resolution of 30 November 1994 relating to the limitations on the admission of third-country nationals to the territory of the Member States for the purpose of pursuing activities as self-employed persons, OJ 1996 C 274/7.

Council resolution of 30 November 1994 on the admission of third-country nationals to the territory of the Member States of the European Union for study purposes, OJ 1996 C 274/10.

Council Recommendation of 30 November 1994 concerning a specimen bilateral readmission agreement between a Member State and a third country, OJ 1996 C 274/20.

Council resolution of 20 June 1995 on minimum guarantees for asylum procedures, OJ 1996 C 274/13.

Joint position on the harmonized application of the definition of the term "refugee" in Article 1 of the Geneva Convention of 28 July 1951 relating to the status of refugees, adopted 4 March 1996, OJ 1996 L 63/2.

Convention relating to extradition between the Member States of the European Union, adopted 27 September 1996, OJ 1996 C 313/12.

Charter of Fundamental Rights of the European Union, adopted 7 December 2000, OJ 2000 C 364/8.

Council Regulation No. 2725/2000 of 11 December 2000 concerning the establishment of "Eurodac" for the comparison of fingerprints for the effective application of the Dublin Convention, OJ 2000 L 316/1.

Council Regulation No. 539/2001 of 15 March 2001 listing the third countries whose nationals must be in possession of visas when crossing the external borders and those whose nationals are exempt from that requirement, OJ 2001 L 081/7.

Council Directive 2001/40/EC of 28 May 2001 on the mutual recognition of decisions on the expulsion of third country nationals, OJ 2001 L 149/34.

Council Directive 2001/51/EC of 28 June 2001 supplementing the provisions of Article 26 of the Convention implementing the Schengen Agreement of 14 June 1985, OJ 2001 L 187/45.

Council Directive 2001/55/EC of 20 July 2001 on minimum standards for giving temporary protection in the event of a mass influx of displaced persons and on measures promoting a balance of efforts between Member States in receiving such persons and bearing the consequences thereof, OJ 2001 L 212/12.

c)   Conference on Security and Cooperation in Europe

Final Act of the Conference on Security and Cooperation in Europe, adopted 1 August 1975, 14 ILM 1292.

Document of the Copenhagen Meetings of the Conference on the Human Dimension of the Conference, adopted 29 June 1990, 29 ILM 1305.

Charter of Paris for a New Europe, adopted 21 November 1991, 30 ILM 190.

2)   African Instruments

Convention of the Organization of African Unity on the Specific Aspects of Refugee Problems in Africa, adopted 10 September 1969, 1000 UNTS 46, entered into force 20 June 1974.

Treaty establishing the Economic Community of West African States, adopted 28 May 1975, 1010 UNTS 17, entered into force 20 June 1975.

African Charter on Human and Peoples' Rights, adopted 27 June 1981, OAU Doc. CAB/LEG/67/3 Rev. 5, 21 ILM 58, entered into force 21 October 1986.

Treaty establishing the African Economic Community, adopted 3 June 1991, 30 ILM 1245, entered into force 12 May 1994.

3)   American Instruments

American Declaration on the Rights and Duties of Man, OAS Res. XXX, adopted 2 May 1948 by the Ninth International Conference of American States, Bogota.

Inter-American Convention on Territorial Asylum, adopted 28 March 1954, OAS Official Records OEA/Ser. XII Treaty Series No. 19, entered into force 24 December 1954.

Inter-American Convention on Diplomatic Asylum, adopted 28 March 1954, OAS Official Records OEA/Ser. X/1 Treaty Series No. 18, entered into force 29 December 1954.

American Convention on Human Rights, adopted 22 November 1969, OAS TS 36, entered into force 18 July 1978.
  Additional Protocol in the Area of Economic, Social and Cultural Rights (Protocol of San Salvador), adopted 17 November 1988, OAS TS 69, entered into force 16 November 1999.

Inter-American Convention on Extradition, adopted 25 February 1981, OAS Official Records OEA/Ser. A/36 Treaty Series No. 60, entered into force 28 March 1982.

Cartagena Declaration on the Problems of Refugees and the Displaced in Central America, adopted 19-22 November 1984.

Inter-American Convention to Prevent and Punish Torture, adopted 9 December 1985, OAS TS 67, entered into force 28 February 1987.

Declaration and Concerted Plan of Action in favor of Central American Refugees, Returnees and Displaced Persons, adopted 31 May 1989, UN Doc. CIREFCA/89/14.

North American Free Trade Agreement, adopted 17 December 1992, 32 ILM 605, entered into force 1 January 1994.

Inter-American Convention on the Prevention, Punishment and Eradication of Violence Against Women (Convention Belem do Para), adopted 9 June 1994, 33 ILM 1535, entered into force 5 March 1995.

4)   Asian Instruments

Comprehensive Plan of Action on Indo-Chinese Refugees, adopted at the International Conference on Indo-Chinese Refugees, 13-14 June 1989, UN Doc. A/CONF.148/2.

Bangkok Declaration on Irregular Migration, Bangkok Symposium on Irregular/Undocumented Migration, held 21-23 April 1999.

INDEX